Mazda
RX-7
Automotive Repair Manual

by Mike Stubblefield and John H Haynes
Member of the Guild of Motoring Writers

Models covered:
All Mazda RX-7 models
1986 through 1991

(61036-2C9)

Haynes Group Limited
Haynes North America, Inc.
www.haynes.com

Acknowledgements

We are grateful for the help and cooperation of the Mazda Motor Company for their assistance with technical information, certain illustrations and vehicle photos. Thanks also to Rotary Engineering of Ventura, California, for technical assistance. Technical writers who contributed to this project include Larry Warren, Bob Henderson and Ken Freund.

© **Haynes North America, Inc. 1989, 1991**

With permission from Haynes Group Limited

A book in the Haynes Automotive Repair Manual Series

ISBN-10: 1-56392-007-7
ISBN-13: 978-1-56392-007-3

Library of Congress Catalog Card Number 91-75878

While every attempt is made to ensure that the information in this manual is correct, no liability can be accepted by the authors or publishers for loss, damage or injury caused by any errors in, or omissions from, the information given.

Contents

Introductory pages

About this manual 5
Introduction to the Mazda RX-7 5
Vehicle identification numbers 6
Buying parts 7
Maintenance techniques, tools and working facilities 7
Booster battery (jump) starting 14
Jacking and towing 15
Automotive chemicals and lubricants 16
Safety first! 17
Conversion factors 18
Troubleshooting 19

Chapter 1
Tune-up and routine maintenance 27

Chapter 2 Part A
Engine 57

Chapter 2 Part B
General engine overhaul procedures 72

Chapter 3
Cooling, heating and air conditioning systems 99

Chapter 4
Fuel and exhaust systems 113

Chapter 5
Engine electrical systems 151

Chapter 6
Emissions control systems 160

Chapter 7 Part A
Manual transmission 175

Chapter 7 Part B
Automatic transmission 185

Chapter 8
Clutch and drivetrain 192

Chapter 9
Brakes 210

Chapter 10
Suspension and steering systems 232

Chapter 11
Body 251

Chapter 12
Chassis electrical system 267

Wiring diagrams 282

Index 297

1986 Mazda RX-7 coupe

About this manual

Its purpose

The purpose of this manual is to help you get the best value from your vehicle. It can do so in several ways. It can help you decide what work must be done, even if you choose to have it done by a dealer service department or a repair shop; it provides information and procedures for routine maintenance and servicing; and it offers diagnostic and repair procedures to follow when trouble occurs.

We hope you use the manual to tackle the work yourself. For many simpler jobs, doing it yourself may be quicker than arranging an appointment to get the vehicle into a shop and making the trips to leave it and pick it up. More importantly, a lot of money can be saved by avoiding the expense the shop must pass on to you to cover its labor and overhead costs. An added benefit is the sense of satisfaction and accomplishment that you feel after doing the job yourself.

Using the manual

The manual is divided into Chapters. Each Chapter is divided into numbered Sections, which are headed in bold type between horizontal lines. Each Section consists of consecutively numbered paragraphs.

At the beginning of each numbered section you will be referred to any illustrations which apply to the procedures in that section. The reference numbers used in illustration captions pinpoint the pertinent Section and the Step within that section. That is, illustration 3.2 means the illustration refers to Section 3 and Step (or paragraph) 2 within that Section.

Procedures, once described in the text, are not normally repeated. When it's necessary to refer to another Chapter, the reference will be given as Chapter and Section number. Cross references given without use of the word "Chapter" apply to Sections and/or paragraphs in the same Chapter. For example, "see Section 8" means in the same Chapter.

References to the left or right side of the vehicle assume you are sitting in the driver's seat, facing forward.

Even though we have prepared this manual with extreme care, neither the publisher nor the author can accept responsibility for any errors in, or omissions from, the information given.

NOTE

A **Note** provides information necessary to properly complete a procedure or information which will make the procedure easier to understand.

CAUTION

A **Caution** provides a special procedure or special steps which must be taken while completing the procedure where the **Caution** is found. Not heeding a **Caution** can result in damage to the assembly being worked on.

WARNING

A **Warning** provides a special procedure or special steps which must be taken while completing the procedure where the **Warning** is found. Not heeding a **Warning** can result in personal injury.

Introduction to the Mazda RX-7

Mazda RX-7 models are available in both hatchback and convertible body styles.

The front-mounted, rotary engine used in the RX-7 is equipped with multi-port fuel injection. The engine drives the rear wheels through either a five-speed manual or four-speed automatic transmission via a driveshaft and independent driveaxles.

Independent suspension, featuring coil springs and struts or shock absorbers, is used at all four wheels, with automatic adjustable suspension available on some models. The rack and pinion steering unit is available with power assist.

All four wheels have power-assisted disc brakes as standard equipment. An ABS (Anti-lock Braking) system is available on later models.

Vehicle identification numbers

Modifications are a continuing and unpublicized process in vehicle manufacturing. Since spare parts manuals and lists are compiled on a numerical basis, the individual vehicle numbers are essential to correctly identify the component required.

Vehicle Identification Number (VIN)

This very important identification number is stamped on a plate attached to the dashboard just inside the windshield on the driver's side of the vehicle **(see illustration)**. The VIN also appears on the Vehicle Certificate of Title and Registration. It contains information such as where and when the vehicle was manufactured, the model year and the body style.

Chassis number

The chassis number is stamped into the engine compartment firewall **(see illustration)**.

Model plate

The model plate is located on the passenger side of the engine compartment firewall **(see illustration)**. The plate contains the VIN number, model and paint code.

Vehicle Certification Plate

The Vehicle Certification Plate (VC label) is affixed to the driver's door pillar **(see illustration)**. The plate contains the name of the manufacturer, the month and year of production, the Gross Vehicle Weight Rating (GVWR) and the certification statement.

Engine number

The engine number is located on the top front housing surface, adjacent to the alternator **(see illustration)**.

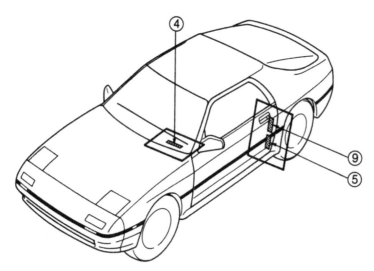

Important vehicle number and label locations

1   Engine number
2   Chassis number
3   Model plate
4   VIN number
5   Tire pressure label
6   Emission Control Information Label
7   Engine oil type label
8   Vacuum hose routing diagram
9   Vehicle Certification Plate

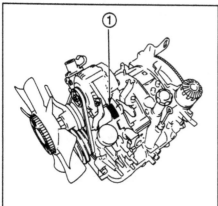

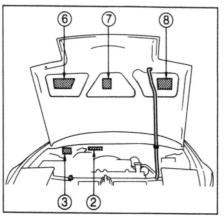

Buying parts

Replacement parts are available from many sources, which generally fall into one of two categories – authorized dealer parts departments and independent retail auto parts stores. Our advice concerning these parts is as follows:

Retail auto parts stores: Good auto parts stores will stock frequently needed components which wear out relatively fast, such as clutch components, exhaust systems, brake parts, tune-up parts, etc. These stores often supply new or reconditioned parts on an exchange basis, which can save a considerable amount of money. Discount auto parts stores are often very good places to buy materials and parts needed for general vehicle maintenance such as oil, grease, filters, spark plugs, belts, touch-up paint, bulbs, etc. They also usually sell tools and general accessories, have con-

venient hours, charge lower prices and can often be found not far from home.

Authorized dealer parts department: This is the best source for parts which are unique to the vehicle and not generally available elsewhere (such as major engine parts, transmission parts, trim pieces, etc.).

Warranty information: If the vehicle is still covered under warranty, be sure that any replacement parts purchased – regardless of the source – do not invalidate the warranty!

To be sure of obtaining the correct parts, have engine and chassis numbers available and, if possible, take the old parts along for positive identification.

Maintenance techniques, tools and working facilities

Maintenance techniques

There are a number of techniques involved in maintenance and repair that will be referred to throughout this manual. Application of these techniques will enable the home mechanic to be more efficient, better organized and capable of performing the various tasks properly, which will ensure that the repair job is thorough and complete.

Fasteners

Fasteners are nuts, bolts, studs and screws used to hold two or more parts together. There are a few things to keep in mind when working with fasteners. Almost all of them use a locking device of some type, either a lockwasher, locknut, locking tab or thread adhesive. All threaded fasteners should be clean and straight, with undamaged threads and undamaged corners on the hex head where the wrench fits. Develop the habit of replacing all damaged nuts and bolts with new ones. Special locknuts

with nylon or fiber inserts can only be used once. If they are removed, they lose their locking ability and must be replaced with new ones.

Rusted nuts and bolts should be treated with a penetrating fluid to ease removal and prevent breakage. Some mechanics use turpentine in a spout-type oil can, which works quite well. After applying the rust penetrant, let it work for a few minutes before trying to loosen the nut or bolt. Badly rusted fasteners may have to be chiseled or sawed off or removed with a special nut breaker, available at tool stores.

If a bolt or stud breaks off in an assembly, it can be drilled and removed with a special tool commonly available for this purpose. Most automotive machine shops can perform this task, as well as other repair procedures, such as the repair of threaded holes that have been stripped out.

Flat washers and lockwashers, when removed from an assembly, should always be replaced exactly as removed. Replace any damaged washers with new ones. Never use a lockwasher on any soft metal surface (such as aluminum), thin sheet metal or plastic.

Fastener sizes

For a number of reasons, automobile manufacturers are making wider and wider use of metric fasteners. Therefore, it is important to be able to tell the difference between standard (sometimes called U.S. or SAE) and metric hardware, since they cannot be interchanged.

All bolts, whether standard or metric, are sized according to diameter, thread pitch and length. For example, a standard 1/2 – 13 x 1 bolt is 1/2 inch in diameter, has 13 threads per inch and is 1 inch long. An M12 – 1.75 x 25 metric bolt is 12 mm in diameter, has a thread pitch of 1.75 mm (the distance between threads) and is 25 mm long. The two bolts are nearly identical, and easily confused, but they are not interchangeable.

In addition to the differences in diameter, thread pitch and length, metric and standard bolts can also be distinguished by examining the bolt heads. To begin with, the distance across the flats on a standard bolt head is measured in inches, while the same dimension on a metric bolt is sized in millimeters (the same is true for nuts). As a result, a standard wrench should not be used on a metric bolt and a metric wrench should not be used on a standard bolt. Also, most standard bolts have slashes radiating out from the center of the head to denote the grade or strength of the bolt, which is an indication of the amount of torque that can be applied to it. The greater the number of slashes, the greater the strength of the bolt. Grades 0 through 5 are commonly used on automobiles. Metric bolts have a property class (grade) number, rather than a slash, molded into their heads to indicate bolt strength. In this case, the higher the number, the stronger the bolt. Property class numbers 8.8, 9.8 and 10.9 are commonly used on automobiles.

Strength markings can also be used to distinguish standard hex nuts from metric hex nuts. Many standard nuts have dots stamped into one side, while metric nuts are marked with a number. The greater the number of dots, or the higher the number, the greater the strength of the nut.

Metric studs are also marked on their ends according to property class (grade). Larger studs are numbered (the same as metric bolts), while smaller studs carry a geometric code to denote grade.

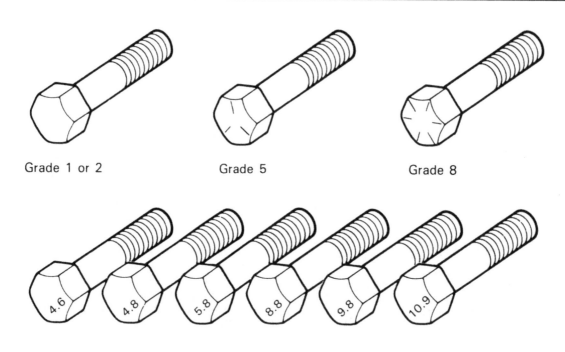

Grade 1 or 2   Grade 5   Grade 8

Bolt strength markings (top – standard/SAE/USS; bottom – metric)

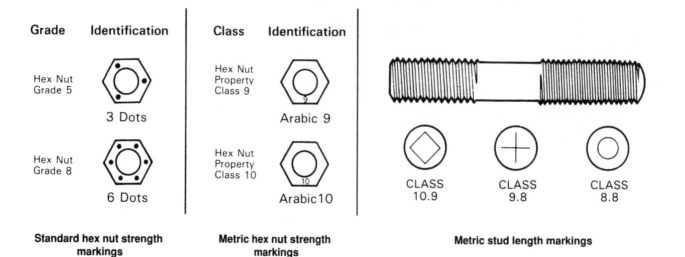

Standard hex nut strength markings   **Metric hex nut strength markings**   **Metric stud length markings**

It should be noted that many fasteners, especially Grades 0 through 2, have no distinguishing marks on them. When such is the case, the only way to determine whether it is standard or metric is to measure the thread pitch or compare it to a known fastener of the same size.

Standard fasteners are often referred to as SAE, as opposed to metric. However, it should be noted that SAE technically refers to a non-metric *fine thread* fastener only. Coarse thread non-metric fasteners are referred to as USS sizes.

Since fasteners of the same size (both standard and metric) may have different strength ratings, be sure to reinstall any bolts, studs or nuts removed from your vehicle in their original locations. Also, when replacing a fastener with a new one, make sure that the new one has a strength rating equal to or greater than the original.

Tightening sequences and procedures

Most threaded fasteners should be tightened to a specific torque value (torque is the twisting force applied to a threaded component such as a nut or bolt). Overtightening the fastener can weaken it and cause it to break, while undertightening can cause it to eventually come loose. Bolts, screws and studs, depending on the material they are made of and their thread diameters, have specific torque values, many of which are noted in the Specifications at the beginning of each Chapter. Be sure to follow the torque recommendations closely. For fasteners not assigned a specific torque, a general torque value chart is presented here as a guide. These torque values are for dry (unlubricated) fasteners threaded into steel or cast iron (not aluminum). As was previously mentioned, the size and grade of a fastener determine the amount of torque that can safely

Metric thread sizes

	Ft-lbs	Nm
M-6	6 to 9	9 to 12
M-8	14 to 21	19 to 28
M-10	28 to 40	38 to 54
M-12	50 to 71	68 to 96
M-14	80 to 140	109 to 154

Pipe thread sizes

	Ft-lbs	Nm
1/8	5 to 8	7 to 10
1/4	12 to 18	17 to 24
3/8	22 to 33	30 to 44
1/2	25 to 35	34 to 47

U.S. thread sizes

	Ft-lbs	Nm
1/4 – 20	6 to 9	9 to 12
5/16 – 18	12 to 18	17 to 24
5/16 – 24	14 to 20	19 to 27
3/8 – 16	22 to 32	30 to 43
3/8 – 24	27 to 38	37 to 51
7/16 – 14	40 to 55	55 to 74
7/16 – 20	40 to 60	55 to 81
1/2 – 13	55 to 80	75 to 108

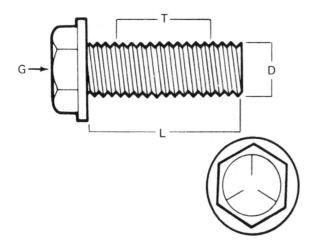

Standard (SAE and USS) bolt dimensions/grade marks

G	Grade marks (bolt length)
L	Length (in inches)
T	Thread pitch (number of threads per inch)
D	Nominal diameter (in inches)

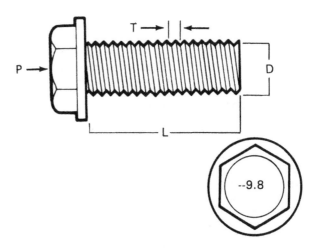

Metric bolt dimensions/grade marks

P	Property class (bolt strength)
L	Length (in millimeters)
T	Thread pitch (distance between threads in millimeters)
D	Diameter

be applied to it. The figures listed here are approximate for Grade 2 and Grade 3 fasteners. Higher grades can tolerate higher torque values.

Fasteners laid out in a pattern, such as cylinder head bolts, oil pan bolts, differential cover bolts, etc., must be loosened or tightened in sequence to avoid warping the component. This sequence will normally be shown in the appropriate Chapter. If a specific pattern is not given, the following procedures can be used to prevent warping.

Initially, the bolts or nuts should be assembled finger-tight only. Next, they should be tightened one full turn each, in a criss-cross or diagonal pattern. After each one has been tightened one full turn, return to the first one and tighten them all one-half turn, following the same pattern. Finally, tighten each of them one-quarter turn at a time until each fastener has been tightened to the proper torque. To loosen and remove the fasteners, the procedure would be reversed.

Component disassembly

Component disassembly should be done with care and purpose to help ensure that the parts go back together properly. Always keep track of the sequence in which parts are removed. Make note of special characteristics or marks on parts that can be installed more than one way, such as a grooved thrust washer on a shaft. It is a good idea to lay the disassembled parts out on a clean surface in the order that they were removed. It may also be helpful to make sketches or take instant photos of components before removal.

When removing fasteners from a component, keep track of their locations. Sometimes threading a bolt back in a part, or putting the washers and nut back on a stud, can prevent mix-ups later. If nuts and bolts cannot be returned to their original locations, they should be kept in a compartmented box or a series of small boxes. A cupcake or muffin tin is ideal for this purpose, since each cavity can hold the bolts and nuts from a particular area (i.e. oil pan bolts, valve cover bolts, engine mount bolts, etc.). A pan of this type is especially helpful when working on assemblies with very small parts, such as the carburetor, alternator, valve train or interior dash and trim pieces. The cavities can be marked with paint or tape to identify the contents.

Whenever wiring looms, harnesses or connectors are separated, it is a good idea to identify the two halves with numbered pieces of masking tape so they can be easily reconnected.

Gasket sealing surfaces

Throughout any vehicle, gaskets are used to seal the mating surfaces between two parts and keep lubricants, fluids, vacuum or pressure contained in an assembly.

Many times these gaskets are coated with a liquid or paste-type gasket sealing compound before assembly. Age, heat and pressure can sometimes cause the two parts to stick together so tightly that they are very difficult to separate. Often, the assembly can be loosened by striking it with a soft-face hammer near the mating surfaces. A regular hammer can be used if a block of wood is placed between the hammer and the part. Do not hammer on cast parts or parts that could be easily damaged. With any particularly stubborn part, always recheck to make sure that every fastener has been removed.

Avoid using a screwdriver or bar to pry apart an assembly, as they can easily mar the gasket sealing surfaces of the parts, which must remain smooth. If prying is absolutely necessary, use an old broom handle, but keep in mind that extra clean up will be necessary if the wood splinters.

After the parts are separated, the old gasket must be carefully scraped off and the gasket surfaces cleaned. Stubborn gasket material can be soaked with rust penetrant or treated with a special chemical to soften it so it can be easily scraped off. A scraper can be fashioned from a piece of copper tubing by flattening and sharpening one end. Copper is recommended because it is usually softer than the surfaces to be scraped, which reduces the chance of gouging the part. Some gaskets can be removed with a wire brush, but regardless of the method used, the mating surfaces must be left clean and smooth. If for some reason the gasket surface is gouged, then a gasket sealer thick enough to fill scratches will have to be used during reassembly of the components. For most applications, a non-drying (or semi-drying) gasket sealer should be used.

Hose removal tips

Warning: *If the vehicle is equipped with air conditioning, do not disconnect any of the A/C hoses without first having the system depressurized by a dealer service department or an air conditioning specialist.*

Hose removal precautions closely parallel gasket removal precautions. Avoid scratching or gouging the surface that the hose mates against or the connection may leak. This is especially true for radiator hoses. Because of various chemical reactions, the rubber in hoses can bond itself to the metal spigot that the hose fits over. To remove a hose, first loosen the hose clamps that secure it to the spigot. Then, with slip-joint pliers, grab the hose at the clamp and rotate it around the spigot. Work it back and forth until it is completely free, then pull it off. Silicone or other lubricants will ease removal if they can be applied between the hose and the outside of the spigot. Apply the same lubricant to the inside of the hose and the outside of the spigot to simplify installation.

As a last resort (and if the hose is to be replaced with a new one anyway), the rubber can be slit with a knife and the hose peeled from the spigot. If this must be done, be careful that the metal connection is not damaged.

If a hose clamp is broken or damaged, do not reuse it. Wire-type clamps usually weaken with age, so it is a good idea to replace them with screw-type clamps whenever a hose is removed.

Tools

A selection of good tools is a basic requirement for anyone who plans to maintain and repair his or her own vehicle. For the owner who has few tools, the initial investment might seem high, but when compared to the spiraling costs of professional auto maintenance and repair, it is a wise one.

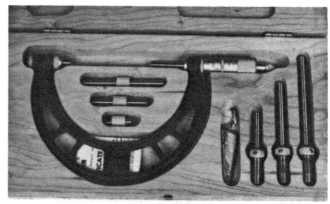

Micrometer set

Dial indicator set

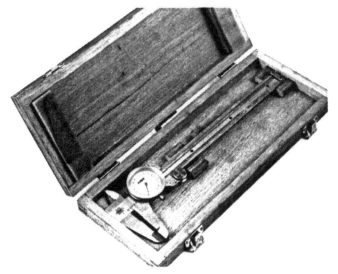

Dial caliper

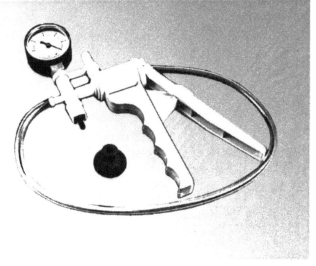

Hand-operated vacuum pump

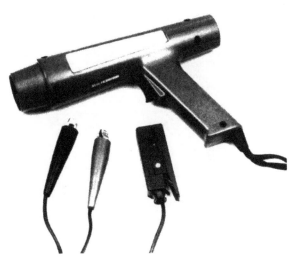

Timing light

Compression gauge with spark plug hole adapter

Damper/steering wheel puller

General purpose puller

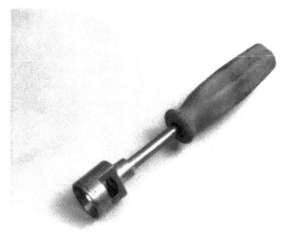

Brake hold-down spring tool

Brake cylinder hone

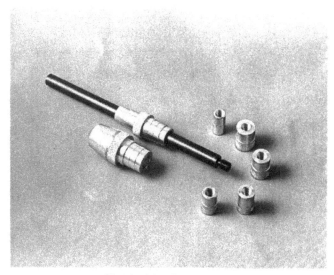

Clutch plate alignment tool

Tap and die set

To help the owner decide which tools are needed to perform the tasks detailed in this manual, the following tool lists are offered: *Maintenance and minor repair, Repair/overhaul and Special.*

The newcomer to practical mechanics should start off with the maintenance and minor repair tool kit, which is adequate for the simpler jobs performed on a vehicle. Then, as confidence and experience grow, the owner can tackle more difficult tasks, buying additional tools as they are needed. Eventually the basic kit will be expanded into the repair and overhaul tool set. Over a period of time, the experienced do-it-yourselfer will assemble a tool set complete enough for most repair and overhaul procedures and will add tools from the special category when it is felt that the expense is justified by the frequency of use.

Maintenance and minor repair tool kit

The tools in this list should be considered the minimum required for performance of routine maintenance, servicing and minor repair work. We recommend the purchase of combination wrenches (box-end and open-end combined in one wrench). While more expensive than open end wrenches, they offer the advantages of both types of wrench.

Combination wrench set (1/4-inch to 1 inch or 6 mm to 19 mm)
Adjustable wrench, 8 inch
Spark plug wrench with rubber insert

Spark plug gap adjusting tool
Feeler gauge set
Brake bleeder wrench
Standard screwdriver (5/16-inch x 6 inch)
Phillips screwdriver (No. 2 x 6 inch)
Combination pliers – 6 inch
Hacksaw and assortment of blades
Tire pressure gauge
Grease gun
Oil can
Fine emery cloth
Wire brush
Battery post and cable cleaning tool
Oil filter wrench
Funnel (medium size)
Safety goggles
Jackstands (2)
Drain pan

Note: *If basic tune-ups are going to be part of routine maintenance, it will be necessary to purchase a good quality stroboscopic timing light and combination tachometer/dwell meter. Although they are included in the list of special tools, it is mentioned here because they are absolutely necessary for tuning most vehicles properly.*

Repair and overhaul tool set

These tools are essential for anyone who plans to perform major repairs and are in addition to those in the maintenance and minor repair tool kit. Included is a comprehensive set of sockets which, though expensive, are invaluable because of their versatility, especially when various extensions and drives are available. We recommend the 1/2-inch drive over the 3/8-inch drive. Although the larger drive is bulky and more expensive, it has the capacity of accepting a very wide range of large sockets. Ideally, however, the mechanic should have a 3/8-inch drive set and a 1/2-inch drive set.

Socket set(s)
Reversible ratchet
Extension – 10 inch
Universal joint
Torque wrench (same size drive as sockets)
Ball peen hammer – 8 ounce
Soft-face hammer (plastic/rubber)
Standard screwdriver (1/4-inch x 6 inch)
Standard screwdriver (stubby – 5/16-inch)
Phillips screwdriver (No. 3 x 8 inch)
Phillips screwdriver (stubby – No. 2)
Pliers – vise grip
Pliers – lineman's
Pliers – needle nose
Pliers – snap-ring (internal and external)
Cold chisel – 1/2-inch
Scribe
Scraper (made from flattened copper tubing)
Centerpunch
Pin punches (1/16, 1/8, 3/16-inch)
Steel rule/straightedge – 12 inch
Allen wrench set (1/8 to 3/8-inch or 4 mm to 10 mm)
A selection of files
Wire brush (large)
Jackstands (second set)
Jack (scissor or hydraulic type)

Note: *Another tool which is often useful is an electric drill with a chuck capacity of 3/8-inch and a set of good quality drill bits.*

Special tools

The tools in this list include those which are not used regularly, are expensive to buy, or which need to be used in accordance with their manufacturer's instructions. Unless these tools will be used frequently, it is not very economical to purchase many of them. A consideration would be to split the cost and use between yourself and a friend or friends. In addition, most of these tools can be obtained from a tool rental shop on a temporary basis.

This list primarily contains only those tools and instruments widely available to the public, and not those special tools produced by the vehicle manufacturer for distribution to dealer service departments. Occasionally, references to the manufacturer's special tools are included in the text of this manual. Generally, an alternative method of doing the job without the special tool is offered. However, sometimes there is no alternative to their use. Where this is the case, and the tool cannot be purchased or borrowed, the work should be turned over to the dealer service department or an automotive repair shop.

Cylinder compression gauge
Micrometers and/or dial calipers
Balljoint separator
Universal-type puller
Impact screwdriver
Dial indicator set
Stroboscopic timing light (inductive pick-up)
Hand operated vacuum/pressure pump
Tachometer/dwell meter
Universal electrical multimeter
Cable hoist
Brake spring removal and installation tools
Floor jack

Buying tools

For the do-it-yourselfer who is just starting to get involved in vehicle maintenance and repair, there are a number of options available when purchasing tools. If maintenance and minor repair is the extent of the work to be done, the purchase of individual tools is satisfactory. If, on the other hand, extensive work is planned, it would be a good idea to purchase a modest tool set from one of the large retail chain stores. A set can usually be bought at a substantial savings over the individual tool prices, and they often come with a tool box. As additional tools are needed, add-on sets, individual tools and a larger tool box can be purchased to expand the tool selection. Building a tool set gradually allows the cost of the tools to be spread over a longer period of time and gives the mechanic the freedom to choose only those tools that will actually be used.

Tool stores will often be the only source of some of the special tools that are needed, but regardless of where tools are bought, try to avoid cheap ones, especially when buying screwdrivers and sockets, because they won't last very long. The expense involved in replacing cheap tools will eventually be greater than the initial cost of quality tools.

Care and maintenance of tools

Good tools are expensive, so it makes sense to treat them with respect. Keep them clean and in usable condition and store them properly when not in use. Always wipe off any dirt, grease or metal chips before putting them away. Never leave tools lying around in the work area. Upon completion of a job, always check closely under the hood for tools that may have been left there so they won't get lost during a test drive.

Some tools, such as screwdrivers, pliers, wrenches and sockets, can be hung on a panel mounted on the garage or workshop wall, while others should be kept in a tool box or tray. Measuring instruments, gauges, meters, etc. must be carefully stored where they cannot be damaged by weather or impact from other tools.

When tools are used with care and stored properly, they will last a very long time. Even with the best of care, though, tools will wear out if used frequently. When a tool is damaged or worn out, replace it. Subsequent jobs will be safer and more enjoyable if you do.

Working facilities

Not to be overlooked when discussing tools is the workshop. If anything more than routine maintenance is to be carried out, some sort of suitable work area is essential.

It is understood, and appreciated, that many home mechanics do not have a good workshop or garage available, and end up removing an engine or doing major repairs outside. It is recommended, however, that the overhaul or repair be completed under the cover of a roof.

A clean, flat workbench or table of comfortable working height is an absolute necessity. The workbench should be equipped with a vise that has a jaw opening of at least four inches.

As mentioned previously, some clean, dry storage space is also required for tools, as well as the lubricants, fluids, cleaning solvents, etc. which soon become necessary.

Sometimes waste oil and fluids, drained from the engine or cooling system during normal maintenance or repairs, present a disposal problem. To avoid pouring them on the ground or into a sewage system, pour the used fluids into large containers, seal them with caps and take them to an authorized disposal site or recycling center. Plastic jugs, such as old antifreeze containers, are ideal for this purpose.

Always keep a supply of old newspapers and clean rags available. Old towels are excellent for mopping up spills. Many mechanics use rolls of paper towels for most work because they are readily available and disposable. To help keep the area under the vehicle clean, a large cardboard box can be cut open and flattened to protect the garage or shop floor.

Whenever working over a painted surface, such as when leaning over a fender to service something under the hood, always cover it with an old blanket or bedspread to protect the finish. Vinyl covered pads, made especially for this purpose, are available at auto parts stores.

Booster battery (jump) starting

Observe these precautions when using a booster battery to start a vehicle:

a) Before connecting the booster battery, make sure the ignition switch is in the Off position.
b) Turn off the lights, heater and other electrical loads.
c) Your eyes should be shielded. Safety goggles are a good idea.
d) Make sure the booster battery is the same voltage as the dead one in the vehicle.
e) The two vehicles MUST NOT TOUCH each other!
f) Make sure the transmission is in Neutral (manual) or Park (automatic).
g) If the booster battery is not a maintenance-free type, rèmove the vent caps and lay a cloth over the vent holes.

Connect the red jumper cable to the positive (+) terminals of each battery.

Connect one end of the black jumper cable to the negative (–) terminal of the booster battery. The other end of this cable should be connected to a good ground on the vehicle to be started, such as a bolt or bracket on the engine block **(see illustration)**. Make sure the cable will not come into contact with the fan, drivebelts or other moving parts of the engine.

Start the engine using the booster battery, then, with the engine running at idle speed, disconnect the jumper cables in the reverse order of connection.

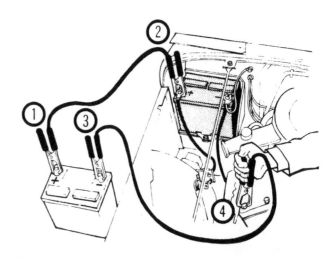

Make the booster battery cable connections in the numerical order shown (note that the negative cable of the booster battery is NOT attached to the negative terminal of the dead battery)

Jacking and towing

Jacking

Warning: *The jack supplied with the vehicle should only be used for raising the vehicle when changing a tire or placing jackstands under the frame. Never work under the vehicle or start the engine while the jack is being used as the only means of support.*

The vehicle must be parked on a level surface with the wheels blocked, the hazard flashers on and the transmission in Park (automatic) or Reverse (manual). Apply the parking brake if the front of the vehicle must be raised. Make sure no one is in the vehicle when using the jack to lift it.

Remove the jack, lug nut wrench and spare tire (if needed) from the vehicle. If a tire is being changed, loosen the lug nuts one-half turn, but leave them in place until the tire is off the ground. Some models have a center cap which must be pried out of the wheel to get at the lug nuts. Convertible models have a special center cap that requires a wrench for removal (the wrench should be in the glove compartment – it's made of plastic, so be very careful not to damage it).

Place the jack under the vehicle in the indicated position **(see illustration)**. Turn the jack handle clockwise until the tire clears the ground. Remove the lug nuts, pull off the wheel and install the spare. Thread the lug nuts back on and tighten them snugly. Don't attempt to tighten them completely until the vehicle is lowered to the ground.

Turn the jack handle counterclockwise to lower the vehicle. Remove the jack and tighten the lug nuts (if loosened or removed) in a criss-cross pattern. If possible, use a torque wrench to tighten them (see Chapter 1 for the torque figures). If you don't have a torque wrench, have the nuts checked by a service station or repair shop as soon as possible.

Stow the tire, jack and wrench and unblock the wheels.

Towing

Vehicles with a manual transmission

The vehicle can be towed with all four wheels on the ground, if the transmission, rear axle and steering system are undamaged. A towing dolly must be used if any of the components are damaged.

Vehicles with an automatic transmission

The vehicle can be towed with all four wheels on the ground if speeds don't exceed 30 mph and the distance is less than 10 miles, otherwise transmission damage can result.

All vehicles

Equipment specifically designed for towing should be used. It should be attached to the main structural members of the vehicle, not the bumpers or brackets. Safety is a major consideration when towing and all applicable state and local laws must be obeyed. A safety chain must be used.

The parking brake must be released and the transmission must be in Neutral. The steering must be unlocked (ignition switch in the Accessory position). Remember that power steering and power brakes won't work with the engine off.

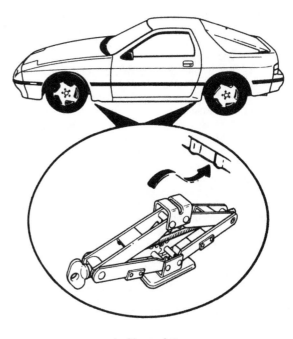

Jacking points

Automotive chemicals and lubricants

A number of automotive chemicals and lubricants are available for use during vehicle maintenance and repair. They include a wide variety of products ranging from cleaning solvents and degreasers to lubricants and protective sprays for rubber, plastic and vinyl.

Cleaners

Carburetor cleaner and choke cleaner is a strong solvent for gum, varnish and carbon. Most carburetor cleaners leave a dry-type lubricant film which will not harden or gum up. Because of this film it is not recommended for use on electrical components.

Brake system cleaner is used to remove grease and brake fluid from the brake system, where clean surfaces are absolutely necessary. It leaves no residue and often eliminates brake squeal caused by contaminants.

Electrical cleaner removes oxidation, corrosion and carbon deposits from electrical contacts, restoring full current flow. It can also be used to clean spark plugs, carburetor jets, voltage regulators and other parts where an oil-free surface is desired.

Demoisturants remove water and moisture from electrical components such as alternators, voltage regulators, electrical connectors and fuse blocks. They are non-conductive, non-corrosive and non-flammable.

Degreasers are heavy-duty solvents used to remove grease from the outside of the engine and from chassis components. They can be sprayed or brushed on and, depending on the type, are rinsed off either with water or solvent.

Lubricants

Motor oil is the lubricant formulated for use in engines. It normally contains a wide variety of additives to prevent corrosion and reduce foaming and wear. Motor oil comes in various weights (viscosity ratings) from 5 to 80. The recommended weight of the oil depends on the season, temperature and the demands on the engine. Light oil is used in cold climates and under light load conditions. Heavy oil is used in hot climates and where high loads are encountered. Multi-viscosity oils are designed to have characteristics of both light and heavy oils and are available in a number of weights from 5W-20 to 20W-50.

Gear oil is designed to be used in differentials, manual transmissions and other areas where high-temperature lubrication is required.

Chassis and wheel bearing grease is a heavy grease used where increased loads and friction are encountered, such as for wheel bearings, balljoints, tie-rod ends and universal joints.

High-temperature wheel bearing grease is designed to withstand the extreme temperatures encountered by wheel bearings in disc brake equipped vehicles. It usually contains molybdenum disulfide (moly), which is a dry-type lubricant.

White grease is a heavy grease for metal-to-metal applications where water is a problem. White grease stays soft under both low and high temperatures (usually from −100 to +190-degrees F), and will not wash off or dilute in the presence of water.

Assembly lube is a special extreme pressure lubricant, usually containing moly, used to lubricate high-load parts (such as main and rod bearings and cam lobes) for initial start-up of a new engine. The assembly lube lubricates the parts without being squeezed out or washed away until the engine oiling system begins to function.

Silicone lubricants are used to protect rubber, plastic, vinyl and nylon parts.

Graphite lubricants are used where oils cannot be used due to contamination problems, such as in locks. The dry graphite will lubricate metal parts while remaining uncontaminated by dirt, water, oil or acids. It is electrically conductive and will not foul electrical contacts in locks such as the ignition switch.

Moly penetrants loosen and lubricate frozen, rusted and corroded fasteners and prevent future rusting or freezing.

Heat-sink grease is a special electrically non-conductive grease that is used for mounting electronic ignition modules where it is essential that heat is transferred away from the module.

Sealants

RTV sealant is one of the most widely used gasket compounds. Made from silicone, RTV is air curing, it seals, bonds, waterproofs, fills surface irregularities, remains flexible, doesn't shrink, is relatively easy to remove, and is used as a supplementary sealer with almost all low and medium temperature gaskets.

Anaerobic sealant is much like RTV in that it can be used either to seal gaskets or to form gaskets by itself. It remains flexible, is solvent resistant and fills surface imperfections. The difference between an anaerobic sealant and an RTV-type sealant is in the curing. RTV cures when exposed to air, while an anaerobic sealant cures only in the absence of air. This means that an anaerobic sealant cures only after the assembly of parts, sealing them together.

Thread and pipe sealant is used for sealing hydraulic and pneumatic fittings and vacuum lines. It is usually made from a teflon compound, and comes in a spray, a paint-on liquid and as a wrap-around tape.

Chemicals

Anti-seize compound prevents seizing, galling, cold welding, rust and corrosion in fasteners. High-temperature anti-seize, usually made with copper and graphite lubricants, is used for exhaust system and exhaust manifold bolts.

Anaerobic locking compounds are used to keep fasteners from vibrating or working loose and cure only after installation, in the absence of air. Medium strength locking compound is used for small nuts, bolts and screws that may be removed later. High-strength locking compound is for large nuts, bolts and studs which aren't removed on a regular basis.

Oil additives range from viscosity index improvers to chemical treatments that claim to reduce internal engine friction. It should be noted that most oil manufacturers caution against using additives with their oils.

Gas additives perform several functions, depending on their chemical makeup. They usually contain solvents that help dissolve gum and varnish that build up on carburetor, fuel injection and intake parts. They also serve to break down carbon deposits that form on the inside surfaces of the combustion chambers. Some additives contain upper cylinder lubricants for valves and piston rings, and others contain chemicals to remove condensation from the gas tank.

Miscellaneous

Brake fluid is specially formulated hydraulic fluid that can withstand the heat and pressure encountered in brake systems. Care must be taken so this fluid does not come in contact with painted surfaces or plastics. An opened container should always be resealed to prevent contamination by water or dirt.

Weatherstrip adhesive is used to bond weatherstripping around doors, windows and trunk lids. It is sometimes used to attach trim pieces.

Undercoating is a petroleum-based, tar-like substance that is designed to protect metal surfaces on the underside of the vehicle from corrosion. It also acts as a sound-deadening agent by insulating the bottom of the vehicle.

Waxes and polishes are used to help protect painted and plated surfaces from the weather. Different types of paint may require the use of different types of wax and polish. Some polishes utilize a chemical or abrasive cleaner to help remove the top layer of oxidized (dull) paint on older vehicles. In recent years many non-wax polishes that contain a wide variety of chemicals such as polymers and silicones have been introduced. These non-wax polishes are usually easier to apply and last longer than conventional waxes and polishes.

Safety first!

Regardless of how enthusiastic you may be about getting on with the job at hand, take the time to ensure that your safety is not jeopardized. A moment's lack of attention can result in an accident, as can failure to observe certain simple safety precautions. The possibility of an accident will always exist, and the following points should not be considered a comprehensive list of all dangers. Rather, they are intended to make you aware of the risks and to encourage a safety conscious approach to all work you carry out on your vehicle.

Essential DOs and DON'Ts

DON'T rely on a jack when working under the vehicle. Always use approved jackstands to support the weight of the vehicle and place them under the recommended lift or support points.

DON'T attempt to loosen extremely tight fasteners (i.e. wheel lug nuts) while the vehicle is on a jack – it may fall.

DON'T start the engine without first making sure that the transmission is in Neutral (or Park where applicable) and the parking brake is set.

DON'T remove the radiator cap from a hot cooling system – let it cool or cover it with a cloth and release the pressure gradually.

DON'T attempt to drain the engine oil until you are sure it has cooled to the point that it will not burn you.

DON'T touch any part of the engine or exhaust system until it has cooled sufficiently to avoid burns.

DON'T siphon toxic liquids such as gasoline, antifreeze and brake fluid by mouth, or allow them to remain on your skin.

DON'T inhale brake lining dust – it is potentially hazardous (see Asbestos below)

DON'T allow spilled oil or grease to remain on the floor – wipe it up before someone slips on it.

DON'T use loose fitting wrenches or other tools which may slip and cause injury.

DON'T push on wrenches when loosening or tightening nuts or bolts. Always try to pull the wrench toward you. If the situation calls for pushing the wrench away, push with an open hand to avoid scraped knuckles if the wrench should slip.

DON'T attempt to lift a heavy component alone – get someone to help you.

DON'T rush or take unsafe shortcuts to finish a job.

DON'T allow children or animals in or around the vehicle while you are working on it.

DO wear eye protection when using power tools such as a drill, sander, bench grinder, etc. and when working under a vehicle.

DO keep loose clothing and long hair well out of the way of moving parts.

DO make sure that any hoist used has a safe working load rating adequate for the job.

DO get someone to check on you periodically when working alone on a vehicle.

DO carry out work in a logical sequence and make sure that everything is correctly assembled and tightened.

DO keep chemicals and fluids tightly capped and out of the reach of children and pets.

DO remember that your vehicle's safety affects that of yourself and others. If in doubt on any point, get professional advice.

Asbestos

Certain friction, insulating, sealing, and other products – such as brake linings, brake bands, clutch linings, torque converters, gaskets, etc. – contain asbestos. *Extreme care must be taken to avoid inhalation of dust from such products since it is hazardous to health.* If in doubt, assume that they *do* contain asbestos.

Fire

Remember at all times that gasoline is highly flammable. Never smoke or have any kind of open flame around when working on a vehicle. But the risk does not end there. A spark caused by an electrical short circuit, by two metal surfaces contacting each other, or even by static electricity built up in your body under certain conditions, can ignite gasoline vapors, which in a confined space are highly explosive. Do not, under any circumstances, use gasoline for cleaning parts. Use an approved safety solvent.

Always disconnect the battery ground (–) cable *at the battery* before working on any part of the fuel system or electrical system. Never risk spilling fuel on a hot engine or exhaust component.

It is strongly recommended that a fire extinguisher suitable for use on fuel and electrical fires be kept handy in the garage or workshop at all times. Never try to extinguish a fuel or electrical fire with water.

Fumes

Certain fumes are highly toxic and can quickly cause unconsciousness and even death if inhaled to any extent. Gasoline vapor falls into this category, as do the vapors from some cleaning solvents. Any draining or pouring of such volatile fluids should be done in a well ventilated area.

When using cleaning fluids and solvents, read the instructions on the container carefully. Never use materials from unmarked containers.

Never run the engine in an enclosed space, such as a garage. Exhaust fumes contain carbon monoxide, which is extremely poisonous. If you need to run the engine, always do so in the open air, or at least have the rear of the vehicle outside the work area.

If you are fortunate enough to have the use of an inspection pit, never drain or pour gasoline and never run the engine while the vehicle is over the pit. The fumes, being heavier than air, will concentrate in the pit with possibly lethal results.

The battery

Never create a spark or allow a bare light bulb near a battery. They normally give off a certain amount of hydrogen gas, which is highly explosive.

Always disconnect the battery ground (–) cable *at the battery* before working on the fuel or electrical systems.

If possible, loosen the filler caps or cover when charging the battery from an external source (this does not apply to sealed or maintenancefree batteries). Do not charge at an excessive rate or the battery may burst.

Take care when adding water to a non maintenance–free battery and when carrying a battery. The electrolyte, even when diluted, is very corrosive and should not be allowed to contact clothing or skin.

Always wear eye protection when cleaning the battery to prevent the caustic deposits from entering your eyes.

Household current

When using an electric power tool, inspection light, etc., which operates on household current, always make sure that the tool is correctly connected to its plug and that, where necessary, it is properly grounded. Do not use such items in damp conditions and, again, do not create a spark or apply excessive heat in the vicinity of fuel or fuel vapor.

Secondary ignition system voltage

A severe electric shock can result from touching certain parts of the ignition system (such as the spark plug wires) when the engine is running or being cranked, particularly if components are damp or the insulation is defective. In the case of an electronic ignition system, the secondary system voltage is much higher and could prove fatal.

Conversion factors

Length (distance)
Inches (in)	X	25.4	= Millimetres (mm)	X	0.0394	= Inches (in)
Feet (ft)	X	0.305	= Metres (m)	X	3.281	= Feet (ft)
Miles	X	1.609	= Kilometres (km)	X	0.621	= Miles

Inches (in)   X   25.4 = Millimetres (mm)   X   0.0394 = Inches (in)
Feet (ft)   X   0.305 = Metres (m)   X   3.281 = Feet (ft)
Miles   X   1.609 = Kilometres (km)   X   0.621 = Miles

Volume (capacity)
Cubic inches (cu in; in³)   X   16.387 = Cubic centimetres (cc; cm³)   X   0.061 = Cubic inches (cu in; in³)
Imperial pints (Imp pt)   X   0.568 = Litres (l)   X   1.76 = Imperial pints (Imp pt)
Imperial quarts (Imp qt)   X   1.137 = Litres (l)   X   0.88 = Imperial quarts (Imp qt)
Imperial quarts (Imp qt)   X   1.201 = US quarts (US qt)   X   0.833 = Imperial quarts (Imp qt)
US quarts (US qt)   X   0.946 = Litres (l)   X   1.057 = US quarts (US qt)
Imperial gallons (Imp gal)   X   4.546 = Litres (l)   X   0.22 = Imperial gallons (Imp gal)
Imperial gallons (Imp gal)   X   1.201 = US gallons (US gal)   X   0.833 = Imperial gallons (Imp gal)
US gallons (US gal)   X   3.785 = Litres (l)   X   0.264 = US gallons (US gal)

Mass (weight)
Ounces (oz)   X   28.35 = Grams (g)   X   0.035 = Ounces (oz)
Pounds (lb)   X   0.454 = Kilograms (kg)   X   2.205 = Pounds (lb)

Force
Ounces-force (ozf; oz)   X   0.278 = Newtons (N)   X   3.6 = Ounces-force (ozf; oz)
Pounds-force (lbf; lb)   X   4.448 = Newtons (N)   X   0.225 = Pounds-force (lbf; lb)
Newtons (N)   X   0.1 = Kilograms-force (kgf; kg)   X   9.81 = Newtons (N)

Pressure
Pounds-force per square inch (psi; lbf/in²; lb/in²)   X   0.070 = Kilograms-force per square centimetre (kgf/cm²; kg/cm²)   X   14.223 = Pounds-force per square inch (psi; lbf/in²; lb/in²)
Pounds-force per square inch (psi; lbf/in²; lb/in²)   X   0.068 = Atmospheres (atm)   X   14.696 = Pounds-force per square inch (psi; lbf/in²; lb/in²)
Pounds-force per square inch (psi; lbf/in²; lb/in²)   X   0.069 = Bars   X   14.5 = Pounds-force per square inch (psi; lbf/in²; lb/in²)
Pounds-force per square inch (psi; lbf/in²; lb/in²)   X   6.895 = Kilopascals (kPa)   X   0.145 = Pounds-force per square inch (psi; lbf/in²; lb/in²)
Kilopascals (kPa)   X   0.01 = Kilograms-force per square centimetre (kgf/cm²; kg/cm²)   X   98.1 = Kilopascals (kPa)

Torque (moment of force)
Pounds-force inches (lbf in; lb in)   X   1.152 = Kilograms-force centimetre (kgf cm; kg cm)   X   0.868 = Pounds-force inches (lbf in; lb in)
Pounds-force inches (lbf in; lb in)   X   0.113 = Newton metres (Nm)   X   8.85 = Pounds-force inches (lbf in; lb in)
Pounds-force inches (lbf in; lb in)   X   0.083 = Pounds-force feet (lbf ft; lb ft)   X   12 = Pounds-force inches (lbf in; lb in)
Pounds-force feet (lbf ft; lb ft)   X   0.138 = Kilograms-force metres (kgf m; kg m)   X   7.233 = Pounds-force feet (lbf ft; lb ft)
Pounds-force feet (lbf ft; lb ft)   X   1.356 = Newton metres (Nm)   X   0.738 = Pounds-force feet (lbf ft; lb ft)
Newton metres (Nm)   X   0.102 = Kilograms-force metres (kgf m; kg m)   X   9.804 = Newton metres (Nm)

Power
Horsepower (hp)   X   745.7 = Watts (W)   X   0.0013 = Horsepower (hp)

Velocity (speed)
Miles per hour (miles/hr; mph)   X   1.609 = Kilometres per hour (km/hr; kph)   X   0.621 = Miles per hour (miles/hr; mph)

Fuel consumption*
Miles per gallon, Imperial (mpg)   X   0.354 = Kilometres per litre (km/l)   X   2.825 = Miles per gallon, Imperial (mpg)
Miles per gallon, US (mpg)   X   0.425 = Kilometres per litre (km/l)   X   2.352 = Miles per gallon, US (mpg)

Temperature
Degrees Fahrenheit = (°C x 1.8) + 32   Degrees Celsius (Degrees Centigrade; °C) = (°F - 32) x 0.56

*It is common practice to convert from miles per gallon (mpg) to litres/100 kilometres (l/100km), where mpg (Imperial) x l/100 km = 282 and mpg (US) x l/100 km = 235

Troubleshooting

Contents

Symptom	Section

Engine

Afterburn (popping noises in exhaust) 9
Engine doesn't return to idle or maintains high idle speed
   at normal operating temperature 6
Engine hard to start when cold, runs roughly when cold
   or stalls when cold 3
Engine hard to start when hot, runs roughly when hot
   or stalls when hot 4
Engine lacks power, accelerates poorly or hesitates 8
Engine idles roughly or erratically 5
Engine rotates but will not start 2
Engine runs rough during deceleration 10
Engine starts but stops immediately, runs roughly at normal
   operating temperature or stalls at normal operating temperature 7
Engine will not rotate when attempting to start 1
Excessive oil consumption 11

Engine electrical system

Battery will not hold a charge 12
Voltage warning light fails to come on when key is turned on 14
Voltage warning light fails to go out 13

Fuel system

Excessive fuel consumption 15
Fuel leakage and/or fuel odor 16

Cooling system

Coolant loss 20
External coolant leakage 19
Overcooling 18
Overheating 17
Poor coolant circulation 21

Clutch

Clutch pedal stays on floor 30
Clutch slips (engine speed increases with no increase
   in vehicle speed) 27
Fluid in area of master cylinder dust cover and on pedal 23
Fluid on slave cylinder 24
Grabbing (chattering) as clutch is engaged 28
High pedal effort 31
Noise in clutch area 29
Pedal feels "spongy" when depressed 25
Pedal travels to floor – no pressure or very little resistance 22
Unable to select gears 26

Manual transmission

Leaks lubricant 37
Noisy in all gears 35
Noisy in Neutral with engine running 33
Noisy in one particular gear 34
Slips out of gear 36
Vibration 32

Automatic transmission

Engine will start in gears other than Park or Neutral 41
Fluid leakage 38
General shift mechanism problems 40
Transmission fluid brown or has a burned smell 39
Transmission slips, shifts roughly, is noisy or has no drive
   in forward or reverse gears 42

Brakes

Brake pedal feels spongy when depressed 50
Brake pedal travels to the floor with little resistance 51
Brake roughness or chatter (pedal pulsates) 45
Dragging brakes 48
Excessive brake pedal travel 47
Excessive pedal effort required to stop vehicle 46
Grabbing or uneven braking action 49
Noise (high-pitched squeal when the brakes are applied) 44
Parking brake does not hold 52
Vehicle pulls to one side during braking 43

Suspension and steering systems

Abnormal noise at the front end 59
Abnormal or excessive tire wear 54
Cupped tires 64
Erratic steering when braking 61
Excessive pitching and/or rolling around corners or
   during braking 62
Excessive play or looseness in steering system 68
Excessive tire wear on inside edge 66
Excessive tire wear on outside edge 65
Hard steering 57
Rattling or clicking noise in rack and pinion 69
Shimmy, shake or vibration 56
Steering, wheel does not return to center position correctly 58
Suspension bottoms 63
Tire tread worn in one place 67
Vehicle pulls to one side 53
Wander or poor steering stability 60
Wheel makes a "thumping" noise 55

This section provides an easy reference guide to the more common problems which may occur during the operation of a vehicle. These problems and their possible causes are grouped under headings denoting various components or systems, such as Engine, Cooling system, etc. They also refer you to the Chapter and/or Section which deals with the problem.

Remember, successful troubleshooting isn't a mysterious black art practiced only by professional mechanics. It's simply the result of the right knowledge combined with an intelligent, systematic approach to a problem. Always use the process of elimination, starting with the simplest solution and working through to the most complex – and never overlook the obvious. Anyone can run the gas tank dry or leave the lights on overnight, so don't assume that it can't happen to you.

Finally, always try to establish a clear idea why a problem has occurred and take steps to ensure that it doesn't happen again. If the electrical system fails because of a poor connection, check all other connections in the system to make sure they don't fail as well. If a particular fuse continues to blow, find out why – don't just replace one fuse after another. Remember, failure of a small component can often be indicative of potential failure or incorrect functioning of a more important component or system.

Engine

Note: *The first step in each of the engine troubleshooting sections is to take the vehicle to a dealer and have the service department extract any trouble codes with a digital code checker. If you wish to purchase your own digital code checker, see the last Section in Chapter 6 for more information.*

1 Engine will not rotate when attempting to start

1 Battery terminal connections loose or corroded or battery discharged or defective (Chapter 1).
2 Automatic transmission not completely engaged in Park (Chapter 7) or clutch not completely depressed (Chapter 8).
3 Broken, loose or disconnected starting circuit wiring (Chapter 5).
4 Starter motor pinion jammed in flywheel ring gear (Chapter 5).
5 Starter pinion or flywheel teeth (Chapter 2) worn or broken.
6 Starter motor or solenoid defective (Chapter 5).
7 Defective ignition switch (Chapter 12).
8 Engine seized; eccentric shaft won't turn (Chapter 2, Part B).

2 Engine rotates but will not start

1 Fuel tank empty or fuel pump strainer clogged (Chapter 4).
2 Battery discharged – engine rotates slowly (Chapter 5).
3 Battery terminal connections loose or corroded (Chapter 1).
4 Defective ignition component(s) (Chapter 5).
5 Worn or defective spark plugs (Chapter 1).
6 Broken, loose or disconnected starting circuit wiring (Chapter 5).
7 Loose crank angle sensor (Chapter 5).
8 Broken, loose or disconnected wires at coil (with igniter) or defective coil (Chapter 5).
9 No fuel (check for pulsations at main fuel hose by hand) (Chapter 4).
10 Primary fuel injector(s) malfunctioning (Chapter 4).
11 Leaking fuel injector, fuel pump, pressure regulator, etc. (Chapter 4).
12 Fuel not reaching fuel rail/low fuel pressure (Chapter 4).
13 Defective fuel system solenoid resistor (Chapter 4).
14 Defective secondary air injection system water thermo sensor (Chapter 6).
15 Faulty fuel pump switch in air flow meter (Chapter 4).
16 Air flow meter malfunctioning (Chapter 4).
17 Incorrect fuel pressure (Chapter 4).

18 Low compression (Chapter 2).
19 Defective control unit (take the vehicle to a dealer).

3 Engine hard to start when cold, runs roughly when cold or stalls when cold

1 Battery discharged or low (Chapter 1).
2 Defective or leaking injector(s) (Chapter 4).
3 No or low fuel pressure (check for pulsations at main fuel hose by hand) (Chapter 4).
4 Faulty fuel system component (Chapter 4).
5 Ignition timing incorrect/malfunctioning ignition system (Chapter 5).
6 Air intake system vacuum leak (Chapter 4).
7 Malfunctioning double throttle system (Chapter 4).
8 Incorrect idle speed (Chapters 1 and 4).
9 Incorrect fast idle operation (Chapter 4).
10 Faulty throttle sensor (Chapter 4).
11 Malfunctioning bypass air control (BAC) system or idle speed control (ISC) system (Chapter 4).
12 Malfunctioning secondary air injection system air control valve (check port air at idle speed) (Chapter 6).
13 Incorrect amount of fuel flow at idle (check variable resistor connection and resistance) (Chapter 4).
14 Bad secondary air injection system water thermo sensor (Chapter 6).
15 Faulty EGR valve or EGR system component (Chapter 6).
16 Defective air flow meter and/or intake air temperature sensor on air flow meter (Chapter 4).
17 Incorrect fuel pressure or malfunctioning fuel pump control system (Chapter 4).
18 Faulty or leaking primary injector(s) (Chapter 4).
19 Incorrect injection volume (Chapter 4).
20 Faulty crankcase and evaporative emission control system purge control valve (Chapter 6).
21 Clogged exhaust system (Chapter 4).
22 Malfunctioning deceleration control system (Chapter 6).
23 Low compression (Chapter 2, Part B).
24 Faulty sub-zero starting assist system (Chapters 1 and 4).
25 Defective control unit or system (take the vehicle to a dealer).

4 Engine hard to start when hot, runs roughly when hot or stalls when hot

1 Air filter clogged (Chapter 4).
2 Fuel not reaching injectors (Chapter 4).
3 Corroded battery terminals – especially ground (Chapter 1).
4 Incorrect ignition timing (Chapter 5).
5 Malfunctioning Electronic Spark Advance system (Chapter 5).
6 Incorrect idle speed (Chapters 1 and 4).
7 Faulty throttle sensor (Chapter 4).
8 Injector(s) malfunctioning (Chapter 3).
9 Faulty (hot start assist system) pressure regulator control solenoid (Chapter 4).
10 Faulty intake air temperature sensor on dynamic chamber (non-turbo) or air intake pipe (turbo) (Chapter 4).
11 Bad secondary air injection system water thermo sensor (Chapter 6).
12 Air intake system air leak (Chapter 4).
13 Malfunction in bypass air control (BAC) system or idle speed control (ISC) system (Chapter 4).
14 Faulty secondary air injection system air control valve (ACV) (Chapter 6).
15 Poor fuel flow at idle (check variable resistor connection and resistor) (Chapter 4).
16 Malfunctioning pressure regulator control system (Chapter 4).
17 Defective air flow meter and/or intake air temperature sensor (Chapter 4).

18 No fuel pressure (check for pulsations at main fuel hose by hand) (Chapter 4).

19 Incorrect fuel pressure (Chapter 4).

20 Faulty fuel pump control system (Chapter 4).

21 Defective fuel system solenoid resistor (Chapter 4).

22 Leaking injector(s) (Chapter 4).

23 Incorrect injection volume (Chapter 4).

24 Faulty crankcase and evaporative emission control system purge control valve (Chapter 6).

25 Low compression pressure (Chapter 2, Part B).

26 Faulty hot start assist system (Chapter 4).

27 Faulty control unit or system (take the vehicle to a dealer).

5 Engine idles roughly or erratically

1 Leaking intake air system (Chapter 4).

2 Incorrect idle speed (Chapters 1 and 4).

3 Incorrect ignition timing (Chapter 5).

4 Malfunctioning Electronic Spark Advance system (Chapter 5).

5 Malfunctioning 6-port induction (6PI) system (Chapter 4).

6 Clogged air filter (Chapter 1).

7 Bad secondary air injection system water thermo sensor (Chapter 6).

8 Faulty atmospheric pressure sensor (Chapter 4).

9 Faulty throttle sensor (Chapter 4).

10 Primary injector(s) malfunctioning (Chapter 4).

11 Malfunctioning fuel pump control system (Chapter 4).

12 By-pass air control (BAC) system/idle speed control (ISC) system malfunctioning (Chapter 4).

13 Defective secondary air injection system air control valve (ACV) (Chapter 6).

14 Faulty fast idle operation (Chapter 4).

15 Poor fuel flow at idle (Chapter 4).

16 Faulty air flow meter and/or intake air temperature sensor (Chapter 4).

17 Defective intake air temperature sensor on dynamic chamber (non-turbo) or air intake pipe (turbo) (Chapter 4).

18 Defective EGR valve (Chapter 6).

19 Incorrect fuel pressure (Chapter 4).

20 Low compression pressure (Chapter 2, Part B).

21 Malfunctioning control unit or control system (take the vehicle to a dealer).

6 Engine doesn't return to idle, or maintains high idle speed at normal operating temperature

1 Throttle cable stuck (Chapter 4).

2 Throttle body throttle valves stuck (Chapter 4).

3 Fast idle cam on throttle body not releasing from roller (Chapter 4).

4 Leaking intake air system (Chapter 4).

5 Bad throttle sensor (Chapter 4).

6 Incorrect idle speed (Chapters 1 and 4).

7 Malfunctioning bypass air control (BAC) system/idle speed control (ISC) system (Chapter 4).

8 Defective bypass air control (BAC) system air bypass solenoid valve (Chapter 4).

9 Incorrect ignition timing (Chapter 5).

10 Defective deceleration control system anti-afterburn valve, dash pot or air bypass valve (Chapter 6).

11 Incorrect fuel pressure (Chapter 4).

12 Malfunctioning pressure regulator control system (Chapter 4).

13 Defective air flow meter and/or intake air temperature sensor (Chapter 4).

14 Malfunctioning control unit and/or control system (take the vehicle to a dealer).

7 Engine starts but stops immediately, runs roughly at normal operating temperature or stalls at normal operating temperature

1 Leaking intake air system (Chapter 4).

2 Loose or dirty electrical connections at distributor, coil or alternator or malfunctioning Electronic Spark Advance (ESA) system (Chapter 5).

3 Insufficient fuel reaching the injector(s) (Chapter 4).

4 Vacuum leak at the gasket between the throttle body and dynamic chamber (Chapter 4).

5 Incorrect ignition timing (Chapter 5).

6 Incorrect idle speed (Chapters 1 and 4).

7 No or low fuel pressure (check for pulsations at main fuel hose by hand) (Chapter 4).

8 Defective fuel system solenoid resistor (Chapter 4).

9 Defective throttle sensor (Chapter 4).

10 Faulty primary fuel injector(s) (Chapter 4).

11 Malfunctioning bypass air control (BAC) system or idle speed control (ISC) system (Chapter 4).

12 Defective crankcase and evaporative emission control system purge control valve (Chapter 6).

13 Defective secondary air injection system air control valve (ACV) or water thermo sensor (Chapter 6).

14 Insufficient fuel flow at idle (check variable resistor connection and resistance) (Chapter 4).

15 Defective EGR valve (Chapter 6).

16 Defective air flow meter and/or intake air temperature sensor (Chapter 4).

17 Incorrect fuel pressure (Chapter 4).

18 Leaking fuel injector(s) (Chapter 4).

19 Incorrect injection volume (Chapter 4).

20 Plugged exhaust system (Chapter 4).

21 Low compression pressure (Chapter 2).

22 Faulty control unit or malfunctioning control system (take the vehicle to a dealer).

8 Engine lacks power, accelerates poorly or hesitates

1 Leaking intake air system (Chapter 4).

2 Malfunctioning 6 port induction (6PI) system or variable dynamic effect intake (Chapter 4).

3 Incorrect ignition timing or malfunctioning electronic spark advance system (Chapter 5).

4 Jumper wire hasn't been removed from the initial set switch connector (used to set idle speed) (Chapters 1 and 4).

5 Accelerator cable incorrectly adjusted or loose (Chapter 4).

6 Stuck double throttle system (Chapter 4).

7 Faulty electronic spark advance knock control system (turbo) (Chapter 5).

8 Defective secondary air injection system air control valve (ACV) or water thermo sensor (Chapter 6).

9 Air cleaner element clogged (Chapter 1).

10 Malfunctioning turbocharger (Chapter 4).

11 Defective waste gate valve (turbo) (Chapter 4).

12 Defective air flow meter, intake air temperature sensor or auxiliary port valve (Chapter 4).

13 Leaking injector(s) or incorrect injection volume (Chapter 4).

14 Defective fuel system boost sensor, pressure sensor or solenoid resistor (Chapter 4).

15 Incorrect fuel pressure/malfunctioning fuel pump control system (Chapter 4).

16 Faulty throttle sensor (Chapter 4).

17 Low compression pressure (Chapter 2, Part B).

18 Plugged exhaust system (Chapter 4).

19 Faulty A/C cut-out control switch (Chapter 4).

20 Malfunctioning control unit and/or control system (take the vehicle to a dealer).

9 Afterburn (popping noises in exhaust)

1 Incorrect ignition timing (Chapter 5).
2 Malfunctioning Electronic Spark Advance system (Chapter 5).
3 Leaking intake air system (Chapter 5).
4 Incorrect idle speed (Chapters 1 and 4).
5 Defective throttle sensor or fuel system pressure sensor (Chapter 4).
6 Defective air control valve (ACV), deceleration control system dash pot or anti-afterburn valve (AAV) (Chapter 6).
7 Malfunctioning bypass air control (BAC) system or idle speed control (ISC) system (Chapter 4).
8 Leaking or faulty injector(s) (Chapter 4).
9 Faulty secondary air injection control system water thermo sensor (Chapter 6).
10 Faulty air flow meter and/or intake air temperature sensor (Chapter 4).
11 Incorrect fuel pressure, malfunctioning fuel pump control system or incorrect fuel flow at idle (Chapter 4).
12 Defective EGR valve (Chapter 6).
13 Incorrect compression pressure (Chapter 2).
14 Faulty control unit and/or control system (take the vehicle to a dealer).

10 Engine runs rough during deceleration

1 Incorrect ignition timing/malfunctioning ignition system (Chapter 5).
2 Air intake system leaks (Chapter 5).
3 Incorrect idle speed (Chapters 1 and 4) or defective throttle sensor (Chapter 4).
4 Faulty secondary air injection system air control valve (ACV) or water thermo sensor (Chapter 6).
5 Defective deceleration control system dash pot (Chapter 6), faulty bypass air control (BAC) system or idle speed control (ISC) system.
6 Malfunctioning primary injector(s) (Chapter 4).
7 Defective air flow meter and/or intake air temperature sensor (Chapter 4).
8 Incorrect fuel pressure/faulty fuel system pressure sensor (Chapter 4).
9 Faulty EGR valve (Chapter 6).
10 Leaking injector(s) (Chapter 4).
11 Defective bypass air control system clutch switch or neutral switch (Chapter 4).
12 Incorrect compression pressure (Chapter 2, Part B).
13 Defective control unit or malfunctioning control system (take the vehicle to a dealer).

11 Excessive oil consumption

1 Check for external oil leaks and puddles under vehicle. Repair as necessary (see Chapter 2, Part A).
2 Check the metering oil pump and lines (see Chapter 2, Part A).
3 If there are no external oil leaks and the metering oil pump is adjusted and functioning properly, the internal engine seals are worn out or defective (see Chapter 2, Part B).

Engine electrical system

12 Battery will not hold a charge

1 Alternator drivebelt defective or not adjusted properly (Chapter 1).
2 Electrolyte level low (Chapter 1).
3 Battery terminal clamps loose or corroded (Chapter 1).
4 Alternator not charging properly (Chapter 5).

5 Loose, broken or faulty wiring in the charging circuit (Chapter 5).
6 Short in vehicle wiring (Chapters 5 and 12).
7 Internally defective battery (Chapters 1 and 5).

13 Voltage warning light fails to go out

1 Faulty alternator or charging circuit (Chapter 5).
2 Alternator drivebelt defective or not adjusted properly (Chapter 1).
3 Alternator voltage regulator inoperative (Chapter 5).

14 Voltage warning light fails to come on when key is turned on

1 Warning light bulb defective (Chapter 12).
2 Fault in the printed circuit, dash wiring or bulb holder (Chapter 12).

Fuel system

15 Excessive fuel consumption

1 Dirty or clogged air filter element (Chapter 1).
2 Incorrect ignition timing (Chapter 5).
3 Emissions system not functioning properly (Chapter 6).
4 Fuel injection internal parts excessively worn or damaged (Chapter 4).
5 Low tire pressure or incorrect tire size (Chapter 1).

16 Fuel leakage and/or fuel odor

1 Leak in a fuel or vapor line (Chapter 4).
2 Tank overfilled.
3 Evaporative canister filter clogged (Chapters 1 and 6).
4 Fuel injector internal parts excessively worn (Chapter 4).

Cooling system

17 Overheating

1 Low coolant level (Chapter 1).
2 Water pump drivebelt defective or out of adjustment (Chapter 1).
3 Radiator core blocked or grille restricted (Chapter 3).
4 Defective thermostat (Chapter 3).
5 Electric cooling fan blades broken or cracked (Chapter 3).
6 Radiator cap not maintaining proper pressure (Chapter 3).
7 Ignition timing incorrect (Chapter 5).

18 Overcooling

Defective thermostat (Chapter 3).

19 External coolant leakage

1 Deteriorated/damaged hoses or loose clamps (Chapters 1 and 3).
2 Water pump seal defective (Chapters 1 and 3).
3 Leaks at radiator core or header tank (Chapter 3).
4 Engine drain or water jacket core plugs leaking (Chapter 2)
5 On 1986 and 1987 models, a Dealer Technical Service Bulletin concerning this problem has been issued (no. 07/87). Contact a dealer service department for assistance.

20 Coolant loss

1   Too much coolant in system (Chapter 1).
2   Coolant boiling away because of overheating (Chapter 3).
3   Internal or external leaks (Chapter 3).
4   Faulty radiator cap (Chapter 3).

21 Poor coolant circulation

1   Inoperative water pump (Chapter 3).
2   Restriction in cooling system (Chapters 1 and 3).
3   Water pump drivebelt defective/out of adjustment (Chapter 1).
4   Thermostat stuck closed (Chapter 3).

Clutch

22 Pedal travels to floor – no pressure or very little resistance

1   Master or slave cylinder defective (Chapter 8).
2   Hose/line ruptured or leaking (Chapter 8).
3   Connections leaking (Chapter 8).
4   No fluid in reservoir (Chapter 1).
5   If fluid is present in master cylinder dust cover, rear master cylinder seal has failed (Chapter 8).
6   Broken release bearing or fork (Chapter 8).

23 Fluid in area of master cylinder dust cover and on pedal

Master cylinder rear seal failure (Chapter 8).

24 Fluid on slave cylinder

Defective slave cylinder plunger seal (Chapter 8).

25 Pedal feels "spongy" when depressed

Air in system (Chapter 8).

26 Unable to select gears

1   Faulty transmission (Chapter 7).
2   Faulty clutch disc (Chapter 8).
3   Fork and bearing not assembled properly (Chapter 8).
4   Faulty pressure plate (Chapter 8).
5   Pressure plate-to-flywheel bolts loose (Chapter 8).

27 Clutch slips (engine speed increases with no increase in vehicle speed)

1   Worn clutch plate (Chapter 8).
2   Clutch plate is contaminated with oil from leaking crankshaft rear main seal (Chapter 8).
3   Clutch plate not seated. It may take 30 or 40 normal starts for a new one to seat.
4   Warped pressure plate or flywheel (Chapter 8).
5   Weak diaphragm spring (Chapter 8).
6   Overheated clutch. Allow it to cool.

28 Grabbing (chattering) as clutch is engaged

1   Clutch plate lining burned/glazed/contaminated with oil (Chapter 8).
2   Worn or loose engine or transmission mounts (Chapters 2 and 7).
3   Clutch plate hub splines worn (Chapter 8).
4   Warped pressure plate or flywheel (Chapter 8).

29 Noise in clutch area

1   Fork shaft improperly installed (Chapter 8).
2   Defective input bearing (Chapter 8).

30 Clutch pedal stays on floor

1   Fork shaft binding in housing (Chapter 8).
2   Broken release bearing or fork (Chapter 8).

31 High pedal effort

1   Fork shaft binding in housing (Chapter 8).
2   Defective pressure plate (Chapter 8).
3   Incorrect master or slave cylinder installed (Chapter 8).

Manual transmission

32 Vibration

1   Rough wheel bearing (Chapters 1 and 10).
2   Damaged driveaxle (Chapter 8).
3   Out-of-round tires (Chapter 1).
4   Tire out-of-balance (Chapters 1 and 10).
5   Worn U-joint (Chapter 8).

33 Noisy in Neutral with engine running

Damaged clutch release bearing (Chapter 8).

34 Noisy in one particular gear

1   Damaged or worn constant mesh gears (Chapter 7).
2   Damaged or worn synchronizers (Chapter 7).

35 Noisy in all gears

1   Low oil level/lubricant (Chapter 1).
2   Damaged or worn bearings (Chapter 7).
3   Worn or damaged input or output gear shaft(s) (Chapter 7).

36 Slips out of gear

1   Worn or improperly adjusted linkage (Chapter 7).
2   Transmission-to-engine bolts loose (Chapter 7).
3   Shift linkage binding (Chapter 7).
4   Input shaft bearing retainer broken or loose (Chapter 7).
5   Dirt between bellhousing and engine (Chapter 7).
6   Worn shift fork (Chapter 7).

37 Leaks lubricant

1   Too much oil in transmission (Chapters 1 and 7).

2   Loose or broken input shaft bearing retainer (Chapter 7).
3   Output shaft seal damaged (Chapter 7).
4   Speedometer gear O-ring damaged (Chapter 7).

Automatic transmission

Note: *Due to the complexity of the automatic transmission, it's difficult for the home mechanic to properly diagnose and service. For problems other than the following, the vehicle should be taken to a dealer service department or a transmission shop.*

38   Fluid leakage

1   Automatic transmission fluid is a deep red color. Fluid leaks should not be confused with engine oil, which can easily be blown by air flow to the transmission.
2   To pinpoint a leak, first remove all built-up dirt and grime from the transmission housing with a degreaser. Then drive the vehicle at low speeds so air flow will not blow the leak far from its source. Raise the vehicle and determine where the fluid is coming from. Common areas where leaks occur are:
  a) Transmission fluid pan (Chapters 1 and 7)
  b) Filler pipe (Chapter 7)
  c) Transmission fluid cooler lines (Chapter 7)
  d) Speedometer gear O-ring (Chapter 7)

39   Transmission fluid brown or has a burned smell

Transmission fluid has been overheated (Chapter 1).

40   General shift mechanism problems

1   Chapter 7, Part B, deals with checking and adjusting the shift linkage on an automatic transmission. Common problems which may be caused by misadjusted linkage are:
  a) Engine starting in gears other than Park or Neutral.
  b) Indicator on shifter pointing to a gear other than the one actually being used.
  c) Vehicle moves when in Park.
2   Refer to Chapter 7, Part B, for the shift linkage adjustment procedure.

41   Engine will start in gears other than Park or Neutral

Neutral start switch malfunctioning (Chapter 7).

42   Transmission slips, shifts roughly, is noisy or has no drive in forward or reverse gears

There are many probable causes for these problems, but the home mechanic should be concerned with only one possibility – low fluid level. Before taking the vehicle to a repair shop, check the level and condition of the fluid as described in Chapter 1. Correct the fluid level as necessary or change the fluid and filter if needed. If the problem persists, have a professional diagnose the probable cause.

Brakes

Note: *Before assuming a brake problem exists, make sure the tires are in good condition and properly inflated (Chapter 1), the front end alignment is correct (Chapter 10) and the vehicle is not loaded with weight in an unequal manner.*

43   Vehicle pulls to one side during braking

1   Incorrect tire pressures (Chapter 1).
2   Front end out of alignment.
3   Unmatched tires on same axle.
4   Restricted brake lines or hoses (Chapter 9).
5   Malfunctioning caliper assembly (Chapter 9).
6   Loose suspension parts (Chapter 10).
7   Loose brake calipers (Chapter 9).

44   Noise (high-pitched squeal when the brakes are applied)

Front and/or rear disc brake pads worn out. The noise comes from the wear sensor metal backing plate rubbing against the disc. Replace pads with new ones immediately and check the disc for damage (Chapter 9).

45   Brake roughness or chatter (pedal pulsates)

1   Excessive lateral runout (Chapter 9).
2   Parallelism not within specifications (Chapter 9).
3   Uneven pad wear caused by caliper not sliding due to improper clearance or dirt (Chapter 9).
4   Defective rotor (Chapter 9).

46   Excessive pedal effort required to stop vehicle

1   Defective power brake booster (Chapter 9).
2   Partial system failure (Chapter 9).
3   Excessively worn brake pads (Chapter 9).
4   Piston in caliper stuck or sluggish (Chapter 9).
5   Brake pads contaminated with oil or grease (Chapter 9).
6   New pads installed and not yet seated. It will take a while for the new pad material to seat against the rotor.

47   Excessive brake pedal travel

1   Partial brake system failure (Chapter 9).
2   Insufficient fluid in master cylinder (Chapters 1 and 9).
3   Air trapped in system (Chapters 1 and 9).

48   Dragging brakes

1   Master cylinder pistons not returning correctly (Chapter 9).
2   Restricted brakes lines or hoses (Chapters 1 and 9).
3   Incorrect parking brake adjustment (Chapter 9).

49   Grabbing or uneven braking action

1   Malfunctioning combination valve (Chapter 9).
2   Malfunctioning power brake booster unit (Chapter 9).
3   Binding brake pedal mechanism (Chapter 9).

50   Brake pedal feels spongy when depressed

1   Air in brake lines (Chapter 9).
2   Master cylinder mounting bolts loose (Chapter 9).
3   Master cylinder defective (Chapter 9).

51   Brake pedal travels to the floor with little resistance

Little or no fluid in the master cylinder reservoir. Caused by leaking caliper piston(s), loose, damaged or disconnected brake lines (Chapter 9).

52 Parking brake does not hold

Parking brake linkage improperly adjusted (Chapters 1 and 9).

Suspension and steering systems

Note: *Before attempting to diagnose the suspension and steering systems, . . .*
   a) Check the tire pressures and look for uneven or unusual tire wear.
   b) Check the steering universal joints from the column to the rack and pinion for loose connections and wear.
   c) Check the front and rear suspension and the rack and pinion assembly for loose and damaged parts.
   d) Look for out-of-round or out-of-balance tires, bent rims and loose and/or rough wheel bearings.

53 Vehicle pulls to one side

1 Mismatched or unevenly worn tires (Chapter 10).
2 Broken or sagging springs (Chapter 10).
3 Wheel alignment incorrect (Chapter 10).
4 Front brakes dragging (Chapter 9).

54 Abnormal or excessive tire wear

1 Wheel alignment incorrect (Chapter 10).
2 Sagging or broken springs (Chapter 10).
3 Tire(s) out-of-balance (Chapter 10).
4 Worn shock absorber (Chapter 10).
5 Overloaded vehicle.
6 Tires not rotated regularly.

55 Wheel makes a "thumping" noise

1 Blister or bump on tire (Chapter 10).
2 Improper shock absorber action (Chapter 10).

56 Shimmy, shake or vibration

1 Tire or wheel out-of-balance or out-of-round (Chapter 10).
2 Loose, worn or out-of-adjustment wheel bearings (Chapters 1 and 10).
3 Worn tie-rod ends (Chapter 10).
4 Worn lower balljoints (Chapter 10).
5 Excessive wheel runout (Chapter 10).
6 Blister or bump on tire (Chapter 10).

57 Hard steering

1 Lack of lubrication at balljoints, tie-rod ends and rack and pinion assembly (Chapter 10).
2 Front wheel alignment incorrect (Chapter 10).
3 Low tire pressure(s) (Chapter 1).

58 Steering wheel does not return to center position correctly

1 Lack of lubrication at balljoints and tie-rod ends (Chapter 10).
2 Binding in balljoints (Chapter 10).
3 Binding in steering column (Chapter 10).

4 Lack of lubricant in rack and pinion assembly (Chapter 10).
5 Front wheel alignment incorrect (Chapter 10).

59 Abnormal noise at the front end

1 Lack of lubrication at balljoints and tie-rod ends (Chapters 1 and 10).
2 Damaged shock absorber mount (Chapter 10).
3 Worn control arm bushings or tie-rod ends (Chapter 10).
4 Loose stabilizer bar (Chapter 10).
5 Loose wheel lug nuts (Chapter 1).
6 Loose suspension bolts (Chapter 10).
7 On 1987 models, a Dealer Technical Service Bulletin concerning this problem has been issued (no. 011/87). Contact a dealer service department for assistance.

60 Wander or poor steering stability

1 Mismatched or unevenly worn tires (Chapter 10).
2 Lack of lubrication at balljoints and tie-rod ends (Chapters 1 and 10).
3 Worn shock absorbers (Chapter 10).
4 Loose stabilizer bar (Chapter 10).
5 Broken or sagging springs (Chapter 10).
6 Wheel alignment incorrect (Chapter 10).

61 Erratic steering when braking

1 Wheel bearings worn (Chapters 1 and 10).
2 Broken or sagging springs (Chapter 10).
3 Leaking wheel cylinder or caliper (Chapter 9).
4 Warped rotors (Chapter 9).

62 Excessive pitching and/or rolling around corners or during braking

1 Loose stabilizer bar (Chapter 10).
2 Worn shock absorbers or mounts (Chapter 10).
3 Broken or sagging springs (Chapter 10).
4 Overloaded vehicle.

63 Suspension bottoms

1 Overloaded vehicle.
2 Worn shock absorbers (Chapter 10).
3 Broken or sagging springs (Chapter 10).

64 Cupped tires

1 Wheel alignment incorrect (Chapter 10).
2 Worn shock absorbers (Chapter 10).
3 Wheel bearings worn (Chapters 1 and 10).
4 Excessive tire or wheel runout (Chapter 10).
5 Worn balljoints (Chapter 10).

65 Excessive tire wear on outside edge

1 Tire pressures incorrect (Chapter 1).
2 Excessive speed in turns.
3 Front end alignment incorrect (excessive toe-in).
4 Suspension arm bent or twisted (Chapter 10).

66 Excessive tire wear on inside edge

1   Tire pressures incorrect (Chapter 1).
2   Front end alignment incorrect (toe-out).
3   Loose or damaged steering components (Chapter 10).

67 Tire tread worn in one place

1   Tires out-of-balance.
2   Damaged or buckled wheel. Inspect and replace if necessary.
3   Defective tire (Chapter 1).

68 Excessive play or looseness in steering system

1   Wheel bearing(s) worn (Chapter 1).
2   Tie-rod end loose or worn (Chapter 10).
3   Rack and pinion loose (Chapter 10).

69 Rattling or clicking noise in rack and pinion

1   Insufficient or improper lubricant in rack and pinion assembly (Chapter 10).
2   Rack and pinion mounts loose (Chapter 10).

Chapter 1 Tune-up and routine maintenance

Contents

Air filter replacement	30
Automatic transmission fluid and filter change	31
Automatic transmission fluid level check	6
Battery check and maintenance	8
Brake check	19
Brake fluid replacement	40
Chassis and body fastener check	27
Clutch/Neutral safety switch check	24
Clutch pedal freeplay and height check and adjustment	14
Cooling system check	9
Cooling system servicing (draining, flushing and refilling)	35
Compression check	See Chapter 2
Differential lubricant change	33
Differential lubricant level check	18
Driveaxle boot check	20
Drivebelt check, adjustment and replacement	22
Engine coolant warning system check	39
Engine oil and filter change	13
Engine oil level warning system check	26
Evaporative emissions control system check	36
Exhaust system check	16
Fluid level checks	4
Front wheel bearing check, repack and adjustment	34
Fuel filter replacement	29
Fuel system check	21
Idle speed check and adjustment	25
Introduction	2
Maintenance schedule	1
Manual transmission lubricant change	32
Manual transmission lubricant level check	17
Power steering fluid level check	7
Seatbelt check	23
Spark plug replacement	37
Spark plug wire check and replacement	38
Sub-zero starting system check	28
Suspension and steering checks	15
Tire and tire pressure checks	5
Tire rotation	12
Tune-up general information	3
Underhood hose check and replacement	10
Wiper blade inspection and replacement	11

Specifications

Recommended lubricants and fluids

Engine oil	
Type	SF, SF/CC or SF/CD
Viscosity	See accompanying chart
Automatic transmission fluid	**Dexron II** automatic transmission fluid
Manual transmission lubricant	
Type	API GL-5 gear lubricant
Viscosity	See accompanying chart
Differential lubricant	
Type	API GL-5 gear lubricant
Viscosity	See accompanying chart
Limited slip differential (all)	SAE 90 limited slip lubricant
Engine coolant	Mixture of water and ethylene glycol-base antifreeze
Brake fluid	DOT-3 or DOT-4 brake fluid
Clutch fluid	DOT-3 or DOT-4 brake fluid
Power steering fluid	**Type F** automatic transmission fluid
Sub-zero starting system fluid	Mixture of 90% ethylene glycol-base antifreeze and 10% water
Wheel bearing grease	NLGI No. 2 moly-base wheel bearing grease

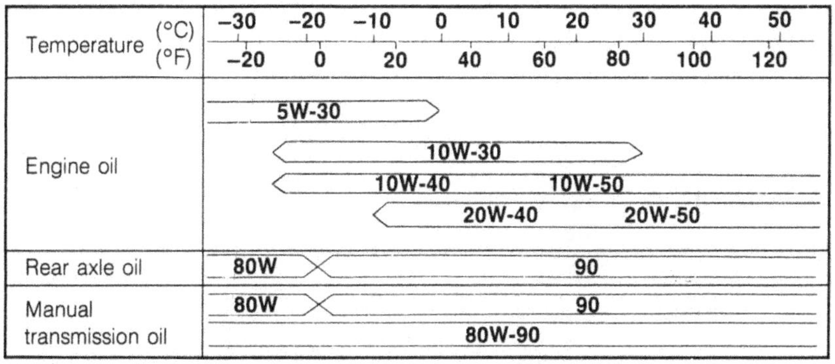

Temperature	(°C)	−30	−20	−10	0	10	20	30	40	50
	(°F)	−20	0	20	40	60	80	100	120	

Engine oil:
- 5W-30
- 10W-30
- 10W-40 / 10W-50
- 20W-40 / 20W-50

Rear axle oil: 80W / 90

Manual transmission oil: 80W / 90 / 80W-90

OIL VISCOSITY CHART

(engine, rear axle [differential] and manual transmission)

Capacities

Engine oil (with filter change, approximate)	5 qts
Cooling system (approximate)	
Non-turbocharged models	7.7 qts
Turbocharged models	9.2 qts
Automatic transmission	7.9 qts
Manual transmission	2.6 qts
Differential	1.3 qts
Fuel tank	16.6 gal

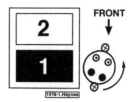

**Cylinder location and
distributor rotation**

General

Engine idle speed	750 ±25 rpm
Radiator pressure cap rating	15 psi

Ignition system

Ignition timing	Refer to Vehicle Emission Control Information label in engine compartment
Spark plug type and gap	
Leading	NGK BUR7EQ or equivalent @ 0.043 to 0.067 inch
Trailing	NGK BUR9EQ or equivalent @ 0.043 to 0.067 inch

Drivebelt deflection

Alternator	1/2 to 3/4-inch
Power steering pump	3/8 to 1/2-inch
Air conditioning compressor	1/4 to 5/16-inch
Air injection pump	
Non-turbocharged models	3/8 to 1/2-inch
Turbocharged models	5/16 to 3/8-inch

Clutch pedal

Height	
Non-turbocharged models	8-5/8 to 8-7/8 inch
Turbocharged models	9-5/16 to 9-1/2 inch
Freeplay	
Non-turbocharged models	1/64 to 1/8-inch
Turbocharged models	3/16 to 1/2-inch

Brakes

Brake pad wear limit	1/8-inch

Torque specifications

	Ft-lbs
Differential (axle) fill plug	10 to 20
Engine oil drain plug	20
Wheel lug nuts	65 to 87
Manual transmission check/fill plug	29 to 43
Manual transmission drain plug	18 to 29
Automatic transmission pan bolts	4 to 5
Spark plugs	9 to 13
Front wheel bearing adjustment	
Spindle nut initial tightening torque	14 to 22
Wheel bearing preload (measured with spring scale)	Initial spring scale torque plus 2.2 ft-lbs
Steering gear-to-frame bolt	23 to 34
Front suspension	
Crossmember-to-body bolt	69 to 86
Stabilizer bracket bolt	13 to 20
Stabilizer control link bolt	27 to 37
Balljoint-to-lower arm nut	69 to 86
Lower suspension arm-to-crossmember bolt	
Front	46 to 69
Rear	43 to 54
Shock absorber-to-steering knuckle bolt	69 to 86
Rear suspension	
Stabilizer bracket bolt	27 to 40
Stabilizer control link bolt	27 to 40
Subframe-to-body bolt	72 to 94
Trailing arm-to-subframe bolt.	46 to 70
Trailing arm-to-control link bolt	27 to 40
Lateral link bolt	22 to 33
Sublink bolts	54 to 69
Shock absorber-to-trailing arm bolt	46 to 69
Seat bracket-to-floor bolt	28 to 38

1 Mazda RX-7 Maintenance schedule

The following maintenance intervals are based on the assumption that the vehicle owner will be doing the maintenance or service work, as opposed to having a dealer service department do the work. Although the time/mileage intervals are loosely based on factory recommendations, most have been shortened to ensure, for example, that such items as lubricants and fluids are checked/changed at intervals that promote maximum engine/driveline service life. Also, subject to the preference of the individual owner interested in keeping his or her vehicle in peak condition at all times, and with the vehicle's ultimate resale in mind, many of the maintenance procedures may be performed more often than recommended in the following schedule. We encourage such owner initiative.

When the vehicle is new it should be serviced initially by a factory authorized dealer service department to protect the factory warranty. In many cases the initial maintenance check is done at no cost to the owner (check with your dealer service department for more information).

Every 250 miles or weekly, whichever comes first

Check the engine oil level (Section 4)
Check the engine coolant level (Section 4)
Check the windshield washer fluid level (Section 4)
Check the brake and clutch fluid levels (Section 4)
Check the tires and tire pressures (Section 5)

Every 3000 miles or 3 months, whichever comes first

All items listed above plus:
Check the automatic transmission fluid level (Section 6)
Check the power steering fluid level (Section 7)
Check and service the battery (Section 8)
Check the cooling system (Section 9)
Inspect and replace, if necessary, all underhood hoses (Section 10)
Inspect and replace, if necessary, the windshield wiper blades (Section 11)
Rotate the tires (Section 12)
Change the engine oil and oil filter (Section 13)*

Every 7500 miles or 6 months, whichever comes first

All items listed above plus:
Check the clutch pedal for proper height and freeplay (Section 14)
Inspect the suspension and steering components (Section 15)
Inspect the exhaust system (Section 16)

Every 15,000 miles or 12 months, whichever comes first

All items listed above plus:
Check the manual transmission lubricant level (Section 17)
Check the differential lubricant level (Section 18)
Inspect the brake system (Section 19)
Check the driveaxle boots (Section 20)
Inspect the fuel system (Section 21)
Check and adjust, if necessary, the engine drivebelts (Section 22)
Check the seatbelts (Section 23)

Check the neutral safety switch (Section 24)
Check and adjust, if necessary, the engine idle speed (Section 25)
Check the engine oil level warning system (Section 26)
Check the tightness of the chassis and body bolts (Section 27)
Check the sub-zero starting system (if equipped) (Section 28)

Every 30,000 miles or 24 months, whichever comes first

All items listed above plus:
Replace the fuel filter (Section 29)*
Replace the air filter (Section 30)*
Change the automatic transmission fluid and filter (Section 31)
Change the manual transmission lubricant (Section 32)
Change the differential lubricant (Section 33)
Check and repack, if necessary, the front wheel bearings (Section 34)
Service the cooling system (drain, flush and refill) (Section 35)
Inspect the evaporative emissions control system (Section 36)
Replace the spark plugs (Section 37)*
Inspect and replace, if necessary, the spark plug and coil wires (Section 38)*
Check the engine coolant warning system (Section 39)
Replace the brake fluid (Section 40)**

*   This item is affected by "severe" operating conditions as described below. If the vehicle in question is operated under "severe" conditions, perform all maintenance indicated with an asterisk (*) at 7500 mile/6 month intervals, except for the following:

Change the engine oil and filter at 2000 mile/two-month intervals
Replace the air filter element at 15,000 mile/15-month intervals

Consider the conditions "severe" if most driving is done. . .
In dusty areas
At low speeds or with extended periods of engine idling
When outside temperatures remain below freezing and most trips are less than four miles

** If most driving is done under one or more of the following conditions, change brake fluid every 15,000 miles or 12 months:
Continuous hard driving
Operation in an extremely humid climate
When brakes are used extensively
Operation in hilly or mountainous terrain

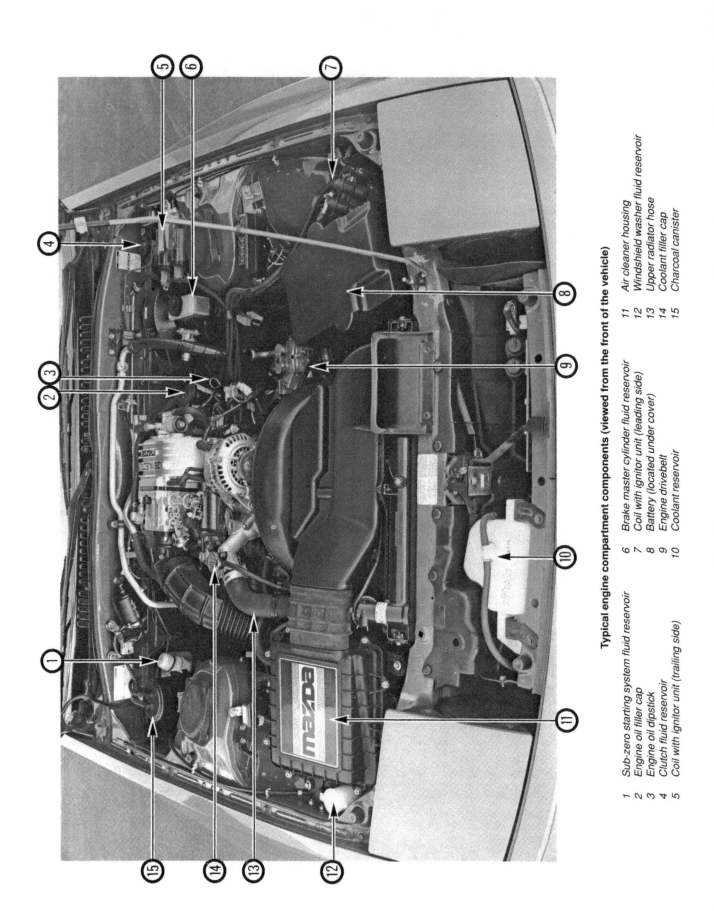

Typical engine compartment components (viewed from the front of the vehicle)

1　Sub-zero starting system fluid reservoir
2　Engine oil filler cap
3　Engine oil dipstick
4　Clutch fluid reservoir
5　Coil with ignitor unit (trailing side)
6　Brake master cylinder fluid reservoir
7　Coil with ignitor unit (leading side)
8　Battery (located under cover)
9　Engine drivebelt
10　Coolant reservoir
11　Air cleaner housing
12　Windshield washer fluid reservoir
13　Upper radiator hose
14　Coolant filler cap
15　Charcoal canister

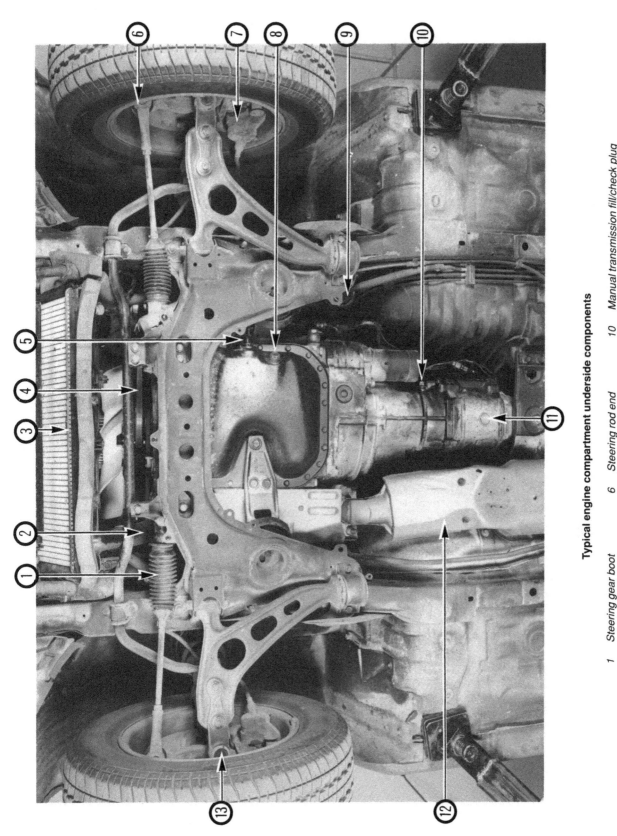

Typical engine compartment underside components

1   Steering gear boot
2   Lower radiator hose
3   Radiator
4   Engine drivebelt
5   Engine oil thermo sensor

6   Steering rod end
7   Disc brake caliper
8   Engine oil drain plug
9   Fuel filter

10   Manual transmission fill/check plug
11   Manual transmission drain plug
12   Exhaust pipe
13   Suspension balljoint

Typical vehicle rear underside components

1 Shock absorber
2 Muffler
3 Inner CV joint boot
4 Fuel tank
5 Differential drain plug

6   Toe control rod boot
7   Outer CV joint boot
8   Suspension bushing
9   Exhaust system hanger
10 Brake caliper

2 Introduction

This Chapter is designed to help the home mechanic maintain the Mazda RX-7 with the goals of maximum performance, economy, safety and reliability in mind.

Included is a master maintenance schedule (page 29), followed by procedures dealing specifically with each item on the schedule. Visual checks, adjustments, component replacement and other helpful items are included. Refer to the accompanying illustrations of the engine compartment and the underside of the vehicle for the locations of various components.

Adhering to the mileage/time maintenance schedule and following the step-by-step procedures, which is simply a preventive maintenance program, will result in maximum reliability and vehicle service life. Keep in mind that it's a comprehensive program – maintaining some items but not others at the specified intervals will not produce the same results.

As you service the vehicle, you will discover that many of the procedures can – and should – be grouped together because of the nature of the particular procedure you're performing or because of the close proximity of two otherwise unrelated components to one another.

For example, if the vehicle is raised, you should inspect the exhaust, suspension, steering and fuel systems while you're under the vehicle. When you're rotating the tires, it makes good sense to check the brakes, since the wheels are already removed. Finally, let's suppose you have to borrow or rent a torque wrench. Even if you only need it to tighten the spark plugs, you might as well check the torque of as many critical fasteners as time allows.

The first step in this maintenance program is to prepare yourself before the actual work begins. Read through all the procedures you're planning to do, then gather up all the parts and tools needed. If it looks like you might run into problems during a particular job, seek advice from a mechanic or an experienced do-it-yourselfer.

3 Tune-up general information

The term tune-up is used in this manual to represent a combination of individual operations rather than one specific procedure.

If, from the time the vehicle is new, the routine maintenance schedule is followed closely and frequent checks are made of fluid levels and high wear items, as suggested throughout this manual, the engine will be kept in relatively good running condition and the need for additional work will be minimized.

More likely than not, however, there will be times when the engine is running poorly due to lack of regular maintenance. This is even more likely if a used vehicle, which has not received regular and frequent maintenance checks, is purchased. In such cases, an engine tune-up will be needed outside of the regular routine maintenance intervals.

The first step in any tune-up or diagnostic procedure to help correct a poor running engine is a cylinder compression check. A compression check (see Chapter 2 Part B) will help determine the condition of internal engine components and should be used as a guide for tune-up and repair procedures. For instance, if a compression check indicates serious internal engine wear, a conventional tune-up will not improve the performance of the engine and would be a waste of time and money. Because of its importance, the compression check should be done by someone with the right equipment and the knowledge to use it properly.

The following procedures are those most often needed to bring a generally poor running engine back into a proper state of tune.

Minor tune-up

Check all engine related fluids (Section 4)
Clean, inspect and test the battery (Section 8)
Check and adjust the drivebelts (Section 22)
Replace the spark plugs (Section 37)
Inspect the spark plug and coil wires (Section 38)
Check the air filter (Section 30)
Check the cooling system (Section 9)
Check all underhood hoses (Section 10)

Major tune-up

All items listed under Minor tune-up plus . . .
Check the ignition system (Chapter 5)
Check the charging system (Chapter 5)
Check the fuel system (Section 21)
Replace the air filter (Section 30)
Replace the spark plug wires (Section 38)

4 Fluid level checks

Refer to illustrations 4.2, 4.4, 4.6, 4.8, 4.14a, 4.14b, 4.17, 4.18 and 4.19
Note: *The following are fluid level checks to be done on a 250 mile or weekly basis. Additional fluid level checks can be found in specific maintenance procedures which follow. Regardless of the intervals, be alert to fluid leaks under the vehicle which would indicate a fault to be corrected immediately.*

1   Fluids are an essential part of the lubrication, cooling, brake, clutch and windshield washer systems. Because the fluids gradually become depleted and/or contaminated during normal operation of the vehicle, they must be periodically replenished. See Recommended lubricants and fluids at the beginning of this Chapter before adding fluid to any of the following components. **Note:** *The vehicle must be on level ground when fluid levels are checked.*

Engine oil

2   The engine oil level is checked with a dipstick that extends through a tube and into the oil pan at the bottom of the engine **(see illustration)**.

4.2   The engine oil dipstick is located at the left rear of the engine compartment

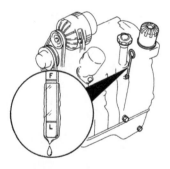

4.4   The engine oil level must be maintained between the marks at all times – it takes one quart of oil to raise the level from the L mark to the F mark

3   The oil level should be checked before the vehicle has been driven, or about 15 minutes after the engine has been shut off. If the oil is checked immediately after driving the vehicle, some of the oil will remain in the upper engine components, resulting in an inaccurate reading on the dipstick.
4   Pull the dipstick from the tube and wipe all the oil from the end with a clean rag or paper towel. Insert the clean dipstick all the way back into the tube, then pull it out again. Note the oil at the end of the dipstick. Add oil as necessary to keep the level between the L mark and the F mark on the dipstick **(see illustration)**.

4.6   Oil is added to the engine after unscrewing the filler cap from the filler tube

5   Do not overfill the engine by adding too much oil, since this may result in oil fouled spark plugs, oil leaks or oil seal failures.
6   Oil is added to the engine after removing a threaded cap **(see illustration)**. An oil can spout or funnel may help to reduce spills.
7   Checking the oil level is an important preventive maintenance step. A consistently low oil level indicates oil leakage through damaged seals, defective gaskets or past worn rings or valve guides. If the oil looks milky in color or has water droplets in it, the internal engine seals may be leaking or the engine block may be cracked. The engine should be checked immediately. The condition of the oil should also be checked. Whenever you check the oil level, slide your thumb and index finger up the dipstick before wiping off the oil. If you see small dirt or metal particles clinging to the dipstick, the oil should be changed (Section 13).

Engine coolant

Warning: *Do not allow antifreeze to come in contact with your skin or painted surfaces of the vehicle. Flush contaminated areas immediately with plenty of water. Don't store new coolant or leave old coolant lying around where it's accessible to children or pets – they're attracted by its sweet taste. Ingestion of even a small amount of coolant can be fatal! Wipe up garage floor and drip pan coolant spills immediately. Keep antifreeze containers covered and repair leaks in your cooling system immediately.*

8   All vehicles covered by this manual are equipped with a pressurized coolant recovery system. A white plastic coolant reservoir located in the engine compartment is connected by a hose to the radiator filler neck **(see illustration)**. If the engine overheats, coolant escapes through a valve in the radiator cap and travels through the hose into the reservoir. As the engine cools, the coolant is automatically drawn back into the cooling system to maintain the correct level.

4.14a   The windshield washer reservoir is located at the right front corner of the engine compartment – flip up the cap to add fluid

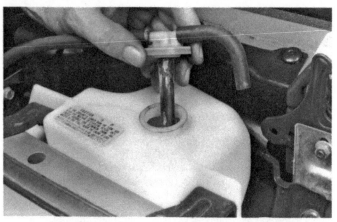

4.8   The coolant reservoir is located in front of the radiator – add coolant after detaching the cap

9   The coolant level in the reservoir should be checked regularly. **Warning:** *Do not remove the radiator cap to check the coolant level when the engine is warm.* The level in the reservoir varies with the temperature of the engine. When the engine is cold, the coolant level should be at or slightly above the FULL mark on the reservoir. If it isn't, allow the engine to cool, then remove the cap from the reservoir and add a 50/50 mixture of ethylene glycol-based antifreeze and water.
10   Drive the vehicle and recheck the coolant level. If only a small amount of coolant is required to bring the system up to the proper level, water can be used. However, repeated additions of water will dilute the antifreeze and water solution. To maintain the proper ratio of antifreeze and water, always top up the coolant level with the correct mixture. An empty plastic milk jug or bleach bottle makes an excellent container for mixing coolant. Do not use rust inhibitors or additives.
11   If the coolant level drops consistently, there may be a leak in the system. Inspect the radiator, hoses, filler cap drain plugs and water pump (see Section 9). If no leaks are noted, have the radiator cap pressure tested by a service station.
12   If you have to remove the radiator cap, wait until the engine has cooled, then wrap a thick cloth around the cap and turn it to the first stop. If coolant or steam escapes, let the engine cool down longer, then remove the cap.
13   Check the condition of the coolant as well. It should be relatively clear. If it's brown or rust colored, the system should be drained, flushed and refilled. Even if the coolant appears to be normal, the corrosion inhibitors wear out, so it must be replaced at the specified intervals.

Windshield and rear window washer fluid

14   Fluid for the windshield washer system is located in a plastic reservoir in the engine compartment **(see illustration)**. The rear window washer fluid reservoir is located next to the spare tire **(see illustration)**.

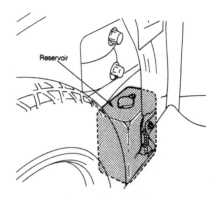

4.14b   The rear window washer fluid reservoir is located next to the spare tire

4.17 Remove the cell caps to check the water level in a conventional battery – if the level is low, add distilled water only

15 In milder climates, plain water can be used in the reservoir but it should be kept no more than 2/3 full to allow for expansion if the water freezes. In colder climates, use windshield washer system antifreeze, available at any auto parts store, to lower the freezing point of the fluid. Mix the antifreeze with water in accordance with the manufacturer's directions on the container. **Caution:** *Don't use cooling system antifreeze – it will damage the vehicle's paint.*
16 To help prevent icing in cold weather, warm the windshield with the defroster before using the washer.

Battery electrolyte

17 All vehicles with which this manual is concerned come equipped with a battery which is permanently sealed (except for vent holes) and has no filler caps. Water doesn't have to be added to these batteries at any time. If a maintenance-type battery is installed, the caps on the top of the battery should be removed periodically to check for a low water level **(see illustration)**. This check is most critical during the warm summer months.

Brake and clutch fluid

18 The brake master cylinder is mounted on the front of the power booster unit in the engine compartment. The clutch cylinder (used on models

with a manual transmission) is mounted adjacent to it on the firewall **(see illustration)**.
19 The fluid inside is readily visible. The level should be above the MIN marks on the reservoirs **(see illustration)**. If a low level is indicated, be sure to wipe the top of the reservoir cover with a clean rag to prevent contamination of the brake and/or clutch system before removing the cover.
20 When adding fluid, pour it carefully into the reservoir to avoid spilling it onto surrounding painted surfaces. Be sure the specified fluid is used, since mixing different types of brake fluid can cause damage to the system. See Recommended lubricants and fluids at the front of this Chapter or your owner's manual. **Warning:** *Brake fluid can harm your eyes and damage painted surfaces, so use extreme caution when handling or pouring it. Do not use brake fluid that has been standing open or is more than one year old. Brake fluid absorbs moisture from the air. Excess moisture can cause a dangerous loss of braking effectiveness.*
21 At this time the fluid and master cylinder can be inspected for contamination. The system should be drained and refilled if deposits, dirt particles or water droplets are seen in the fluid.
22 After filling the reservoir to the proper level, make sure the cover is on tight to prevent fluid leakage.
23 The brake fluid level in the master cylinder will drop slightly as the pads at each wheel wear down during normal operation. If the master cylinder requires repeated fluid additions to keep it at the proper level, it's an indication of leakage in the brake system, which should be corrected immediately. Check all brake lines and connections (see Section 19 for more information).
24 If, upon checking the master cylinder fluid level, you discover one or both reservoirs empty or nearly empty, the brake system should be bled (see Chapter 9).

---

5 Tire and tire pressure checks

Refer to illustrations 5.2, 5.3, 5.4a, 5.4b and 5.8

1 Periodic inspection of the tires may spare you the inconvenience of being stranded with a flat tire. It can also provide you with vital information regarding possible problems in the steering and suspension systems before major damage occurs.
2 The original tires on this vehicle are equipped with 1/2-inch side bands that will appear when tread depth reaches 1/16-inch, but they don't appear until the tires are worn out. Tread wear can be monitored with a simple, inexpensive device known as a tread depth indicator **(see illustration)**.

4.18 Keep the clutch fluid level between the MIN and MAX marks – unscrew the cap to add fluid

4.19 Since the brake fluid reservoir is translucent, the level is easily checked – unscrew the cap to add fluid

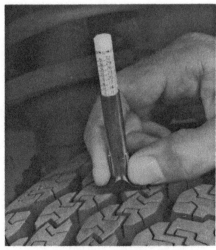

5.2 Use a tire tread depth indicator to monitor tire wear – they are available at auto parts stores and service stations and cost very little

Condition	Probable cause	Corrective action	Condition	Probable cause	Corrective action
Shoulder wear	• Underinflation (both sides wear) • Incorrect wheel camber (one side wear) • Hard cornering • Lack of rotation	• Measure and adjust pressure. • Repair or replace axle and suspension parts. • Reduce speed. • Rotate tires.	Feathered edge **Toe wear**	• Incorrect toe	• Adjust toe-in.
Center wear	• Overinflation • Lack of rotation	• Measure and adjust pressure. • Rotate tires.	**Uneven wear**	• Incorrect camber or caster • Malfunctioning suspension • Unbalanced wheel • Out-of-round brake drum • Lack of rotation	• Repair or replace axle and suspension parts. • Repair or replace suspension parts. • Balance or replace. • Turn or replace. • Rotate tires.

5.3   This chart will help you determine the condition of the tires, the probable cause(s) of abnormal wear and the corrective action necessary

3   Note any abnormal tread wear **(see illustration)**. Tread pattern irregularities such as cupping, flat spots and more wear on one side than the other are indications of front end alignment and/or balance problems. If any of these conditions are noted, take the vehicle to a tire shop or service station to correct the problem.

4   Look closely for cuts, punctures and embedded nails or tacks. Sometimes a tire will hold air pressure for a short time or leak down very slowly after a nail has embedded itself in the tread. If a slow leak persists, check the valve stem core to make sure it's tight **(see illustration)**. Examine the tread for an object that may have embedded itself in the tire or for a "plug" that may have begun to leak (radial tire punctures are repaired with a plug that's installed in a puncture). If a puncture is suspected, it can be easily verified by spraying a solution of soapy water onto the puncture area **(see illustration)**. The soapy solution will bubble if there's a leak. Unless the puncture is unusually large, a tire shop or service station can usually repair the tire.

5   Carefully inspect the inner sidewall of each tire for evidence of brake fluid leakage. If you see any, inspect the brakes immediately.

6   Correct air pressure adds miles to the lifespan of the tires, improves mileage and enhances overall ride quality. Tire pressure cannot be accurately estimated by looking at a tire, especially if it's a radial. A tire pressure gauge is essential. Keep an accurate gauge in the vehicle. The pressure gauges attached to the nozzles of air hoses at gas stations are often inaccurate.

7   Always check tire pressure when the tires are cold. Cold, in this case, means the vehicle has not been driven over a mile in the three hours preceding a tire pressure check. A pressure rise of four to eight pounds is not uncommon once the tires are warm.

5.4a   If a tire loses air on a steady basis, check the valve core first to make sure it's snug (special inexpensive wrenches are commonly available at auto parts stores)

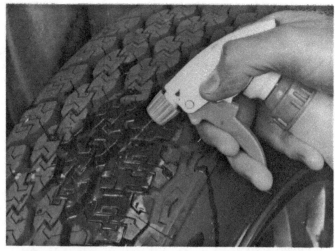

5.4b   If the valve core is tight, raise the corner of the vehicle with the low tire and spray a soapy water solution onto the tread as the tire is turned slowly – leaks will cause small bubbles to appear

5.8 To extend the life of your tires, check the air pressure at least once a week with an accurate gauge (don't forget the spare!)

8   Unscrew the valve cap protruding from the wheel or hubcap and push the gauge firmly onto the valve stem **(see illustration)**. Note the reading on the gauge and compare the figure to the recommended tire pressure shown on the placard on the driver's side door pillar. Be sure to reinstall the valve cap to keep dirt and moisture out of the valve stem mechanism. Check all four tires and, if necessary, add enough air to bring them up to the recommended pressure.

9   Don't forget to keep the spare tire inflated to the specified pressure (refer to you owner's manual or the tire sidewall). Note that the pressure recommended for the compact spare is higher than for the tires on the vehicle.

---

6   Automatic transmission fluid level check

Refer to illustration 6.3

1   The automatic transmission fluid level should be carefully maintained. Low fluid level can lead to slipping or loss of drive, while overfilling can cause foaming and loss of fluid.

2   With the parking brake set, start the engine, then move the shift lever through all the gear ranges, ending in Park. The fluid level must be checked with the vehicle level and the engine running at idle. **Note**: *Incor-*

rect fluid level readings will result if the vehicle has just been driven at high speeds for an extended period, or in hot weather in city traffic. If any of these conditions apply wait until the fluid has cooled (about 30 minutes).

3   With the transmission at normal operating temperature, remove the dipstick from the filler tube. The dipstick is located at the rear of the engine compartment **(see illustration)**.

4   Carefully touch the fluid at the end of the dipstick to determine if it is cool, warm or hot. Wipe the fluid from the dipstick with a clean rag and push it back into the filler tube until the cap seats.

5   Pull the dipstick out again and note the fluid level.

6   The fluid level must be kept between the F and L marks on the dipstick. If additional fluid is required, add it directly into the tube using a funnel. It takes about one pint to raise the level from the L mark to the F mark with a hot transmission, so add the fluid a little at a time and keep checking the level until it's correct.

7   The condition of the fluid should also be checked along with the level. If the fluid at the end of the dipstick is a dark reddish–brown color, or if it smells burned, it should be changed. If you are in doubt about the condition of the fluid, purchase some new fluid and compare the two for color and smell.

---

7   Power steering fluid level check

Refer to illustration 7.6

1   Unlike manual steering, the power steering system relies on fluid which may, over a period of time, require replenishing.

2   The fluid reservoir for the power steering pump is located on the pump body at the front of the engine.

3   For the check, the front wheels should be pointed straight ahead and the engine should be off.

4   Use a clean rag to wipe off the reservoir cap and the area around the cap. This will help prevent any foreign matter from entering the reservoir during the check.

5   Twist off the cap and check the temperature of the fluid at the end of the dipstick with your finger to make sure it's cool.

6   Wipe off the fluid with a clean rag, reinsert the dipstick, then withdraw it and read the fluid level. The level should be between the H and L marks on the dipstick **(see illustration)**. Never allow the fluid level to drop below the L mark.

7   If additional fluid is required, pour the specified type directly into the reservoir, using a funnel to prevent spills.

8   If the reservoir requires frequent fluid additions, all power steering hoses, hose connections and the power steering pump should be carefully checked for leaks.

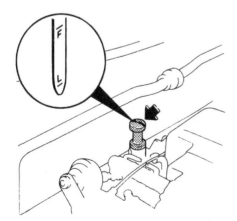

6.3 The automatic transmission dipstick is located at the rear of the engine compartment – the fluid level should be kept between the L and F marks on the dipstick

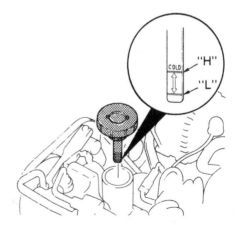

7.6 The power steering fluid reservoir is located near the front of the engine – keep the level between the H and L marks on the dipstick

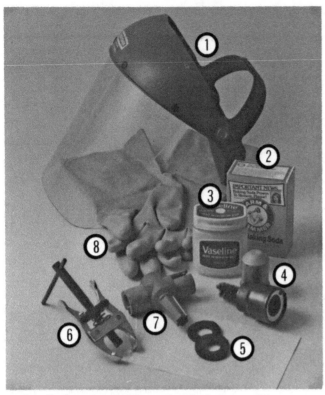

8.1   Tools and materials required for battery maintenance

1 **Face shield/safety goggles** – *When removing corrosion with a brush, the acidic particles can easily fly up into your eyes*
2 **Baking soda** – *A solution of baking soda and water can be used to neutralize corrosion*
3 **Petroleum jelly** – *A layer of this on the battery posts will help prevent corrosion*
4 **Battery post/cable cleaner** – *This wire brush cleaning tool will remove all traces of corrosion from the battery posts and cable clamps*
5 **Treated felt washers** – *Placing one of these on each post, directly under the cable clamps, will help prevent corrosion*
6 **Puller** – *Sometimes the cable clamps are very difficult to pull off the posts, even after the nut/bolt has been completely loosened. This tool pulls the clamp straight up and off the post without damage.*
7 **Battery post/cable cleaner** – *Here is another cleaning tool which is a slightly different version of number 4 above, but it does the same thing*
8 **Rubber gloves** – *Another safety item to consider when servicing the battery; remember that's acid inside the battery!*

---

8   Battery check and maintenance

Refer to illustrations 8.1, 8.6a, 8.6b, 8.7a and 8.7b

1 A routine preventive maintenance program for the battery in your vehicle is the only way to ensure quick and reliable starts. But before performing any battery maintenance, make sure you have the proper equipment necessary to work safely around the battery **(see illustration)**.
2 There are also several precautions that should be taken whenever battery maintenance is performed. Before servicing the battery, always turn the engine and all accessories off and disconnect the cable from the negative terminal of the battery.
3 The battery produces hydrogen gas, which is both flammable and explosive. Never create a spark, smoke or light a match around the battery. Always charge the battery in a ventilated area.

8.6a   Battery terminal corrosion usually appears as light, fluffy powder

4 Electrolyte contains poisonous and corrosive sulfuric acid. Do not allow it to get in your eyes, on your skin or on your clothes. Never ingest it. Wear protective safety glasses when working near the battery. Keep children away from the battery.
5 Note the external condition of the battery. If the positive terminal and cable clamp on your vehicle's battery is equipped with a rubber protector, make sure it's not torn or damaged. It should completely cover the terminal. Look for an corroded or loose connections, cracks in the case or cover or loose hold-down clamps. Also check the entire length of each cable for cracks and frayed conductors.
6 If corrosion, which looks like white, fluffy deposits **(see illustration)** is evident, particularly around the terminals, the battery should be removed for cleaning. Loosen the cable clamp bolts with a wrench, being careful to remove the ground cable first, and slide them off the terminals **(see illustration)**. Then remove the hold-down clamp nuts, detach the clamp and lift the battery from the engine compartment.
7 Clean the cable clamps thoroughly with a battery brush or a terminal cleaner and a solution of warm water and baking soda **(see illustration)**. Wash the terminals and the top of the battery case with the same solution, but make sure the solution doesn't get into the battery. When cleaning the cables, terminals and battery top, wear safety goggles and rubber gloves to prevent any solution from coming in contact with your eyes or hands. Wear old clothes too – even diluted, sulfuric acid splashed onto clothes will burn holes in them. If the terminals have been extensively corroded, clean them up with a terminal cleaner **(see illustration)**. Thoroughly wash all cleaned areas with plain water.
8 Before reinstalling the battery into the engine compartment, inspect the plastic battery carrier. If it's dirty or covered with corrosion, remove it and clean it in the same solution of warm water and baking soda. Inspect the metal brackets which support the carrier to make sure that they are not covered with corrosion If they are, wash them off. If corrosion is extensive, sand the bracket down to bare metal and spray them with a zinc-based primer (available in spray cans at auto paint and body supply stores).
9 Reinstall the battery carrier and the battery back into the engine compartment. make sure that no parts or wires are laying on the carrier during installation of the battery.
10 Install a pair of specially treated felt washers around the terminals (available at auto parts stores), then coat the terminals and the cable clamps with petroleum jelly or grease to prevent further corrosion. Install the cable clamps and tighten the bolts, being careful to install the negative cable last.
11 Install the hold-down clamp and nuts. Tighten the nuts only enough to hold the battery firmly in place. Overtightening the nuts can crack the battery case.
12 Further information on the battery, charging and jump starting can be found in Chapter 5 and at the front of this manual.

8.6b   Removing a cable from the battery post with a wrench – sometimes a special battery pliers is required for this procedure if corrosion has caused deterioration of the nut hex (always remove the ground cable first and hook it up last!)

8.7a   Regardless of the type of tool used on the battery post, a clean, shiny surface should be the result

8.7b   When cleaning the cable clamps, all corrosion must be removed (the inside of the clamp is tapered to match the taper on the post, so don't remove too much material)

9   Cooling system check

Refer to illustrations 9.3 and 9.4

1   Many major engine failures can be attributed to a faulty cooling system. If the vehicle is equipped with an automatic transmission, the cooling system also cools the transmission fluid and thus plays an important role in prolonging transmission life.

2   The cooling system should be checked with the engine cold. Do this before the vehicle is driven for the day or after the engine has been shut off for at least three hours.

3   Remove the coolant filler cap **(see illustration)** by turning it to the left until it reaches a stop. If you hear a hissing sound (indicating there is still pressure in the system), wait until this stops. Now press down on the cap with the palm of your hand and continue turning to the left until the cap can be removed. Thoroughly clean the cap, inside and out, with clean water. Also clean the filler neck where the cap attaches. All traces of corrosion should be removed. The coolant inside the radiator should be relatively transparent. If it is rust colored, the system should be drained and refilled (see Section 35). If the coolant level is not up to the top, add additional anti-freeze/coolant mixture (see Section 4).

4   Carefully check the large upper and lower radiator hoses along with the smaller diameter heater hoses which run from the engine to the fire-wall. On some models the heater return hose runs directly to the radiator. Inspect each hose along its entire length, replacing any hose which is cracked, swollen or shows signs of deterioration. Cracks may become more apparent if the hose is squeezed **(see illustration)**. Regardless of condition, it's a good idea to replace hoses with new ones every two years.

5   Make sure that all hose connections are tight. A leak in the cooling system will usually show up a white or rust colored deposits on the areas adjoining the leak. If wire-type clamps are used at the ends of the hoses, it may be a good idea to replace them with more secure screw-type clamps.

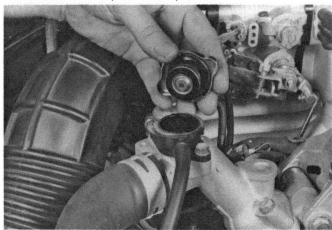

9.3   After allowing the engine to cool completely, remove the coolant filler cap – inspect the cap's rubber gasket and the sealing surface in the filler neck

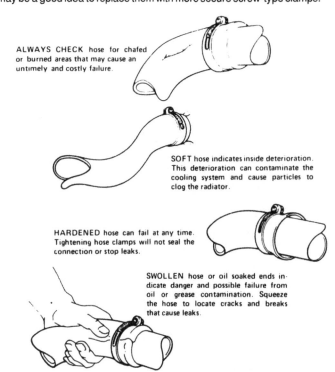

ALWAYS CHECK hose for chafed or burned areas that may cause an untimely and costly failure.

SOFT hose indicates inside deterioration. This deterioration can contaminate the cooling system and cause particles to clog the radiator.

HARDENED hose can fail at any time. Tightening hose clamps will not seal the connection or stop leaks.

SWOLLEN hose or oil soaked ends indicate danger and possible failure from oil or grease contamination. Squeeze the hose to locate cracks and breaks that cause leaks.

9.4   Hoses, like drivebelts, have a habit of failing at the worst possible time – to prevent the inconvenience of a blown radiator or heater hose, inspect them carefully as shown here

6   Use compressed air or a soft brush to remove bugs, leaves, etc. from the front of the radiator or air conditioning condenser. Be careful not to damage the delicate cooling fins or cut yourself on them.

7   Every other inspection, or at the first indication of cooling system problems, have the cap and system pressure tested. If you don't have a pressure tester, most gas stations and repair shops will do this for a minimal charge.

10   Underhood hose check and replacement

General

1   **Caution:** *Replacement of air conditioning hoses must be left to a dealer service department or air conditioning shop that has the equipment to depressurize the system safely. Never remove air conditioning components or hoses until the system has been depressurized.*

2   High temperatures in the engine compartment can cause the deterioration of the rubber and plastic hoses used for engine, accessory and emission systems operation. Periodic inspection should be made for cracks, loose clamps, material hardening and leaks. Information specific to the cooling system hoses can be found in Section 9.

3   Some, but not all, hoses are secured to the fittings with clamps. Where clamps are used, check to be sure they haven't lost their tension, allowing the hose to leak. If clamps aren't used, make sure the hose has not expanded and/or hardened where it slips over the fitting, allowing it to leak.

Vacuum hoses

4   It's quite common for vacuum hoses, especially those in the emissions system, to be color coded or identified by colored stripes molded into them. Various systems require hoses with different wall thicknesses, collapse resistance and temperature resistance. When replacing hoses, be sure the new ones are made of the same material.

5   Often the only effective way to check a hose is to remove it completely from the vehicle. If more than one hose is removed, be sure to label the hoses and fittings to ensure correct installation.

6   When checking vacuum hoses, be sure to include any plastic T-fittings in the check. Inspect the fittings for cracks and the hose where it fits over the fitting for distortion, which could cause leakage.

7   A small piece of vacuum hose (1/4-inch inside diameter) can be used as a stethoscope to detect vacuum leaks. Hold one end of the hose to your ear and probe around vacuum hoses and fittings, listening for the "hissing" sound characteristic of a vacuum leak. **Warning**: *When probing with the vacuum hose stethoscope, be very careful not to come into contact with moving engine components such as the drivebelt, cooling fan, etc.*

Fuel hose

Warning: *There are certain precautions which must be taken when inspecting or servicing fuel system components. Work in a well ventilated area and do not allow open flames (cigarettes, appliance pilot lights, etc.) or bare light bulbs near the work area. Mop up any spills immediately and do not store fuel soaked rags where they could ignite. On vehicles equipped with fuel injection, the fuel system is under pressure, so if any fuel lines are to be disconnected, the pressure in the system must be relieved first (see Chapter 4 for more information).*

8   Check all rubber fuel lines for deterioration and chafing. Check especially for cracks in areas where the hose bends and just before fittings, such as where a hose attaches to the fuel filter.

9   High quality fuel line, usually identified by the word Fluroelastomer printed on the hose, should be used for fuel line replacement. Never, under any circumstances, use unreinforced vacuum line, clear plastic tubing or water hose for fuel lines.

10   Spring-type clamps are commonly used on fuel lines. These clamps often lose their tension over a period of time, and can be "sprung" during removal. Replace all spring-type clamps with screw clamps whenever a hose is replaced.

Metal lines

11   Sections of metal line are often used for fuel line between the fuel pump and fuel injection unit. Check carefully to be sure the line has not been bent or crimped and that cracks have not started in the line.

12   If a section of metal fuel line must be replaced, only seamless steel tubing should be used, since copper and aluminum tubing don't have the strength necessary to withstand normal engine vibration.

13   Check the metal brake lines where they enter the master cylinder and brake proportioning unit (if used) for cracks in the lines or loose fittings. Any sign of brake fluid leakage calls for an immediate thorough inspection of the brake system.

11   Wiper blade inspection and replacement

Refer to illustrations 11.6, 11.7, 11.9a and 11.9b

1   The windshield wiper and blade assembly should be inspected periodically for damage, loose components and cracked or worn blade elements.

2   Road film can build up on the wiper blades and affect their efficiency, so they should be washed regularly with a mild detergent solution.

3   The action of the wiping mechanism can loosen the bolts, nuts and fasteners, so they should be checked and tightened, as necessary, at the same time the wiper blades are checked.

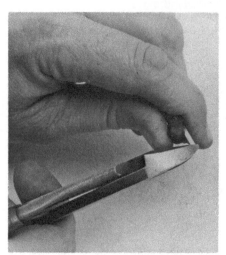

11.7   Wire cutters or needle-nose pliers can be used to pull the two support rods out of the blade element

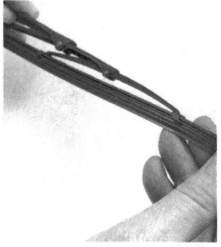

11.9a   Insert the new element into the blade assembly

11.6   Press the retaining tab in, then slide the wiper blade assembly down and out of the hook in the end of the wiper arm

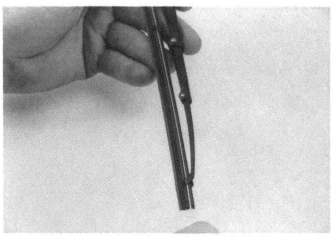

11.9b   Slide the support rods into the grooves in the element until they lock the element in the blade assembly

4   If the wiper blade elements (sometimes called inserts) are cracked, worn or warped, they should be replaced with new ones.
5   Pull the wiper blade/arm assembly away from the glass.
6   Depress the retaining tab and slide the blade assembly off the wiper arm **(see illustration)**.
7   Bend the end of the element out of the way and pull out the two support rods **(see illustration)**. Slide the element out of the blade assembly.
8   Compare the new element with the old for length, design, etc.
9   Slide the new element into place **(see illustration)**. Insert the support rods into the element to lock it in place **(see illustration)**.
10   Reinstall the blade assembly on the arm, wet the windshield and check for proper operation.

---

12   Tire rotation

Refer to illustrations 12.2a and 12.2b

1   The tires should be rotated at the specified intervals and whenever uneven wear is noticed.
2   Refer to the accompanying illustrations for the preferred tire rotation patterns.
3   Refer to the information in *Jacking and towing* at the front of this manual for the proper procedures to follow when raising the vehicle and changing a tire. If the brakes are to be checked, don't apply the parking brake as stated. Make sure the tires are blocked to prevent the vehicle from rolling as it's raised.
4   Preferably, the entire vehicle should be raised at the same time. This can be done on a hoist or by jacking up each corner and then lowering the vehicle onto jackstands placed under the frame rails. Always use four jackstands and make sure the vehicle is safely supported.

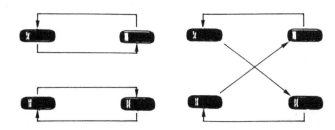

12.2a   Recommended rotation pattern for radial tires

12.2b   Recommended rotation pattern for bias ply tires

5   After rotation, check and adjust the tire pressures as necessary and be sure to check the lug nut tightness.
6   For additional information on the wheels and tires, see Chapter 10.

---

13   Engine oil and filter change

Refer to illustrations 13.3, 13.9, 13.13 and 13.17

1   Frequent oil changes are the most important preventive maintenance procedures that can be done by the home mechanic. As engine oil ages, it becomes diluted and contaminated, which leads to premature engine wear.
2   Although some sources recommend oil filter changes every other oil change, we feel that the minimal cost of an oil filter and the relative ease with which it is installed dictate that a new filter be installed every time the oil is changed.
3   Gather together all necessary tools and materials before beginning this procedure **(see illustration)**.
4   You should have plenty of clean rags and newspaper hand to mop up any spills. Access to the underside of the vehicle is greatly improved if the vehicle can be lifted on a hoist, driven onto ramps or supported by jackstands. **Warning:** *Do not work under a vehicle which is supported only by a bumper, hydraulic or scissors-type jack.*

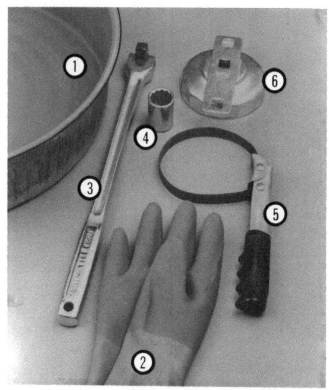

13.3   These tools are required when changing the engine oil and filter

1   **Drain pan** – *It should be fairly shallow in depth, but wide to prevent spills*
2   **Rubber gloves** – *When removing the drain plug and filter, you will get oil on your hands (the gloves will prevent burns)*
3   **Breaker bar** – *Sometimes the oil drain plug is tight and a long breaker bar is needed to loosen it*
4   **Socket** – *To be used with the breaker bar or a ratchet (must be the correct size to fit the drain plug – 6-point preferred)*
5   **Filter wrench** – *This is a metal band-type wrench, which requires clearance around the filter to be effective*
6   **Filter wrench** – *This type fits on the bottom of the filter and can be turned with a ratchet or breaker bar (different size wrenches are available for different types of filters)*

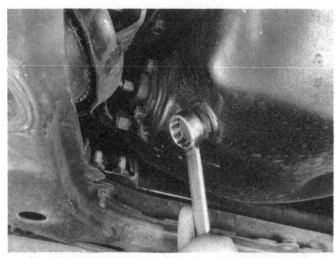

13.9   The oil drain plug is located at the bottom of the pan and should be removed using either a socket or box-end wrench – DO NOT use an open-end wrench, as the corners on the bolt can be easily rounded off

13.13   Use an oil filter wrench to loosen the filter, but hand tighten the new filter when installing it

13.17   Lubricate the oil filter gasket with clean engine oil before installing the filter on the engine

5   If this is your first oil change, get under the vehicle and familiarize yourself with the locations of the oil drain plug and the oil filter. The engine and exhaust components will be warm during the actual work, so note how they are situated to avoid touching them when working under the vehicle.

6   Warm the engine to normal operating temperature. If the new oil or any tools are needed, use this warm-up time to gather everything necessary for the job. The correct type of oil for your application can be found in Recommended lubricants and fluids at the beginning of this Chapter.

7   With the engine oil warm (warm engine oil will drain better and more built-up sludge will be removed with it), raise and support the vehicle. Make sure it's safely supported!

8   Move all necessary tools, rags and newspapers under the vehicle. Set the drain pan under the drain plug. Keep in mind that the oil will initially flow from the pan with some force; position the pan accordingly.

9   Being careful not to touch any of the hot exhaust components, use a wrench to remove the drain plug near the bottom of the oil pan **(see illustration)**. Depending on how hot the oil is, you may want to wear gloves while unscrewing the plug the final few turns.

10   Allow the old oil to drain into the pan. It may be necessary to move the pan as the oil flow slows to a trickle.

11   After all the oil has drained, wipe off the drain plug with a clean rag. Small metal particles may cling to the plug and would immediately contaminate the new oil.

12   Clean the area around the drain plug opening and reinstall the plug. Tighten the plug securely with the wrench. If a torque wrench is available, use it to tighten the plug.

13   Use the filter wrench to loosen the oil filter **(see illustration)**. Chain or metal band filter wrenches may distort the filter canister, but is doesn't matter since the filter will be discarded anyway.

14   Completely unscrew the old filter. Be careful; it may contain some residual oil. Empty the oil inside the filter into the drain pan.

15   Compare the old filter with the new one to make sure they're the same type.

16   Use a clean rag to remove all oil, dirt and sludge from the area where the oil filter mounts to the engine. Check the old filter to make sure the rubber gasket isn't stuck to the engine. If the gasket is stuck to the engine, remove it.

17   Apply a light coat of clean oil to the rubber gasket on the new oil filter **(see illustration)**.

18   Attach the new filter to the engine, following the tightening directions printed on the filter canister or packing box. Most filter manufacturers recommend against using a filter wrench due to the possibility of overtightening and damage to the seal.

19   Remove all tools, rags, etc. from under the vehicle, being careful not to spill the oil in the drain pan, then lower the vehicle.

20   Move to the engine compartment and locate the oil filler cap.

21   Pour the fresh oil through the filler opening, using a funnel to prevent spills.

22   Pour the specified amount of fresh oil into the engine. Wait a few minutes to allow the oil to drain into the pan, then check the level on the oil dipstick (see Section 4 if necessary). If the oil level is above the L mark, start the engine and allow the new oil to circulate

23   Run the engine for only about a minute and then shut it off. Immediately look under the vehicle and check for leaks at the oil pan drain plug and around the oil filter. If either is leaking, tighten with a bit more force.

24   With the new oil circulated and the filter now completely full, recheck the level on the dipstick and add more oil, if necessary.

25   During the first few trips after an oil change, make it a point to check frequently for leaks and proper oil level.

26   The old oil drained from the engine cannot be reused in its present state and should be disposed of. Oil reclamation centers, auto repair shops and gas stations will normally accept the oil, which can be refined and used again. After the oil has cooled it can be drained into a suitable container (capped plastic jugs, topped bottles, milk cartons, etc.) for transport to one of these disposal sites.

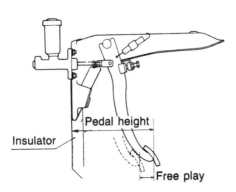

14.1   Clutch pedal freeplay and height measurement details

15.4a   Push on the tie-rod end and balljoint boots to check for
damage and leaking grease

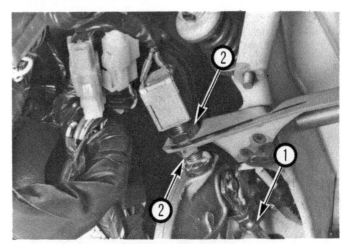

14.2   To adjust the clutch pedal freeplay, loosen the locknut
(1) and rotate the clutch pushrod – to adjust the pedal height,
loosen the locknuts (2) and rotate the clutch safety switch

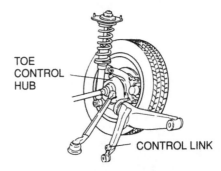

15.4b   Check the rear suspension toe control hub and control
link bushings for damage

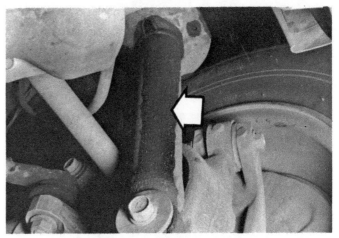

15.4c   Inspect the shock absorbers for leaking fluid (arrow),
indicating the need for replacement

14   Clutch pedal freeplay and height check and adjustment

Refer to illustrations 14.1 and 14.2

1   Press down lightly on the clutch pedal and, with a small steel ruler, measure the distance that it moves freely before the clutch resistance is felt **(see illustration)**. The freeplay should be within the specified limits. If it isn't, it must be readjusted.

2   Loosen the locknut on the pedal end of the clutch pushrod **(see illustration)**.

3   Rotate the pushrod until pedal freeplay is correct.

4   Tighten the locknut.

5   After adjusting the pedal freeplay, check the pedal height.

6   If pedal height is incorrect, loosen the locknuts and rotate the clutch safety switch until the height is correct **(see illustration 14.2)**. Tighten the locknuts.

15   Suspension and steering checks

Refer to illustrations 15.4a, 15.4b, 15.4c and 15.4d

1   Indications of a fault in these systems are excessive play in the steering wheel before the front wheels react, excessive sway around corners, body movement over rough roads or binding at some point as the steering wheel is turned.

2   Raise the front of the vehicle periodically and visually check the suspension and steering components for wear. Because of the work to be done, make sure the vehicle cannot fall from the stands.

3   Check the wheel bearings. Do this by spinning the front wheels. Listen for any abnormal noises and watch to make sure the wheel spins true (doesn't wobble). Grab the top and bottom of the tire and pull in-and-out on it. Notice any movement which would indicate a loose wheel bearing assembly. If the bearings are suspect, refer to Section 34 and Chapter 10 for more information.

4   From under the vehicle check for loose bolts, broken or disconnected parts and deteriorated rubber bushings on all suspension and steering components **(see illustrations)**. Look for grease or fluid leaking from the steering assembly **(see illustration)**. Check the power steering hoses and connections for leaks.

5   Have an assistant turn the steering wheel from side-to-side and check the steering components for free movement, chafing and binding. If the steering doesn't react with the movement of the steering wheel, try to determine where the slack is located.

15.4d   Push on the steering boots to check for cracks and leaking grease

17.1a   Use an open end wrench to unscrew the manual transmission check and fill plug(s) – on non-turbocharged models (shown), check the lubricant level and add lubricant at the same opening

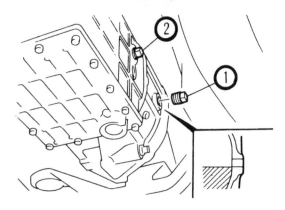

17.1b   On turbocharged models, check the lubricant level at the check plug opening (1) – if it's low, add lubricant at the fill plug opening (2)

16   Exhaust system check

1   With the engine cold (at least three hours after the vehicle has been driven), check the complete exhaust system from the manifold to the end of the tailpipe. Be careful around the catalytic converter, which may be hot even after three hours. The inspection should be done with the vehicle on a hoist to permit unrestricted access. If a hoist isn't available, raise the vehicle and support it securely on jackstands.
2   Check the exhaust pipes and connections for signs of leakage and/or corrosion indicating a potential failure. Make sure that all brackets and hangers are in good condition and tight.
3   Inspect the underside of the body for holes, corrosion, open seams, etc. which may allow exhaust gases to enter the passenger compartment. Seal all body openings with silicone or body putty.
4   Rattles and other noises can often be traced to the exhaust system, especially the hangers, mounts and heat shields. Try to move the pipes, mufflers and catalytic converter. If the components can come in contact with the body or suspension parts, secure the exhaust system with new brackets and hangers.

17   Manual transmission lubricant level check

Refer to illustrations 17.1a and 17.1b
1   The manual transmission has inspection and fill plug(s) which must be removed to check the lubricant level **(see illustrations)**. If the vehicle is raised to gain access to the plug(s), be sure to support it safely on jackstands – DO NOT crawl under a vehicle which is supported only by a jack!
2   Remove the inspection plug from the transmission and use your little finger to reach inside the housing to feel the lubricant level. The level should be at or near the bottom of the plug hole.
3   If it isn't, add the recommended lubricant through the fill plug hole with a hand pump, syringe or squeeze bottle.
4   Install and tighten the plug and check for leaks after the first few miles of driving.

18   Differential lubricant level check

Refer to illustration 18.2
1   The differential has a check/fill plug which must be removed to check the oil level. If the vehicle is raised to gain access to the plug, be sure to support it safely on jackstands – DO NOT crawl under the vehicle when it's supported only by the jack.
2   Remove the lubricant check/fill plug from the side of the differential and insert your little finger in the hole **(see illustration)**.

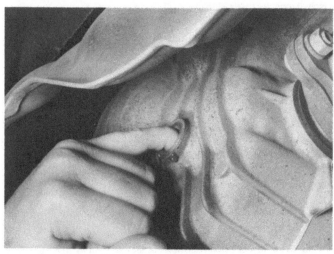

18.2   Use your little finger as a dipstick to make sure the differential lubricant level is even with the bottom of the opening

3   The lubricant level should be at the bottom of the plug opening. If not, use a syringe to add the recommended lubricant until it just starts to run out of the opening. On some models a tag may be located in the area of the plug which gives information regarding lubricant type, particularly on models equipped with a limited slip differential.

4   Install the plug and tighten it securely.

19   Brake check

Refer to illustration 19.6

Warning: *Brake system dust contains asbestos, which is hazardous to your health. DO NOT blow it out with compressed air and DO NOT inhale it. DO NOT use gasoline or solvents to remove the dust. Use brake system cleaner or denatured alcohol only.*

Note: *For detailed photographs of the brake system, refer to Chapter 9.*

1   In addition to the specified intervals, the brakes should be inspected every time the wheels are removed or whenever a defect is suspected.

2   To check the brakes, raise the vehicle and place it securely on jackstands. Remove the wheels (see *Jacking and towing* at the front of the manual, if necessary).

Front and rear disc brakes

3   Disc brakes are used on these models. Extensive rotor damage can occur if the pads are not replaced when needed.

4   These vehicles are equipped with wear sensors attached to the inner pads on the front wheels. When the pad wears to the specified limit, the metal sensor rubs against the rotor and makes a squealing sound.

5   The disc brake calipers, which contain the pads, are visible with the wheels removed. There is an outer pad and an inner pad in each caliper. All pads should be inspected.

6   Each caliper has a "window" to inspect the pads. Check the thickness of the pad lining by looking into the caliper at each end and down through the inspection window at the top of the housing **(see illustration)**. If the wear sensor is very close to the rotor or the pad material has worn to about 1/8-inch or less, the pads should be replaced.

7   If you're unsure about the exact thickness of the remaining lining material, remove the pads for further inspection or replacement (refer to Chapter 9).

8   Before installing the wheels, check for leakage and/or damage (cracks, splitting, etc.) around the brake hose connections. Replace the hose or fittings as necessary (see Chapter 9).

9   Check the condition of the rotor. Look for score marks, deep scratches and burned spots. If these conditions exist, the hub/rotor assembly should be removed for servicing (see Section 34).

Parking brake

10   The parking brake operates from a handle between the seats and locks the rear brake system. The easiest, and most obvious method of periodically checking the operation of the parking brake assembly is to park the vehicle on a steep hill with the parking brake set and the transmission in Neutral. If the parking brake cannot prevent the vehicle from rolling, it's in need of adjustment (see Chapter 9).

20   Driveaxle boot check

Refer to illustration 20.2

1   The driveaxle boots are very important because they prevent dirt, water and foreign material from entering and damaging the constant velocity (CV) joints. Oil and grease can cause the boot material to deteriorate prematurely, so it's a good idea to wash the boots with soap and water.

2   Inspect the boots for tears and cracks as well as loose clamps **(see illustration)**. If there is any evidence of cracks or leaking lubricant, they must be replaced as described in Chapter 8.

21   Fuel system check

Warning: *There are certain precautions to take when inspecting or servicing the fuel system components. Work in a well ventilated area and don't allow open flames (cigarettes, appliance pilot lights, etc.) in the work area. Mop up spills immediately and don't store fuel soaked rags where they could ignite. On fuel injection equipped models the fuel system is under pressure. No components should be disconnected until the pressure has been relieved (see Chapter 4).*

1   The fuel tank is located under the rear of the vehicle.

2   The fuel system is most easily checked with the vehicle raised on a hoist so the components underneath the vehicle are readily visible and accessible.

3   If the smell of gasoline is noticed while driving or after the vehicle has been in the sun, the system should be thoroughly inspected immediately.

4   Remove the gas tank cap and check for damage, corrosion and an unbroken sealing imprint on the gasket. Replace the cap with a new one if necessary.

5   With the vehicle raised, check the gas tank and filler neck for punctures, cracks and other damage. The connection between the filler neck and the tank is especially critical. Sometimes a rubber filler neck will leak due to loose clamps or deteriorated rubber, problems a home mechanic can usually rectify. **Warning:** *Do not, under any circumstances, try to repair a fuel tank yourself (except rubber components). A welding torch or any open flame can easily cause the fuel vapors to explode if the proper precautions are not taken!*

19.6   Look through the caliper inspection window to inspect the brake pads – the pad lining, which rubs against the disc, can also be inspected by looking at each end of the caliper

20.2   Push on the driveaxle boots to check for cracks

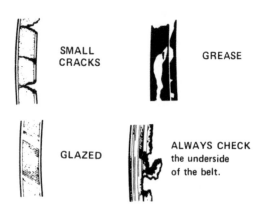

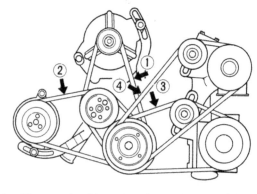

22.3   Here are some of the more common problems associated with drivebelts (check the belts very carefully to prevent an untimely breakdown)

22.4a   Measure the drivebelt deflection at the points shown

1	Alternator	3	Air conditioning compressor
2	Air pump	4	Power steering pump

6   Carefully check all rubber hoses and metal lines leading away from the fuel tank. Look for loose connections, deteriorated hoses, crimped lines and other damage. Follow thw lines to the front of the vehicle, carefully inspecting them all the way. Repair or replace damaged sections as necessary.

7   If a fuel odor is still evident after the inspection, refer to Section 36.

22   Drivebelt check, adjustment and replacement

Refer to illustrations 22.3, 22.4a, 22.4b and 22.9

1   The drivebelts, or V-belts as they are often called, are located at the front of the engine and play an important role in the overall operation of the engine and accessories. Due to their function and material makeup, the belts are prone to failure after a period of time and should be inspected and adjusted periodically to prevent major engine damage.

2   The number of belts used on a particular vehicle depends on the accessories installed. Drivebelts are used to turn the alternator, power steering pump, water pump and air conditioning compressor. Depending on the pulley arrangement, more than one of these components may be driven by a single belt.

3   With the engine off, locate the drivebelts at the front of the engine. Using your fingers (and a flashlight, if necessary), move along the belts checking for cracks and separation of the belt plies. Also check for fraying and glazing, which gives the belt a shiny appearance **(see illustration)**. Both sides of each belt should be inspected, which means you will have to twist the belt to check the underside. Check the pulleys for nicks, cracks, distortion and corrosion.

4   Check the tension of the belts by pushing on them at the indicated points **(see illustration)**. Push firmly with your thumb and see how much the belt moves (deflects) **(see illustration)**. A rule of thumb is that if the distance from pulley center-to-pulley center is between 7 and 11-inches, the belt should deflect 1/4-inch. If the belt travels between pulleys spaced 12-to-16 inches apart, the belt should deflect 1/2-inch.

5   If adjustment is needed, either to make the belt tighter or looser, it's done by moving the belt-driven accessory on the bracket.

6   For each component except the air conditioning compressor there will be an adjusting bolt and a pivot bolt. Both bolts must be loosened slightly to enable you to move the component.

7   After the two bolts have been loosened, move the component away from the engine to tighten the belt or toward the engine to loosen the belt. Hold the accessory in position and check the belt tension. If it's correct, tighten the two bolts until just snug, then recheck the tension. If the tension is all right, tighten the bolts.

8   It will often be necessary to use some sort of pry bar to move the accessory while the belt is adjusted. If this must be done to gain the proper leverage, be very careful not to damage the component being moved or the part being pried against.

9   On the air conditioning compressor, adjust the belt by turning the belt idler adjusting bolt **(see illustration)**.

10   To replace a belt, follow the above procedures for drivebelt adjustment, but slip the belt off the pulleys and remove it. Since belts tend to wear out more or less at the same time, it's a good idea to replace all of them at the same time. Mark each belt and the corresponding pulley grooves so the replacement belts can be installed properly.

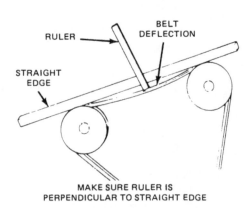

22.4b   Drivebelt tension can be checked with a straightedge and ruler

22.9   Adjust the air conditioning compressor drivebelt tension by turning the idler adjusting bolt (arrow)

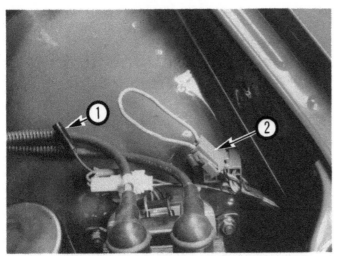

25.1   Hook up a tachometer to the one-wire connector (1) (leading side coil shown, trailing side similar), then connect a jumper wire between the two terminals of the initial set electrical connector (2)

11   Take the old belts with you when purchasing new ones in order to make a direct comparison for length, width and design.
12   Adjust the belts as described earlier in this Section.

23   Seatbelt check

1   Check the seatbelts, buckles, latch plates and guide loops for any obvious damage or signs of wear.
2   Make sure the seatbelt reminder light comes on when the key is turned on.
3   The seatbelts are designed to lock up during a sudden stop or impact, yet allow free movement during normal driving. The retractors should hold the belt against your chest while driving and rewind the belt when the buckle is unlatched.
4   If any of the above checks reveal problems with the seatbelt system, replace parts as necessary.

24   Clutch/Neutral safety switch check

Warning: *During the following checks there is a chance that the vehicle could lunge forward, possibly causing damage or injuries. Allow plenty of room around the vehicle, apply the parking brake firmly and hold down the regular brake pedal during the checks.*

1   These models are equipped with a clutch/Neutral safety switch which prevents the engine from starting unless the clutch pedal is depressed (manual transmission) or the shift lever is in Neutral or Park (automatic transmission).
2   On automatic transmission vehicles, try to start the vehicle in each gear. The engine should crank only in Park or Neutral.
3   If equipped with a manual transmission, place the shift lever in Neutral. The engine should crank only with the clutch pedal depressed.
4   Make sure the steering column lock allows the key to go into the Lock position only when the shift lever is in Park (automatic transmission) or Reverse (manual transmission).
5   The ignition key should come out only in the Lock position.

25   Idle speed check and adjustment

Refer to illustrations 25.1, 25.5 and 25.6

1   Following the manufacturer's instructions, connect a tachometer to the engine. On most models this is accomplished by connecting the tachometer to the one-wire electrical connector on the trailing side coil **(see**

25.5   On non-turbocharged models, turn the air adjust screw on the top of the throttle body to adjust the idle speed

illustration). **Note:** *the trailing side coil is identified by its blue spark plug wire boots.* If the tachometer does not operate properly, connect it to the black one-wire electrical connector on the leading side coil. On inductive type tachometers, connect only to the spark plug wires on the trailing side coil or incorrect readings will result.
2   Before checking or adjusting the idle speed, turn off all accessories and warm up the engine to normal operating temperature.
3   Check the throttle sensor (see Chapter 4).
4   Connect a jumper wire to the terminals of the initial set electrical connector **(see illustration 25.1)**.
5   On non-turbocharged engines, remove the blind cap and adjust the idle speed by turning the air adjust screw on the top of the throttle body **(see illustration)**.
6   On turbocharged engines, remove the blind cap from the Bypass Air Control (BAC) valve and adjust the idle speed by turning the air adjust screw **(see illustration)**.
7   Install the blind cap and disconnect the jumper wire from the initial set coupler. If the jumper wire is left in place, engine performance will be reduced, so be sure to remove it.

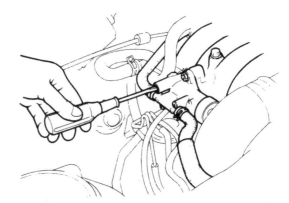

25.6   On turbocharged models, adjust the idle speed at the BAC valve

26   Engine oil level warning system check

Refer to illustrations 26.2 and 26.5

1   Turn the ignition switch on and make sure the oil level warning light comes on. When the engine is started, the warning light should go off.

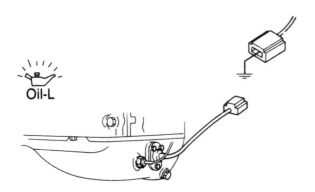

26.2   With the oil level sensor unplugged and the connector terminal grounded, the oil level warning light and buzzer should come on

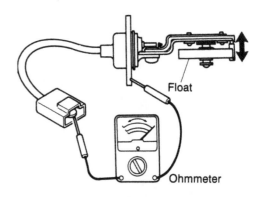

26.5   Check the oil level sensor to make sure there is continuity when the float is lowered

2   With the engine idling, unplug the connector from the oil level sensor and ground the terminal (see illustration). The oil level warning light should come on and the buzzer should sound.
3   To further check the system, unscrew the three mounting bolts and remove the sensor from the oil pan. Some oil may drain out, so position a drain pan or rags beneath the sensor before removing it.
4   Check the oil holes of the oil chamber to make sure they are not clogged. Clean the oil holes with solvent, if necessary.

5   Connect an ohmmeter to the sensor and move the float up and down to check for continuity (see illustration). When the float is raised, the ohmmeter should not show continuity. When it is lowered, there should be continuity. If the sensor fails either test, replace it with a new one.

27   Chassis and body fastener check

Tighten the following parts securely: front seat mounting bolts, front suspension member–to–body mounting bolts and nuts and rear suspension mounting bolts.

28   Sub–zero starting system check

Refer to illustrations 28.1, 28.2 and 28.3
1   Make sure the starting assist fluid level is near the top of the reservoir (see illustration). If it's not, fill it with a mixture of 90% ethylene glycol anti-freeze and 10% water.
2   To test the operation of the system, first unplug the electrical connector marked S from the starter motor. Unscrew the nut and bolt and remove the starting fluid valve (see illustration).
3   Unplug the electrical connector from the oil thermo unit on the oil pan and ground the connector (see illustration).
4   Press the silver air bleed button on the starting assist fluid reservoir while an assistant turns the ignition key to the Start position. Make sure starting assist fluid spurts from the starting fluid valve. If it does not, re-place the assembly.
5   Reinstall the starting fluid valve and reconnect the thermo valve and starter motor S connector wires.

28.1   Keep the starting assist fluid level near the top of the reservoir (arrow) – unscrew the cap to add more fluid

28.2   To remove the starting fluid valve, unscrew the nut and bolt (arrows)

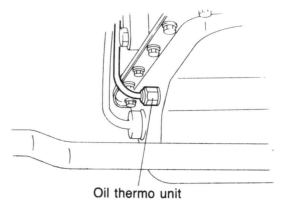

Oil thermo unit

28.3   Disconnect the wire to the oil thermo unit and ground the wire harness terminal

29.5   Squeeze the tabs with pliers and slide the clamps off the fuel filter, then pull the fuel lines off

29.6   The word OUT should face toward the engine

29   Fuel filter replacement

Refer to illustrations 29.5 and 29.6

Warning: *Gasoline is extremely flammable, so take extra precautions when working on any part of the fuel system. Do not smoke or allow open flames or bare light bulbs in or near the work area. Also, don't work in a garage where a natural gas appliance such as a water heater or clothes dryer is present.*

1   The fuel filter is located on the left side frame rail, near the engine.
2   Depressurize the fuel system (see Chapter 4)
3   Raise the vehicle and support it securely on jackstands.
4   With the engine cold, place a container, newspapers or rags under the fuel filter.
5   Disconnect the fuel lines, remove the retaining nuts and detach the filter from the frame **(see illustration)**.
6   Install the new filter by reversing the removal procedure. Make sure the word OUT on the filter points toward the engine, not the fuel tank **(see illustration)**.

30   Air filter replacement

Refer to illustrations 30.2a, 30,2b, 30.4 and 30.7

1   At the specified intervals, the air filter should be replaced with a new one.
2   The filter is located in the right front corner of the engine compartment and is replaced by unscrewing the bolts from the filter housing, lifting off the cover and detaching the rubber connector **(see illustrations)**.

3   While the cover is off, be careful not to drop anything down into the air cleaner assembly.
4   Lift the air filter element straight up and out of the housing **(see illustration)**. Don't turn the element over until it is clear of the housing as debris could fall in and possibly jam the measuring plate. Wipe out the inside of the air cleaner housing with a clean rag.

30.2a   Remove the retaining bolts (arrows) from the filter cover. . .

30.2b . . . and lift the cover up to detach the rubber connector from the air intake pipe

30.4   Lift the filter element out of the housing and move it away before turning it over

30.7   Push on the hose between the air filter housing and the fuel injection unit to check for cracks which could cause air leaks and poor performance

5   Place the new filter in the air cleaner housing. Make sure it seats properly in the bottom of the housing.
6   Install the cover.
7   Check the condition of the hose between the air filter housing and the fuel injection unit **(see illustration)**. Leaks in this hose can cause idle and driveability problems.

31   Automatic transmission fluid and filter change

Refer to illustration 31.10

1   At the specified time intervals, the transmission fluid should be drained and replaced. Since the fluid will remain hot long after driving, perform this procedure only after the engine has cooled down completely.
2   Before beginning work, purchase the specified transmission fluid (see Recommended lubricants and fluids at the front of this Chapter) and a new filter.
3   Other tools necessary for this job include jackstands to support the vehicle in a raised position, a drain pan capable of holding at least eight pints, newspapers and clean rags.
4   Raise the vehicle and support it securely on jackstands.
5   With a drain pan in place, remove the front and side pan mounting bolts.
6   Loosen the rear pan bolts approximately four turns.
7   Carefully pry the transmission pan loose with a screwdriver, allowing the fluid to drain.

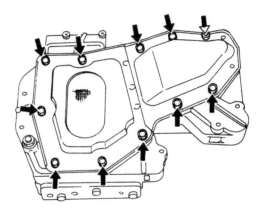

31.10   Automatic transmission filter retaining bolt locations (arrows)

8   Remove the remaining bolts, pan and gasket. Carefully clean the gasket surface of the transmission to remove all traces of the old gasket and sealant.
9   Drain the fluid from the transmission pan, clean it with solvent and dry it with compressed air.
10   Remove the filter from the mount inside the transmission **(see illustration)**.
11   Install a new filter.
12   Make sure the gasket surface on the transmission pan is clean, then install a new gasket. Put the pan in place against the transmission and, working around the pan, tighten each bolt a little at a time until the final torque figure is reached.
13   Lower the vehicle and add the specified amount of automatic transmission fluid through the filler tube (Section 6).
14   With the transmission in Park and the parking brake set, run the engine at a fast idle, but don't race it.
15   Move the gear selector through each range and back to Park. Check the fluid level.
16   Check under the vehicle for leaks during the first few trips.

32   Manual transmission lubricant change

Refer to illustrations 32.3a and 32.3b

1   Raise the vehicle and support it securely on jackstands.
2   Move a drain pan, rags, newspapers and wrenches under the transmission.
3   Remove the transmission drain plug(s) at the bottom of the case **(see illustrations)** and allow the lubricant to drain into the pan.

32.3a   Location of the drain plug on a non-turbocharged model manual transmission (arrow)

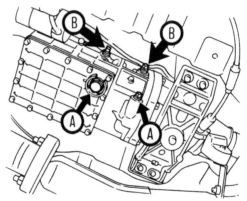

32.3b   Turbocharged models have two drain plugs (A) and two fill plugs (B) which must be removed to drain and refill the transmission case

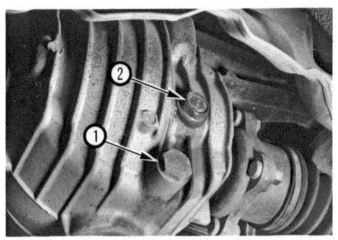

33.2   The differential drain plug (1) and fill plug (2) are located at the rear of the differential

4   After the lubricant has drained completely, reinstall the plug(s) and tighten them securely.
5   Remove the fill plug(s) from the side of the transmission case and add the correct amount of the specified lubricant (see Section 17). Reinstall the fill plug(s).
6   Lower the vehicle.
7   Drive the vehicle a short distance, then check the drain and fill plugs for leakage.

33   Differential lubricant change

Refer to illustration 33.2

1   Raise the vehicle and support it securely on jackstands. Move a drain pan, rags, newspapers and wrenches under the vehicle.
2   Remove the fill plug from the differential (**see illustration**).
3   Remove the drain plug and allow the differential lubricant to drain completely. After the lubricant has drained, install the plug and tighten it securely.
4   Use a hand pump, syringe or funnel to fill the differential housing with the specified lubricant until it's level with the bottom of the fill plug hole.
5   Install the fill plug and tighten it securely.

34.6   Dislodge the dust cap by working around the outer circumference with a hammer and chisel – be careful; the hub is aluminum and can be easily damaged

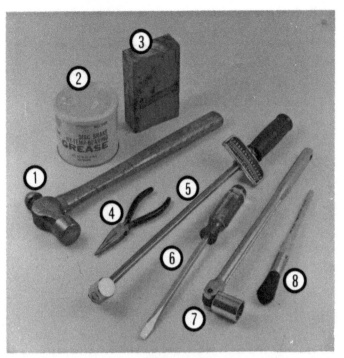

34.1   Tools and materials needed for front wheel bearing maintenance

1   *Hammer – A common hammer will do just fine*
2   *Grease – High-temperature grease which is formulated specially for front wheel bearings should be used*
3   *Wood block – If you have a scrap piece of 2x4, it can be used to drive the new seal into the hub*
4   *Needle-nose pliers – Used to straighten and remove the cotter pin in the spindle*
5   *Torque wrench – This is very important in this procedure; if the bearing is too tight, the wheel won't turn freely – if it's too loose, the wheel will "wobble" on the spindle. Either way, it could mean extensive damage.*
6   *Screwdriver – Used to remove the seal from the hub (a long screwdriver would be preferred)*
7   *Socket/breaker bar – Needed to loosen the nut on the spindle if it's extremely tight*
8   *Brush – Together with some clean solvent, this will be used to remove old grease from the hub and spindle*

34   Front wheel bearing check, repack and adjustment

Refer to illustrations 34.1, 34.6, 34.7, 34.8, 34.9 and 34.24

1   In most cases the front wheel bearings will not need servicing until the brake pads are changed. However, the bearings should be checked whenever the front of the vehicle is raised for any reason. Several items, including a torque wrench and special geases, are required for this procedure (**see illustration**).
2   With the vehicle securely supported on jackstands, spin each wheel and check for noise, rolling resistance and free play.
3   Grasp the top of each tire with one hand and the bottom with the other. Move the wheel in-and-out on the spindle. If there's any noticable movement, the bearings should be checked and then repacked with grease or replaced if necessary.
4   Remove the wheel.
5   Remove the brake caliper and hang it out of the way on a piece of wire, then remove the caliper bracket (see Chapter 9).
6   Pry the dust cap out of the hub using a screwdriver or hammer and chisel (**see illustration**).

34.7   Use wire cutters or needle-nose pliers to straighten the cotter pin and pull it out

34.9   Dislodge the outer bearing and extract it from the hub

7   Straighten the bent ends of the cotter pin, then pull the cotter pin out of the nut lock **(see illustration)**. Discard the cotter pin and use a new one during reassembly.
8   Remove the nut lock, spindle nut and washer from the end of the spindle **(see illustration)**.
9   Pull the hub assembly out slightly, then push it back into its original position. This should force the outer bearing off the spindle enough so it can be removed **(see illustration)**.
10   Pull the hub off the spindle.
11   Use a screwdriver to pry the seal out of the rear of the hub. As this is done, note how the seal is installed.
12   Remove the inner wheel bearing from the hub.
13   Use solvent to remove all traces of the old grease from the bearings, hub and spindle. A small brush may prove helpful; however, make sure no bristles from the brush embed themselves inside the bearing rollers. Allow the parts to air dry.
14   Carefully inspect the bearings for cracks, heat discoloration, worn rollers, etc. Check the bearing races inside the hub for wear and damage. If the bearing races are defective, the hub should be replaced with a new one. Note that the bearings and races come as matched sets and old bearings should never be installed on new races.
15   Use high-temperature front wheel bearing grease to pack the bearings. Work the grease completely into the bearings, forcing it between the rollers, cone and cage from the back side.
16   Apply a thin coat of grease to the spindle at the outer bearing seat, inner bearing seat, shoulder and seal seat.
17   Put a small quantity of grease inboard of each bearing race inside the hub. Using your finger, form a dam at these points to provide extra grease availability and to keep thinned grease from flowing out of the bearing.

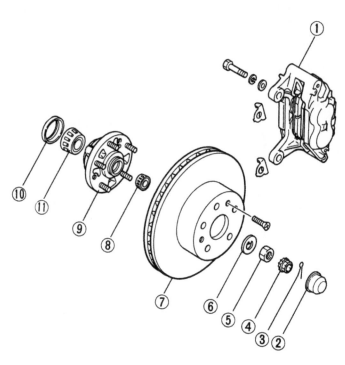

34.8   Front hub and wheel bearing components – exploded view

1	Brake caliper assembly	7	Brake disc
2	Dust cap	8	Outer wheel bearing
3	Cotter pin	9	Hub
4	Nut lock	10	Inner wheel bearing seal
5	Spindle nut	11	Inner wheel bearing
6	Washer		

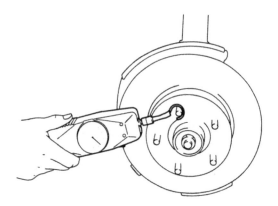

34.24   Use a pull scale to measure the initial torque required to turn the hub

18   Place the grease-packed inner bearing into the rear of the hub and put a little more grease outboard of the bearing.
19   Place a new seal over the inner bearing and tap the seal evenly into place with a hammer and block of wood until it's flush with the hub.
20   Carefully place the hub assembly onto the spindle and push the grease-packed outer bearing into position.
21   Install the washer and spindle nut. Tighten the nut to the initial torque listed in this Chapter's specifications.
22   Spin the hub in a forward direction to seat the bearings and remove any grease or burrs which could cause excessive bearing play later.
23   Loosen the spindle nut until it's just loose, no more.
24   Attach a pull scale to a wheel stud and note the initial torque required to turn the hub **(see illustration)**.

35.3   Unscrew the bleeder plug (arrow) using a phillips screwdriver

35.4   Also use a phillips screwdriver to remove the drain plug at the bottom of the radiator

25   Using a wrench, tighten the nut until the pull scale indicates the pre-load listed in this Chapter's specifications. Install the nut lock, then install a new cotter pin through the hole in the spindle and slots in the nut lock. If the nut lock slots don't line up, loosen the nut slightly until they do.
26   Bend the ends of the cotter pin until they're flat against the nut. Cut off any extra length which could interfere with the dust cap.
27   Install the dust cap, tapping it into place with a hammer.
28   Install the bracket and caliper (see Chapter 9).
29   Install the tire/wheel assembly on the hub and tighten the lug nuts.
30   Grasp the top and bottom of the tire and check the bearings in the manner described earlier in this Section.
31   Lower the vehicle.

35   Cooling system servicing (draining, flushing and refilling)

Refer to illustrations 35.3, 35.4 and 35.5
Warning: *Antifreeze is a corrosive and poisonous solution, so be careful not to spill any of the coolant mixture on the vehicle's paint or your skin. If this happens, rinse immediately with plenty of clean water. Consult local authorities regarding proper disposal procedures for antifreeze before draining the cooling system. In many areas, reclamation centers have been established to collect used oil and coolant mixtures.*

1   Periodically, the cooling system should be drained, flushed and re-filled to replenish the antifreeze mixture and prevent formation of rust and corrosion, which can impair the performance of the cooling system and cause engine damage. When the cooling system is serviced, all hoses, clamps and the filler cap should be checked and replaced if necessary (see Section 9).
2   Apply the parking brake and block
the wheels. If the vehicle has just been driven, wait several hours to allow the engine to cool down before beginning this procedure.
3   Once the engine is completely cool, remove the coolant filler cap and bleeder plug **(see illustration)**.
4   Move a large container under the radiator drain to catch the coolant, then remove the drain plug **(see illustration)**.
5   After the coolant stops flowing out of the radiator, move the container under the engine block drain plug. Remove the plug **(see illustration)** and allow the coolant in the block to drain.
6   While the coolant is draining, check the condition of the radiator hoses, heater hoses and clamps.
7   Replace any damaged clamps or hoses.
8   Once the system is completely drained, flush the radiator with fresh water from a garden hose until it runs clear at the drain. The flushing action of the water will remove sediments from the radiator but will not remove rust and scale from the engine and cooling tube surfaces.

35.5   The engine block drain plug is located on the left side of the engine

9   These deposits can be removed with a chemical cleaner. Follow the procedure outlined in the manufacturer's instructions. If the radiator is se-verely corroded, damaged or leaking, it should be removed (see Chapter 3) and taken to a radiator repair shop.
10   Remove the overflow hose from the coolant recovery reservoir. Drain the reservoir and flush it with clean water, then reconnect the hose.
11   Install and tighten the radiator drain and the block drain plug.
12   Place the heater temperature control in the maximum heat position.
13   Slowly add new coolant (a 50/50 mixture of water and antifreeze) through the filler neck until it begins flowing out the bleeder plug hole. In-stall the bleeder plug and add coolant to the reservoir up to the lower mark.
14   Leave the filler cap off and run the engine in a well-ventilated area until the thermostat opens (the upper radiator hose will become hot). Add cool-ant as necessary to bring the level to the lip of the filler neck. Install the filler cap.
15   Start the engine, allow it to reach normal operating temperature and check for leaks.

36   Evaporative emissions control system check

Refer to illustration 36.2
1   The function of the evaporative emissions control system is to draw fuel vapors from the gas tank and fuel system, store them in a charcoal canister and route them to the intake manifold during normal engine oper-ation.

36.2   The charcoal canister is located at the right rear corner of the engine compartment – inspect the canister and the various hoses attached to it for any damage

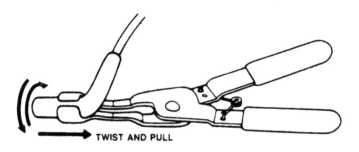

TWIST AND PULL

37.6   When removing the spark plug wires, pull only on the boot and twist it back-and-forth

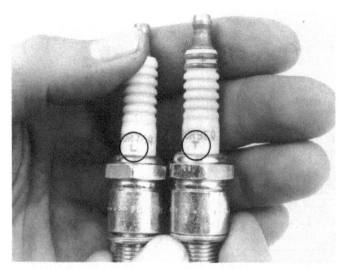

37.9   These models use two different types of spark plugs: Leading (marked L) and trailing (marked T) – leading plugs go into the lower spark plug holes and trailing plugs go in the upper holes

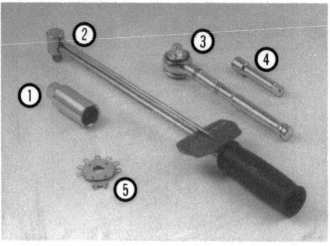

37.2   Tools required for changing spark plugs

1   *Spark plug socket* – *This will have special padding inside to protect the spark plug's porcelain insulator*
2   *Torque wrench* – *Although not mandatory, using this tool is the best way to ensure the plugs are tightened properly*
3   *Ratchet* – *Standard hand tool to fit the spark plug socket*
4   *Extension* – *Depending on model and accessories, you may need special extensions and universal joints to reach one or more of the plugs*
5   *A **spark plug gap gauge** like this is not necessary for rotary-engined vehicles.*

2   The most common symptom of a fault in the evaporative emissions system is a strong fuel odor in the engine compartment. If a fuel odor is detected, inspect the charcoal canister, located in the engine compart-ment **(see illustration)**. Check the canister and all hoses for damage and deterioration.
3   The evaporative emissions control system is explained in more detail in Chapter 6.

37   Spark plug replacement

Refer to illustrations 37.2, 37.6, 37.9 and 37.10
1   Open the hood.
2   In most cases, the tools necessary for spark plug replacement include a spark plug socket which fits onto a ratchet (spark plug sockets are padded inside to prevent damage to the porcelain insulators on the new plugs) and various extensions **(see illustration)**. A special plug wire re-moval tool is available for separating the wire boots from the spark plugs, but it isn't absolutely necessary. A torque wrench should be used to tighten the new plugs.
3   The best approach when replacing the spark plugs is to purchase the new ones in advance and replace them one at a time. When buying the new spark plugs, be sure to obtain the correct plug type for your particular engine. This information can be found on the Emission Control Informa-tion label located under the hood and in the factory owner's manual. If dif-ferences exist between the plug specified on the emissions label and in the owner's manual, assume that the emissions label is correct.
4   Allow the engine to cool completely before attempting to remove any of the plugs.
5   While you're waiting for the engine to cool, check the new plugs for defects. Check for cracks in the porcelain insulator (if any are found, the plug should not be used).
6   With the engine cool, remove the spark plug wire from one spark plug. Pull only on the boot at the end of the wire – do not pull on the wire. A plug wire removal tool should be used if available **(see illustration)**.
7   If compressed air is available, use it to blow any dirt or foreign material away from the spark plug hole. A common bicycle pump will also work. The idea here is to eliminate the possibility of debris falling into the cylinder as the spark plug is removed.

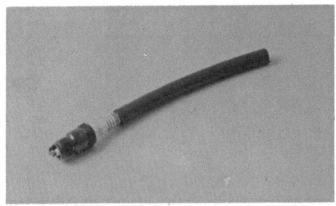

37.10   A length of 3/16-inch ID rubber hose will save time and prevent damaged threads when installing the spark plugs

8   Place the spark plug socket over the plug and remove it from the engine by turning it in a counterclockwise direction.
9   These vehicles use two different types of spark plugs: Leading plugs (installed in the lower spark plug holes) and trailing plugs (installed in the upper spark plug holes). Leading and trailing spark plugs and their associated holes are marked with a T or an L **(see illustration)**. Don't mix them up!
10   Before installing the spark plugs, apply a small amount of anti-seize compound to the spark plug threads. Thread one of the new plugs into the hole until you can no longer turn it with your fingers, then tighten it with a torque wrench (if available) or the ratchet. It might be a good idea to slip a short length of rubber hose over the end of the plug to use as a tool to thread it into place **(see illustration)**. The hose will grip the plug well enough to turn it, but will start to slip if the plug begins to cross-thread in the hole – this will prevent damaged threads and the accompanying repair costs.
11   Before pushing the spark plug wire onto the end of the plug, inspect it following the procedure in Section 38.
12   Attach the plug wire to the new spark plug, again using a twisting motion on the boot until it's seated on the spark plug.
13   Repeat the procedure for the remaining spark plugs, replacing them one at a time to prevent mixing up the spark plug wires.

---

38   Spark plug wire check and replacement

Refer to illustration 38.6

1   The spark plug wires should be checked at the recommended intervals and whenever new spark plugs are installed in the engine.

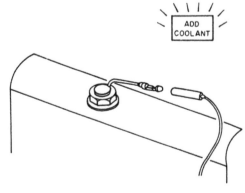

39.2   When the coolant level sensor (located on top of the radiator) is unplugged with the ignition switch in the On position, the coolant level warning light should come on

38.6   The number one spark plug wires are marked with a white band and their corresponding coil terminals are marked with a white dot (arrows)

2   The wires should be inspected one at a time to prevent mixing up the order, which is essential for proper engine operation.
3   Disconnect the plug wire from one spark plug. To do this, grab the rubber boot, twist slightly and pull the wire free. Do not pull on the wire itself, only on the rubber boot **(see illustration 37.6)**.
4   Check inside the boot for corrosion, which will look like a white crusty powder. Push the wire and boot back onto the end of the spark plug. It should be a tight fit on the plug. If it isn't, remove the wire and use a pair of pliers to carefully crimp the metal connector inside the boot until it fits securely on the end of the spark plug.
5   Using a clean rag, wipe the entire length of the wire to remove any built-up dirt and grease. Once the wire is clean, check for holes, burned areas, cracks and other damage. Don't bend the wire excessively or the conductor inside might break.
6   To help you avoid mixing them up, the spark plug wires are color coded. The boots of the leading (lower) spark plugs are black and the trailing (upper) spark plug boots are blue. The number one boots are identified with a white band and the coils are identified with a corresponding white dot **(see illustration)**.
7   Disconnect the wire from the coil. Again, pull only on the rubber boot. Check for corrosion and a tight fit in the same manner as the spark plug end. Reattach the wire to the coil.
8   Check the remaining spark plug wires one at a time, making sure they are securely fastened at the coil and the spark plug when the check is complete.
9   If new spark plug wires are required, purchase a new set for your specific engine mode. Wire sets are available pre-cut, with the rubber boots already installed. Remove and replace the wires one at a time to avoid mix-ups in the firing order, which can severely affect engine performance.

---

39   Engine coolant warning system check

Refer to illustrations 39.2 and 39.7

1   Turn the ignition switch to the on position. The coolant level warning light on the dashboard should come on. Start the engine; it should go off.
2   Unplug the electrical connector from the level sensor on top of the radiator **(see illustration)**. The warning light should come on after 9 to 16 seconds and a buzzer should sound when the engine is idling.
3   Cool the engine completely (allow the vehicle to sit for at least four hours). Remove the filler cap to relieve any pressure in the cooling system.
4   Unscrew the sensor from the radiator. Plug the opening to prevent coolant leakage.
5   Inspect the sensor for cracks and damage. Replace it if either is found.
6   Start the engine.

7   Reattach the electrical connector to the sensor and ground the tip of the sensor **(see illustration)**. Make sure the coolant level warning light goes out. If it does not, the sensor is defective and must be replaced with a new one.

40   Brake fluid replacement

1   Because brake fluid absorbs moisture which could ultimately cause corrosion of the brake components, and air, which could make the braking system less effective, the fluid should be replaced at the specified intervals. This job can be accomplished for a nominal fee by a properly equipped brake shop using a pressure bleeder. The task can also be done by the home mechanic with the help of an assistant. To bleed the air and old fluid and replace it with fresh fluid from sealed containers, refer to the brake bleeding procedure in Chapter 9.

2   If there is any possibility that incorrect fluid has been used in the system, drain all the fluid and flush the system with alcohol. Replace all piston seals and cups, as they will be affected and could possibly fail under pressure.

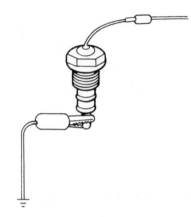

39.7   The coolant level warning light should go off when the tip of the sensor is grounded

Chapter 2 Part A   Engine

Contents

Compression test . . . . See Chapter 2B	General information 1
Drivebelt check, adjustment and replacement . . . . See Chapter 1	Intake manifold – removal and installation 3
Engine mounts – check and replacement 11	Metering oil pump – check, removal and installation 9
Engine oil and filter change . . . . See Chapter 1	Oil pan – removal and installation 8
Engine overhaul – general information . . . . See Chapter 2B	Oil pump – removal and installation 10
Engine – removal and installation . . . . See Chapter 2B	Rear eccentric shaft oil seal – replacement 7
Exhaust manifold – removal and installation 4	Repair operations possible with the engine in the vehicle 2
Front eccentric shaft oil seal – replacement 5	Spark plug replacement . . . . See Chapter 1
Flywheel/driveplate – removal and installation 6	Water pump – removal and installation . . . . See Chapter 3

Specifications

General

Eccentric shaft bypass valve protrusion at 140°F (60°C)	0.24 in (6 mm) minimum
Oil pressure control valve (in front cover) spring free length	2.87 in (73.0 mm)
Metering oil pump discharge (at 2,000 rpm for 5 min.)	
Turbo	5.2 to 6.6 cc
Non-turbo	4.5 to 5.5 cc
Metering oil pump rod clearance	0 to 0.039 in (0 to 1 mm)
Pulley hub protrusion (maximum)	0.0961 in (2.44 mm)

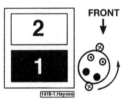

Cylinder location and distributor rotation

Torque specifications*

	Ft-lbs	Nm
Counterweight locknut (automatic transmission)	290 to 360	390 to 490
Driveplate-to-counterweight bolts (automatic transmission)	32 to 45	43 to 61
Eccentric shaft pulley-to-hub bolts	5.8 to 8.0	8 to 11
Eccentric shaft-to-hub bolt	80 to 98	108 to 132
Exhaust manifold-to-engine nuts	23 to 24	31 to 46
Flywheel nut (manual transmission)	290 to 360	390 to 490
Front cover bolts	12 to 17	16 to 23
Intake manifold-to-engine bolts and nuts	14 to 19	19 to 25
Left engine mount bracket-to-engine nuts	41 to 59	55 to 80
Metering oil nozzle	12 to 17	6 to 23
Metering oil pump bolts	5.8 to 8.0	8 to 11
Oil pressure control valve cap	29 to 36	39 to 49
Oil strainer (pickup) bolts	5.1 to 7.2.	7 to 10
Oil pan-to-engine bolts	5.8 to 8.0	8 to 11
Oil pump-to-engine bolts	5.1 to 7.2	7 to 10
Oil pump sprocket nut	23 to 34	31 to 46
Pressure regulator valve bolt	65 to 80	88 to 108
Right engine mount bracket-to-engine bolts	46 to 69	63 to 93

Note: Refer to Part B for additional torque specifications.

1   General information

This Part of Chapter 2 is devoted to in-vehicle repair procedures for the model 13B rotary engine. Information concerning engine removal and installation, as well as engine overhaul, is in Part B of this Chapter.

The following repair procedures are based on the assumption that the engine is installed in the vehicle. If the engine has been removed from the vehicle and mounted on a stand, many of the steps included in this Part of Chapter 2 will not apply.

The Specifications included in this Part of Chapter 2 apply only to the procedures in this Part. The Specifications necssary for rebuilding the engine are found in Part B.

2   Repair operations possible with the engine in the vehicle

Many repair operations can be accomplished without removing the engine from the vehicle.

Clean the engine compartment and the exterior of the engine with some type of degreaser before any work is done. It will make the job easier and help keep dirt out of the internal areas of the engine.

Depending on the components involved, it may be helpful to remove the hood to improve access to the engine as repairs are performed (refer to Chapter 11 if necessary). Cover the fenders to prevent damage to the paint. Special pads are available, but an old bedspread or blanket will also work.

If vacuum, exhaust, oil or coolant leaks develop, indicating a need for gasket or seal replacement, the repairs can generally be made with the engine in the vehicle. The intake and exhaust manifold gaskets, oil pan gasket and eccentric shaft oil seals are all accessible with the engine in place.

Exterior engine components, such as the intake and exhaust manifolds, oil pan, oil pump, flywheel/driveplate, oil metering pump, water pump, starter motor, alternator, crank angle sensor and fuel system components can be removed for repair with the engine in place.

Repair of internal engine components requires engine removal and disassembly. See Chapter 2, Part B for those procedures.

3   Intake manifold – removal and installation

Refer to illustrations 3.7a, 3.7b, 3.9 and 3.10

1   Relieve the fuel system pressure (see Chapter 4).

2   Disconnect the negative cable from the battery.
3   On vehicles equipped with antilock brakes, remove the ABS unit for access (see Chapter 9).
4   On turbocharged models, remove the intercooler, throttle body, surge tank and fuel rail (see Chapter 4).

Non-turbo models only

5   Remove the throttle body, dynamic chamber and extension manifold (1986 through 1988) or VDI manifold (1989) (see Chapter 4).
6   Remove the auxiliary port valve actuators (see Chapter 4).

All models

7   Mark the air hoses **(see illustrations)** and then remove them.
8   Remove the air control valve (see Chapter 6).
9   Disconnect and set aside the oil metering lines **(see illustration)**.
10   Unbolt the intake manifold **(see illustrations)** and separate it from the engine.
11   Thoroughly clean the intake manifold and engine gasket mating surfaces, removing all traces of old gasket material. On turbo models, remove the O-rings.
12   Inspect the intake manifold for cracks and damage. If the gasket was leaking, have the manifold checked for warpage by an automotive machine shop and resurfaced, if necessary.

3.7a   Mark the hoses with paint and make corresponding marks where they connect (arrows) to allow proper reassembly (non-turbo model shown)

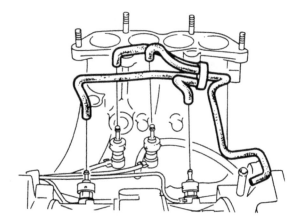

3.7b   The molded hoses on turbo models hold their shape, but marking them prevents any chance of assembly error

3.9   Unscrew the oil metering nozzles (arrow) to remove the oil metering lines (turbo model shown, non-turbo similar)

3.10   On non-turbo models, loosen the metal tube bolt (1),
then, on all models, remove the manifold mounting nuts and
bolts (2) – the upper left mounting bolt in this photo is
not visible

4.4a   On non-turbo models, remove the heat shield nuts on the
side of the manifold, . . .

4.4b . . . remove the two upper heat shield bolts located under the
center of the intake manifold, . . .

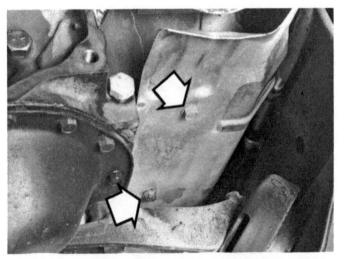

4.4c . . . then raise the vehicle and remove the lower heat shield
bolts (arrows)

13   On non-turbo models, install the auxiliary port valves as described in
Chapter 4.
14   Using a new gasket (and O-rings on turbo models), install the manifold and finger tighten the fasteners.
15   Working back and forth diagonally, tighten the manifold nuts/bolts in
three steps to the torque listed in this Chapter's specifications.
16   Reinstall the remaining parts in the reverse order of removal. **Note:**
*The oil metering lines are color coded. The line to the front inlet port is blue
and the line to the rear inlet port is green.*
17   Run the engine and check for vacuum leaks and proper operation.

---

4   Exhaust manifold – removal and installation

Refer to illustrations 4.4a, 4.4b, 4.4c, 4.4d, 4.8 and 4.10
Warning: *Allow the engine to cool completely before following this
procedure.*
1   Disconnect the negative cable from the battery.
2   On vehicles equipped with antilock brakes, remove the ABS unit for
access (see Chapter 9).
3   Remove the oxygen sensor (see Chapter 6) and, on non-turbo models, remove the auxiliary port valve actuators and air control valve (see
Chapter 4).

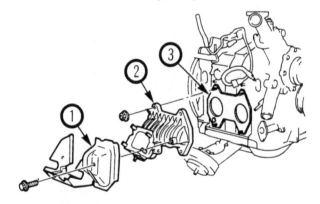

4.4d   **Exploded view of turbo exhaust manifold components**
1   Heat shield   2   Exhaust manifold   3   Gasket

4   Remove the heat shield from the exhaust manifold (**see illustrations**). On non-turbo models you must raise the vehicle to access the lower heat shield bolts. Support the vehicle securely on jackstands while it is
raised and leave it raised for Steps 7 and 8.

4.8   The exhaust manifold is attached to the engine with four nuts (arrows) – raise the vehicle and remove the lower two first, then lower the vehicle to remove the upper two (non-turbo model shown, turbo models are similar)

4.10   The hole in the exhaust manifold gasket must be aligned with the port in the engine casting (arrow)

5   On turbo models, remove the turbo wastegate actuator and the turbo-charger (see Chapter 4).

6   Apply penetrating oil to the manifold and exhaust pipe mounting nuts and allow it to soak in.

7   On non-turbo models, detach the exhaust pipe at the manifold outlet flange.

8   If not already done, raise the vehicle and support it securely on jack-stands. Remove the lower manifold nuts, then lower the vehicle and re-move the upper nuts **(see illustration)**. Lift the manifold from the engine compartment.

9   Clean the mating surfaces, removing all traces of old gasket material. If the gasket was blown out, have an automotive machine shop check the manifold for warpage and resurface it, if necessary.

10   Slip a new gasket over the studs on the engine, ensuring the gasket is aligned properly **(see illustration)**.

11   Install the exhaust manifold using new nuts. Working back and forth in several steps, tighten the nuts to the torque listed in this Chapter's specifi-cations.

12   Reinstall the remaining parts in the reverse order of removal.

13   Run the engine and check for exhaust leaks.

5.5   Remove the pulley mounting bolts (arrows)

---

5   Front eccentric shaft oil seal – replacement

Refer to illustrations 5.5, 5.6a, 5.6b, 5.8, 5.10 and 5.11

1   Disconnect the negative cable from the battery.

2   Remove the radiator and shroud (see Chapter 3).

3   Remove the cooling fan and pulley (see Chapter 3).

4   Remove the drivebelts (see Chapter 1).

5   Remove the eccentric shaft pulley **(see illustration)**.

6   Hold the eccentric shaft hub from turning **(see illustration)**, remove the eccentric shaft-to-hub bolt and pull out the relief valve assembly from behind the bolt **(see illustration)**. **Note:** *If the eccentric shaft bolt on 1986 and 1987 non-turbo models is found to be loose, there is an improved type available (no. N31811420A). Refer to dealer service bulletin Cat. 1, 034/88.*

7   Slip the front hub off the eccentric shaft and set it aside.

8   Carefully pry the old seal out of the front cover **(see illustration)**.

9   Clean and inspect the seal bore and lip contact surface. Replace the front hub if a groove is worn into it where it contacts the seal lip.

10   Gently tap a new seal into place with a hammer and socket **(see illus-tration)**. Be sure the spring side is facing in.

11   Lubricate the seal lips with engine oil and install the hub. Ensure the key is in place in the eccentric shaft and the keyway in the hub is aligned with it **(see illustration)**.

12   Install the remaining parts in the reverse order of removal. Be sure to tighten the eccentric shaft-to-hub bolt to the specified torque.

13   After reassembly, start the engine and check for oil leaks.

5.6a   The eccentric shaft hub may be held stationary with a chain wrench

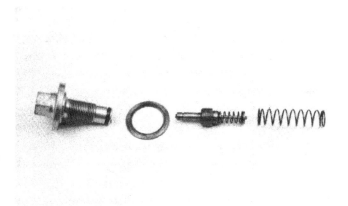

5.6b The relief valve components must be installed in this order

5.8 Wrap the tip of a screwdriver with tape, then carefully pry out the old seal without scratching the shaft or seal bore

5.10 Using a hammer and a large socket, gently tap the new seal into position

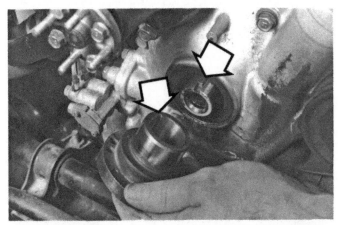

5.11 Align the keyway in the hub with the key in the eccentric shaft (arrows)

6 Flywheel/driveplate – removal and installation

Refer to illustrations 6.4, 6.5, 6.6, 6.8, 6.9, 6.11, 6.12, 6.13, 6.14, 6.15 and 6.17

Removal

1 Remove the transmission (see Chapter 7).
2 On manual transmission equipped models, remove the clutch assembly (see Chapter 8).
3 The eccentric shaft is tapered where the flywheel/driveplate fits onto

it. A keyway and key index the flywheel/driveplate on the eccentric shaft.
4 The eccentric shaft nut is very tight and requires special tools for removal and installation. A 54 mm (2 1/8-inch) socket and breaker bar (Mazda no. 490820035 or equivalent) may be used to remove the eccentric shaft nut **(see illustration)**.
5 The eccentric shaft must be prevented from turning while the nut is removed or installed. Mazda has a ring gear brake (no. 49F011101 or equivalent) available for manual transmission equipped models. A counter weight stopper (no. 491881055 or equivalent) is available for automatic transmission equipped models **(see illustration)**.

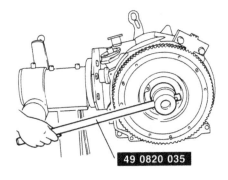

6.4 Special Mazda eccentric shaft nut tool

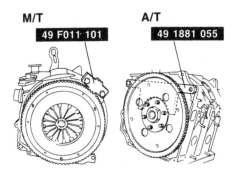

6.5 Special Mazda tools for holding the eccentric shaft stationary

6.6   Special aftermarket tools can be substituted for the Mazda tools – the tool being used to loosen the nut uses the ring gear to provide torque multiplication – a tool for holding the ring gear stationary is in the technician's left hand

6.9   With the nut backed off but not removed, alternately pry against the flywheel and turn it until the flywheel pops loose

6   If the special Mazda tools mentioned above are not available, after-market companies sell tools that will also work (see illustration).

Manual transmission models

7   Once the eccentric shaft nut has been loosened, back it off until about four threads remain meshed (this will prevent the flywheel from falling off suddenly).

8   Use a puller (Mazda no. 490839305A or equivalent) to break the flywheel loose from the tapered shaft (see illustration).

9   If a puller is not available, pry against the flywheel until it pops loose (see illustration).

10   Remove the key from the shaft and keep it in a safe place for reinstallation.

Automatic transmission models

11   Unbolt the retainer and driveplate (see illustration).

12   Install the counterweight stopper (no. 491881055 or equivalent) and remove the eccentric shaft nut (see illustration).

13   Use a puller (Mazda no. 490839305A or equivalent) to break the counterweight loose from the tapered shaft (see illustration). Remove the key from the shaft and keep it in a safe place for reinstallation.

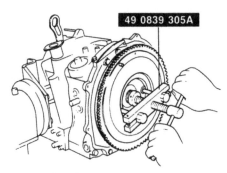

6.8   A two-bolt puller, such as this special Mazda tool, is preferred for loosening the flywheel – be sure to protect the eccentric shaft threads

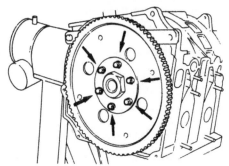

6.11   Remove the bolts (arrows), then the retainer and driveplate

6.12   Mazda counterweight stopper (tool no. 491881055)

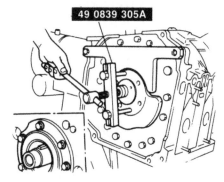

6.13   Remove the counterweight with a two-bolt puller – be sure to protect the end of the eccentric shaft

Installation

14   Inspect the eccentric shaft oil seal for damage and evidence of leakage. Replace it, if necessary (see Section 7). Seat the key in the keyway of the eccentric shaft (see illustration).

6.14   The key (arrow) must be fully seated in the keyway

6.15   During installation, align the keyway with the key (arrows) on the flywheel (shown) or counterweight (automatic transmission models)

15   Align the keyway with the key as you slide the counterweight (automatic transmission models) or flywheel (manual transmission models) onto the shaft **(see illustration)**.

16   Apply thread locking compound to the eccentric shaft threads and sealant to the inner face of the nut.

17   Using the tools described above, install the eccentric shaft nut and tighten it to the torque listed in this Chapter's specifications **(see illustration)**.

18   On automatic transmission models, install the driveplate so the holes in the driveplate and counterweight are aligned. Install the bolts and tighten them to the torque listed in this Chapter's specifications.

19   On manual transmission models, install the clutch assembly (see Chapter 8) and the transmission. On automatic transmission models, install the transmission and torque converter. See Chapter 7 for transmission installation instructions.

6.17   If a torque multiplying device is used, reduce the torque wrench setting accordingly – this special tool provides a multiplication factor of 12.5, so, if the specified torque were 300, you would set the torque wrench to 24

---

7   Rear eccentric shaft oil seal – replacement

Refer to illustrations 7.3 and 7.5

1   Remove the transmission (see Chapter 7).
2   Remove the flywheel or driveplate (see Section 6).
3   Carefully pry out the old seal **(see illustration)**.
4   Thoroughly clean and inspect the seal bore and the seal lip contact surface on the flywheel (manual transmission equipped models) or counterweight (automatic transmission equipped models).
5   Lubricate the lip of the new seal with engine oil and gently tap it into position with a soft-face hammer **(see illustration)**.

6   Reinstall the flywheel or driveplate.
7   Install the transmission as described in Chapter 7.
8   Run the engine and check for oil leaks at the rear of the engine.

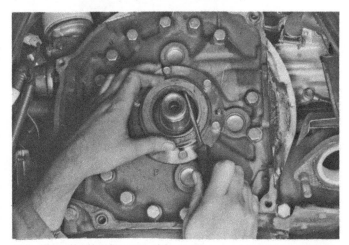

7.3   Wrap the tip of a screwdriver with tape and use it to carefully pry the old seal out – avoid scratching the shaft or housing

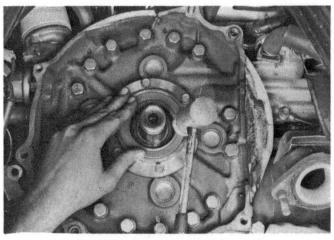

7.5   Gently tap the new seal into place with a soft-face hammer

8.6   The oil level sensor and oil thermo unit are mounted on the left side of the oil pan (arrows) – view is from below the vehicle

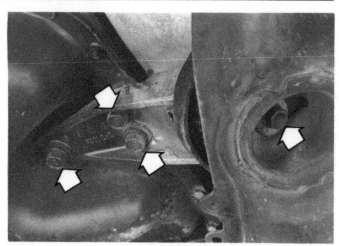

8.7   To remove the right engine mount and bracket, unscrew the bracket bolts and stud nut (arrows)

8.8   The front row of oil pan bolts can be removed with a swivel socket and long extension

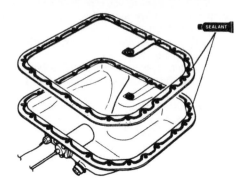

8.11   If the vehicle was originally equipped with an oil pan gasket, apply a bead of sealer to the oil pan flange and to the engine side of the new gasket

8.12   If the vehicle was not originally equipped with a gasket, apply a bead of silicone sealer to the flange inside of the bolt holes – if the sealer is applied outside the bolt holes, oil will leak around the bolts

8   Oil pan – removal and installation

Refer to illustrations 8.6, 8.7, 8.8, 8.11 and 8.12

Removal

1   Disconnect the negative cable from the battery.
2   Remove the cooling fan from the water pump (see Chapter 3).
3   Raise the front of the vehicle and support it securely on jackstands.
4   Remove the lower splash pan.
5   Drain the engine oil and change the oil filter (see Chapter 1).
6   Unplug the oil level sensor and oil thermo unit electrical connectors **(see illustration)**.
7   Support the engine and remove the right engine mount and bracket **(see illustration). Note:** *The engine may be supported from above with a hoist (see Chapter 2, Part B, Section 5) or from below with a jack and wood block under the transmission.*
8   Remove the oil pan mounting bolts **(see illustration)** and carefully pry the oil pan loose from the engine.
9   Thoroughly clean the oil pan and gasket mating surfaces, removing all traces of old gasket material or sealant. Remove any traces of oil with lacquer thinner or acetone and a clean cloth.
10   Inspect the oil pan and flanges for damage, cracks and distortion. Replace it if any of these conditions are found. Check for stripped mounting bolts and stripped threads in the mounting bolt holes. Replace the bolts or repair the threads, as necessary.

Installation

11   If the vehicle originally used a gasket to seal the oil pan, obtain a new gasket and apply a 4 to 6 mm bead of RTV sealer (Mazda no. 852777739 or equivalent) to the flange of the oil pan and the engine side of the new gasket **(see illustration)**.
12   If the vehicle was not equipped with an oil pan gasket, apply a 4 to 6 mm bead of RTV sealer (Mazda no. 852777739 or equivalent) around the flange of the oil pan **(see illustration). Note:** *Whether you use a gasket or not, install the oil pan immediately after applying the sealer – do not allow it to dry.*
13   Position the oil pan onto the engine and install the right engine mount. Install the bolts finger tight.
14   Working diagonally from the center out, gradually tighten the oil pan mounting bolts – and the two engine mount bolts along the oil pan flange – in several steps to the torque listed in this Chapter's specifications.

15 Reinstall the remaining parts in the reverse order of removal.
16 Add engine oil (see Chapter 1), start the engine and check for leaks and proper oil pressure.
17 Shut the engine off and recheck the oil level with the vehicle on a level surface.

9   Metering oil pump – check, removal and installation

Refer to illustrations 9.2, 9.4, 9.5, 9.6, 9.7a, 9.7b, 9.8, 9.13, 9.15 and 9.17

1 The metering oil pump lubricates the engine rotor seals by injecting engine oil into the intake airstream.
2 The pump is located at the lower right front corner of the engine **(see illustration)**.
3 Some pumps have an external mechanical control linkage while others have electrical controls. An electrically controlled pump may be identified by the wiring harness leading to it. Due to the complexity of the circuitry, we recommend taking electrically controlled pumps to a dealer service department for diagnosis.

Check (models with a mechanically controlled pump)

4 Inspect the oil lines for damage or kinks. Remove the oil nozzles one at a time and blow through them in both directions **(see illustration)**. The air must pass only in one direction.
5 Move the fast idle cam as shown **(see illustration)** to force the cam down.
6 Check the clearance of the rod and lever **(see illustration)** and compare it to this Chapter's specifications. Adjust it, if necessary, by adding or subtracting washers until the clearance between the lever and washers is as specified.

7 Next, warm the engine to normal operating temperature, shut the engine off, remove two oil lines at the pump and connect two test lines in their place (you can fabricate the test lines from two banjo fittings and lengths of plastic hose) **(see illustrations)**. **Caution:** *Do not operate the engine with all lines disconnected.*
8 Place the ends of the test lines in a measuring cup and hold the linkage rod in the full up position. Have an assistant run the engine at 2,000 RPM for five minutes. Oil will collect in the measuring cup **(see illustration)**. Compare the amount collected with this Chapter's specifications. **Warning:** *Stay clear of the fan and drivebelts while the engine is running.*

9.2   The metering oil pump is located at the lower right front corner of the engine

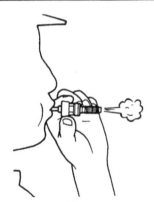

9.4   You should be able to blow through the oil nozzles only in the direction shown

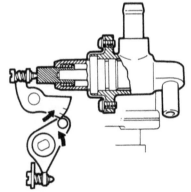

9.5   Move the fast-idle cam (mounted adjacent to the throttle body) as shown to force the cam down

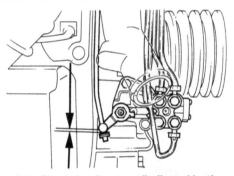

9.6   Check the clearance (indicated by the arrows) between the metering pump rod and lever; compare it with this Chapter's specifications – adjust the clearance by adding or removing washers

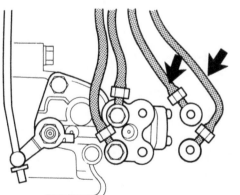

9.7a   Disconnect the two front oil lines . . .

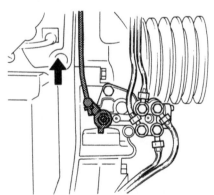

9.7b   . . . then connect two test lines – make sure the linkage rod is in the full up position (arrow) while the engine is running

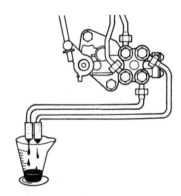

9.8   Collect the discharged oil in a measuring cup during the test

9.13   Mechanically controlled metering oil pump (lower radiator hose removed for clarity)

1	*Linkage adjustment washer and cotter pin*	*2*	*Oil line banjo bolts*
		3	*Pump mounting bolts*

9   If pump output is not as specified, readjust the pump (see Step 6). If adjustment does not correct the problem, replace the pump (see below).

Removal *(all models)*

10   Disconnect the negative cable from the battery.
11   If necessary for clearance, remove the air injection pump (see Chapter 6), drain the cooling system (see Chapter 1) and remove the lower radiator hose.
12   If the pump has electrical controls, unplug the connector at the pump.
13   On mechanically controlled pumps, disconnect the throttle body-to-pump linkage at the pump end by removing the cotter pin **(see illustration)**.
14   Remove the oil line banjo bolts, detach the oil lines and remove the two oil pump mounting bolts.

Installation

15   Clean the mating surfaces and install a new O-ring in the pump housing **(see illustration)**.
16   Reinstall the pump and linkage or electrical connector.

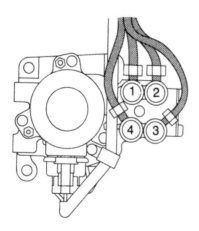

9.17   Connect the oil lines so the color codes of the tube ends match the numbers as shown

1	*White*	*3*	*Green*
2	*Blue*	*4*	*Yellow*

9.15   Install a new O-ring in the pump housing

17   Reconnect the oil lines by matching the color codes on the tube ends with the position numbers shown **(see illustration)**.
18   If removed, reinstall the air pump and lower radiator hose and add coolant.
19   Adjust the linkage and check the pump's output, as described above.

---

10   Oil pump – removal and installation

Refer to illustrations 10.1, 10.2, 10.4, 10.5, 10.8, 10.9, 10.10a, 10.10b, 10.11, 10.12a, 10.12b, 10.14, 10.16, 10.20, 10.24a, 10.24b and 10.29

1   Remove the front eccentric shaft pulley and hub as described in Section 5. Position the eccentric shaft so its key is aligned with the timing pointer **(see illustration)**.
2   Remove the water pump (see Chapter 3) and the water pump housing **(see illustration)**.
3   Remove the crank angle sensor (see Chapter 5).
4   Unbolt the air conditioning compressor (see Chapter 3) and (if equipped) power steering pump (see Chapter 10) and brackets **(see illustration)**. Set them aside without disconnecting the hoses.
5   Disconnect the oil line from the left side of the front cover **(see illustration)**.
6   Remove the metering oil pump (see Section 9).

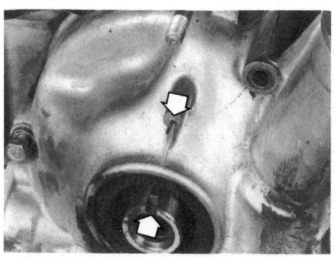

10.1   Align the eccentric shaft key with the timing pointer

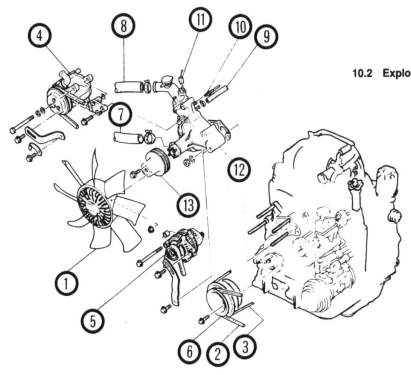

10.2 Exploded view of water pump and related components

1 Cooling fan
2 Power steering pump drivebelt
3 Air conditioning compressor drivebelt
4 Air pump and drivebelt
5 Alternator and drivebelt
6 Eccentric shaft pulley
7 Lower radiator hose
8 Upper radiator hose
9 Coolant bypass hose
10 Water thermo sensor conenctor
11 Water thermo switch connector (models with automatic transmission)
12 Water pump and housing
13 Cooling fan pulley

10.4 Exploded view of front cover and oil pump components

1 Cooling fan
2 Air pump drivebelt
3 Alternator drivebelt
4 Power steering pump and drivebelt
5 Air conditioning compressor and drivebelt
6 Crank angle sensor
7 Air conditioning compressor/ power steering pump bracket
8 Oil pipe
9 Metering oil pump
10 Oil pan
11 Eccentric shaft pulley lock bolt
12 Eccentric shaft bypass valve and spring
13 Eccentric shaft pulley
14 Front cover
15 Crank angle sensor drive gear
16 Oil pump drive sprocket/ driven sprocket and chain
17 Oil pump

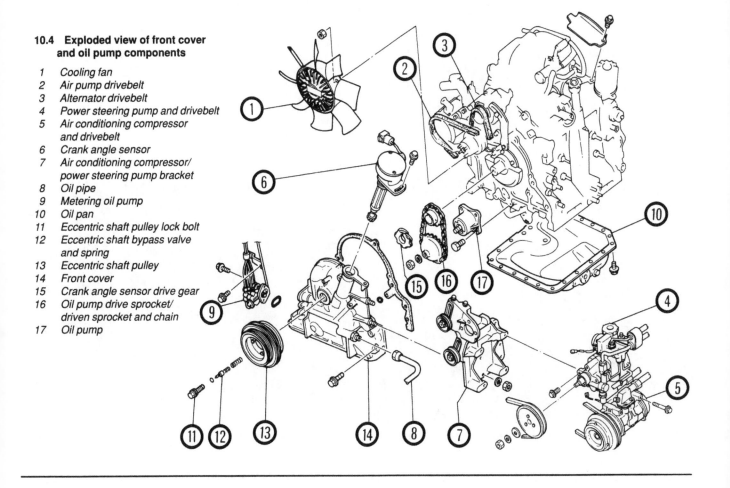

10.5   Disconnect the oil line (arrow) from the left side of the front cover

10.8   Pry against the casting protrusion (arrow) – DO NOT pry between the cover and engine housing

10.9   Slip the crank angle sensor drive gear (arrow) off the eccentric shaft

7   Remove the oil pan (see Section 8).

8   Unbolt the front cover and carefully pry it loose from the engine **(see illustration)**.

9   Slip the crank angle sensor drive gear off the eccentric shaft **(see illustration)**.

10   Flatten the locking tab **(see illustration)**, remove the oil pump shaft nut and pull the oil pump chain and sprockets off as an assembly **(see illustration)**.

11   Unbolt the oil pump from the engine **(see illustration)**.

12   Unscrew the cap on the oil pressure control valve **(see illustration)** and remove the spring and plunger **(see illustration)**.

13   Clean and visually inspect the spring and plunger. Measure the free length of the spring. Compare the measurement with this Chapter's specifications and replace it, if necessary.

14   Thoroughly clean all parts, including the metering oil pump driven gear **(see illustration)**. Remove any traces of old gasket material and inspect for cracks, wear and damage.

15   Reinstall the oil pressure control valve plunger and spring and tighten the cap to the specified torque.

16   Wrap the tip of a screwdriver with tape and use it to pry the old eccentric shaft oil seal out of the front cover. Gently drive a new seal into place using a large socket and a hammer **(see illustration)**.

10.10a   Flatten the locking tab (arrow) with a small hammer and chisel

10.10b   The oil pump chain and sprockets can be removed as an assembly

10.11   Remove the oil pump mounting bolts (arrows)

10.12a   Unscrew the cap (arrow) . . .

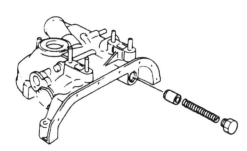

10.12b   . . . then remove the oil pressure control valve spring and plunger

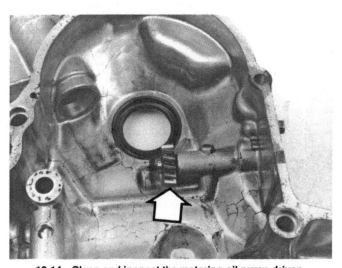

10.14   Clean and inspect the metering oil pump driven gear (arrow)

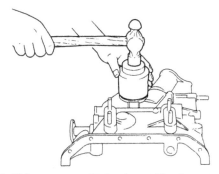

10.16   Drive a new seal into place with a hammer and a large socket

17   Install the oil pump and tighten the bolts to the specified torque.
18   Slip the chain and sprockets into position over the keys in the shafts (if the engine has high mileage, replace the chain and sprockets with new ones). Install a new locking tab and nut. Tighten the nut to the specified torque, then bend the locking tab to lock the nut.
19   Slip the crank angle sensor drive gear onto the eccentric shaft with the chamfered surface facing the engine.
20   Apply petroleum jelly to a new O-ring and install it in the oil passage hole (see illustration).
21   Apply a bead of RTV sealant to the engine housing and front cover mating surfaces. Place a new gasket over the engine housing locating dowels. Position the front cover on the engine. Install the accessory brackets and finger tighten the bolts.

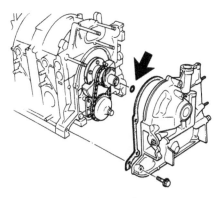

10.20   Apply petroleum jelly to a new O-ring (arrow) and install it in the oil passage hole

22   Tighten the front cover mounting bolts to the torque listed in this Chapter's specifications, working diagonally from the center out.
23   Cut away the part of the gasket which projects out from the oil pan surface.
24   Check the pulley boss protrusion from the eccentric shaft end:
     a) Temporarily install the lock bolt and tighten it by hand only.

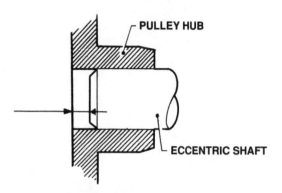

10.24a   Measure the pulley hub protrusion (arrows) and compare it to this Chapter's specifications

b) Remove the lock bolt and measure the pulley hub protrusion **(see illustration)**. If it exceeds the limit in this Chapter's specifications, the needle bearing located behind the eccentric shaft balance weight may be wedged by the spacer **(see illustration)**. Correct the problem before proceeding. **Caution:** *To prevent the needle bearing from being wedged by the spacer, do not move the eccentric shaft and the balance weight before tightening the eccentric shaft lock bolt.*

25   Apply thread locking compound to the threads and apply sealer to the flange surface of the eccentric shaft bolt.

26   Apply engine oil to a new O-ring and install it on the bolt.

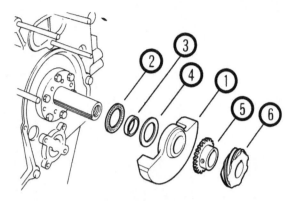

10.24b   Eccentric shaft balance weight and related components – exploded view

1	Balance weight	4	Thrust washer
2	Needle bearing	5	Oil pump drive sprocket
3	Spacer	6	Crank angle sensor drive gear

27   Install the eccentric shaft valve components, then the bolt. Tighten the bolt to the specified torque.

28   Reinstall the remaining parts in the reverse order of removal.

29   Add oil, run the engine and check for oil pressure and leaks in the lubricating system **(see illustration)**.

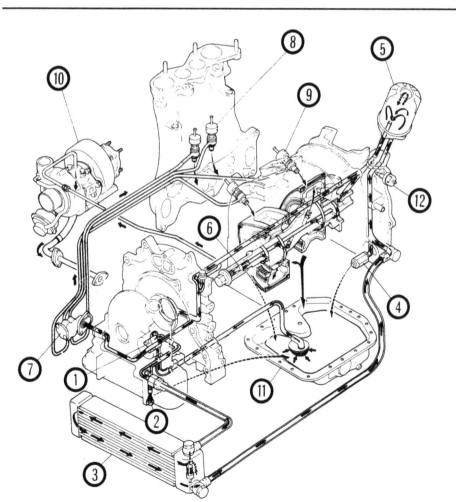

10.29   Lubrication system (turbo shown non-turbo similar)

1   Oil pump
2   Oil pressure control valve
3   Oil cooler
4   Oil pressure regulator valve
5   Oil filter
6   Eccentric shaft bypass valve
7   Metering oil pump
8   Manifold oil nozzle
9   Housing oil nozzle
10   Turbocharger
11   Oil pan
12   Oil pressure sending unit

11   Engine mounts – check and replacement

Refer to illustration 11.7

Warning: *Do not place any part of your body under the engine when it is supported by a jack only.*

1   Engine mounts seldom require attention, but broken or deteriorated mounts should be replaced immediately or the added strain placed on the driveline components may cause damage.

Check

2   During the check, the engine must be raised slightly to remove the weight from the mounts.

3   Raise the vehicle and support it securely on jackstands, then position the jack under the engine oil pan. Place a large block of wood between the jack head and the oil pan, then carefully raise the engine just enough to take the weight off the mounts.

4   Check the mounts to see if the rubber is cracked, hardened or separated from the metal plates. Sometimes the rubber will split right down the center. Rubber preservative may be applied to the mounts to slow deterioration.

5   Check for relative movement between the mount plates and the engine or frame (use a large screwdriver or pry bar to attempt to move the mounts). If movement is noted, lower the engine and tighten the mount fasteners.

Replacement

6   Disconnect the negative battery cable from the battery, then raise the vehicle and support it securely on jackstands.

11.7   Each mount is attached to its engine bracket with a nut (arrow) – left mount shown, right mount attachment is similar

7   Remove the nut from the mount **(see illustration)**.

8   Raise the engine slightly, then remove the mount-to-frame nut and detach the mount **(see illustration 8.7)**.

9   Installation is the reverse of removal. Use Locktite on the nuts and be sure to tighten them securely.

Chapter 2   Part B
General engine overhaul procedures

Contents

Apex seal and spring – inspection 14
Compression check 3
Corner seal and spring – inspection 16
Eccentric shaft – inspection 17
Eccentric shaft end play – adjustment 20
Engine components – cleaning 8
Engine overhaul – disassembly sequence 7
Engine overhaul – general information 2
Engine overhaul – reassembly of internal components 19
Engine rebuilding alternatives 6
Engine – removal and installation 5
Engine removal – methods and precautions 4

Final assembly and installation 22
Front and rear oil seals – replacement 18
Front bearing and oil pump assemblies – installation 21
General information 1
Housings – inspection and overhaul 9
Initial start-up and break-in after overhaul 23
Oil seal and spring – inspection and replacement 13
Rotor bearing – replacement 12
Rotor – inspection and repair 11
Side seal and spring – inspection 15
Stationary gears and main bearings – replacement 10

Specifications

General
Displacement .... 654cc (40.0 cu in) x 2 rotors
Compression pressure
  Limit .... 85 psi at 250 rpm
  Max. permissible difference between chambers .... 21 psi

Oil pressure
At idle .... 14 to 54 psi
At 3000 rpm .... 64 to 78 psi

Side housings (front, intermediate and rear)
Oil seal wear limit .... 0.0008 in (0.02 mm)
Overlapping oil seal wear limit .... 0.0004 in (0.01mm)
Limit of warpage .... 0.0016 in (0.04 mm)
Side seal and outside oil seal wear limit .... 0.0039 in (0.10 mm)

Rotor housing
Width .... 3.1485 to 3.1500 in (79.970 to 80.010 mm)
Max. permissible difference in width .... 0.0024 in (0.06 mm)

Rotor
Width .... 3.142 to 3.144 in (79.80 to 79.85 mm)
Clearance of side housing and rotor
  Standard .... 0.0047 to 0.0083 in (0.12 to 0.21 mm)
  Limit .... 0.004 in (0.10 mm)

Apex seal
Warpage limit . . . .   0.0024 in (0.06 mm)
Width . . . .   0.0752 to 0.0763 in (1.910 to 1.939 mm)
Height
   Standard . . . .   0.315 in (8.0 mm)
   Limit . . . .   0.256 in (6.5 mm)
Clearance of apex seal and side housing . . . .   0.0051 to 0.0067 in (0.13 to 0.17 mm)
Clearance of apex seal and rotor groove
   Standard . . . .   0.0024 to 0.004 in (0.062 to 0.102 mm)
   Limit . . . .   0.006 in (0.15 mm)

Apex seal spring
Free height (short)
   Standard . . . .   0.130 in (3.3 mm)
   Limit . . . .   0.067 in (1.7 mm)
Free height (long)
   Standard . . . .   0.246 in (6.25 mm) or more
   Limit . . . .   0.181 in (4.6 mm)

Side seal
Thickness . . . .   0.0260 to 0.0270 in (0.661 to 0.686 mm)
Height . . . .   0.1122 to 0.1240 in (2.85 to 3.15 mm)
Clearance of side seal and rotor groove
   Standard . . . .   0.0011 to 0.0031 in (0.028 to 0.078 mm)
   Limit . . . .   0.0039 in (0.10 mm)
Clearance of side seal and corner seal
   Standard . . . .   0.0020 to 0.0060 in (0.05 to 0.15 mm)
   Limit . . . .   0.016 in (0.40 mm)
Side seal protrusion (minimum) . . . .   0.020 in (0.5 mm)

Oil seal
Height . . . .   0.220 to 0.228 in (5.6 to 5.8 mm)
Width limit of oil seal lip . . . .   0.020 in (0.5 mm)
Oil seal protrusion (minimum) . . . .   0.020 in (0.5 mm)

Corner seal
Outer diameter . . . .   0.4327 to 0.4336 in (10.990 to 11.014 mm)
Height . . . .   0.268 to 0.276 in (6.8 to 7.0 mm)
Corner seal protrusion (minimum) . . . .   0.020 in (0.5 mm)

Main bearing clearance
Standard . . . .   0.0016 to 0.0031 in (0.04 to 0.08 mm)
Wear limit . . . .   0.0039 in (0.10 mm)

Rotor bearing clearance
Standard . . . .   0.0016 to 0.0031 in (0.04 to 0.08 mm)
Wear limit . . . .   0.0039 in (0.10 mm)

Eccentric shaft
Eccentricity of rotor journal . . . .   0.591 in (15.0 mm)
Main journal diameter . . . .   1.6918 to 1.6923 in (42.970 to 42.985 mm)
Rotor journal diameter . . . .   2.9122 to 2.9128 in (73.970 to 73.985 mm)
Max. permissible runout . . . .   0.0047 in (0.12 mm)
End play
   Standard . . . .   0.0016 to 0.0028 in (0.04 to 0.07 mm)
   Limit . . . .   0.0035 in (0.09 mm)
Main bearing inner diameter . . . . :   1.6939 to 1.6949 in (43.025 to 43.050 mm)
Rotor bearing inner diameter . . . .   2.9144 to 2.9154 in (74.025 to 74.050 mm)

Torque Specifications*

	Ft-lbs	Nm
Left engine mount bracket-to-engine bolts	41 to 59	55 to 80
Oil filter pedestal bolts	5.7 to 7.9	8 to 11
Oil inlet pipe (turbo only)	14 to 19	19 to 25
Right engine mount bracket-to-engine bolts	46 to 69	63 to 93
Stationary gear attaching bolts (front and rear)	12 to 17	16 to 23
Tension bolts	23 to 29	31 to 39

* Note: *See Chapter 2, Part A for additional torque specifications*

1   General information

Included in this portion of Chapter 2 are the general overhaul procedures for the internal engine components.

The information ranges from advice concerning preparation for an overhaul and the purchase of replacement parts to detailed, step-by-step procedures covering removal and installation of internal engine components and the inspection of parts.

The following Sections have been written based on the assumption that the engine has been removed from the vehicle. For information concerning in-vehicle engine repair, as well as removal and installation of the external components necessary for the overhaul, see Part A of this Chapter and Section 7 of this Part.

The specifications included in this Part are only those necessary for the inspection and overhaul procedures which follow. Refer to Part A for additional Specifications.

2   Engine overhaul – general information

Refer to illustration 2.4

It's not always easy to determine when, or if, an engine should be completely overhauled, as a number of factors must be considered.

High mileage is not necessarily an indication that an overhaul is needed, while low mileage doesn't preclude the need for an overhaul. Frequency of servicing is probably the most important consideration. An engine that's had regular and frequent oil and filter changes, as well as other required maintenance, will most likely give many thousands of miles of reliable service. Conversely, a neglected engine may require an overhaul very early in its life.

Excessive oil consumption is an indication that rotor apex and side seals are in need of attention. Make sure that oil leaks aren't responsible before deciding that the internal components are bad. The harder the car is driven, the more oil it will use. Consumption of one quart of oil in 1000 to 2000 miles is considered normal, while 700 to 800 miles per quart in normal driving is excessive. Perform a compression check to determine the extent of the work required (see Section 3).

Double check the oil pressure with a gauge installed in place of the oil pressure sending unit **(see illustration)** and compare it with this Chapter's specifications. If it's extremely low, the bearings and/or oil pump are probably worn out.

Loss of power, rough running, grinding or metallic engine noise, excessive smoke and high fuel consumption rates may also point to the need for an overhaul, especially if they're all present at the same time. If a com-

plete tune-up doesn't remedy the situation, major mechanical work is the only solution.

An engine overhaul involves restoring the internal parts to the specifications of a new engine. During an overhaul, worn or damaged parts are replaced and the seals and bearings are changed. While the engine is being overhauled, other components, such as the crank angle sensor, starter and alternator, can be rebuilt as well. The end result should be like a new engine that will give many trouble free miles. **Note:** *Critical cooling system components such as the hoses, drivebelts, thermostat and water pump MUST be replaced with new parts when an engine is overhauled. The radiator should be checked carefully to ensure that it isn't clogged or leaking (see Chapter 3). Also, we don't recommend overhauling the oil pumps – always install new ones when an engine is rebuilt.*

Before beginning the engine overhaul, read through the entire procedure to familiarize yourself with the scope and requirements of the job. Overhauling an engine isn't difficult, but it is time consuming. Plan on the vehicle being tied up for a minimum of two weeks, especially if parts must be taken to an automotive machine shop for repair or reconditioning. Check on availability of parts and make sure that any necessary special tools and equipment are obtained in advance. Most work can be done with typical hand tools, although a number of precision measuring tools are required for inspecting parts to determine if they must be replaced. Often an automotive machine shop will handle the inspection of parts and offer advice concerning reconditioning and replacement. **Note:** *Always wait until the engine has been completely disassembled and all components, especially the engine housings, have been inspected before deciding what service and repair operations must be performed by an automotive machine shop.* Since the condition of the housings will be a major factor to consider when determining whether to overhaul the original engine or buy a rebuilt one, never purchase parts or have machine work done on other components until the engine has been thoroughly inspected. As a general rule, time is the primary cost of an overhaul, so it doesn't pay to install worn or substandard parts.

As a final note, to ensure maximum life and minimum trouble from a rebuilt engine, everything must be assembled with care in a spotlessly clean environment.

3   Compression check

Refer to illustrations 3.1 and 3.6
Note: *The engine must be at normal operating temperature and the battery must be fully charged for this check.*

1   A compression check will tell you what mechanical condition your engine is in. Specifically, it can tell you if the compression is down due to leakage caused by worn seals or scuffed housing surfaces. **Note:** *This procedure tells how to check compression with a conventional compression gauge. A dealer service department can check compression more accurately using a special tester* **(see illustration)**.

2   Begin by cleaning the area around the spark plugs before you remove

2.4   Remove the oil pressure sending unit (arrow) to connect the mechanical gauge – the sending unit is located below the oil filter

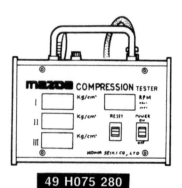

3.1   A Mazda dealer can perform a more accurate compression test using this special tester

3.6   An ordinary compression tester may be used – remove the check valve so it won't hold a reading

them (compressed air should be used, if available, otherwise a small brush or even a bicycle tire pump will work). The idea is to prevent dirt from getting into the chambers as the compression check is being done.

3   Remove the two upper spark plugs from the engine (see Chapter 1).

4   Block the throttle wide open.

5   Unplug the crank angle sensor (see Chapter 5). The fuel pump circuit should also be disabled (see Chapter 4).

6   Remove the check valve and install the compression gauge in the front upper spark plug hole **(see illustration)**, so it won't hold a reading.

7   Using the starter motor, crank the engine over at least seven revolutions and watch the gauge. The compression gauge needle should make three even bounces as the eccentric shaft makes one revolution. Two low bounces followed by a high one indicates a burned apex seal. A single low bounce usually indicates a faulty side seal. Record the gauge readings obtained.

8   Repeat the procedure for the rear upper spark plug hole and compare the results with this Chapter's specifications.

---

4   Engine removal – methods and precautions

If you've decided that an engine must be removed for overhaul or major repair work, several preliminary steps should be taken.

Locating a suitable place to work is extremely important. Adequate work space, along with storage space for the vehicle, will be needed. If a shop or garage isn't available, at the very least a flat, level, clean work surface made of concrete or asphalt is required.

Cleaning the engine compartment and engine before beginning the removal procedure will help keep tools clean and organized.

An engine hoist or A-frame will also be necessary. Make sure the equipment is rated in excess of the combined weight of the engine and accessories. Safety is of primary importance, considering the potential hazards involved in lifting the engine out of the vehicle.

If the engine is being removed by a novice, a helper should be available Advice and aid from someone more experienced would also be helpful. There are many instances when one person cannot simultaneously perform all of the operations required when lifting the engine out of the vehicle.

Plan the operation ahead of time. Arrange for or obtain all of the tools and equipment you'll need prior to beginning the job. Some of the equipment necessary to perform engine removal and installation safely and with relative ease are (in addition to an engine hoist) a heavy duty floor jack, complete sets of wrenches and sockets as described in the front of this manual, wooden blocks and plenty of rags and cleaning solvent for mopping up spilled oil, coolant and gasoline. If the hoist must be rented, make sure that you arrange for it in advance and perform all of the operations possible without it beforehand. This will save you money and time.

Plan for the vehicle to be out of use for quite a while. A machine shop will be required to perform some of the work which the do–it–yourselfer can't accomplish without special equipment. These shops often have a busy schedule, so it would be a good idea to consult them before removing the engine in order to accurately estimate the amount of time required to rebuild or repair components that may need work.

Always be extremely careful when removing and installing the engine. Serious injury can result from careless actions. Plan ahead, take your time and a job of this nature, although major, can be accomplished successfully.

---

5   Engine – removal and installation

Refer to illustrations 5.5, 5.12, 5.20, 5.24 and 5.25

Warning: *The air conditioning system is under high pressure! Have a dealer service department or service station discharge the system before disconnecting any A/C system hoses or fittings.*

Removal

1   Refer to Chapter 4 and relieve the fuel system pressure, then disconnect the negative cable from the battery.

2   Cover the fenders and cowl and remove the hood (see Chapter 11). special pads are available to protect the fenders, but an old bedspread or blanket will also work.

3   Remove the air cleaner assembly (see Chapter 4).

4   Drain the cooling system (see Chapter 1).

5   Label the vacuum lines, emission system hoses, wiring connectors, ground straps and fuel lines, to ensure correct reinstallation, then detach them. Pieces of masking tape with numbers or letters written on them work well **(see Illustration)**. If there's any possibility of confusion, make a sketch of the engine compartment and clearly label the lines, hoses and wires.

6   Label and detach all coolant hoses from the engine.

7   Remove the cooling fan, shroud, radiator and oil cooler (see Chapter 3).

8   Remove the drivebelts (see Chapter 1).

9   **Warning:** *Gasoline is extremely flammable, so extra precautions must be taken when working on any part of the fuel system. DO NOT smoke or allow open flames or bare light bulbs near the vehicle. Also, don't work in a garage if a natural gas appliance with a pilot light is present.* Disconnect the fuel lines running from the engine to the chassis (see Chapter 4). Plug or cap all open fittings/lines.

10   Disconnect the throttle linkage (and TV linkage/speed control cable, if equipped) from the engine (see Chapter 4).

11   On power steering equipped vehicles, unbolt the power steering pump (see Chapter 10). Leave the lines/hoses attached and make sure the pump is kept in an upright position in the engine compartment (use wire or rope to restrain it out of the way).

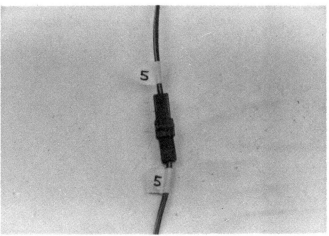

5.5   Label both ends of each wire before disconnecting it

5.12   Unbolt the compressor and secure it to the inner fender with the hoses still attached

5.20   Position the hoist and take up the slack in the chain

12   On air conditioned vehicles, unbolt the compressor (see Chapter 3) and set it aside **(see illustration)**. Do not disconnect the hoses.
13   Drain the engine oil (see Chapter 1) and remove the filter.
14   Remove the starter motor (see Chapter 5).
15   Remove the alternator (see Chapter 5).
16   Unbolt the exhaust system from the engine (see Chapter 4).
17   If you're working on a vehicle with an automatic transmission, refer to Chapter 7 and remove the torque converter-to-driveplate fasteners.
18   Support the transmission with a jack. Position a block of wood between them to prevent damage to the transmission. Special transmission jacks with safety chains are available – use one if possible.
19   Attach an engine sling or a length of chain to the lifting brackets on the engine.
20   Roll the hoist into position and connect the sling to it. Take up the slack in the sling or chain, but don't lift the engine **(see illustration)**. **Warning:** *DO NOT place any part of your body under the engine when it's supported only b a hoist or other lifting device.*
21   Remove the transmission-to-engine block bolts.
22   Remove the engine mount-to-frame nuts.
23   Recheck to be sure nothing is still connecting the engine to the transmission or vehicle. Disconnect anything still remaining.
24   Raise the engine slightly. Carefully work it forward to separate it from the transmission. If you're working on a vehicle with an automatic transmission, be sure the torque converter stays in the transmission (clamp a pair of locking pliers to the housing to keep the converter from sliding out). If you're working on a vehicle with a manual transmission, the input shaft must be completely disengaged from the clutch. Slowly raise the engine out of the engine compartment **(see illustration)**. Check carefully to make sure nothing is hanging up.
25   Mount the engine on an engine stand **(see illustration)**.

Installation

26   Check the engine and transmission mounts. If they're worn or damaged, replace them.
27   If you're working on a manual transmission equipped vehicle, install the clutch and pressure plate (see Chapter 7). Now is a good time to install a new clutch.
28   Carefully lower the engine into the engine compartment – make sure the engine mounts line up.
29   If you're working on an automatic transmission equipped vehicle, guide the torque converter into the crankshaft following the procedure in Chapter 7.
30   If you're working on a manual transmission equipped vehicle, apply a dab of high-temperature grease to the input shaft and guide it into the crankshaft pilot bearing until the bellhousing is flush with the engine block.
31   Install the transmission-to-engine bolts and tighten them securely. **Caution:** *DO NOT use the bolts to force the transmission and engine together!*
32   Reinstall the remaining components in the reverse order of removal.
33   Add coolant, oil, power steering and transmission fluid as needed.
34   Run the engine and check for leaks and proper operation of all accessories, then install the hood and test drive the vehicle.
35   Have the air conditioning system recharged and leak tested if it was discharged for any reason.

5.24   Lift the engine high enough to clear the front of the vehicle

5.25   Attach the engine stand adaptor and secure it to the engine stand before lowering the hoist

6   Engine rebuilding alternatives

The do-it-yourselfer is faced with a number of options when performing an engine overhaul. The decision to replace the engine housings, rotors and eccentric shaft depends on a number of factors, with the number one consideration being the condition of the housings. Other considerations are cost, access to machine shop facilities, parts availability, time required to complete the project and the extent of prior mechanical experience on the part of the do-it-yourselfer.

Some of the rebuilding alternatives include:

Individual parts – If the inspection procedures reveal that the engine housings and most engine components are in reusable condition, purchasing individual parts may be the most economical alternative. The housings, eccentric shaft, gear and rotor assemblies should all be inspected carefully. Even if the engine shows little wear, the seals and bearings should be replaced.

Rebuilt engine – A rebuilt engine consists of the eccentric shaft, rotors and housings, oil pump, sprockets and chain, water pump and oil metering pump. All components are installed with new bearings, seals and gaskets incorporated throughout. The installation of manifolds and exter-nal parts is all that's necessary. Some suppliers require the old engine in exchange.

Give careful thought to which alternative is best for you and discuss the situation with local automotive machine shops, auto parts dealers and experienced rebuilders before ordering or purchasing replacement parts.

7   Engine overhaul – disassembly sequence

External components

Refer to illustrations 7.3a, 7.3b, 7.3c, 7.3d and 7.3e.

1   It's much easier to disassemble and work on the engine if it's mounted on a portable engine stand. A stand can often be rented quite cheaply from an equipment rental yard.

2   If a stand isn't available, it's possible to disassemble the engine with it blocked up on the floor. Be extra careful not to tip or drop the engine when working without a stand.

3   If you're going to obtain a rebuilt engine, all external components **(see illustrations)** must come off first, to be transferred to the replacement en-

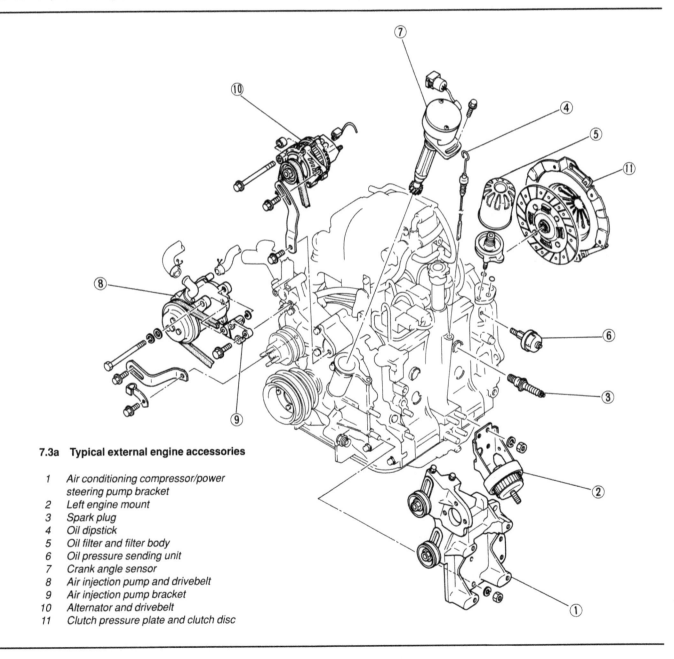

7.3a   Typical external engine accessories

1   Air conditioning compressor/power
    steering pump bracket
2   Left engine mount
3   Spark plug
4   Oil dipstick
5   Oil filter and filter body
6   Oil pressure sending unit
7   Crank angle sensor
8   Air injection pump and drivebelt
9   Air injection pump bracket
10 Alternator and drivebelt
11 Clutch pressure plate and clutch disc

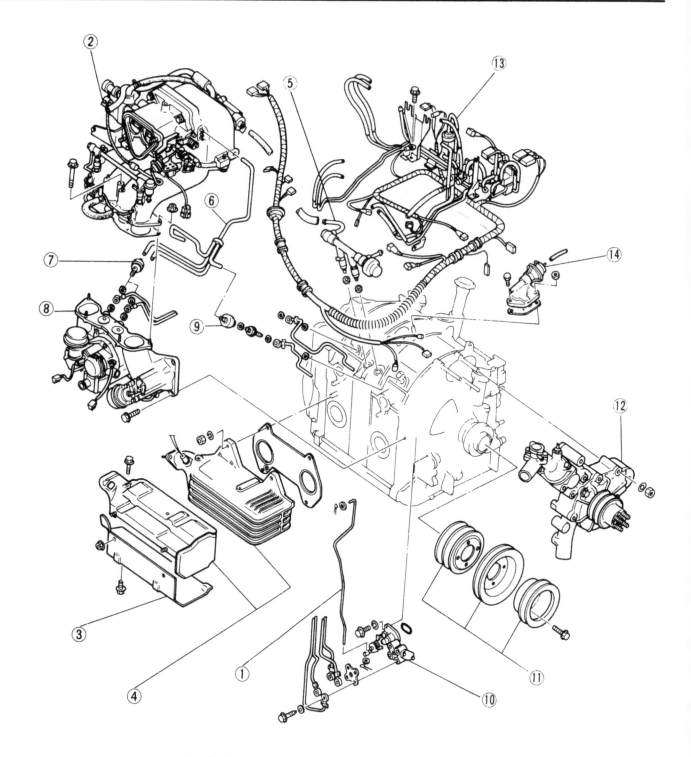

7.3b   Typical external engine components – non-turbo models

1	Metering oil pump connecting rod	8	Intake manifold
2	Throttle and dynamic chamber	9	Housing oil nozzle and metering oil tube
3	Exhaust manifold heat shield	10	Metering oil pump
4	Exhaust manifold and upper heat shield	11	Eccentric shaft pulley
5	Fuel injector and delivery pipe	12	Water pump
6	Air hose	13	Engine harness and vacuum pipes
7	Manifold oil nozzle and metering oil tube	14	EGR valve

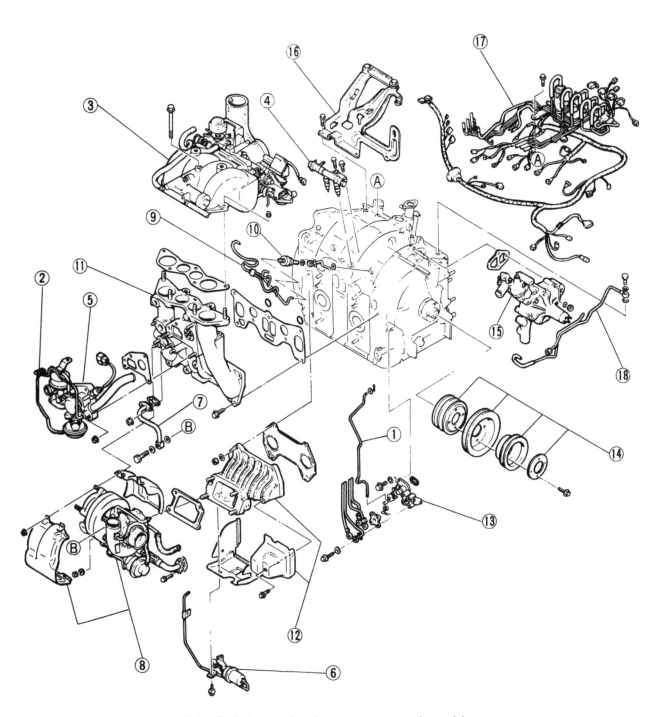

7.3c Typical external engine components – turbo models

1	Metering oil pump connecting rod	10	Housing oil nozzle and
2	Vacuum pipes		manifold oil nozzle
3	Throttle and dynamic chamber	11	Intake manifold
4	Primary fuel injector and	12	Exhaust manifold and insulator
	distribution pipe	13	Metering oil pump
5	Air control valve	14	Eccentric shaft pulley
6	Switching actuator	15	Water pump
7	Water pipe	16	Dynamic chamber bracket
8	Turbocharger and insulator	17	Engine harness and vacuum piping
9	Air hose	18	Oil inlet pipe

7.3d   The engine mounting brackets must be removed prior to engine disassembly (left side shown)

7.3e   Remove the bolts (arrows) and lift off the oil strainer/pickup tube

gine, just as they will if you're doing a complete engine overhaul yourself. These include:

    Alternator and brackets
    Emissions control components
    Crank angle sensor, spark plug wires and spark plugs
    Thermostat and housing cover
    Water pump and housing
    EFI components
    Intake/exhaust manifolds (and turbocharger, if equipped)
    Oil filler tube
    Oil filter
    Engine mounts and brackets
    Clutch and flywheel/driveplate
    Oil pan and oil strainer/pickup tube
    Metering oil pump
    Front engine cover
    Chain and sprockets
    Oil pump

Note: *When removing the external components from the engine, pay close attention to details that may be helpful or important during installation. Note the installed position of gaskets, seals, spacers, pins, brackets, washers, bolts and other small items. Refer to Chapter 3 and Chapter 2, Part A for information on removing major components.*

4   See Section 6 for information which will help you decide whether to rebuild your own engine or purchase one already rebuilt.

Internal components

Refer to illustrations 7.7, 7.8a, 7.8b, 7.8c, 7.9, 7.10, 7.11, 7.13, 7.14, 7.15, 7.16, 7.17a, 7.17b, 7.18a, 7.18b, 7.18c, 7.21, 7.22 and 7.23

5   Use this procedure if: 1) you are planning to overhaul the engine yourself or 2) you need to inspect the internal engine components to decide whether or not to overhaul it yourself. If you have already decided to purchase a rebuilt engine, disregard this procedure.

6   Before removing internal engine components, make sure the following items are available. Also, refer to Section 19 for a list of tools and materials needed for engine reassembly.

    Common hand tools
    Small cardboard boxes or plastic bags for storing parts
    Gasket scraper
    Feeler gauges
    Bolt-type puller
    Micrometers
    Scribe
    Dial indicator set
    Tap and die set
    Wire brushes
    Oil gallery brushes
    Cleaning solvent

7.7   Tension bolt LOOSENING sequence

7.8a   Once the tension bolts are removed, separate the rear housing with a soft-face hammer and lift it off

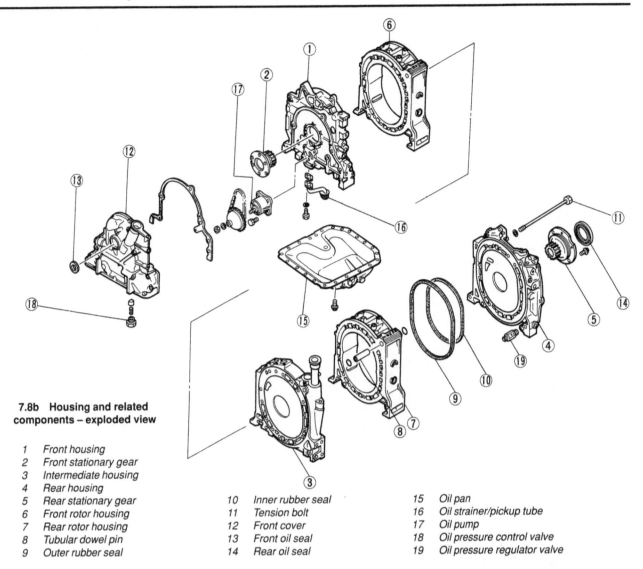

7.8b   Housing and related components – exploded view

1   Front housing
2   Front stationary gear
3   Intermediate housing
4   Rear housing
5   Rear stationary gear
6   Front rotor housing
7   Rear rotor housing
8   Tubular dowel pin
9   Outer rubber seal

10   Inner rubber seal
11   Tension bolt
12   Front cover
13   Front oil seal
14   Rear oil seal

15   Oil pan
16   Oil strainer/pickup tube
17   Oil pump
18   Oil pressure control valve
19   Oil pressure regulator valve

7.8c   Mark the front and rear rotor housings for later identification

7.9   Remove the O-ring from the dowel pin

7   Remove the 18 tension bolts securing the rear housing. It is important that these bolts be loosened a little at a time and in the sequence shown **(see illustration)**.

8   Carefully lift the rear housing off the rotor housing **(see illustrations)**. If there are any seals stuck to the inside surfaces of the rear housing reinstall them in their respective positions. Mark the rotor housings for later

identification **(see illustration)**.

9   Remove the rubber seals from the housing and the O-ring on one of the dowel pins now exposed **(see illustration)**.

10   The two dowel pins must now be removed from the rotor housing. These pins go through the rotor housing and into the intermediate housing. To remove them, thread a 12 x 1.75 mm bolt into the dowel, then use a

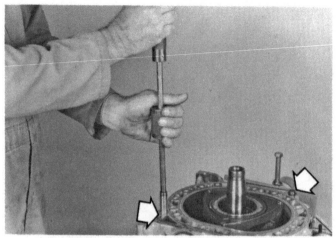

7.10   Slip the two dowel pins (arrows) out with a puller

7.11   As you lift the rotor housing, the rubber seals may stick to the housing

slide hammer puller **(see illustration)** to pull the dowel up. Hold onto the housing to prevent movement as the dowel is forced up and out. As the

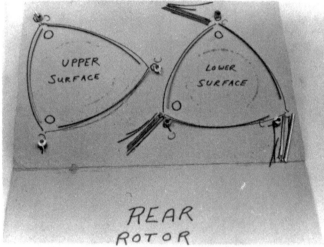

7.13   Sketch a diagram of all the parts for each rotor to keep them organized and identified ("upper surface" and "lower surface" in this diagram refer to the rotor's installed position when the engine is on the stand, front facing down)

dowel pins are not in very tight, it may be possible to use vise-grips on the threaded bolt to pull the pins free.

11   The rear rotor housing can now be lifted off the eccentric shaft and rotor **(see illustration)**. If any of the rotor seals fall off during this operation, replace them on the rotor in their original positions.

12   Remove the rubber seals and the O-ring on the other side of the rotor housing and set the housing aside.

13   At this point it is imperative that a system be set up to identify each of the many seals for the rotors. You can use dividers inside a cardboard box to form compartments for each seal, or you can draw a rough sketch of each rotor on a large piece of cardboard or paper **(see illustration)** and place each seal on the drawing. Make sure the box or sketch includes both sides of each rotor.

14   Clean the face of the rotor and take note of the round indentations located near two of the three apexes. Mark the rotor **(see illustration)** at the corner without an indentation. Use the indentations and the paint marks to identify each seal as it is removed from the rotor.

15   The rear rotor can now be lifted off the eccentric shaft **(see illustration)**. Place it gear side down on a clean surface and remove the side seals and springs from this side of the rotor. Again, place them in the proper location in the box or on the sketch .

16   Remove the components of each apex seal **(see illustration)** and place them in the compartmented box or on the sketch.

17   Remove all corner seals and corner seal springs **(see illustration 7.16)**, then remove the side seals and side seal springs **(see illustrations)**. Place them in the proper locations in the box or on the sketch.

7.14   Scratch or paint marks on the rear rotor (R for rear and Up) to speed assembly·

7.15   Lift the rotor straight up off the eccentric shaft

7.16   Rotating components – exploded view

1   Front rotor
2   Rear rotor
3   Apex seal (1986 through 1988 models)
4   Corner seal
5   Side seal
6   Outer oil seal
7   Inner oil seal
8   Eccentric shaft
9   Oil bypass valve
10   Eccentric shaft pulley
11   Drive gear (for crank angle sensor)
12   Oil pump drive sprocket
13   Balance weight
14   Thrust washer
15   Needle bearing
16   Spacer
17   Plate
18   Thrust plate
19   Oil jet valve
20   Pilot bearing (manual
        transmission only)
21   Oil seal (manual transmission only)
22   Counterweight (automatic
        transmission only)
23   Driveplate (automatic
        transmission only))
24   Back plate (automatic
        transmission only)
25   Flywheel (manual transmission only)

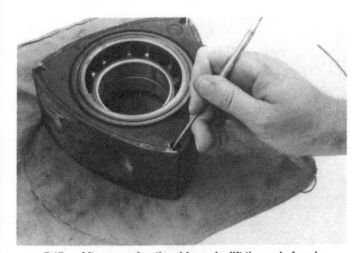

7.17a   After removing the side seals, lift the end of each
side seal spring with a scribe . . .

7.17b   . . . and push it out with an old side seal

18   Using a scribe or a small screwdriver, pry the inner and outer oil seals out of their grooves on the rotor faces. Pry the seals out a little at a time, working completely around their circumference **(see illustrations)**. Place each seal and its respective O-ring and spring together in the box or on the sketch.

19   Remove the oil seals, O-rings and springs from the other side of the rotor following the same procedures.

20   The stripped rotor can now be placed with its corresponding components.

21   Using the puller or vise-grips, pull the tubular dowels off the intermediate housing **(see illustration)**. Hold the housing in place as the dowels are forced out.

22   Have an assistant slightly lift the eccentric shaft (about an inch) while you lift the intermediate housing clear of the rear rotor journals **(see illustration)**. Set the intermediate housing aside.

23   The eccentric shaft can now be carefully lifted out of the remaining components and set aside **(see illustration)**.

24   The front rotor housing and front rotor are removed in the same manner as the rear rotor and housing. Be sure that each seal and spring is properly identified and placed in the proper box or on the sketch.

7.18a   Use a scribe to lift the inner oil seal first ...

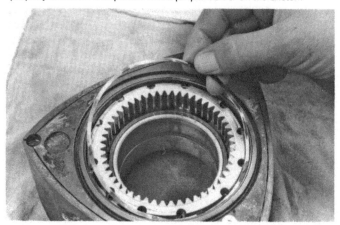

7.18b   ... then remove the inner oil seal spring

7.18c   Next, lift out the outer oil seal and spring

7.21   Remove the remaining dowel with a puller tool (shown) or a bolt and locking pliers

7.22   Have an assistant push up on the eccentric shaft as you lift the intermediate housing

7.23   Carefully lift the eccentric shaft straight out of the housing

8 Engine components – cleaning

Warning: *Do not smoke and avoid all sources of ignition when using flammable solvents.*

1 Rather than cleaning all of the components together, the rotors, housings, seals and springs should be cleaned individually to prevent mix-ups in the identifying process. Remove each part from the compartmented box or sketch, clean it, then replace it immediately before the next part is done.

2 Remove all carbon from the surfaces of the rotors using a carbon remover or emery paper. Wash the rotors in cleaning solvent and dry them with compressed air, if available. **Warning:** *Wear eye protection when using compressed air.* Pay close attention to the recessed grooves where the oil seals and apex seals seat. The apex seal grooves should be perfectly clean with no sharp burrs which could prevent the seals from expanding against the housings.

3 The front, rear and intermediate housings have a finished surface which can be damaged if it is not cleaned properly. Use a soft cloth soaked with kerosene to remove any carbon on the machined surfaces. The leftover sealing agent used to mate the housings can be removed with a brush soaked in kerosene.

4 Before cleaning the rotor housings, check for traces of gas or coolant leakage along the inner margin of each side face. This will indicate a failure in the rubber sealing gaskets. carbon should be removed from the inner surfaces with a soft cloth soaked in kerosene. Remove all deposits and rust from the cooling water passages. Remove any excess sealing agent with a brush soaked in kerosene.

5 Clean each seal and spring one at a time using kerosene. **Caution:** *Never use emery paper or a wire brush as they will damage the delicate surfaces.*

6 Wash all parts in cleaning solvent to remove all traces of grit, then lightly oil them with penetrating oil to prevent rust from forming while the parts await reassembly.

7 Cover all parts to keep away any dust and make sure that all parts are located in a place where they cannot be accidentally jostled and mixed-up.

9 Housings – inspection and overhaul

Refer to illustrations 9.1a, 9.1b, 9.2a, 9.2b, 9.2c, 9.2d, 9.3, 9.5a, 9.5b, 9.8a and 9.8b

1 The front, intermediate and rear housings should be checked for warpage by placing a straightedge along the surfaces and using a feeler gauge. Place the straightedge in four positions across the machined surface, measuring the distance between the straightedge and the housing surface **(see illustrations)**. If any of the housings are warped beyond the limit in this Chapter's specifications, they should be resurfaced by an automotive machine shop or replaced.

2 A dial indicator mounted to a gauge body must be used to check for stepped wear on the front, intermediate and rear housings **(see illustrations)**. The stepped wear measurements indicate the amount of material which has been worn off the housings from the rotors as they turn on the

9.1a   A straightedge and feeler gauge are used to check the housings for warpage

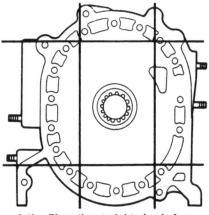
9.1b   Place the straightedge in four positions as shown here

9.2a   A dial indicator can be used to check for stepped wear on the housings

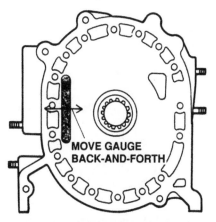
9.2b   Check for stepped wear by the side seal, . . .

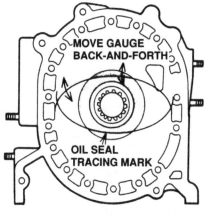
9.2c   . . . inside and outside the oil seal tracing mark . . .

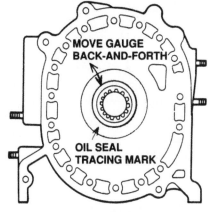
9.2d   . . . and by the oil seal

9.3   Inspect the stationary gears on the front and rear housings for wear and damage

9.5a   Measure the inside diameter of the bearing with a telescoping gauge or inside micrometer

eccentric shaft. If the necessary tools are not available, the housings should be taken to an automotive machine shop or a Mazda dealer. There are three critical areas to be checked for stepped wear: 1) where the side seal of the rotor contacts the housing, 2) inside the oil seal tracing mark and 3) outside the oil seal tracing mark on the housing (see illustrations). Wear caused by the side seals and oil seals should not exceed the limits in this Chapter's specifications. Again, an automotive machine shop can re-surface the housings although it may prove to be more economical to re-place them if the limits are exceeded.

3   Check the stationary gears in the front and rear housings for cracked, scored or worn teeth. Replace them, if necessary, following the proce-dures outlined later in this Chapter (see illustration).

4   Check the main bearings in the front and rear housings for wear and damage. Replace them following the procedures outlined later in this Chapter.

5   The clearance of the main bearings is checked by first measuring the inner diameter of the bearing with an inside micrometer, then the outside diameter of the eccentric shaft journal on which it rides (see illustrations). The difference between these two measurements is the clearance. If the bearing clearance exceeds the specification, the bearing should be re-placed following the procedures outlined later in this Chapter.

6   Next, replace the soft plugs (freeze plugs) located in the front and rear housings. They may not be bad now, but due to their inaccessibility after the engine is assembled and installed they should be replaced while the engine is torn down. Pull the old ones out with a slide hammer, coat the sealing surfaces of the new ones with non-hardening sealant, then drive

them in using a large socket, extension and hammer.

7   Check the chrome-plated surface on the rotor housing for scoring, flaking and other damage. If any of these conditions exist, replace the rotor housing(s).

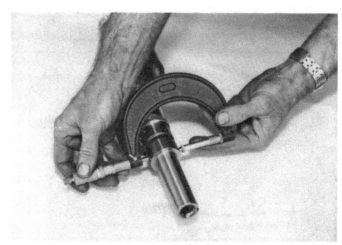

9.5b   Then check the diameter of the eccentric shaft journal and subtract the two to determine main bearing clearance

9.8a   Measuring the width of a rotor housing

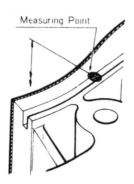

Measuring Point

9.8b   Measure the width at a point close to the inner, running surface

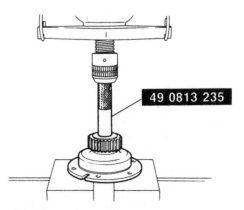

49 0813 235

10.3   The main bearing may be pressed out of the stationary gear with Mazda tool no. 490813235 without the adapter ring – a piece of pipe or a hardwood dowel will also work

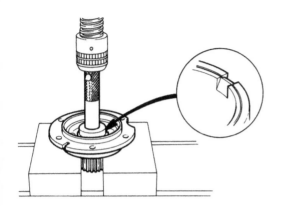
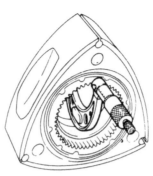

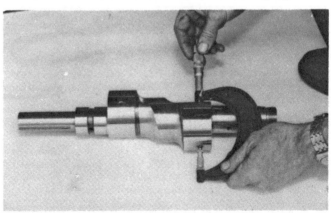

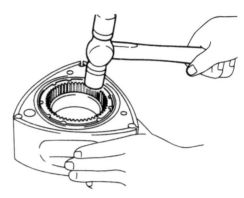

10.5 Position the new main bearing on the stationary gear so that the bearing lug is aligned with the slot of the stationary gear, then press it into position (installation tool shown is Mazda tool 490813235 with adapter ring – a large socket should also work)

11.3a Measure the rotor width at three points on the internal gear adjacent to the apexes

11.3b If the clearance is less than specified, reseat the internal gear with a plastic hammer

8   Check the width of each rotor housing with a micrometer **(see illustration)**. Measure the width at a number of points around the circumference of the housing and write down each measurement. Place the micrometer at a point close to the inner, running surface of the housings **(see illustration)**. The difference between the largest measurement and the smallest should not exceed the limit in this Chapter's specifications. If it does, the rotor housing(s) should be replaced as they cannot be repaired.

---

10 Stationary gears and main bearings – replacement

Refer to illustrations 10.3 and 10.5

1   The engine main bearings are pressed into the stationary gears located on the front and rear housings. The removal and installation process is the same for the front and rear except that the rear main bearing has an O-ring which is installed in a groove in the stationary gear.
2   Remove the stationary gear attaching bolts, then remove the gear and bearing assembly from the housing. Remove the assembly from the housing by using a hydraulic press, or by pounding it free with a piece of hardwood and a hammer.
3   Mazda tool no. 490813235, a piece of pipe or a hardwood dowel can then be used to remove the bearing from the stationary gear. A hydraulic press is advisable **(see illustration)** although a large vise will also do the job.
4   Clean the inside of the stationary gear, where the bearing rides, and the outside of the new bearing. Smooth any rough spots with emery cloth.
5   Press the new bearing into the stationary gear, aligning the lug of the bearing and the slot of the stationary gear **(see illustration)**.
6   On the rear housing, apply a thin coat of petroleum jelly to the new O-ring and place it in the groove of the stationary gear.
7   Apply sealant to the stationary gear flange and install the assembly in the housing, aligning the slot of the stationary gear flange and the dowel pin on the housing.
8   Tighten the attaching bolts to the torque listed in this Chapter's specifications.

---

11 Rotor – inspection and repair

Refer to illustrations 11.3a, 11.3b, 11.5a and 11.5b

1   Carefully inspect the rotor and replace it if it is severely worn or damaged.
2   Check the internal gear for cracked, scored, worn or chipped teeth.
3   To arrive at the clearance between the side housing and the rotor, measure the width of the rotor at three locations **(see illustration)** and compare these measurements with the measurements written down previously for the width of the rotor housing **(see illustration 9.8a)**. The differ-

11.5a Measure the inside diameter of the rotor bearing . . .

11.5b . . . and subtract the diameter of the eccentric shaft journal to determine the bearing clearance

ence between rotor width and the side housing width gives you the clearance. If the clearance is more than the limit in this Chapter's specifications, replace the rotor assembly. If the clearance is less than the standard specification, it indicates that the internal gear has come out slightly and can be lightly tapped further into the rotor with a plastic hammer **(see illustration)**. Recheck the rotor width to make certain that it's now within specifications.
4   Check the rotor bearing for wear, flaking, scoring and other damage. If any of these conditions are found, replace the bearing as outlined later in this Chapter.
5   Check the rotor bearing clearance by measuring the inside diameter of both bearings with an inside micrometer, then subtracting the outer diameter of the eccentric shaft journal **(see illustrations)**. If the bearing clearance exceeds the limit in this Chapter's specifications, replace the rotor bearings.

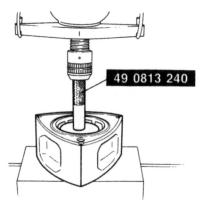

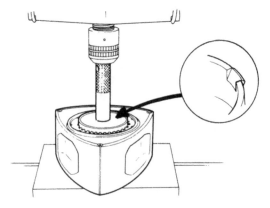

12.1   Removing the bearing with a hydraulic press and Mazda tool 490813240 (do not use the adaptor ring) – a piece of pipe or a hardwood dowel could substitute for the Mazda tool

12.3   Position the rotor with the internal gear facing up and press the new bearing in until it is flush with the rotor boss (Mazda tool 490813240 with adapter shown) – be sure to align the oil hole in the bearing with the slot in the rotor bore

12   Rotor bearing – replacement

Refer to illustrations 12.1 and 12.3

1   The rotor bearing is essentially a sleeve pressed into the rotor. A hydraulic press, large vise or other equipment must be used to securely support the rotor as the bearing is pressed out. The rotor should have its internal gear facing down during the bearing removal process **(see illustration)**. Be careful not to damage the rotor or internal gear. If you lack the equipment, take it to a dealer or automotive machine shop.

2   Clean the inner surfaces of the rotor and outer surface of the bearing. Smooth any rough spots with emery cloth.

3   Place the rotor with its gear side up and press the new bearing into place, making sure the oil hole in the bearing matches up with the slot in the rotor bore **(see illustration)**.

13   Oil seal and spring – inspection and replacement

Refer to illustration 13.2

1   Check the oil seal for wear and damage. Replace it, if necessary.

2   Check the width of the oil seal lip with a micrometer to ensure the seal has not been widened through use. Width should not exceed the limit in this Chapter's specifications **(see illustration)**.

3   Replace the oil seal springs in their respective grooves and assemble the oil seals using new neoprene O-rings. Additional information on installing the oil seals can be found in Section 19.

4   Check for free movement of the oil seals by pressing on them with your finger. The seals should move freely in their grooves. If they don't, check that the seals and grooves are perfectly clean.

5   Check that the oil seals protrude from the rotor the amount listed in this Chapter's specifications. If the protrusion is less than specified, this indicates a failure in the oil seal spring. Replace the oil seal spring(s).

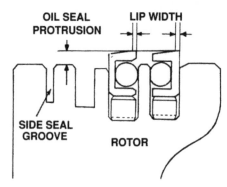

13.2   Checking the lip width and protrusion of the rotor oil seals

14   Apex seal and spring – inspection

Refer to illustrations 14.2, 14.3, 14.4, 14.5 and 14.6

1   Check the apex seals and accompanying side pieces for wear, cracking and damage. Replace them if any of these conditions are found.

2   Measure the height of the apex seals with a micrometer **(see illustration)**. Replace the apex seals if the height is less than specified.

3   To check the apex seals for warping, take the seals from one rotor at a time and measure them one against the other. Measure the clearance between the top surfaces of the seals by placing them top-to-top **(see illustration)**. The gap should not exceed the limit in this Chapter's specifications. If it does, replace all three seals. Take care not to mix any of the seals from one rotor with those of the other when measuring.

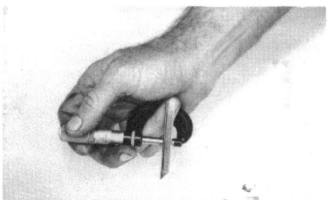

14.2   Measuring the height of an apex seal

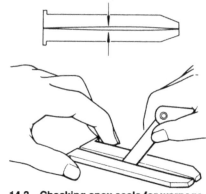

14.3   Checking apex seals for warpage

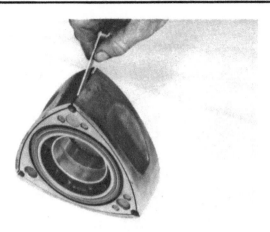

14.4   With an apex seal installed in its corresponding rotor groove, the clearance can be checked with a feeler gauge

4   Place each apex seal into its respective groove and use feeler gauges to check the clearance between the seal and the rotor groove. Insert the feeler gauge until it touches the bottom of the groove **(see illustration)**. If the clearance is greater than the limit in this Chapter's specifications, replace all the apex seals.
5   If new apex seals are being used, check the clearance between the apex seals and the side housing. Do this by measuring the overall length of each apex seal with a micrometer **(see illustration)** and subtracting this from the rotor housing width. Compare the clearance with the figure listed in this Chapter's specifications. If necessary, the apex seals can be shortened with emery paper.
6   Lay each apex seal spring on a flat surface and check for free height **(see illustration)**. If the free height of the spring is less than the height listed in this Chapter's specifications, replace the spring.

---

15   Side seal and spring – inspection

Refer to illustrations 15.2, 15.3, 15.4 and 15.5
1   Place each side seal and side seal spring into its respective groove in the rotor and check for free movement by pressing on it with your finger. If it does not move freely, make sure the seal, spring and groove are perfectly clean.
2   Check the protrusion of each side seal by measuring it with a dial or vernier caliper **(see illustration)**. If the protrusion is not within the limits listed in this Chapter's specifications, replace the side seal ring.
3   Check the clearance between the side seal and the groove in the rotor with a feeler gauge **(see illustration)**. If the clearance is less than the minimum listed in this Chapter's specifications, replace the side seal.

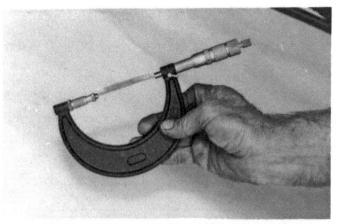

14.5   Measuring the overall length of an apex seal to arrive at the clearance between the seal and the housing

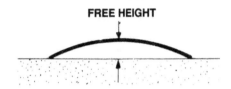

FREE HEIGHT

14.6   Measuring the free height of an apex seal spring

15.2   Measuring the protrusion of a rotor side seal

4   With the side seals and corner seals in their proper locations in the rotor, check the clearance between the side seals and the corner seals with a feeler gauge **(see illustration)**. If the clearance is less than the limit listed in this Chapter's specifications, replace the side seals.

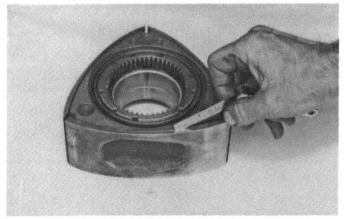

15.3   Checking the side seal-to-rotor clearance

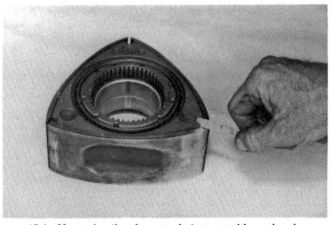

15.4   Measuring the clearance between a side seal and a corner seal

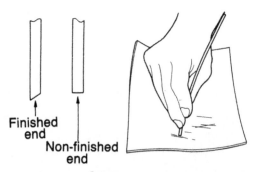

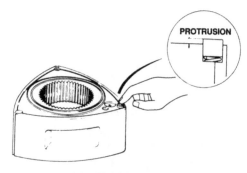

15.5   Adjust the clearance betwen the side seal and corner seal by carefully grinding down the round end

16.2   Checking a corner seal

5   If the side seals have been replaced, the gap between the side seals and the corner seals may have to be adjusted. A small amount can be ground off the round end of the side seal to arrive at the specified clearance **(see illustration)**.

16   Corner seal and spring – inspection

Refer to illustrations 16.2 and 16.4

1   Place each corner seal and its accompanying spring into the rotor.
2   Check for free movement by pressing on each seal with your finger **(see illustration)**.
3   Check the protrusion of the corner seal from the rotor surface with a dial or vernier caliper. Replace the corner seal spring if the protrusion is less than the figure listed in this Chapter's specifications.
4   Check the corner seal bores for wear with a corner seal gauge (Mazda tool no. 490839165 or equivalent) **(see illustration)**, or take the rotors to a dealer service department for inspection.
   a) If neither end of the gauge goes into the bore, use the original corner seal.
   b) If only one end of the gauge goes into the bore, replace the corner seal.
   c) If both ends of the gauge go into the bore, replace the rotor.

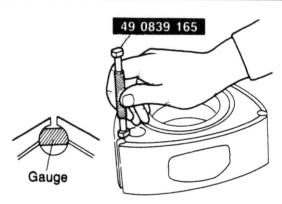

16.4   Use this special tool to check the corner seal bores

17   Eccentric shaft – inspection

Refer to illustrations 17.3 and 17.4

1   Check the shaft for cracks, scratches, wear and damage.
2   Check that the oil passages are open.
3   The eccentric shaft can be checked for runout by mounting it in V-blocks and using a dial indicator **(see illustration)**. Turn the shaft through one complete revolution, noting the reading on the indicator. The runout is one half of the difference between the highest and lowest readings. If the runout is more than the limit listed in this Chapter's specifications, replace the shaft with a new one.
4   Check the oil jet in the side of the eccentric shaft. Remove the plug with a screwdriver and pull out the spring and steel ball **(see illustration)**. Check the spring for weakness and sticking. Check the steel ball for damage. Before reassembly, clean all parts and make sure the cavity in the eccentric shaft is not plugged.
5   On manual transmission models, inspect the pilot bearing (located in the flywheel end of the eccentric shaft) and replace it, if necessary. Replace the pilot bearing oil seal and lubricate the bearing with high-temperature grease.

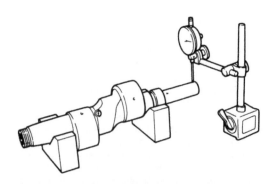

17.3   With the eccentric shaft supported by V-blocks, measure runout at the end of the shaft

18   Front and rear oil seals – replacement

Refer to illustrations 18.4a and 18.4b

1   The front oil seal in the front cover and the rear oil seal in the rear stationary gear should always be replaced during an engine rebuild.

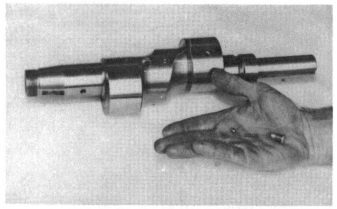

17.4   The oil jet plug, spring and steel ball must be removed from the side of the eccentric shaft

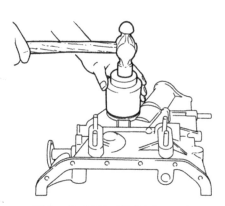

18.4a   Installing the front cover oil seal . . .

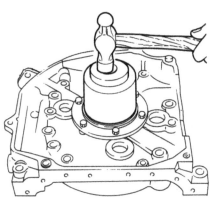

18.4b   . . . and the rear stationary gear oil seal

19.3a   The rounded ends of the springs go into the stopper holes in the oil seal grooves (arrows)

2   Pry the seals out of their bores using a curved seal remover or a screwdriver with its tip wrapped with tape.
3   Clean the seal bores in the engine and the outside of the new seals.
4   Place the new seals in position and use a hammer and a socket or piece of hardwood to drive the seal in until it's flush with the surface (see illustrations). Do not hammer directly on the seal. Do not use sealant on the seal.

19   Engine overhaul – reassembly of internal components

Refer to illustrations 19.3a, 19.3b, 19.4a, 19.4b, 19.5, 19.6a, 19.6b, 19.10, 19.11, 19.14, 19.15a, 19.15b, 19.20, 19.21, 19.26, 19.27a, 19.27b, 19.27c, 19.27d, 19.29, 19.30a, 19.30b, 19.36, 19.40, 19.49a and 19.49b

1   Before beginning engine reassembly, make sure you have all the necessary new parts, gaskets and seals as well as the following items on hand:
   Common hand tools
   3/8 and 1/2-inch drive torque wrenches
   A dial indicator set
   Feeler gauges
   A fine-toothed file
   Petroleum jelly
   New engine oil
   Moly-based grease or engine assembly lube
   Gasket sealant
   Thread locking compound
   Flywheel/driveplate holding and tightening tools
2   The O-rings located inside the oil seals of the rotors should always be replaced when overhauling an engine. In addition, any components found defective during the inspection process should be replaced with new ones.

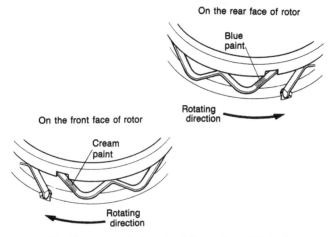

19.3b   The squared-off ends of the springs fit into the stopper holes of the oil seals

3   With the rotor resting on a clean surface, install the oil seal springs in their respective grooves. If these parts were properly identified and stored during disassembly, this will be an easy task. If the springs have become mixed up and/or are being replaced, the springs with the cream paint mark should be installed on the front faces of both the front and rear rotors. The springs with blue paint marks go on the rear faces. The rounded end of the spring fits into the stopper hole inside the groove and the squared-off end will fit inside a notch in the oil seal (see illustrations).
4   Install a new O-ring in each oil seal, being careful not to stretch the O-ring out of shape (see illustrations).

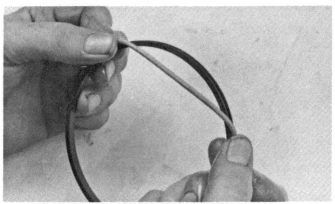

19.4a   Install the outside O-rings without excessive twisting or stretching

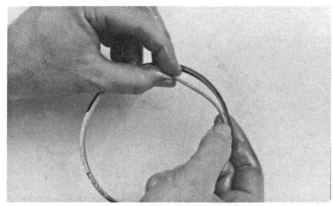

19.4b   Install the inside O-rings without twisting or cutting them

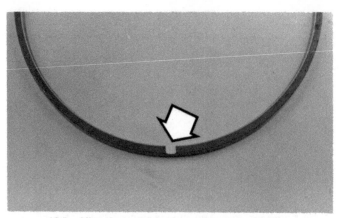

19.5   Align the notch in the seal (arrow) with the squared-off end of the spring

5   Align the inner oil seal in the groove so that the notch in the seal **(see illustration)** will be pressed onto the squared-off edge of the oil seal spring, which is sticking up.

6   Press the seal into the groove using an old oil seal or your fingers **(see illustrations)**. Press evenly around the circumference of the seal, until it is firmly seated. Be careful not to deform the lip of the oil seal.

7   Install the outer oil seal in the same fashion.

8   Install the oil seals on the opposite side of the rotor and the oil seals on the other rotor using the same procedure.

9   Confirm the smooth movement of all oil seals by pressing lightly with your fingers. They should move freely inside the rotor grooves.

1986 through 1988 models

10   If the old apex seals are being reused, clean the surfaces with lacquer thinner where adhesive is to be applied **(see illustration)**.

11   Assemble the apex seal and side piece with anaerobic bonding adhesive (Loctite 312 and Primer NF, or equivalent) so the sliding surfaces and side surfaces are flush. Cut away any adhesive that protrudes, then measure the overall length **(see illustration)**.

1989 and later models

12   For the apex seals and side pieces to seal properly without gouging the rotor housing on initial start-up, 1989 and later models require a part called an assist piece. The assist piece is made of a carbon material which disintegrates inside the engine after start-up. Its function is to relieve some of the spring tension of the apex seal spring during initial running after an overhaul.

13   Using a sharp knife or single-edged razor blade, cut the assist piece to a length of 0.08 to 0.10-inch (2.0 to 2.8 mm).

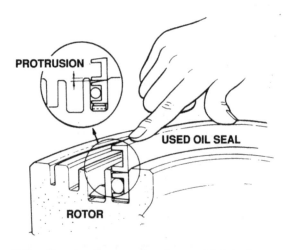

19.6a   Pressing the new oil seal assembly into the rotor with a used oil seal

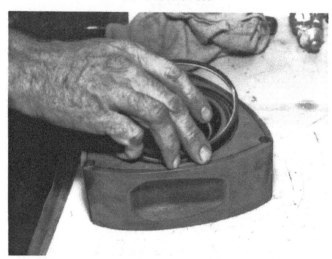

19.6b   The oil seals may be pressed in by hand if you're careful – apply even pressure

14   Peel off the paper stuck to the assist piece (if equipped) and stick it to the apex seal, as shown **(see illustration)**. Do this, one at a time, to all apex seals and return each seal to its proper location in your identifying box or sketch.

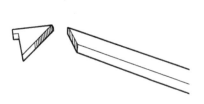

19.10   Clean the shaded areas with lacquer thinner prior to applying bonding adhesive (1986 through 1988 models)

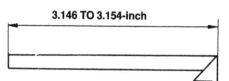

19.11   Assemble the apex seals and side pieces as shown and measure the overall length (1986 through 1988 models only)

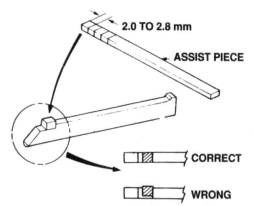

19.14   Peel off the paper on the assist piece and stick the assist piece on the apex seal (1989 and later models)

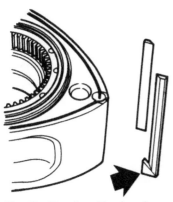

19.15a   Position the side piece (arrow) on the rear side of the rotor (1986 through 1988 models only)

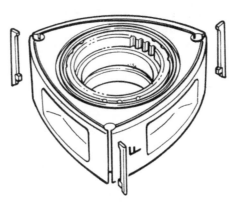

19.15b   Install the apex seals in the rotor without the springs (1989 and later models shown)

19.20   Place the assembled rotor onto the front housing and mesh its internal gear with the stationary gear on the housing

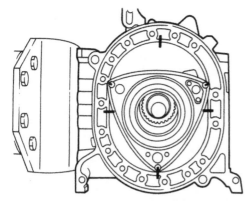

19.21   Position the rotor with one apex pointed towards one of the four positions shown – the top position is best

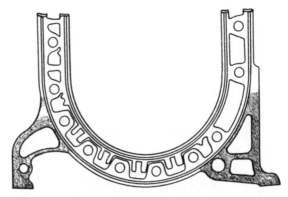

19.26   Apply sealant to the shaded areas just before installation

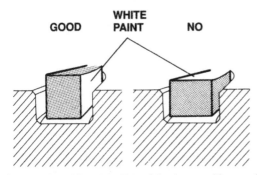

19.27a   The wider white line of the inner rubber seal should face the combustion chamber

19.27b   The seam on the rubber seal is marked with a stripe about one inch long

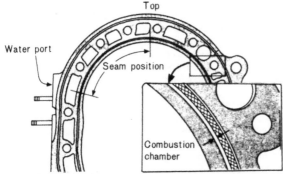

19.27c   When the rubber seal is installed, the seam must be between the top of the engine and the water port

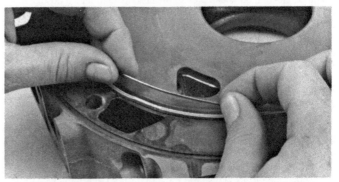

19.27d   The protective piece is a thin metal strip which is installed outside the O-ring adjacent to the exhaust ports

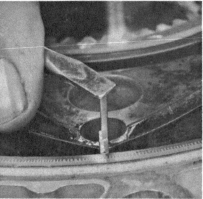

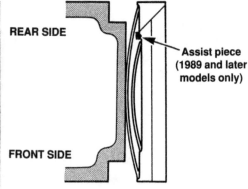

19.29   Use a rubber mallet to push the tubular dowel pins through the rotor housing and into the front housing

19.30a   Install the short apex seal spring first, then the long one

19.30b   The short and long apex seal springs must be seated as shown in this cutaway side view)

REAR SIDE

Assist piece (1989 and later models only)

FRONT SIDE

19.36   Carefully lower the intermediate housing over the eccentric shaft and onto the dowel pins

19.40   With the rotor positioned as shown, set the rear rotor housing into place

All models

15   Working on the front rotor install the three apex seals without their respective springs **(see illustrations)**.

16   On the front face (the one with the internal gear) of the front rotor, place the corner seal springs and corner seals into their proper bores.

17   Install the side seal springs and side seals into their grooves on the front of the rotor.

18   Confirm the smooth movement of all seals by pressing with your finger.

19   Mount the front housing on the engine stand.

20   Place the front rotor assembly on the front housing **(see illustration)**, being careful that none of the seals are dislodged from their positions.

21   Mesh the internal gear and stationary gear so that the rotor is in the same location as when disassembled. The rotor is easiest to install with one apex pointed towards one of the four positions shown **(see illustration)**.

22   Lubricate the front rotor journal and main journal on the eccentric shaft with engine oil.

23   Insert the eccentric shaft carefully to avoid damaging the rotor bearing or main bearing.

24   At this point it will be necessary to apply sealant to the front rotor housing where it will mate to the front housing. Since the housings are not really cinched into place until the tension bolts are tightened later on, check the setting time of the sealant being used.

25   To have the entire engine assembly cinched before the sealant sets, it's a good idea to assemble the remaining rotor before any sealant is applied. Double-check that all components are clean and ready to install and that all necessary tools are at your disposal.

26   Apply sealant to the front side of the front rotor housing **(see illustration)**, working it around with your fingers to get a smooth, even coat.

27   Also on the front side of the front rotor housing, install new rubber seals and a new O-ring in the recessed area where the dowel pin goes. The wider white line of the inner rubber seal should face the combustion chamber **(see illustration)** and the seam of the seal should be positioned in the area between the top point of the engine and the water ports **(see illustrations)**. Use Vaseline to hold the O-ring and rubber seals in place, as the housing will be inverted. Do not use grease for this. Install the protective piece **(see illustration)**, if equipped.

28   Invert the front rotor housing and carefully place it onto the front housing. Make sure the rubber seal and O-ring do not come out of place.

29   Put some engine oil into the two tubular dowels and push them through the rotor housing and into the front housing. You can use a rubber mallet to push them into place **(see illustration)**.

30   The apex seal springs can then be pushed into position at each apex of the front rotor **(see illustrations)**.

31   Install the corner seal springs, corner seals, side seal springs and side seals into their proper locations on the rear side of the front rotor previously installed.

32   Fit each triangular shaped side piece in its original position. Confirm the apex seal spring and assist piece (if equipped) are working properly and the side piece is not resting against the rotor housing surface.

33   Check that all seals are properly installed on the rotor and that there is smooth movement by pressing with your finger. If so, the eccentric shaft can be set into place.

34   Apply sealant to the rear side of the front rotor housing and install the new rubber seals and O-ring in the same fashion as previously described

19.49a   Tightening sequence for the tension bolts – note that bolt no. 17 is longer

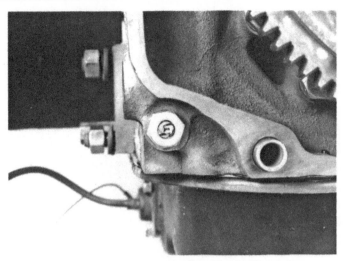

19.49b   Bolt no. 17 may be identified by the mark on its head

for the other side. Remember the wide white line of the sealing rubber goes in and the seam in the rubber is positioned between the top and water port.

35   Apply engine oil or engine assembly lube to each of the rotor seals and the inside surface of the rotor housing. Make sure that there is no foreign matter in the front rotor housing.

36   With an assistant pulling slightly up on the eccentric shaft (no more than an inch), install the intermediate housing over the eccentric shaft and onto the front rotor housing **(see illustration)**. Align the dowel pins and use a rubber mallet to fully seal the intermediate housing against the front rotor housing.

37   The rear rotor with its apex seals and front side components installed is then lifted over the eccentric shaft and into position on the intermediate housing. One of its apexes should be towards the bottom of the engine, exactly opposite from the front rotor. Do not drop any of the seals into the openings at the sides of the housing.

38   Apply sealant to the front side of the rear rotor housing, smoothing it with your fingers.

39   As with the front rotor housing, use Vaseline to hold the rubber seals and O-rings in place on the front of the housing as it is inverted and set into place. The same rules apply to the wide white line and seam on the rubber seal.

40   Invert the rear rotor housing and place it in position over the rear rotor **(see illustration)**. Check that the rubber seal and O-ring remain in position.

41   Apply engine oil to the two dowel pins and hammer them through the rear rotor housing and into the intermediate housing using a rubber mallet.

42   Insert each apex seal spring into its proper bore.

43   Install each corner seal spring, corner seal, side seal spring and side seal on the rear side of the rotor. Check for free movement.

44   Install each triangular side piece and check for free movement.

45   Apply sealant to the rear side of the rear rotor housing, then place a new O-ring and rubber seal on this side following the same cautions about the wide while line and seam.

46   Apply engine oil to the rotor seals and the sliding inside surface of the rear rotor housing. Check that no dirt or foreign matter has entered the rotor or rotor housing.

47   Coat the stationary gear and main bearing with engine oil and install the rear housing on the rear rotor housing. Tap with a rubber mallet to properly seat the two housings.

48   Install a new O-ring on each of the tension bolts and lightly coat the threads with oil.

49   Install the tension bolts with new sealing washers and tighten them finger tight only. Note that bolt number 17 is longer than the rest **(see illustrations)**.

50   Tighten the bolts in the proper order and a little at a time. The tightening should be done in about three steps to prevent any warping of the housings. Once all the bolts are tightened to the torque listed in this Chapter's specifications, go around in a circular order to make sure none of the bolts have been forgotten.

51   Turn the eccentric shaft to make sure it rotates smoothly.

---

20   Eccentric shaft end play – adjustment

Refer to illustrations 20.3, 20.4 and 20.5

1   It is important to check the eccentric shaft end play after any major work is performed on the engine. The front cover need not be in place, but the front pulley must be temporarily installed.

2   Install the eccentric shaft pulley on the shaft and tighten the attaching bolt to the torque specified in Chapter 2, Part A. It may be necessary to use a flywheel brake of some kind to prevent the shaft from turning as this is done.

3   The best way to measure end play is with a dial indicator mounted on the flywheel/driveplate with the stem contacting the housing. The flywheel is then moved back and forth by hand and the reading is obtained **(see illustration)**.

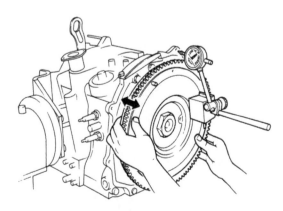

20.3   Move the eccentric shaft back and forth and measure the movement with a dial indicator

20.4   Measuring the eccentric shaft end play by prying the flywheel back and forth and measuring the movement with a feeler gauge

4   A cruder method can be used if a dial indicator is not available. Use the steel 'eye' bolted to the rear housing designed for lifting the engine out of the car. Turn the lifting eye and bolt around and thread a nut onto the bolt so that the steel just touches the flywheel when it is pried all the way out from the engine. Then push in the flywheel and measure the gap that the flywheel has moved with a feeler gauge **(see illustration)**.

5   If the end play is not within the range listed in this Chapter's specifications, the oil pump and bearing assemblies must be removed and the spacer replaced with a thinner or thicker one **(see illustration)**.

---

21   Front bearing and oil pump assemblies – installation

Refer to illustrations 21.1, 21.2, 21.3a and 21.3b

1   Slide the thrust plate, spacer and needle bearing onto the front of the eccentric shaft. Apply grease to hold the components in place **(see illustration)**.

2   Place the bearing housing on the front housing and tighten the attaching bolts **(see illustration)**.

3   Ensure the key is seated in the keyway, then slide the needle bearing, thrust plate and balance weight over the end of the shaft **(see illustrations)**.

4   Install the oil pump assembly, including the chain and sprockets and front cover (See Chapter 2, Part A, Section 10).

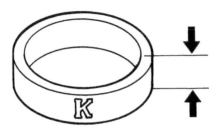

SPACER STAMP AND THICKNESS

Stamp	Thickness mm (in)	Stamp	Thickness mm (in)
S	8.12 (0.3197)	Y	8.04 (0.3165)
T	8.10 (0.3189)	V	8.02 (0.3157)
X	8.08 (0.3181)	Z	8.00 (0.3150)
K	8.06 (0.3173)		

20.5   If the end play is less than the standard listed in this Chapter's specifications, replace the spacer with a thicker one – if the end play is more than the standard replace the spacer with a thinner one

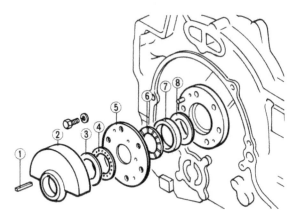

21.1   Exploded view of front bearing and balance weight components

1	Key	5	Bearing housing
2	Balance weight	6	Needle bearing
3	Thrust plate	7	Spacer
4	Needle bearing	8	Thrust plate

21.2   Tighten the bearing housing bolts to the specified torque

21.3a   Use grease to hold the needle bearing in place against the bearing housing

21.3b   Before sliding the balance weight over the eccentric shaft, attach the thrust plate to the back of it with a film of grease

22.17a   Non-turbo engine – front view

22   Final assembly and installation

Refer to illustrations 22.17a, 22.17b, 22.17c and 22.17d

Note: *See Section 7 for additional illustrations.*

1   Reinstall the flywheel/driveplate as described in Chapter 2, Part A.
2   On manual transmission equipped vehicles, install the clutch disc and pressure plate (see Chapter 8).
3   Mount the oil strainer (pickup) with a new gasket and tighten the bolts to the specified torque.
4   Install the oil pan and right engine mount and bracket as described in Chapter 2, Part A.
5   On turbo models, mount the oil filler pipe and attach the turbo oil inlet pipe to the front housing, using new washers.
6   Install the EGR valve (see Chapter 6).
7   Attach the left engine mount and bracket (see Section 7).
8   Attach the metering oil pump and oil metering nozzles and route the oil lines (see Chapter 2, Part A).
9   Using new O-rings, install the oil filter pedestal on the rear housing. Tighten the pedestal bolts to the torque listed in this Chapter's specifications.
10   Install a new oil filter and the spark plugs (see Chapter 1).
11   Bolt the eccentric shaft pulleys into place, referring to Chapter 2, Part A for the torque specification.
12   Install the water pump housing and water pump (see Chapter 3). Don't forget to use shims on the studs where the gasket does not mount. Tighten the water pump housing fasteners to the torque listed in this Chapter's specifications.
13   Mount the intake and exhaust manifolds as described in Chapter 2,

22.17b   Non-turbo engine – left side view

Part A. Install the turbocharger at this time, if equipped (see Chapter 4).
14   Install the crank angle sensor, alternator brackets and alternator (see Chapter 5).
15   Install the air pump brackets and air pump (see Chapter 6).
16   If removed, reinstall the sending units for oil pressure and coolant temperature. Use a light coating of sealer on the threads and tighten them securely.
17   Attach the remaining components that were detached during engine removal **(see illustrations)**.
18   Install the engine as described in Section 5, then refer to Section 23 for start-up and break-in information.

22.17c   Non-turbo engine – right side view

22.17d   Non-turbo engine – rear view

23   Initial start-up and break-in after overhaul

Warning: *Have a fire extinguisher handy when starting the engine for the first time.*

1   Once the engine has been installed in the vehicle, double-check the engine oil and coolant levels.

2   With the spark plugs out of the engine and the ignition system disabled (see Section 3), crank the engine until oil pressure registers on the gauge or the light goes out.

3   Install the spark plugs, hook up the plug wires and restore the ignition system functions (Section 3).

4   Start the engine. It may take a few moments for the fuel system to build up pressure, but the engine should start without a great deal of effort. **Note:** *If backfiring occurs through the throttle body, recheck the ignition timing.*

5   After the engine starts, it should be allowed to warm up to normal operating temperature. While the engine is warming up, make a thorough check for fuel, oil and coolant leaks.

6   Shut the engine off and recheck the engine oil and coolant levels.

7   Drive the vehicle gently for the first 600 miles (vary cruising speeds keep the engine speed low) and keep a constant check on the oil level. It is not unusual for an engine to use extra oil during the break-in period.

8   At approximately 600 miles, change the oil and filter.

9   For the next few hundred miles, drive the vehicle normally. Do not pamper it or abuse it, then consider the engine broken in.

Chapter 3   Cooling, heating and air conditioning systems

Contents

Air conditioning and heater control assembly – removal
    and installation 13
Air conditioning system – check and maintenance 14
Air conditioning compressor – removal and installation 16
Air conditioning condenser – removal and installation 17
Air conditiioning receiver/drier – removal and
    installation 15
Antifreeze – general information 2
Blower unit – removal and installation 11
Coolant level check .... See Chapter 1
Coolant reservoir – removal and installation 7
Coolant temperature sending unit – check and replacement 10
Cooling system check .... See Chapter 1

Cooling system servicing (draining, flushing
    and refilling) .... See Chapter 1
Drivebelt check, adjustment and replacement .... See Chapter 1
Engine cooling fan and clutch – check and replacement 4
General information 1
Heater core – removal and installation 12
Oil cooler – removal and installation 6
Radiator – removal and installation 5
Thermostat – check and replacement 3
Underhood hose check and replacement .... See Chapter 1
Water pump – check 8
Water pump – replacement 9

Specifications

General

Cooling system capacity .... See Chapter 1
Drivebelt deflection .... See Chapter 1
Radiator pressure cap rating .... 11 to 15 psi
Thermostat opening temperature .... 177 to 183 F
Oil cooler bypass valve protrusion (minimum) .... 0.2 in (5 mm) at 65°C (149°F)
Fan-to-shroud clearance .... 3/4 to 1 in (15 to 25 mm)

Torque specifications

	Ft-lbs	Nm
Mechanical cooling fan nuts	5.8 to 8.0	8 to 11
Thermostat cover bolts		
1986 through 1988	14 to 17	19 to 23
1989	5 to 7	7 to 10
Water pump attaching bolts	13 to 20	18 to 26

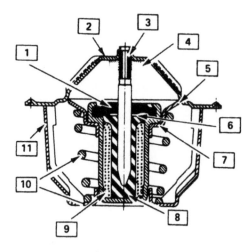

1.2   Pellet type thermostat

1	Flange seal	5	Valve seat	8	Rubber diaphragm
2	Flange	6	Teflon seal	9	Wax pellet
3	Piston	7	Valve	10	Coil spring
4	Nut			11	Frame

1   General information

Refer to illustrations 1.2 and 1.3

Engine cooling system

All vehicles covered by this manual employ a pressurized engine cooling system with thermostatically controlled coolant circulation.
An impeller type water pump mounted on the front of the block pumps coolant through the engine. The coolant flows around the combustion chambers and toward the rear of the engine. Cast-in coolant passages direct coolant near the intake ports, exhaust ports and spark plug areas.

A wax pellet type thermostat is located in a housing near the front of the engine. During warm up, the closed thermostat prevents coolant from circulating through the radiator. As the engine nears normal operating temperature, the thermostat opens and allows hot coolant to travel through the radiator, where it's cooled before returning to the engine **(see illustration)**.

The cooling system is sealed by a pressure type radiator cap, which raises the boiling point of the coolant and increases the cooling efficiency of the radiator. If the system pressure exceeds the cap pressure relief value, the excess pressure in the system forces the spring-loaded valve inside the cap off its seat and allows the coolant to escape through the overflow tube into a coolant reservoir. When the system cools the excess coolant is automatically drawn from the reservoir back into the radiator **(see illustration)**.

The coolant reservoir does double duty as both the point at which fresh coolant is added to the cooling system to maintain the proper fluid level and as a holding tank for overheated coolant.

This type of cooling system is known as a closed design because coolant that escapes past the pressure cap is saved and reused.

Heating system

The heating system consists of a blower fan and heater core located in the heater box, the hoses connecting the heater core to the engine cooling system and the heater/air conditioning control head on the dashboard. Hot engine coolant is circulated through the heater core. When the heater mode is activated, a flap door opens to expose the heater box to the passenger compartment. A fan switch on the control head activates the blower motor, which forces air through the core, heating the air.

Air conditioning system

The air conditioning system consists of a condenser mounted in front of the radiator, an evaporator mounted adjacent to the heater core, a com-

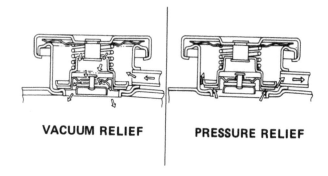

VACUUM RELIEF   PRESSURE RELIEF

1.3   Pressure-type radiator cap

pressor mounted on the engine, a filter-drier (accumulator) which contains a high pressure relief valve and the plumbing connecting all of the above components.

A blower fan forces the warmer air of the passenger compartment through the evaporator core (sort of a radiator-in-reverse), transferring the heat from the air to the refrigerant. The liquid refrigerant boils off into low pressure vapor, taking the heat with it when it leaves the evaporator.

2   Antifreeze – general information

Warning: *Do not allow antifreeze to come in contact with your skin or painted surfaces of the vehicle. Rinse off spills immediately with plenty of water. Antifreeze, if consumed, can be fatal. Children and pets are attracted to its sweet taste, so keep antifreeze containers covered and repair leaks in your cooling system as soon as they are noticed. Wipe up garage floor and drip pan coolant spills immediately*

The cooling system should be filled with a water/ethylene glycol based antifreeze solution, which will prevent freezing down to at least – 20 degrees F, or lower if local climate requires it. It also provides protection against corrosion and increases the coolant boiling point.

The cooling system should be drained, flushed and refilled at the specified intervals (see Chapter 1). Old or contaminated antifreeze solutions are likely to cause damage and encourage the formation of rust and scale in the system. Use distilled water with the antifreeze.

Before adding antifreeze, check all hose connections, because antifreeze tends to search out and leak through very minute openings. Engines don't normally consume coolant, so if the level goes down, find the cause and correct it.

The exact mixture of antifreeze-to-water which you should use depends on the relative weather conditions. The mixture should contain at least 50 percent antifreeze, but should never contain more than 70 percent antifreeze. Consult the mixture ratio chart on the antifreeze container before adding coolant. Hydrometers are available at most auto parts stores to test the coolant. Use antifreeze which meets the vehicle manufacturer's specifications.

3   Thermostat – check and replacement

Warning: *Do not remove the radiator cap, drain the coolant or replace the thermostat until the engine has cooled completely.*

Check

1   Before assuming the thermostat is to blame for a cooling system problem, check the coolant level, drivebelt tension (see Chapter 1) and temperature gauge operation.
2   If the engine seems to be taking a long time to warm up (based on heater output or temperature gauge operation), the thermostat is probably stuck open. Replace the thermostat with a new one.

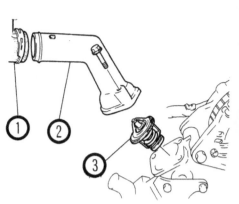

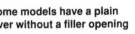

3.10a Remove the bolts (arrows) to detach the thermostat housing cover – note that this one has a cap and filler opening incorporated in it

3.10b Some models have a plain housing cover without a filler opening

1   *Hose*
2   *Thermostat housing cover*
3   *Thermostat*

3.13 Position the thermostat with the spring side in and the jigglepin (arrow) near the top

3   If the engine runs hot, use your hand to check the temperature of the upper radiator hose. If the hose isn't hot, but the engine is, the thermostat is probably stuck closed, preventing the coolant inside the engine from escaping to the radiator. Replace the thermostat. **Caution:** *Don't drive the vehicle without a thermostat. The computer may stay in open loop and emissions and fuel economy will suffer.*

4   If the upper radiator hose is hot, it means that the coolant is flowing and the thermostat is open. Consult the Troubleshooting Section at the front of this manual for cooling system diagnosis.

Replacement

Refer to illustrations 3.10a, 3.10b and 3.13

5   Disconnect the negative battery cable from the battery.

6   Drain the cooling system (see Chapter 1). If the coolant is relatively new or in good condition, save it and reuse it.

7   Follow the upper radiator hose to the engine to locate the thermostat housing.

8   Loosen the hose clamp, then detach the hose from the fitting. If it's stuck, grasp it near the end with a pair of Channelock pliers and twist it to break the seal, then pull it off. If the hose is old or deteriorated, cut it off and install a new one.

9   If the outer surface of the large fitting that mates with the hose is deteriorated (corroded, pitted, etc.) it may be damaged further by hose removal. If it is, the thermostat housing cover will have to be replaced.

10   Remove the bolts and detach the housing cover **(see illustrations)**. If the cover is stuck, tap it with a soft-face hammer to jar it loose. Be prepared for some coolant to spill as the gasket seal is broken.

11   Note how it's installed (which end is facing up), then remove the thermostat.

12   Stuff a rag into the engine opening, then remove all traces of old gasket material and sealant from the housing and cover with a gasket scraper. Remove the rag from the opening and clean the gasket mating surfaces with lacquer thinner or acetone.

13   Install the new thermostat in the housing. Make sure the correct end faces up – the spring end is normally directed into the engine and the jiggle pin is positioned near the top **(see illustration)**.

14   Apply a thin, uniform layer of RTV sealant to both sides of the new gasket and position it on the housing.

15   Install the cover and bolts. Tighten the bolts to the torque listed in this Chapter's specifications.

16   Reattach the hose to the fitting and tighten the hose clamp securely.

17   Refill the cooling system (see Chapter 1).

18   Start the engine and allow it to reach normal operating temperature,

then check for leaks and proper thermostat operation (as described in Steps 2 through 4).

---

4   Engine cooling fan and clutch – check and replacement

Warning: *To avoid possible injury or damage, DO NOT operate the engine with a damaged fan. Do not attempt to repair fan blades – replace a damaged fan with a new one.*

Removal and installation

Electric fan

Refer to illustration 4.4

1   Disconnect the negative battery cable from the battery.

2   Remove the fan wire harness from the clips.

3   Insert a small screwdriver into the connector to lift the lock tab and unplug the fan wire harness.

4   Unbolt the fan bracket assembly **(see illustration)**, then carefully lift it out of the engine compartment.

5   If you are replacing the motor, transfer the fan to the new unit.

6   To remove the bracket from the fan motor, remove the mounting nuts.

7   Installation is the reverse of removal.

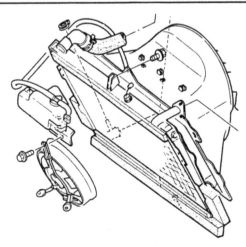

4.4 The optional electric cooling fan is mounted in front of the radiator

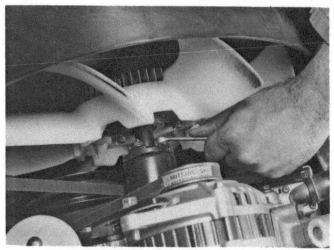

4.9   Loosen or tighten the fan mounting nuts with the drivebelts in place – this prevents the water pump pulley from turning

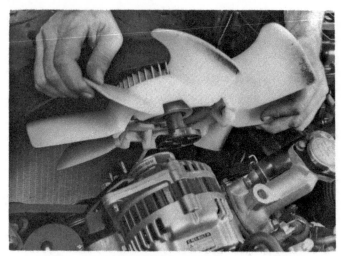

4.10   The cooling fan just fits between the shroud and the engine

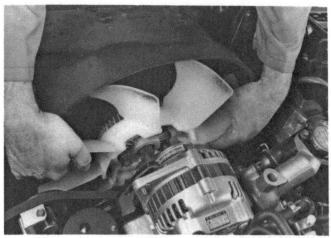

4.16   Check for excessive play by rocking the fan blades back and forth

Mechanical fan with viscous clutch

Refer to illustrations 4.9 and 4.10

8   Disconnect the negative battery cable.

9   Remove the nuts attaching the fan/clutch assembly to the water pump hub **(see illustration)**.

10   Lift the fan/clutch assembly out of the engine compartment **(see illustration)**.

11   Carefully inspect the fan blades for damage and defects. Replace it if necessary.

12   At this point, the fan may be unbolted from the clutch, if necessary. If the fan clutch is stored, position it with the radiator side facing down.

13   Installation is the reverse of removal Be sure to tighten the fan and clutch mounting nuts evenly and to the torque listed in this Chapter's specifications.

Check

Electric fan

14   To test the motor, unplug the electrical connector at the motor and use jumper wires to connect the fan directly to the battery. If the fan still doesn't work, replace the motor.

15   If the motor tested OK, the fault lies in the coolant temperature switch or the wiring which connects the components. Carefully check all wiring and connections. If no obvious problems are found, further diagnosis should be done by a dealer service department or repair shop.

Mechanical fan with viscous clutch

Refer to illustration 4.16

16   Disconnect the negative battery cable and rock the fan back and forth by hand to check for excessive bearing play **(see illustration)**.

17   With the engine cold, turn the fan blades by hand. The fan should turn freely.

18   Visually inspect for substantial fluid leakage from the clutch assembly. If problems are noted, replace the clutch assembly.

19   With the engine completely warmed up, turn off the ignition switch and disconnect the negative battery cable from the battery.

Turn the fan by hand. Some drag should be evident. If the fan turns easily, replace the fan clutch.

5 Radiator – removal and installation

Refer to illustrations 5.2, 5.5a, 5.5b, 5.6a, 5.6b and 5.9

Warning: *Wait until the engine is completely cool before beginning this procedure.*

1   Remove the battery and battery box (See Chapter 5).

2   Drain the cooling system (see Chapter 1). If the coolant is relatively new or in good condition, save it and reuse it. While the coolant is draining, remove the air intake duct **(see illustration)**.

3   Loosen the hose clamps, then detach the hoses from the radiator fittings. If they're stuck, grasp each hose near the end with a pair of Channelock pliers and twist it to break the seal, then pull it off – be careful not to distort the radiator fittings! If the hoses are old or deteriorated, cut them off and install new ones.

4   On models with the filler neck on the radiator, disconnect the reservoir hose from the radiator filler neck.

5   Disconnect the wiring from the radiator **(see illustrations)**.

6   Remove the five clips that attach the shroud to the radiator **(see illustration)** and lift the shroud from the engine compartment **(see illustration)**.

7   If the vehicle is equipped with an automatic transmission, disconnect the cooler hoses from the radiator **(see illustration 5.2)**. Use a drip pan to catch spilled fluid.

8   Plug the lines and fittings.

9   Remove the radiator mounting bolts **(see illustration)**.

10   Carefully lift out the radiator. Don't spill coolant on the vehicle or scratch the paint.

11   With the radiator removed, it can be inspected for leaks and damage. If it needs repair, have a radiator shop or dealer service department perform the work as special techniques are required.

12   Bugs and dirt can be removed from the radiator with compressed air and a soft brush. Don't bend the cooling fins as this is done.

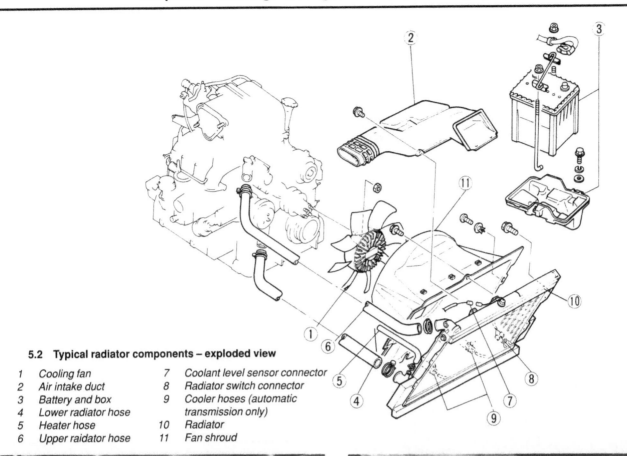

5.2   Typical radiator components – exploded view

1	Cooling fan	7	Coolant level sensor connector
2	Air intake duct	8	Radiator switch connector
3	Battery and box	9	Cooler hoses (automatic
4	Lower radiator hose		transmission only)
5	Heater hose	10	Radiator
6	Upper raidator hose	11	Fan shroud

5.5a   Disconnect the coolant level sensor (arrow) and move the wiring harness aside

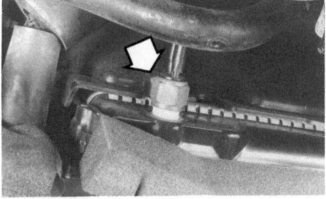

5.5b   Unplug the wires from the switch (arrow) located at the lower left corner of the radiator (viewed from below)

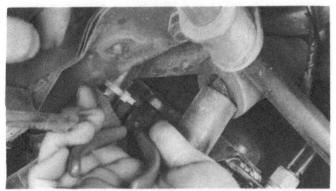

5.6a   The fan shroud is attached on three sides with reusable plastic clips – pinch the tabs on the front side together with needle-nose pliers, then push the clips out the other side

5.6b   Tilt the fan shroud to clear the hose fitting and lift it from the engine compartment

5.9   The radiator mounting bolts are located on the sides (arrows)

13   Check the radiator mounts for deterioration and make sure they are in place when the radiator is installed.
14   Installation is the reverse of the removal procedure. Make sure the fan-to-shroud clearance is as listed in this Chapter's specifications.

6.5a   The lower fitting (arrow) is accessible from under the vehicle

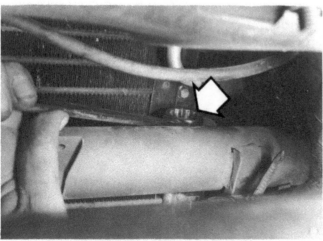

6.5b   The upper hose fitting (arrow) is situated between the radiator and a tubular cross-brace

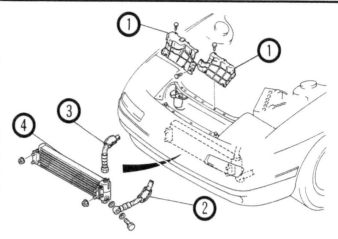

6.4   Oil cooler – exploded view

1	Radiator grill upper cover	3	Oil outlet hose
2	Oil inlet hose	4	Oil cooler

15   After installation, fill the cooling system with the proper mixture of anti-freeze and water. Refer to Chapter 1 if necessary.
16   Start the engine and check for leaks. Allow the engine to reach normal operating temperature, indicated by the upper radiator hose becoming hot. Recheck the coolant level and add more if required.
17   If you're working on an automatic transmission equipped vehicle, check and add fluid as needed.

6   Oil cooler – removal and installation

Refer to illustrations 6.4, 6.5a, 6.5b, 6.6, 6.7 and 6.8
Warning: *Wait until the engine is completely cool before beginning this procedure.*
1   Disconnect the negative cable from the battery.
2   Raise the front of the vehicle and support it securely on jackstands.
3   Unbolt the lower splash pan and set it aside.
4   Remove the radiator grille upper covers **(see illustration)**.
5   Detach the upper and lower hoses **(see illustrations)** and plug the open fittings. Have a drip pan ready to catch spills.
6   Remove the mounting nuts **(see illustration)** and lower the oil cooler from the vehicle.

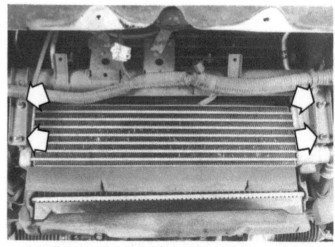

6.6   The mounting nuts (arrows) are located at both ends of the oil cooler

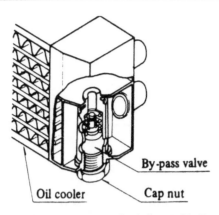

6.7 The oil cooler bypass valve is located in the bottom of the oil cooler

6.8 Submerge the bypass valve in hot water for several minutes, then measure the stem protrusion

7   Clean and inspect the oil cooler, checking for damage, cracks and leakage. Unscrew the bypass valve **(see illustration)** and flush the cooler with clean solvent.

8   The bypass valve may be tested by holding it in hot water (149 degrees F) for several minutes and measuring the protrusion of the stem **(see illustration)**. Compare the measurement to this Chapter's specifications and replace the valve if the protrusion is out of specification. If you are replacing the oil cooler, transfer the bypass valve to the new cooler.

9   Install the cooler in the reverse order of removal. Check the engine oil level and add oil as needed.

10   Start the engine and check for oil pressure and leakage.

7   Coolant reservoir – removal and installation

Refer to illustration 7.1

1   Pull the reservoir lid off with the hoses still attached and set it aside **(see illustration)**.

2   Remove the two mounting bolts and lift the reservoir from the vehicle.

3   Installation is the reverse of removal.

8   Water pump – check

Refer to illustration 8.4

1   A failure in the water pump can cause serious engine damage due to overheating.

2   There are three ways to check the operation of the water pump while it's installed on the engine. If the pump is defective, it should be replaced with a new or rebuilt unit.

3   With the engine running at normal operating temperature, squeeze the upper radiator hose. If the water pump is working properly, a pressure surge should be felt as the hose is released. **Warning:** Keep your hands away from the fan blades!

4   Water pumps are equipped with weep or vent holes. If a failure occurs in the pump seal, coolant will leak from the hole. In most cases you'll need a flashlight to find the hole on the water pump from underneath to check for leaks **(see illustration)**.

5   If the water pump shaft bearings fail there may be a howling sound at the front of the engine while it's running. Shaft wear can be felt if the water pump pulley is rocked up and down. Don't mistake drivebelt slippage, which causes a squealing sound, for water pump bearing failure.

9   Water pump – replacement

Refer to illustrations 9.4, 9.6 and 9.14

Warning: *Wait until the engine is completely cool before beginning this procedure.*

1   Disconnect the negative battery cable from the battery.

2   Drain the cooling system (see Chapter 1). If the coolant is relatively new or in good condition, save it and reuse it.

3   Remove the cooling fan and shroud (see Sections 4 and 5).

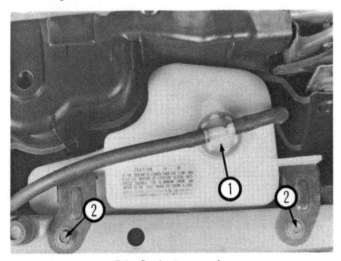

7.1   Coolant reservoir

1   *Lid*   2   *Mounting bolts*

8.4   A "weep hole" (arrow) is located on the underside of the water pump (shown with pulley and fan removed for clarity)

9.4   Loosen the water pump pulley bolts (arrows) and remove the pulley – the water pump drivebelt will loosen and can be removed when the pulley is removed

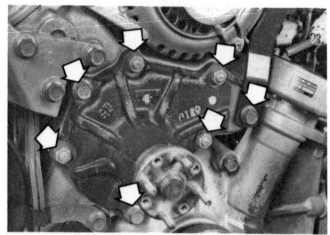

9.6   View of water pump with pulley removed shows locations of nuts and bolts and alternator bracket (arrows)

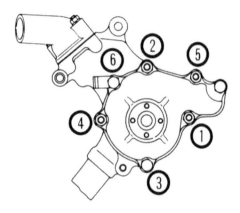

9.14   Water pump nut and bolt tightening sequence

10.1   The coolant temperature sending unit (arrow) is located below and just forward of the oil filter (fuel lines detached for clarity)

4   Remove the drivebelts (see Chapter 1) and the pulley at the end of the water pump shaft **(see illustration)**.

5   Remove all accessory brackets from the water pump.

6   Remove the bolts and nuts and detach the water pump from the engine. Note the locations of the various lengths and different types of bolts and nuts as they're removed to ensure correct installation **(see illustration)**.

7   Clean the bolt threads and the threaded holes in the engine to remove corrosion and sealant.

8   Compare the new pump to the old one to make sure they're identical.

9   Remove all traces of old gasket material from the engine with a gasket scraper.

10   Clean the engine and new water pump mating surfaces with lacquer thinner or acetone.

11   Apply a thin coat of RTV sealant to the engine side of the new gasket.

12   Apply a thin layer of RTV sealant to the gasket mating surface of the new pump, then carefully mate the gasket and the pump. Slip a couple of bolts through the pump mounting holes to hold the gasket in place.

13   Carefully attach the pump and gasket to the engine and thread the bolts into the holes finger tight.

14   Install the remaining bolts and nuts (if they also hold an accessory bracket in place, be sure to reposition the bracket at this time). Tighten them to the torque listed in this Chapter's Specifications, using 1/4–turn increments. Don't overtighten them or the pump may be distorted. Be sure the nuts/bolts are tightened in the sequence shown **(see illustration)**.

15   Reinstall all parts removed for access to the pump.

16   Refill the cooling system and check the drivebelt deflection (See Chapter 1). Run the engine and check for leaks.

10   Coolant temperature sending unit – check and replacement

Refer to illustration 10.1

Warning: *Wait until the engine is completely cool before beginning this procedure.*

1   The coolant temperature indicator system is composed of a temperature gauge mounted in the instrument panel and a coolant temperature sending unit mounted on the engine **(see illustration)**.

Some vehicles have more than one sending unit, but only one is used for the indicator system. **Warning:** *If the vehicle is equipped with an electric cooling fan, stay clear of the fan blades, which can come on at any time.*

2   If an overheating indication occurs, check the coolant level in the system and then make sure the wiring between the gauge and the sending unit is secure and all fuses are intact.

3   Test the circuit by grounding the wire to the sending unit while the ignition is on (engine not running for safety). If the gauge deflects full scale, replace the sending unit.

4   A constant HOT indication may be due to a grounded wire between the gauge and the sending unit, a defective sending unit or a faulty gauge. Check the coolant to make sure it's the proper type.

5   If the sending unit must be replaced, simply unscrew it from the engine and install the replacement. Use sealant on the threads. Make sure the engine is cool before removing the defective sending unit. There will be some coolant loss as the unit is removed, so be prepared to catch it. Check the level after the replacement has been installed.

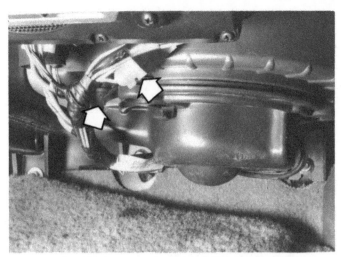

**11.3a   The blower motor is located under the right
side of the dash panel – disconnect the electrical
connector and the flexible tube (arrows) ...**

**11.3b   ... then remove the mounting screws located
around the perimeter of the blower motor cover**

**11.3c   Once the screws are removed, lower the
blower motor out of the housing**

**11.4   The blower fan is attached to the motor shaft
by a nut (arrow)**

11   Blower unit – removal and installation

Refer to illustrations 11.3a, 11.3b, 11.3c and 11.4
1   Disconnect the negative cable from the battery.
2   The blower unit is located in the passenger compartment below the
right side of the dash panel.
3   Disconnect the flexible tube and electrical connector from the blower
unit **(see illustration)**, then remove the mounting screws **(see illustration)** and lower the unit from the housing **(see illustration)**.
4   If the motor is being replaced, remove the nut **(see illustration)** and
transfer the fan to the new motor prior to installation.
5   Installation is the reverse of removal. Check for proper operation.

12   Heater core – removal and installation

Refer to illustrations 12.3, 12.6, 12.7 and 12.8
1   Disconnect the negative cable from the battery.
2   Drain the cooling system (see Chapter 1).
3   Working in the engine compartment, disconnect the heater hoses
(see illustration) where they enter the firewall.

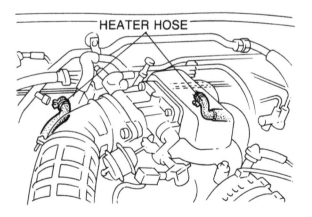

**12.3   Loosen the clamps, then detach the heater hoses from the
firewall fittings**

4   Remove the instrument panel and the center console (see Chapters
11 and 12).
5   Remove the heater controls (see Section 13).

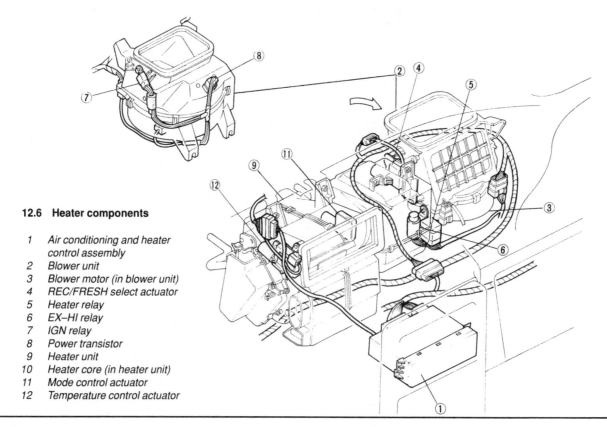

12.6 Heater components

1 *Air conditioning and heater*
   control assembly
2 *Blower unit*
3 *Blower motor (in blower unit)*
4 *REC/FRESH select actuator*
5 *Heater relay*
6 *EX–HI relay*
7 *IGN relay*
8 *Power transistor*
9 *Heater unit*
10 *Heater core (in heater unit)*
11 *Mode control actuator*
12 *Temperature control actuator*

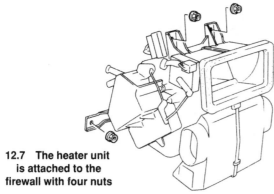

**12.7 The heater unit
is attached to the
firewall with four nuts**

6   Label and detach the air ducts, wiring hoses and controls still attached to the heater unit **(see illustration)**.
7   Unscrew the nuts and remove the heater unit **(see illustration)**.
8   Remove the screws and clips and separate the two halves of the heater unit case **(see illustration)**. Take out the old heater core and install the new one.
9   Reassemble the heater unit and check the operation of the air control doors. If any parts bind, correct the problem before installation.
10   Reinstall the remaining parts in the reverse order of removal.
11   Refill the cooling system, reconnect the battery and run the engine. Check for leaks and proper system operation.

**13   Air conditioning and heater control assembly – removal
        and installation**

Refer to illustrations 13.3 and 13.4
1   Disconnect the negative cable from the battery.
2   Remove the instrument cluster and radio (see Chapter 12).
3   Remove the air conditioning and heater control mounting screws **(see illustration)**.

4   Pull out the control unit as far as possible without stretching the wiring harnesses. Unplug the two electrical connectors behind the control unit **(see illustration)**.
5   Reach through the instrument cluster opening and unplug the remaining air conditioning and heater control connector plug near the left defroster duct below the windshield (illustration 12.6 shows the location of this cable and connector).
6   Installation is the reverse of removal.

---

14   Air conditioning system – check and maintenance

Refer to illustrations 14.1, 14.7, 14.10 and 14.12
Warning: *The air conditioning system is under high pressure. Do not loosen any hose fittings or remove any components until after the system has been discharged by a dealer service department or service station. Always wear eye protection when disconnecting air conditioning system fittings.*

Check

1   The following maintenance checks should be performed on a regular basis to ensure that the air conditioner continues to operate at peak efficiency.

a) Check the compressor drivebelt. If it's worn or deteriorated, replace it (see Chapter 1).
b) Check the drivebelt tension and, if necessary, adjust it (see Chapter 1).
c) Check the system hoses. Look for cracks, bubbles, hard spots and deterioration. Inspect the hoses and all fittings for oil bubbles and seepage. If there's any evidence of wear, damage or leaks, replace the hose(s).
d) Inspect the condenser fins for leaves, bugs and other debris. Use a "fin comb" or compressed air to clean the condenser.
e) Make sure the system has the correct refrigerant charge.
f) The evaporator housing drain tube **(see illustration)** can become clogged, trapping water and causing a sloshing sound in the vehicle.

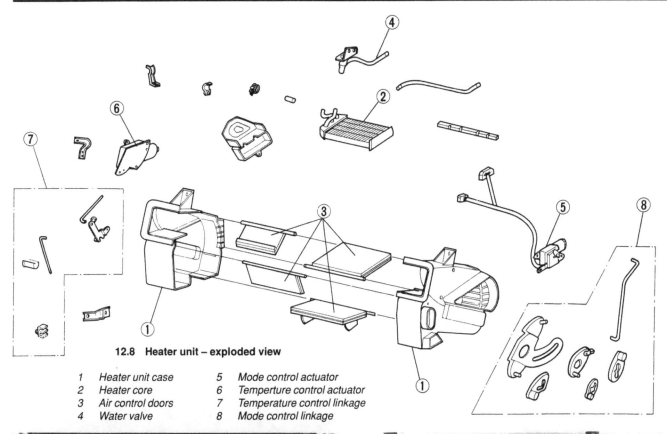

12.8 Heater unit – exploded view

1	Heater unit case	5	Mode control actuator
2	Heater core	6	Temperture control actuator
3	Air control doors	7	Temperature control linkage
4	Water valve	8	Mode control linkage

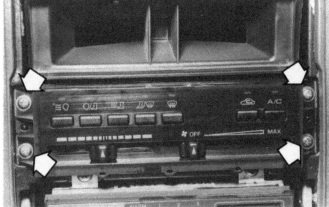

13.3 The air conditioning and heater control is attached to the dash by four screws (arrows)

13.4 This rear view of the control unit shows the locations of the two connectors on the back of the housing (arrows)

2   It's a good idea to operate the system for about 10 minutes at least once a month, particularly during the winter. Long term non-use can cause hardening, and subsequent failure, of the seals.

3   Because of the complexity of the air conditioning system and the special equipment necessary to service it, in–depth troubleshooting and repairs are not included in this manual (refer to the Haynes Automotive Heating and Air Conditioning manual for further information). However, simple checks and component replacement procedures are provided in this Chapter.

4   The most common cause of poor cooling is simply a low system refrigerant charge. If a noticeable drop in cool air output occurs, one of the following quick checks will help you determine if the refrigerant level is low.

5   Warm the engine up to normal operating temperature.

6   Place the air conditioning temperature selector at the coldest setting and put the blower at the highest setting. Open the doors (to make sure the air conditioning system doesn't cycle off as soon as it cools the passenger compartment).

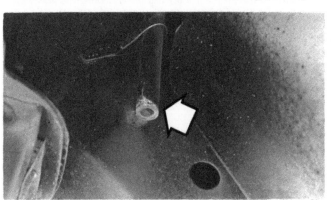

14.1 The evaporator housing drain tube (arrow) is located on the inner side of the right front frame rail at the firewall – push a wire through it to check for obstructions

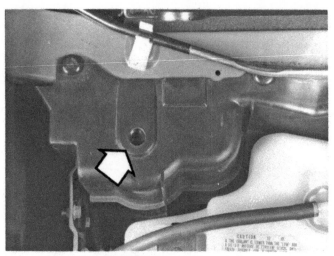

14.7   The sight glass is visible through the opening (arrow) in the receiver/drier cover

14.10   Connect the charging kit to the low pressure side – distinguished by its larger diameter tubing

14.12   Place a thermometer in the center vent to monitor output temperature

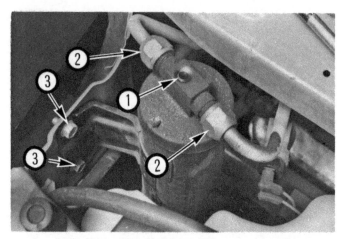

15.4   View of receiver/drier with cover removed

1   Sight glass
2   Refrigerant line fittings
3   Mounting bracket bolts

7   With the compressor engaged – the clutch will make an audible click and the center of the clutch will rotate – inspect the sight glass, if equipped **(see illustration)**. If the refrigerant looks foamy, it's low. Charge the system as described later in this Section.

8   If there's no sight glass, feel the inlet and outlet pipes at the compressor. One side should be cold and one hot. If there's no perceptible difference between the two pipes, there's something wrong with the compressor or the system. It might be a low charge – it might be something else. Take the vehicle to a dealer service department or an automotive air conditioning shop.

Adding refrigerant

9   Buy an automotive charging kit at an auto parts store. A charging kit includes a 14-ounce can of refrigerant, a tap valve and a short section of hose that can be attached between the tap valve and the system low side service valve. Because one can of refrigerant may not be sufficient to bring the system charge up to the proper level, it's a good idea to buy a few additional cans. Make sure that one of the cans contains red refrigerant dye. If the system is leaking, the red dye will leak out with the refrigerant and help

you pinpoint the location of the leak. **Warning:** *Never add more than three cans of refrigerant to the system.*

10   Hook up the charging kit by following the manufacturer's instructions **(see illustration)**. **Warning:** *DO NOT hook the charging kit hose to the system high side!*

11   Warm up the engine and turn on the air conditioner. Keep the charging kit hose away from the fan and other moving parts.

12   Place a thermometer in the dashboard vent nearest the evaporator **(see illustration)** and add refrigerant until the indicated temperature is around 40 to 45-degrees F.

15   Air conditioning receiver/drier – removal and installation

Refer to illustration 15.4

Warning: *The air conditioning system is under high pressure. DO NOT disassemble any part of the system (hose, compressor, line fittings, etc.) until after the system has been depressurized by a dealer service department or service station.*

1   Have the air conditioning system discharged (see Warning above).

16.3   Detach the compressor clutch electrical connector by pinching the clasp together and pulling the plug out

NIPPONDENSO COMPRESSOR

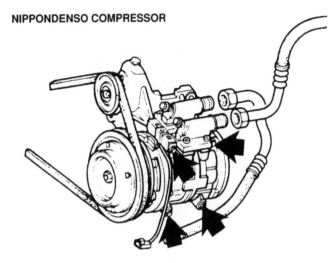

SANDEN COMPRESSOR

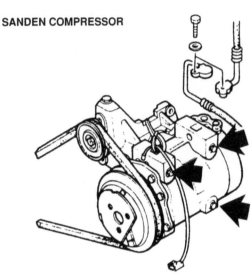

2   Disconnect the negative battery cable from the battery.
3   Remove the plastic receiver/drier cover **(see illustration 14.7)** by pushing in the clip pins, then prying the clips out of the radiator support.
4   Disconnect the refrigerant lines from the receiver/drier **(see illustration)**.
5   Plug the open fittings to prevent entry of dirt and moisture.
6   Loosen the mounting bracket bolts and lift the receiver/drier out.
7   If a new receiver/drier is being installed, pour the oil out of the old unit into a measuring cup, noting the amount. Add fresh refrigerant oil to the new receiver/drier equal to the amount removed from the old unit, plus one ounce.
8   Installation is the reverse of removal.
9   Take the vehicle back to the shop that discharged it. Have the air conditioning system evacuated, charged and leak tested.

16.5   The vehicle may be equipped with either of these compressors – the refrigerant lines are shown disconnected and the arrows point to the mounting bolts

16   Air conditioning compressor – removal and installation

Refer to illustrations 16.3 and 16.5

Warning: *The air conditioning system is under high pressure. DO NOT disassemble any part of the system (hoses, compressor, line fittings, etc.) until after the system has been depressurized by a dealer service department or service station.*

Note: *The receiver/drier (see Section 15) should be replaced whenever the compressor is replaced.*

1   Have the system discharged (see Warning above).
2   Disconnect the negative battery cable from the battery.
3   Disconnect the compressor clutch electrical connector **(see illustration)**.
4   Remove the drivebelt (see Chapter 1).
5   Disconnect the refrigerant lines from the rear of the compressor **(see illustration)**. Plug the open fittings to prevent entry of dirt and moisture.
6   Unbolt the compressor from the mounting brackets and lift it out of the vehicle.
10   Have the system evacuated, recharged and leak tested by the shop that discharged it.
7   If a new compressor is being installed, follow the directions with the compressor regarding the draining of excess oil prior to installation.
8   The clutch may have to be transferred from the original to the new compressor.
9   Installation is the reverse of removal. Replace all O-rings with new

ones specifically made for air conditioning system use and lubricate them with refrigerant oil.
10   Have the system evacuated, recharged and leak tested by the shop that discharged it.

17   Air conditioning condenser – removal and installation

Refer to illustrations 17.5 and 17.6

Warning: *The air conditioning system is under high pressure. DO NOT disassemble any part of the system (hoses, compressor, line fittings, etc.) until after the system has been depressurized by a dealer service department or service station.*

Note: *The receiver/drier (see Section 15) should be replaced whenever the condenser is replaced.*

1   Have the air conditioning system discharged (see Warning above).
2   Remove the battery (see Chapter 5).
3   Drain the cooling system (see Chapter 1).
4   Remove the radiator (see Section 5).

17.5   The refrigerant lines (arrow) connect to the top left and bottom right corners of the condenser

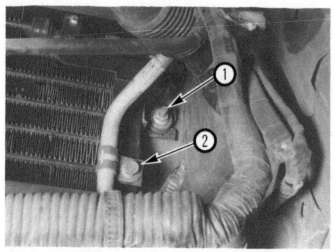

17.6   Remove the condenser bracket mounting nuts (1) (located on the front side of the condensor at the left and right edges) and the line bracket bolt (2)

5   Disconnect the refrigerant lines from the condenser **(see illustration)**.
6   Remove the mounting nuts from the condenser brackets and the line bracket bolt from the condensor **(see illustration)**.
7   Lift the condenser out of the vehicle and plug the lines to keep dirt and moisture out.
8   If the original condenser will be reinstalled, store it with the line fittings on top to prevent oil from draining out
9   If a new condenser is being installed, pour one ounce of refrigerant oil into it prior to installation.
10   Reinstall the components in the reverse order of removal. Be sure the rubber grommets are in place on the condenser mounting brackets.
11   Have the system evacuated, recharged and leak tested by the shop that discharged it.

Chapter 4   Fuel and exhaust systems

Contents

Air cleaner – removal and installation 7
Air filter replacement .... See Chapter 1
Air flow meter – removal, installation and check 8
Atmospheric pressure sensor – check and replacement 23
Auxiliary port valve system – description, inspection and
    component replacement 15
Boost/pressure sensor – check and replacement 22
Bypass air control (BAC) system (1986 through 1988 models) ... 9
Dynamic chamber/surge tank – removal and installation 13
EGI main fuse – check and replacement 20
EGI main relay – check and replacement 21
Engine idle speed check and adjustment .... See Chapter 1
Exhaust system check .... See Chapter 1
Exhaust system servicing – general information 26
Extension manifold or VDI manifold – removal, installation
    and VDI component check (non-turbo models only) 14
Fuel filter replacement .... See Chapter 1
Fuel injection system – general information 1

Fuel injectors – check and replacement 18
Fuel pressure regulator – check and replacement 16
Fuel pressure relief and fuel system priming 2
Fuel pump/fuel pressure – check 3
Fuel pump – removal and installation 4
Fuel system check .... See Chapter 1
Fuel tank cleaning and repair – general information 6
Fuel tank – removal and installation 5
Hot start assist system (1986 through 1988 models) 24
Idle speed control system (1989 models only) 10
Pulsation damper – check and replacement 17
Solenoid resistor – check and replacement 19
Sub-zero starting system check .... See Chapter 1
Throttle body – check and component replacement 12
Throttle cable – check, adjustment and replacement 11
Turbocharger and control system – check
    and component replacement 25

Specifications

Fuel injector resistance

1986 and 1987	1.5 to 3 ohms
1988 and later	12 to 16 ohms

Fuel Pressure

Fuel system pressure	34.1 to 39.8 psi
Fuel system hold pressure	18 psi
Fuel pump pressure	
EGI	64 to 85.3 psi
Turbo	71.1 to 92.4 psi
Fuel pump hold pressure	57 psi
Pressure regulator check (at idle)	
1986 through 1988	
Vacuum hose detached	35.6 to 37.0 psi
Vacuum hose attached	28.4 psi
1989 on	
Vacuum hose detached	27 to 33 psi
Vacuum hose attached	21 psi

Throttle body

Number one secondary throttle valve clearance
  EGI
      manual transmission .... 0.02 to 0.03 in (0.5 to 0.7 mm)
      automatic transmission .... 0.03 to 0.06 in (0.8 to 1.4 mm)
  Turbo .... 0.04 to 0.07 in (1.1 to 1.7 mm)
Fast idle clearance .... 0.016 to 0.02 in (0.4 to 0.5 mm)
Double throttle diaphragm clearance (automatic transmission) ... 0.09 to 0.13 in (2.2 to 3.2 mm)
Throttle cable freeplay .... 0.04 to 0.12 in (1 to 3 mm)
Auxiliary port valve actuator operating pressure
  1986 through 1988
      Starting to open .... 1.2 psi
      Fully open .... 2.1 psi
  1989
      Starting to open .... 0.85 psi
      Fully open .... 1.4 psi
VDI actuator operating pressure (1989 models only) .... 2.8 psi

Torque specifications

	Ft-lbs	Nm
Throttle body and dynamic chamber nuts/bolts	14 to 19	19 to 25
Turbocharger nuts/bolts	32.0 to 40.0	44 to 54
Front catalytic converter nuts/bolts	32.5 to 39.7	44 to 54

---

1   Fuel injection system – general information

Refer to illustrations 1.1a, 1.1b, 1.1c, 1.1d, 1.1e, 1.1f, 1.1g, 1.1h, 1.1i, 1.1j, 1.1k and 1.1l

All engines are equipped with electronic fuel injection (EGI) **(see illustrations)**. The EGI system consists of three basic sub-systems – the air intake system, the fuel system and the electronic control system.

Air intake system

The air intake system on non–turbo models consists of the air filter housing, the air flow meter, the throttle body, the dynamic chamber, the intake manifold and either an extension manifold or Variable Dynamic Effect Intake (VDI) manifold. All components except the intake manifold are covered in this Chapter; for information on removing and installing the intake manifold, refer to Chapter 2.

The air intake system on turbo models consists of the air filter housing, the air flow meter, the intercooler, the throttle body, the surge tank and the intake manifold.

All components except the intake manifold are covered in this Chapter. For information on removing and installing the intake manifold, refer to Chapter 2.

The throttle valves inside the throttle body are actuated by the throttle cable. When you depress the accelerator pedal, the throttle plates open and airflow through the intake system increases. A flap inside the air flow meter opens wider as the air flow increases. A potentiometer attached to the pivot shaft of the flap measures the angle of the flap (how much it's open) and converts this to a voltage signal which it sends to the computer. An intake air temperature sensor also sends an electrical signal to the computer. The air intake temperature is compared to a "map" – stored in computer memory – of the ideal injector opening duration for the prevailing operating conditions, and the computer alters injector duration accordingly.

Fuel system

An electric fuel pump, located inside the fuel tank, supplies fuel under constant pressure to two fuel rails, each of which distributes fuel to two injectors. One fuel rail supplies the two primary injectors and the other supplies the two secondary injectors. A pulsation damper smoothes out the pulses of the electric fuel pump. A regulator controls the pressure in the fuel rails. The amount of fuel actually injected into the intake ports is precisely controlled by an electronic control unit (computer).

Electronic control system

Besides altering the injector opening duration as described above, the electronic control unit performs a number of other tasks related to fuel and emissions control. It accomplishes these tasks by comparing data relayed to it by a wide array of information sensors located throughout the engine compartment, comparing this information to its stored map and altering engine operation by controlling a number of different actuators. Since special equipment is required, most troubleshooting and repairing of the electronic control system is beyond the scope of the home mechanic.

Turbocharger

Some of the vehicles covered by this manual are turbocharged. Refer to Section 25 for check and component replacement procedures for the turbocharger and its control system.

Warranty information

These vehicles are covered by a Federally-mandated extended warranty (5 years or 50,000 miles at the time this manual was written) which covers nearly every fuel system component in this Chapter. Before working on the fuel system, check with a dealer service department for warranty terms on your particular vehicle.

---

2   Fuel pressure relief and fuel system priming

Refer to illustration 2.6

Warning: *Gasoline is extremely flammable, so take extra precautions when you work on any part of the fuel system. Don't smoke or allow open flames or bare light bulbs near the work area. Also, don't work in a garage where a natural gas-type appliance with a pilot light is present. Finally, when you perform any kind of work on the fuel tank, wear safety glasses and have a Class B type fire extinguisher on hand. If you spill any fuel on your skin, clean it off immediately with soap and water.*

Relieving fuel pressure

1   Start the engine.
2   Detach the fuel pump connector (see Section 4).
3   Wait for the engine to stall, then turn off the ignition key.
4   Remove the fuel filler cap to relieve the fuel tank pressure.

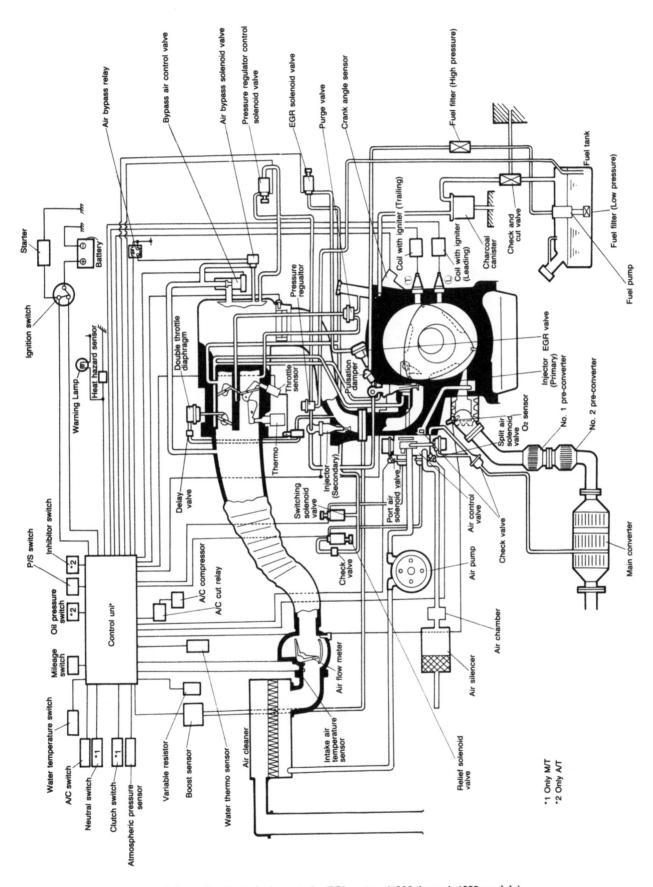

1.1a   Schematic of a typical non-turbo EGI system (1986 through 1988 models)

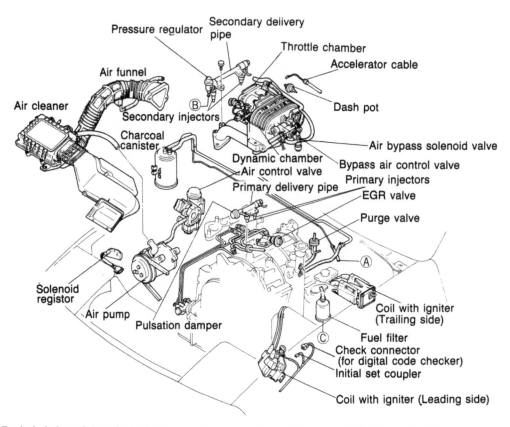

1.1b   Exploded view of the principal components of a non-turbo EGI system (1986 through 1988 models) (1 of 2)

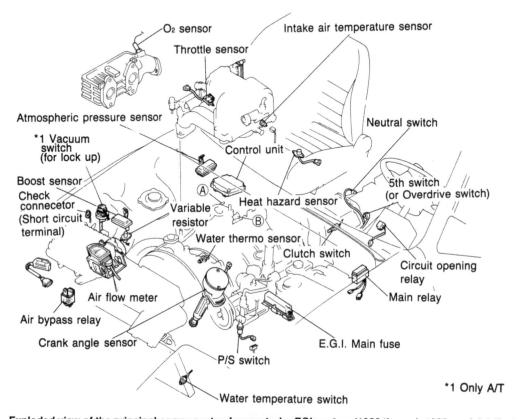

1.1c   Exploded view of the principal components of a non-turbo EGI system (1986 through 1988 models) (2 of 2)

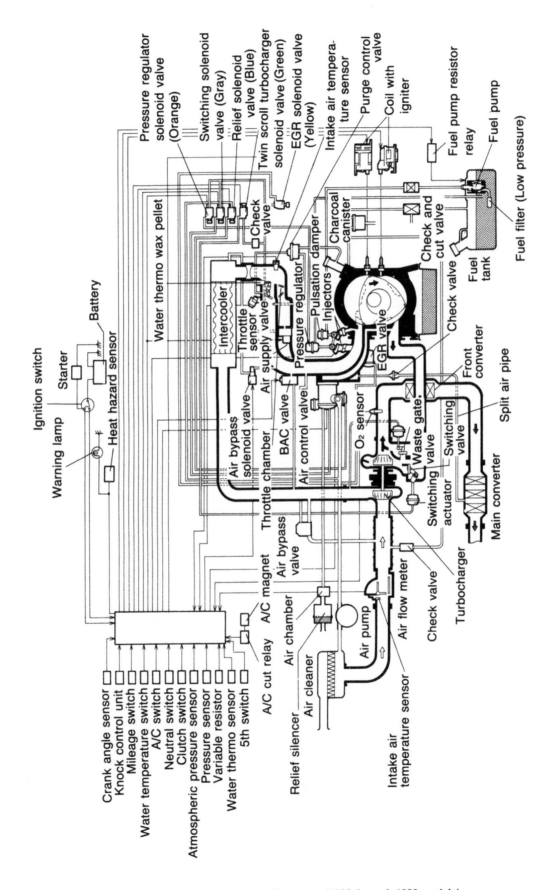

1.1d   Schematic of a typical turbo EGI system (1986 through 1988 models)

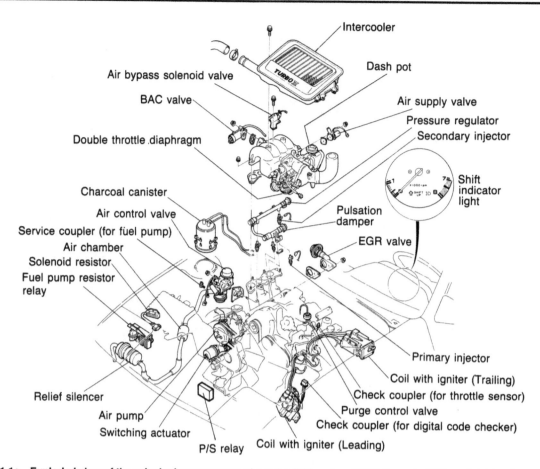

1.1e   Exploded view of the principal components of a turbo EGI system (1986 through 1988 models) (1 of 2)

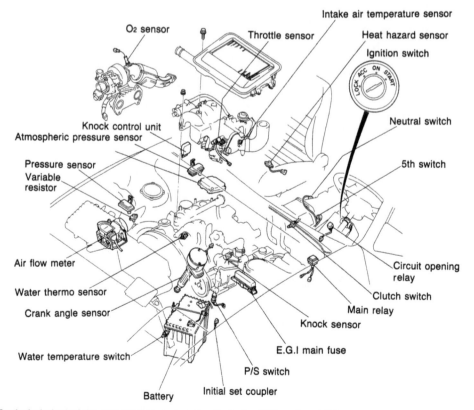

1.1f   Exploded view of the principal components of a turbo EGI system (1986 through 1988 models) (2 of 2)

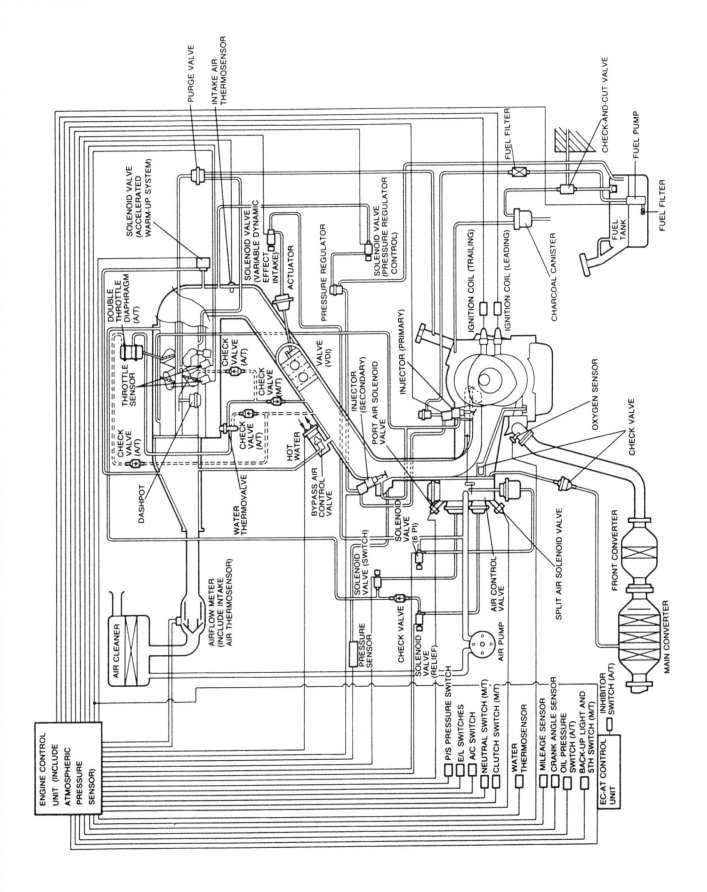

1.1g Schematic of a 1989 non-turbo EGI system (later models similar)

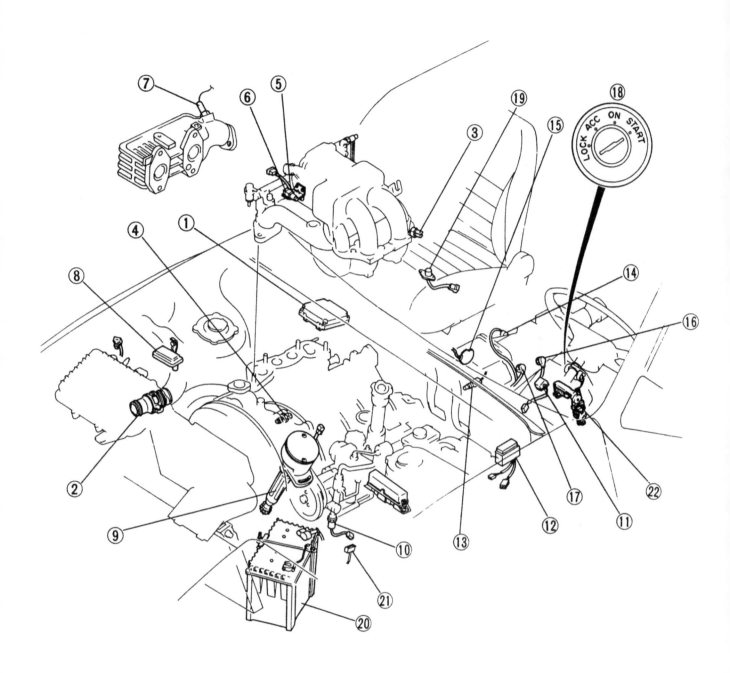

1.1h　Exploded view of EGI system input devices (1989 non-turbo model shown, later models similar)

1	Engine control unit	10	Power steering pressure switch	16	Back-up light and fifth gear switch
2	Air flow meter/intake air thermosensor	11	Circuit opening relay		(manual transmission only)
3	Intake air thermosensor	12	Main relay	17	Oil pressure switch
4	Water thermosensor	13	Clutch switch		(automatic transmission only)
5	Narrow range throttle sensor		(manual transmission only)	18	Ignition switch
6	Full range throttle sensor	14	Neutral switch	19	Heat hazard sensor
7	Oxygen sensor		(manual transmission only)	20	Battery
8	Pressure sensor	15	Inhibitor switch	21	Green one-pin test connector
9	Crank angle sensor		(automatic transmission only)	22	Mileage sensor

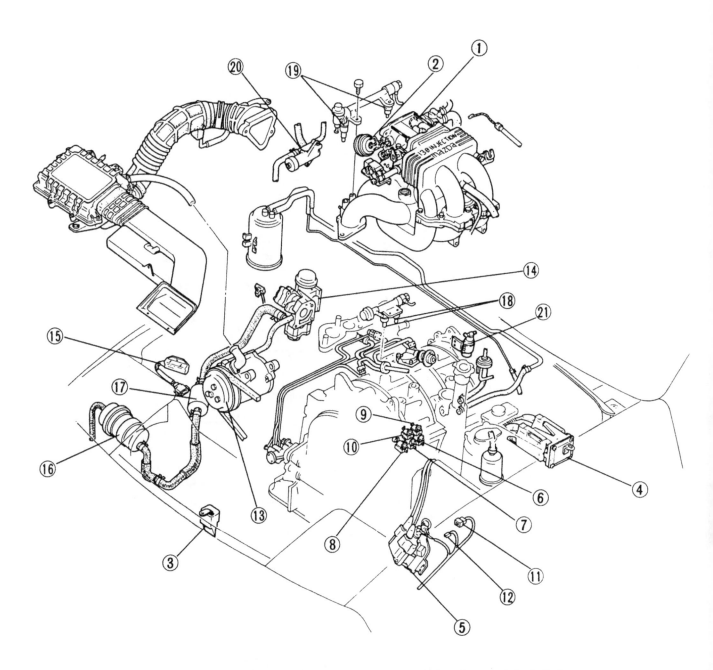

1.1i Exploded view of 1989 non-turbo EGI system output devices (later models similar)

1 Dashpot
2 Double throttle diaphragm
3 Air conditioning relay
4 Trailing ignition coil
5 Leading ignition coil
6 Relief solenoid valve
7 Switching solenoid valve
8 Pressure regulator control (PRC) solenoid valve
9 Variable Dynamic Effect Intake (VDI) solenoid valve
10 6 port induction (6PI) solenoid valve
11 Green six-pin check connector
12 Yellow two-pin check connector
13 Air pump
14 Air control valve (ACV)
15 Fuel pump resistor relay
16 Relief silencer
17 Air chamber
18 Primary injector
19 Secondary injector
20 Bypass Air Control (BAC) valve
21 Accelerated warm-up system solenoid valve

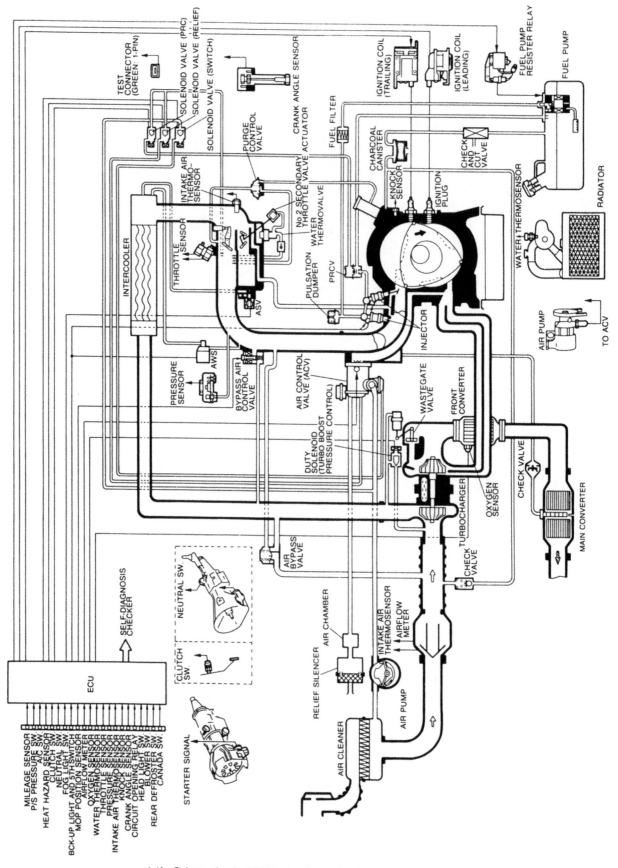

1.1j Schematic of a 1989 turbo EGI system (later models similar)

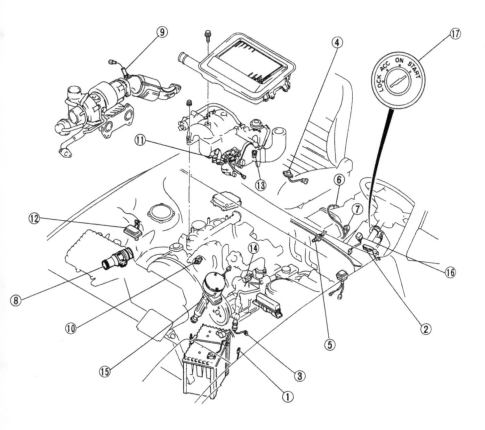

1.1k   Exploded view of 1989 turbo EGI system input devices (later models similar)

1   Green one-pin test connector
2   Mileage sensor
3   Power steering pressure switch
4   Heat hazard sensor
5   Clutch switch
6   Neutral switch
7   Back-up light and fifth gear switch
8   Airflow meter/intake air thermosensor
9   Oxygen sensor
10   Water thermosensor
11   Full range and narrow range throttle sensor
12   Pressure sensor
13   Engine intake air thermosensor
14   Knock sensor
15   Crank angle sensor
16   Circuit opening relay
17   Ignition switch

1.1l   Exploded view of 1989 turbo EGI system output devices (later models similar)

1   Intercooler
2   Air supply valve solenoid valve
3   Dashpot
4   Double throttle diaphragm
5   Air conditioning relay
6   Trailing ignition coil
7   Leading ignition coil
8   Relief solenoid valve
9   Pressure Regulator Control (PRC) solenoid valve
10   Switching solenoid valve
11   Turbo boost pressure control duty solenoid valve
12   Green six-pin self-diagnosis check connector
13   Air pump
14   Air control valve (ACV)
15   Yellow two-pin fuel pump check connector
16   Fuel pump resistor relay
17   Relief silencer
18   Air chamber
19   Primary injector
20   Secondary injector
21   Bypass air control (BAC) solenoid valve
22   Accelerated warm-up system solenoid valve

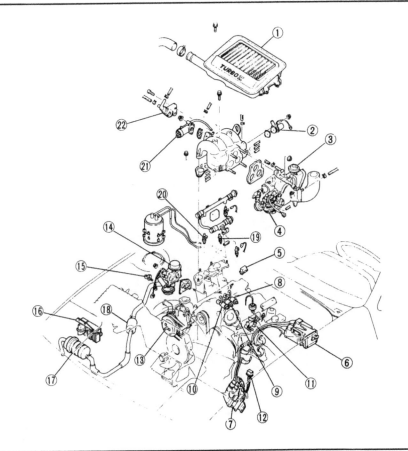

2.6   Bridge the terminals of the check connector with a jumper wire

Priming the fuel system

5   To avoid excessive cranking when you first start the engine after the fuel pressure has been relieved, prime the system.

6   Using a jumper wire, bridge the terminals of the yellow, two-pin check connector **(see illustration)**.

7   Turn the ignition switch to On for about 10 seconds, then check for leaks.

8   Turn the ignition switch to Off and remove the jumper wire.

---

3   Fuel pump/fuel pressure – check

Warning: *Gasoline is extremely flammable, so take extra precautions when you work on any part of the fuel system. Don't smoke or allow open flames or bare light bulbs near the work area. Also, don't work in a garage where a natural gas-type appliance with a pilot light is present. Finally, when you perform any kind of work on the fuel tank, wear safety glasses and have a Class B type fire extinguisher on hand. If you spill any fuel on your skin, clean it off immediately with soap and water.*

Note: *The following checks assume the fuel filter is in good condition. If you doubt the condition of your fuel filter, replace it (see Chapter 1).*

Fuel pump operational check

1   Bridge the terminals of the yellow, two-pin check connector **(see illustration 2.6)**

3.5   Detach the fuel feed hose (arrow)

2   Have an assistant turn the ignition key to On while you listen at the fuel tank (the fuel pump is inside the fuel tank). You should hear a whirring sound for a few seconds.

1) If there is no whirring sound, there is a problem in the fuel pump circuit. Check the EGI main fuse first (see Section 20).

2) If the whirring sound continues for a long period of time, the fuel system is probably not pressurizing properly. Check the fuel system pressure (see below).

Fuel system pressure check

Refer to illustrations 3.5 and 3.6

3   Relieve the system fuel pressure (see Section 2).

4   Detach the cable from the negative battery terminal.

5   Detach the fuel feed hose from the primary fuel rail **(see illustration)**.

6   Using a tee (three-way) fitting, a short section of high-pressure fuel hose and clamps, attach a fuel pressure gauge without disturbing normal fuel flow **(see illustration)**.

7   Attach the cable to the negative battery terminal.

8   Bridge the terminals of the yellow, two-pin check connector with a jumper wire **(see illustration 2.6)**.

9   Turn the ignition switch to On.

10   Note the fuel pressure and compare it with this Chapter's specifications.

11   If the system fuel pressure is less than specified:

1) Inspect the system for a fuel leak. Repair any leaks and recheck the fuel pressure.

2) If there are no leaks, install a new fuel filter and recheck the fuel pressure.

3) If the pressure is still low, check the fuel pump pressure (see below) and the fuel pressure regulator (see Section 16).

12   If the pressure is higher than specified, replace the fuel pressure regulator.

13   Turn the ignition switch to Off, wait five minutes and recheck the pressure. Compare the reading with the hold pressure listed in this Chapter's specifications. If the hold pressure is less than specified:

1) Inspect the fuel system for a fuel leak. Repair any leaks and recheck the fuel pressure.

2) Check the fuel pump pressure (see below).

3) Check the fuel pressure regulator (see Section 16).

4) Check the injectors (see Section 18).

Fuel pump pressure check

Refer to illustration 3.16

14   Relieve the system fuel pressure (see Section 2).

15   Detach the cable from the negative battery terminal.

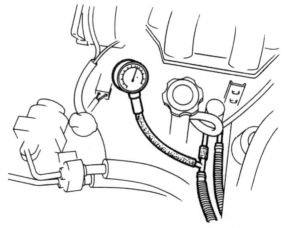

3.6   Install a fuel pressure gauge between the fuel filter and the pulsation damper with a tee fitting, as shown

16   Detach the fuel feed hose from the primary fuel rail and attach a fuel pressure gauge (**see illustration**).
17   Attach the cable to the negative battery terminal.
18   Using a jumper wire, bridge the terminals of the yellow, two-pin check connector (**see illustration 2.6**).
19   Turn the ignition switch to On to operate the fuel pump.
20   Note the pressure reading on the gauge and compare the reading to the fuel figure listed in this Chapter's specifications.
21   If the indicated pressure is less than specified, inspect the fuel line for leaks between the pump and gauge. If no leaks are found, replace the fuel pump.
22   Turn the ignition key to Off and wait five minutes. Note the reading on the gauge and compare it to the hold pressure listed in this Chapter's specifications. If the hold pressure is less than specified, check the fuel lines between the pump and gauge for leaks. If no leaks are found, replace the fuel pump.
23   Remove the jumper wire and gauge and reconnect the fuel line.

3.16   Detach the fuel feed hose and attach a fuel pressure gauge to the hose

---

4   Fuel pump – removal and installation

Refer to illustrations 4.5, 4.6 and 4.7

Warning: *Gasoline is extremely flammable, so take extra precautions when you work on any part of the fuel system. Don't smoke or allow open flames or bare light bulbs near the work area. Also, don't work in a garage where a natural gas-type appliance with a pilot light is present. Finally, when you perform any kind of work on the fuel tank, wear safety glasses and have a Class B type fire extinguisher on hand. If you spill any fuel on your skin, clean it off immediately with soap and water.*

1   Relieve the system fuel pressure (see Section 2).
2   Remove the fuel tank filler cap to relieve pressure in the tank.
3   Lift up the mat in the cargo space.
4   Remove the carpeting that covers the left rear corner of the cargo space and the left shock tower.
5   Locate the fuel pump connector on the back side of the left shock tower (**see illustration**), pop it loose from the tower with a screwdriver and disconnect it.
6   Remove the fuel pump cover screws (**see illustration**), push the grommet through the cover and slide the cover off the floor and over the fuel pump lead.
7   Label, then detach the fuel feed and return hoses (**see illustration**).
8   Remove the fuel pump mounting screws.
9   Lift the fuel pump from the fuel tank.
10   Installation is the reverse of removal. If the gasket between the fuel pump and fuel tank is dried, cracked or damaged, replace it.

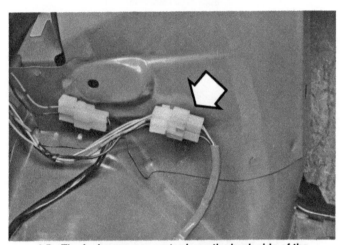

4.5   The fuel pump connector is on the back side of the left shock tower – trace the lead from the fuel pump to be sure you have the right one

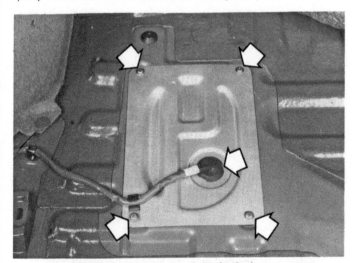

4.6   Remove the four screws from the fuel pump cover and push the grommet through its hole in the cover (arrows); slide the cover over the lead

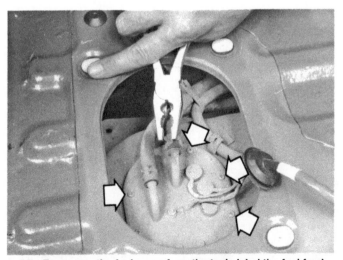

4.7   To remove the fuel pump from the tank, label the fuel feed and return hoses, compress the hose clamps with pliers, slide them back, detach the hoses from the pipes, then remove the fuel pump mounting screws (arrows) (only four of the eight mounting screws are visible in this photo); lift out the pump carefully

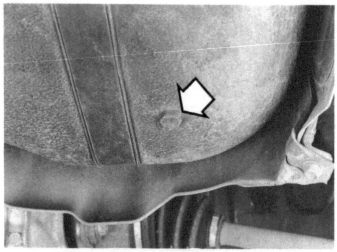

5.4   Before you remove the tank, remove the fuel tank drain plug (arrow) and drain the residual fuel into an approved container

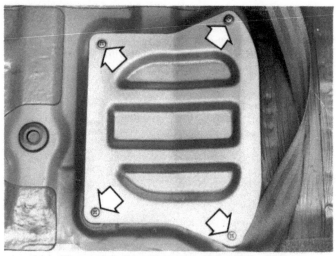

5.6a   To get at the fuel filler neck and breather hose, lift up the carpet in the cargo space, remove the screws (arrows) and remove the access cover . . .

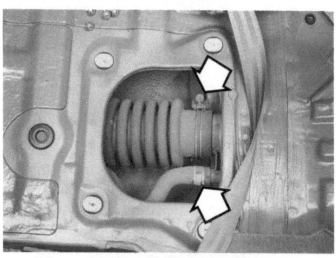

5.6b   . . . then detach the filler neck and breather hose clamps (arrows) and slide both hoses off their pipes

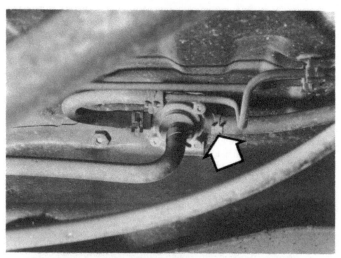

5.8   From underneath the vehicle, locate the evaporative system check valve at the right front corner of the fuel tank and detach the vapor hose (arrow)

5.10a   To remove the heat shield from the front of the fuel tank, remove the two lower bolts (lower left bolt shown) . . .

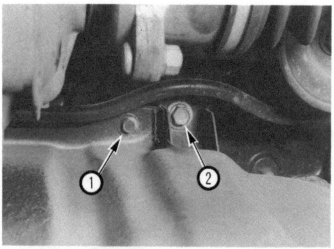

5.10b   . . . and the two upper bolts (1) (upper left bolt shown) – remove both tank strap bolts (2) to detach the tank from the vehicle (left bolt shown)

5   Fuel tank – removal and installation

Refer to illustrations 5.4, 5.6a, 5.6b, 5.8, 5.10a and 5.10b

Warning: *Gasoline is extremely flammable, so take extra precautions when you work on any part of the fuel system. Don't smoke or allow open flames or bare light bulbs near the work area. Also, don't work in a garage where a natural gas-type appliance with a pilot light is present. Finally, when you perform any kind of work on the fuel tank, wear safety glasses and have a Class B type fire extinguisher on hand. If you spill any fuel on your skin, clean it off immediately with soap and water.*

Note: *To avoid draining large amounts of fuel, make sure the fuel tank is nearly empty before beginning this procedure.*

1   Remove the fuel tank filler cap to relieve fuel tank pressure.
2   Relieve the system fuel pressure (see Section 2).
3   Detach the cable from the negative battery terminal.
4   Remove the drain plug **(see illustration)** and drain the fuel into an approved container.
5   Unplug the fuel pump electrical connector and detach the fuel feed and return hoses (see Section 4).
6   Remove the access panel and detach the fuel filler neck and breather hose **(see illustrations)**.
7   Raise the vehicle and place it securely on jackstands.
8   From underneath the vehicle, detach the vapor hose from the evaporative system check valve **(see illustration)**.
9   Support the tank with a floor jack or jackstands. Position a block of wood between the jack head and the fuel tank to protect the tank.
10 Remove the heat shield from the front of the fuel tank **(see illustrations)**.
11 Unbolt both fuel tank retaining straps **(see illustration 5.10b)** and pivot them down until they're hanging out of the way.
12 Lower the tank just enough so you can see the top and make sure you have detached everything. Finish lowering the tank and remove it from the vehicle.
13 Installation is the reverse of removal.

6   Fuel tank cleaning and repair – general information

1   All repairs to the fuel tank or filler neck should be carried out by a professional who has experience in this critical and potentially dangerous work. Even after cleaning and flushing of the fuel system, explosive fumes can remain and ignite during repair of the tank.
2   If the fuel tank is removed from the vehicle, it should not be placed in an area where sparks or open flames could ignite the fumes coming out of the tank. Be especially careful inside garages where a natural gas–type appliance is located, because the pilot light could cause an explosion.

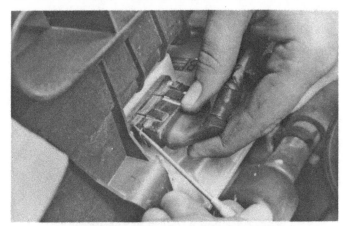

7.5   The connector for the air flow meter, which is located on the side of the air cleaner housing, isn't visible until you remove the air intake duct

7   Air cleaner – removal and installation

Refer to illustrations 7.2 and 7.5

1   Detach the cable from the negative battery terminal.
2   Detach the air intake duct from the air cleaner **(see illustration)**.
3   Detach the hose to the air pump.
4   Detach the duct between the air cleaner and the throttle body.
5   Unplug the air flow meter electrical connector **(see illustration)**.
6   Remove the three air cleaner mounting bolts **(see illustration 7.2)** and lift the air cleaner assembly from the engine compartment.

8   Air flow meter – removal, installation and check

Removal and installation
1986 through 1988 models
Refer to illustration 8.2

1   Remove the air cleaner assembly (see Section 7).
2   Remove the four bolts and detach the air flow meter from the bottom of air cleaner housing **(see illustration)**.
3   Installation is the reverse of removal.

7.2   Air cleaner attachment details

1 Air intake duct	3 Duct between the air cleaner
2 Air pump hose	and throttle body
	4 Mounting bolts

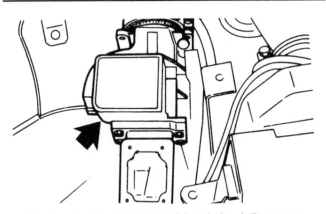

8.2   Remove the four bolts and detach the air flow meter (arrow) from the bottom of the air cleaner housing

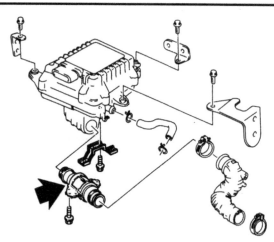

8.5   Attachment details for the 1989 and later model air flow meter (arrow)

1989 and later models

Refer to illustration 8.5

4   Remove the air cleaner assembly (see Section 7).
5   Unbolt the air flow meter from the air cleaner housing **(see illustration)**.
6   Installation is the reverse of removal.

Check

7   Checking the air flow meter requires special equipment. Take the meter to a dealer service department.

---

9   Bypass Air Control (BAC) system (1986 through 1988 models)

Check
BAC system

Refer to illustration 9.2

1   Warm up the engine and run it at idle speed.
2   Have an assistant watch the vehicle's tachometer while you unplug the BAC valve electrical connector **(see illustration)**.

9.2   The BAC valve is located on the side of the dynamic chamber – to check the BAC system, unplug the electrical connector and see if the engine speed decreases – to remove the BAC valve, detach the air hose on top, the two coolant hoses (one has already been detached in this photo) and the two mounting nuts (lower nut not visible)

3   Verify the engine speed decreases when the electrical connector is unplugged.
4   If the engine speed does not decrease, check the individual components of the system, as discussed below.

BAC valve

Refer to illustration 9.6

5   Unplug the BAC valve electrical connector **(see illustration 9.2)**.
6   Check the valve resistance with an ohmmeter **(see illustration)**. It should be about 10.7 to 12.3 ohms. If it isn't, replace the BAC valve (see Step 37 below).
7   Connect a jumper lead from the positive battery terminal to one of the BAC valve terminals. Connect a jumper lead from the other BAC valve terminal to ground.
8   The valve should click when the jumper leads are attached. If it doesn't, replace the valve (see Step 37 below).

Air bypass solenoid valve
Voltage signal check

Refer to illustrations 9.10 and 9.11

9   Locate the air bypass solenoid valve on the dynamic chamber, underneath the BAC valve (refer to the illustrations in Section 1).
10   Buy a 2 k–ohm resistor at an electronics store. Separate the male and female sides of the solenoid valve connector and use the resistor to bridge the terminals of the of the female side **(see illustration)**.
11   Insert a voltmeter probe into the backside of the female terminal with the brown/yellow wire and connect the other voltmeter probe to ground **(see illustration)**.
12   Start the engine and verify there is no voltage for 17 seconds and 12 volts after 17 seconds.
13   If the voltage signal is incorrect, there is a problem in either the control unit or the wiring between the control unit and the solenoid valve. Check the wiring first (refer to the wiring diagrams at the end of this manual). If the wiring is okay, take the vehicle to a dealer service department for further testing. Troubleshooting the control unit requires special equipment.

Resistance check

Refer to illustration 9.15

14   Unplug the solenoid valve connector **(see illustration 9.10)**.
15   Using an ohmmeter, verify the solenoid valve resistance is between 9.2 and 11.3 ohms (16.2 to 19.8 ohms on turbocharged models) **(see illustration)**.
16   If the resistance is not as specified, replace the solenoid valve.

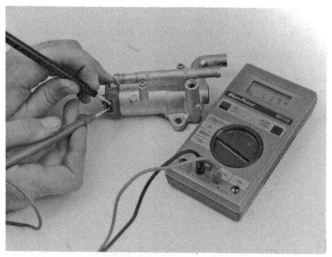

9.6   To check the BAC valve, measure the resistance between the connector terminals with an ohmmeter (valve removed for clarity

Air bypass relay (non-turbo models only)

Refer to illustration 9.18

17   Locate the air bypass relay in the front of the engine compartment and remove it. The illustrations in Section 1 may help you locate the relay.

18   Using jumper wires, connect terminal A to the battery positive terminal. Ground terminal B. Using an ohmmeter, verify there is continuity at terminals C and D **(see illustration)**.

19   Disconnect the battery from the relay and verify there is no continuity between terminals C and D.

20   If the continuity is not as specified, replace the relay.

Power steering switch

Refer to illustration 9.21

21   Locate the power steering switch in the front of the engine compartment **(see illustration)**

22   Start the engine and allow it to idle.

23   Unplug the power steering switch connector and connect an ohmmeter **(see illustration 9.21)**.

24   Turn the steering wheel to the left, then to the right. There should be continuity when the wheel is turned to the left or right, but no continuity when it's pointed straight ahead.

25   If the indicated continuity is not as specified, replace the switch.

9.10   Attach a 2 k-ohm resistor (available at any electronics store) to the terminals of the female side of the connector

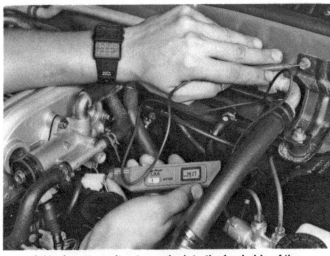

9.11   Insert a voltmeter probe into the backside of the terminal with the brown/yellow wire; connect the other probe to ground

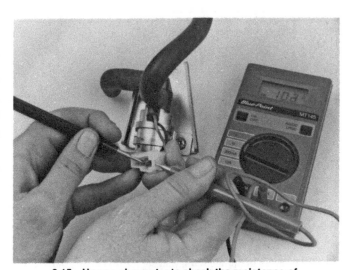

9.15   Use an ohmmeter to check the resistance of the solenoid valve

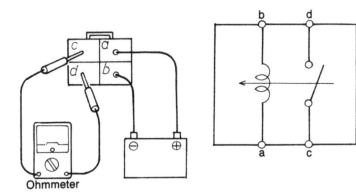

9.18   Attach a jumper wire between the positive battery terminal and terminal A of the relay, ground terminal B and, with an ohmmeter, verify there is continuity between terminals C and D

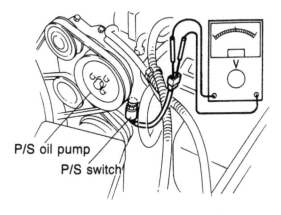

9.21   Locate the power steering switch and hook up an ohmmeter to its electrical connector

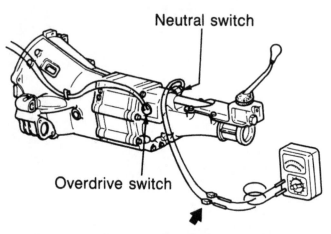

9.27   From underneath the vehicle, locate the neutral switch lead, unplug the connector and check the continuity of the terminals with an ohmmeter – in Neutral, there should be continuity; in all other gears, there should be no continuity

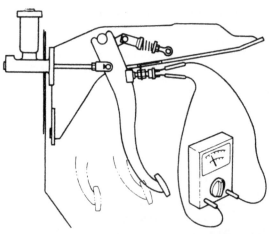

9.30   The clutch switch is located near the top of the clutch pedal – unplug its electrical connector and hook up an ohmmeter

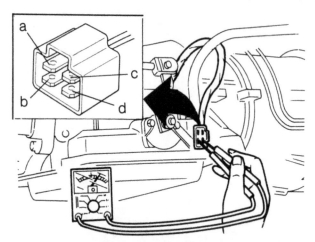

9.34   From underneath the vehicle, locate the inhibitor switch, unplug its electrical connector, then hook up an ohmmeter to terminals C and D

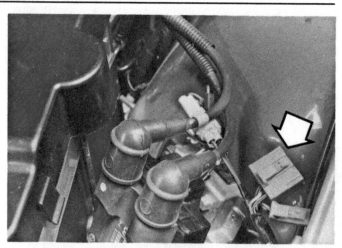

10.2   The check connector (arrow) is located near the leading coil – ground the number one pin (the one with the green wire connected to it)

Neutral switch (manual transmission only)

Refer to illustration 9.27

26   Raise the vehicle and place it securely on jackstands.
27   From underneath the vehicle, locate the neutral switch, unplug its connector(s) and connect an ohmmeter **(see illustration)**.
28   Check the continuity of the switch in all gear positions. In Neutral, there should be continuity; in all other gears, there should be no continuity.
29   If there is continuity in any gear other than Neutral, replace the switch.

Clutch switch (manual transmission only)

Refer to illustration 9.30

30   From inside the vehicle, locate the clutch switch at the clutch pedal. Unplug the clutch switch connector and attach an ohmmeter **(see illustration)**.
31   Depress the clutch pedal; the ohmmeter should show continuity. Release the pedal; there should be no continuity.
32   If the continuity is not as specified, replace the switch.

Inhibitor switch (automatic transmission only)

Refer to illustration 9.34

33   Raise the vehicle and support it securely on jackstands.
34   From underneath the vehicle, locate the inhibitor switch on the transmission. Unplug its connector and connect an ohmmeter to terminals C and D **(see illustration)**.

35   Check for continuity in each gear selector position. In Park and Neutral, there should be continuity; in all other positions, there should be no continuity.
36   If the continuity is not as specified, replace the switch.

BAC valve replacement

37   Drain the engine coolant (see Chapter 1).
38   Detach the air and coolant hoses from the valve **(see illustration 9.2)**.
39   Remove the BAC valve mounting nuts **(see illustration 9.2)** and detach the valve.
40   Remove all traces of old gasket material from the mating surfaces.
41   Installation is the reverse of removal. Be sure to use a new gasket.

---

10   Idle speed control system (1989 models only)

System check

Refer to illustrations 10.2 and 10.3

1   Warm up the engine and run it at idle speed.
2   Ground the number 1 (green wire) pin of the test connector **(see illustration)**.

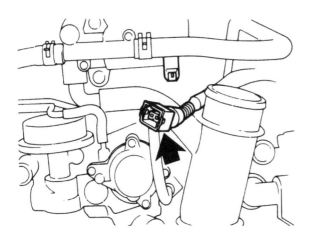

10.3   Unplug the solenoid valve electrical connector (arrow)

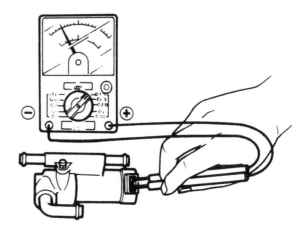

10.8   Hook up an ohmmeter as shown to check the
resistance of the BAC solenoid valve

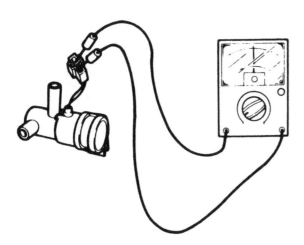

10.11   Hook up an ohmmeter as shown to check the resistance of
the AWS solenoid valve

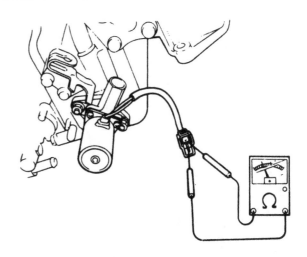

10.14   To check the air supply solenoid valve on a turbo model,
unplug the electrical connector and measure the resistance with
an ohmmeter

3   Have an assistant observe the vehicle's tachometer while you unplug
the solenoid valve connector **(see illustration)**.
4   Verify that the engine speed decreases when the connector is unplugged.
5   Reattach the solenoid valve connector.
6   If the system does not perform as described, check the following components.

Bypass air control (BAC) solenoid valve

Refer to illustration 10.8

7   Unplug the solenoid valve connector **(see illustration 10.3)**.
8   Measure the resistance of the solenoid with an ohmmeter **(see illustration)**. It should be about 10.7 to 12.3 ohms.
9   Connect a jumper wire between the positive battery terminal and one
of the solenoid valve terminals. Ground the other solenoid valve terminal.
You should hear a click from the solenoid valve.
10   If the valve fails either test, replace it.

Accelerated warm-up system (AWS) solenoid valve

Refer to illustration 10.11

11   Unplug the connector from the solenoid valve and measure its resistance with an ohmmeter **(see illustration)**. It should be 9.3 to 11.3 ohms.
12   Connect a jumper wire between the positive battery terminal and one
of the solenoid valve terminals. Ground the other terminal. You should
hear a click from the solenoid valve.
13   If the valve fails either test, replace it.

Air supply valve (ASV) solenoid valve (turbocharged models only)

Refer to illustration 10.14

14   Unplug the electrical connector from the air supply valve and hook up
an ohmmeter **(see illustration)**.
15   Measure resistance. It should be about 16.5 to 23.5 ohms.
16   Connect a jumper wire between the positive battery terminal and one
of the solenoid valve terminals. Ground the other terminal. You should
hear a click from the solenoid valve.
17   If the valve fails either test, replace it.

11   Throttle cable – check, adjustment and replacement

Check

Refer to illustration 11.1

1   Separate the air intake duct from the throttle body **(see illustration)**.

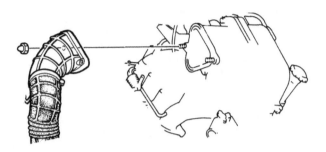

11.1   The air intake duct is attached to the throttle body by two nuts

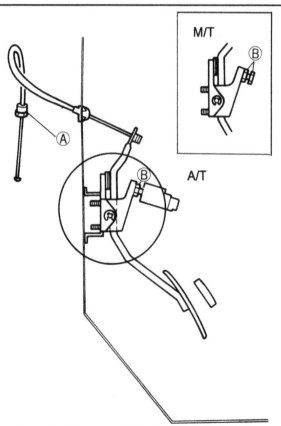

11.5   To adjust the throttle cable freeplay, loosen the locknut and turn the adjuster nut (A) (located at the rear of the throttle body) – if the throttle valves aren't fully open when you fully depress the accelerator pedal, loosen locknut (B), adjust the throttle valve opening with stop bolt (B), then tighten locknut (B)

2   Have an assistant depress the accelerator pedal to the floor while you watch the throttle valves. They should move to their fully open (horizontal) positions.

3   Release the accelerator pedal and make sure the throttle valves return smoothly to their fully closed position.

Adjustment

Refer to illustration 11.5

4   Warm the engine to normal operating temperature and turn it off. Depress the accelerator pedal to the floor twice, then check the cable freeplay at the throttle body. Compare it to the value listed in this Chapter's specifications.

5   If the freeplay isn't within specifications, adjust it with nut A **(see illustration)**.

6   Have an assistant help you verify the throttle valves are fully open when the accelerator pedal is depressed to the floor. If they're not, adjust the opening with stop bolt B **(see illustration 11.5)**.

Replacement

Note: *You'll need a flashlight for the under-dash portion of the following procedure*

7   Detach the cable from the negative battery terminal.

8   Loosen the cable adjuster locknuts and detach the cable from its support bracket located behind the throttle body.

9   Rotate the throttle linkage to put some slack in the throttle cable and detach the cable from the linkage.

10   Working from underneath the driver's side of the dash, reach up and detach the throttle cable from the top of the accelerator pedal. The cable end is sheathed in a small plastic bushing that pops out of the grooved upper end of the pedal.

11   With a flashlight, trace the path of the cable up to the firewall. You will see the cable disappear through a small plastic grommet with locking tabs on the top and bottom. Depress these tabs and push the grommet through the firewall.

12   Pull the cable through the firewall, from the engine compartment side.

13   Installation is the reverse of removal.

12   Throttle body – check and component replacement

Throttle valve clearance check and adjustment

Refer to illustrations 12.2 and 12.3

1   Detach the air intake duct from the throttle body **(see illustration 11.1)** and move the duct out of the way.

2   Have an assistant depress the accelerator while you watch the throttle valves. When the number one secondary throttle valve just starts to open, measure the clearance between the primary throttle valve and the throttle body bore with the shank of an appropriately sized drill **(see illustration)**. Compare your measurement with the figure listed in this Chapter's specifications.

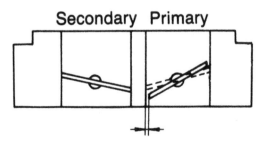

12.2   When the number one secondary throttle valve starts to open, check the clearance between the primary throttle valve and the wall of the throttle bore

3   If the clearance is not within specification, bend the tab **(see illustration)** until the proper clearance is obtained.

Fast idle check and adjustment

Refer to illustrations 12.5, 12.6, 12.8 and 12.9

Note: *Unless it has been tampered with, fast idle adjustment is unnecessary. The engine temperature should be about 77-degrees F for this procedure.*

4   Start the engine.

5   Verify the matching mark on the fast idle cam is aligned with the center of the cam roller **(see illustration)**.

6   If the matching mark and the center of the cam roller aren't aligned, turn the cam adjusting screw **(see illustration)** until they're correctly aligned.

7   With the matching mark aligned, check the clearance between the primary throttle valve and the throttle bore **(see illustration 12.2)**. Compare your measurement to the fast idle clearance listed in this Chapter's specifications.

8   To adjust the clearance, turn the fast idle adjusting screw **(see illustration)**.

9   Once the engine has warmed up to normal operating temperature, verify the rod extends fully and the idle cam separates from the roller **(see illustration)**.

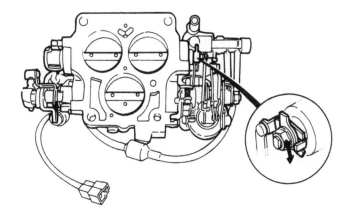

12.3   If the clearance between the primary throttle valve and the wall of the throttle bore is incorrect, bend the tab (inset) as shown

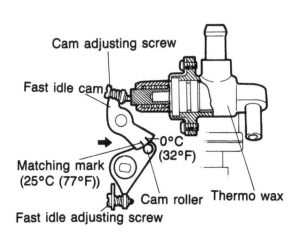

12.5   With the engine temperature about 77°F, verify the matching mark on the fast idle cam is aligned with the center of the cam roller

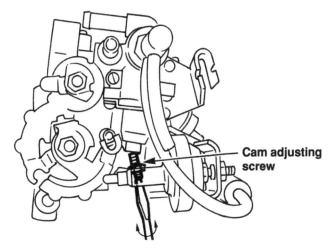

12.6   If the matching mark and the center of the cam roller aren't aligned, turn the cam adjusting screw until they are

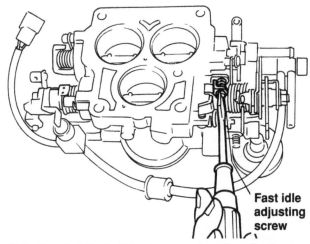

12.8   To adjust the fast idle clearance, turn the adjusting screw

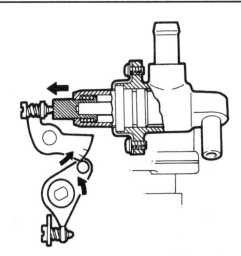

12.9   Once the engine has warmed up, verify the rod extends as far as it will go and the idle cam separates from the roller

12.10   After unplugging the hoses, unscrew the water thermo valve (arrow)

Water thermo valve check and replacement

Refer to illustrations 12.10, 12.12a and 12.12b

10   Unplug the vacuum hoses and remove the water thermo valve from the throttle body **(see illustration)**. Place rags beneath the valve to catch any coolant that may spill.

11   Immerse the thermo valve in a Pyrex-type container of water, heat the water gradually and note the temperature.

12   Blow through port A and note whether air passes out ports B and C at the indicated temperatures **(see illustrations)**.

13   Replace the thermo valve if necessary. **Note:** *Whether you are installing the old valve or a new one, be sure to seal the threads with teflon tape to prevent coolant leaks.*

Throttle body removal and installation

Refer to illustrations 12.16 and 12.20

14   Detach the cable from the negative battery terminal.

15   If your vehicle is a non-turbo model, detach the air intake duct from the throttle body and set it aside **(see illustration 11.1).**

16   If your vehicle is turbocharged, remove the intercooler **(see illustration).**

17   Detach the accelerator cable from the throttle body (see Section 11).

18   Detach the cruise control cable, if equipped.

19   Clearly label all electrical connectors, then unplug them.

20   Detach the metering oil pump connecting rod **(see illustration).**

21   Clearly label all vacuum hoses, then detach them.

22   Clearly label the coolant hoses, then detach them.

23   Remove the throttle body mounting nuts and detach the throttle body from the dynamic chamber.

24   Cover the dynamic chamber opening with a clean cloth to prevent dust or dirt from entering while the throttle body is removed.

25   Installation is the reverse of removal. Be sure to tighten the throttle body mounting nuts to the torque listed in this Chapter's specifications and adjust the accelerator cable (see Section 11) when you're done.

---

13   Dynamic chamber/surge tank – removal and installation

Refer to illustration 13.2

1   There are three reasons to remove the dynamic chamber/surge tank. Each requires a different strategy:

  a) You're replacing the dynamic chamber or surge tank. To do this, remove the throttle body first (see Section 12), then the chamber/tank (begin at Step 2 in this section). This removal order is recommended because it's easier to break the throttle body mounting bolts loose while the chamber/tank is still bolted to the extension manifold.

  b) You're replacing the extension manifold (1986 through 1988 models), the variable dynamic effect intake (VDI) manifold (1989 models) or the inlet manifold (turbo models). In this case, remove the throttle body and chamber/tank as an assembly. To do so, follow Steps 14 through 22 in Section 12, then proceed to Step 2 in this Section.

  c) You're stripping the engine block for disassembly. In this case, remove the throttle body and dynamic chamber, along with the extension manifold or VDI manifold as a single assembly. Follow Steps 14 through 22 in Section 12 and Steps 1 through 8 (extension manifold) or 10 through 14 (VDI manifold) in Section 14.

2   Remove the two mounting bolts and three nuts from the underside of the dynamic chamber/surge tank **(see illustration)**. Detach the chamber/tank and remove its gasket.

3   Using a putty knife, scrape off all traces of old gasket material from the gasket mating surfaces.

4   Installation is the reverse of removal. Be sure to use a new gasket.

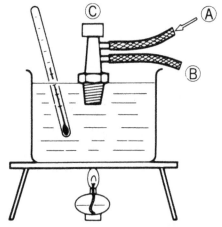

12.12a   To check the water thermo valve on a vehicle equipped with a manual transmission, blow through port A and verify air comes out port B while the temperature is below 140-degrees F – above 140-degrees F, air should come out port C

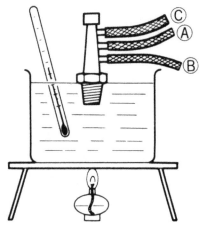

12.12b   To check the water thermo valve on a vehicle equipped with an automatic transmission, blow through port A and verify air comes out port C while the temperature is below 154-degrees F – above 154-degrees F, air should come out port B

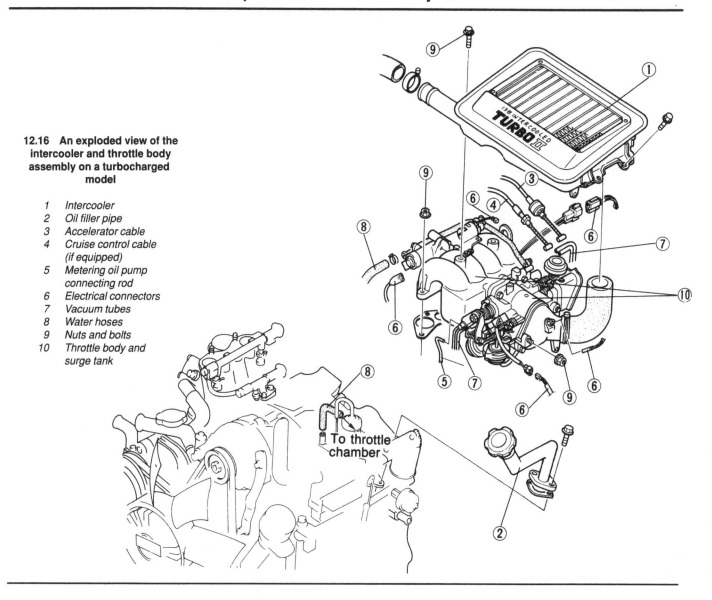

12.16   An exploded view of the intercooler and throttle body assembly on a turbocharged model

1   Intercooler
2   Oil filler pipe
3   Accelerator cable
4   Cruise control cable (if equipped)
5   Metering oil pump connecting rod
6   Electrical connectors
7   Vacuum tubes
8   Water hoses
9   Nuts and bolts
10 Throttle body and surge tank

To throttle chamber

12.20   To detach the metering oil pump connecting rod (arrow), remove the cotter pin and washer and pull the rod out of the lever

13.2   To separate the extension manifold from the dynamic chamber, remove the nuts and bolts (arrows) (assembly removed from the vehicle for clarity)

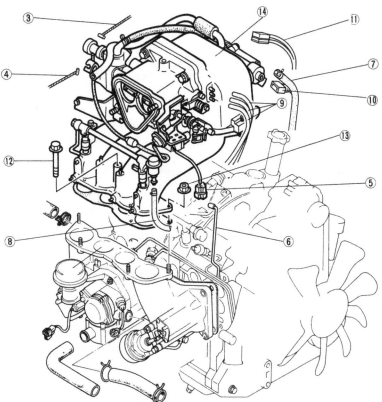

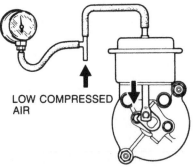

14.3   Exploded view of the throttle body, dynamic chamber and extension manifold assembly

3   Accelerator cable
4   Cruise control cable (if equipped)
5   Throttle sensor connector
6   Metering oil pump connecting rod
7   Water hoses
8   Fuel hoses
9   Vacuum hoses
10   Bypass air control valve connector
11   Connector for the intake air temperature sensor
12   Bolts
13   Nuts
14   Dynamic chamber

LOW COMPRESSED AIR

14.15   To check the VDI actuator, detach the air hose from the actuator, hook up a pressure gauge with a tee fitting and apply low pressure compressed air to the actuator

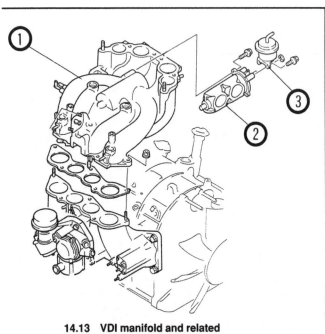

14.13   VDI manifold and related components – exploded view

1   Manifold
2   Valve
3   Actuator

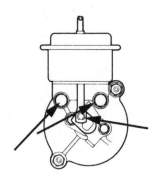

14.19   To remove the VDI actuator, remove the attaching nuts and pry off the retaining clip (arrows)

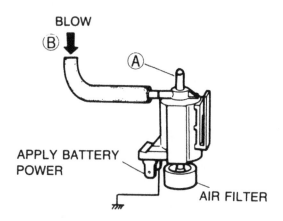

14.29 With no power applied to the solenoid terminals, air should flow out the air filter when you blow through port B – with battery power applied, air should flow out port A when you blow through port B

---

14 Extension manifold or VDI manifold – removal, installation and VDI component check (non-turbo models only)

Extension manifold (1986 through 1988 models) removal and installation

Refer to illustration 14.3

1   If you're replacing the extension manifold, first remove the throttle body and dynamic chamber as an assembly (see Section 13), then proceed to the next step. If you're stripping the engine for disassembly, remove the extension manifold with the dynamic chamber and throttle body still attached (see Steps 14 through 22 in Section 12, then proceed to the next Step).

2   Relieve the system fuel pressure (see Section 2).

3   Clearly label, then detach, all electrical connectors and vacuum hoses **(see illustration)**.

4   If you're replacing the extension manifold, remove the secondary fuel rail and injector assembly. If you're replacing the intake manifold or stripping the engine for overhaul, detach the fuel lines from the fuel rail. See Section 18 for either procedure.

5   If you're replacing the extension manifold, remove the sub-zero starting assist device (non-California models only) (see Chapter 1).

6   Remove the extension manifold mounting nuts **(see illustration 14.3)**.

7   Remove the extension manifold and gasket. Use a gasket scraper or putty knife to remove off all traces of old gasket material from the gasket mating surfaces. Be careful not to scratch the soft aluminum surfaces.

8   Installation is the reverse of removal. Be sure to use a new gasket and tighten the mounting nuts securely.

Variable dynamic effect intake (VDI) manifold (1989 and later models)
Description

9   On 1989 models, a variable dynamic effect intake (VDI) manifold is used in place of an extension manifold. This manifold and its associated VDI system components force additional air into each combustion chamber by generating pressure waves in the intake tracts. The following Steps tell how to remove and install the manifold and how to check and replace the components of the VDI system.

Removal and installation

Refer to illustration 14.13

10   If you're replacing the VDI manifold, first remove the throttle body and dynamic chamber as an assembly (see Section 13), then proceed to the next Step. If you're stripping the engine for disassembly, remove the VDI

manifold with the dynamic chamber and throttle body still attached (see Steps 14 through 22 in Section 12, then proceed to the next Step).

11   Clearly label, then detach all vacuum hoses, electrical connectors and brackets.

12   If you're replacing the VDI manifold, remove the secondary fuel rail and injector assembly. If you're replacing the intake manifold or stripping the engine for overhaul, detach the fuel lines from the fuel rail. See Section 18 for either procedure.

13   Remove the mounting nuts **(see illustration)** and lift off the VDI manifold. Using a gasket scraper or putty knife, remove all traces of old gasket material. Be careful not to scratch the soft aluminum surfaces.

14   Installation is the reverse of removal. Be sure to use a new gasket and tighten the mounting nuts securely.

Component check and replacement
Actuator

Refer to illustrations 14.15 and 14.19

15   Detach the air hose from the actuator and, using a tee (three-way) fitting, hook up a pressure gauge and apply low-pressure compressed air **(see illustration)**.

16   Check the operation of the actuator. At 2.8 psi, the actuator should be fully open. If it's not, move the actuator rod by hand to make sure there is no mechanical bind.

17   If there's no mechanical bind and the actuator doesn't operate properly, proceed to the next step and replace it.

18   Remove the VDI manifold (see above).

19   Remove the actuator attaching nuts and pry off the retaining clip **(see illustration)**.

20   Pull off the actuator and gasket.

21   Installation is the reverse of removal. Be sure to use a new gasket and tighten the attaching nuts securely.

VDI valve

22   Remove the throttle body (see Section 12) and dynamic chamber (see Section 13).

23   Remove the VDI manifold (see Step 10).

24   Remove the actuator (see Step 18).

25   Remove the VDI valve **(see illustration 14.13)**.

26   Check the valve for cracks, damage or binding. Replace the valve if any of these conditions are found.

27   Installation is the reverse of removal.

VDI solenoid valve

Refer to illustration 14.29

28   Locate the VDI solenoid valve at the front left corner of the engine **(see illustration 1.1i)**.

29   Detach the vacuum hoses from the solenoid valve and blow through the solenoid valve from port B. Air should pass through the valve and flow from the air filter **(see illustration)**.

30   Detach the electrical connector from the solenoid valve and attach a jumper lead between the battery positive terminal and one of the solenoid's terminals. Ground the other solenoid terminal. Blow through the solenoid valve from port B. Air should pass through the valve and flow out port A.

---

15 Auxiliary port valve system – description, inspection and component replacement

General description

Refer to illustration 15.2

1   To permit optimum performance at all engine speeds, the 13B rotary engine uses an auxiliary port valve system. This system controls airflow through two auxiliary intake ports (one for each rotor chamber).

2   The auxiliary port is opened and closed by a rotating cylindrical valve operated by an actuator, which in turn is activated by the air pump, via a solenoid valve. At lower engine speeds, the auxiliary valves are closed, maintaining high gas velocities in the intake system and thereby maximizing engine performance. As the engine speed increases, rising pressure in the line between the air pump and the air control valve opens a solenoid

valve which in turn activates a pair of actuators. These actuators retract their linkage rods and rotate their respective auxiliary port valves into an open position, allowing the additional air necessary for maximum engine performance at higher speeds **(see illustration)**.

Solenoid valve check and replacement

Refer to illustration 15.4

3   Locate the solenoid valve **(see illustration 1.1i).**
4   Detach the vacuum hose and blow through port B of the solenoid valve **(see illustration)**. Verify air passes through the valve and out the air filter.
5   Detach the solenoid valve electrical connector.
6   Apply battery voltage to the solenoid valve terminals, blow through the solenoid valve from port B and verify air passes through the valve and out port A.
7   If the solenoid valve fails either test, replace it.

Actuator check and replacement

Refer to illustrations 15.8, 15.12 and 15.14

8   Detach the air hose from the actuator and, using a Tee (three–way) fitting, hook up a pressure gauge **(see illustration)**.
9   Apply low pressure compressed air to the actuator and check its operation, noting the pressure at which it begins to open and the pressure at which it's fully open (its linkage rod will be fully retracted). Compare your findings with this Chapter's specifications

10   If the actuator doesn't operate properly or the pressures are not as specified, replace the actuator.
11   Remove the extension manifold or VDI manifold (see Section 14).
12   Remove the actuator attaching nuts and pry off the retaining clip **(see illustration)**.
13   Slide the lever off the shaft and remove the actuator.
14   Installation is the reverse of removal. Be sure to rotate the lever and verify it moves smoothly before you install the new actuator **(see illustration)**.

Auxiliary port valve replacement

Refer to illustrations 15.21 and 15.23

15   Remove the throttle body, dynamic chamber and extension manifold or VDI manifold. See Sections 12, 13 and 14 for the proper procedure.
16   Detach the oil nozzles from the manifold (see Chapter 2A).
17   Clearly label all vacuum and air hoses, then detach them.
18   Clearly label all electrical connectors, then unplug them.
19   Remove the actuators (see above).
20   Remove the intake manifold (see Chapter 2A).
21   Remove the auxiliary port valve(s) **(see illustration)**.
22   Inspect the valve(s) for cracks or damage. Be sure to replace either valve if it's damaged or worn.
23   Installation is the reverse of removal. Make sure the thick part of the valve shafts align with the matching mark on the gasket as shown **(see illustration)**.

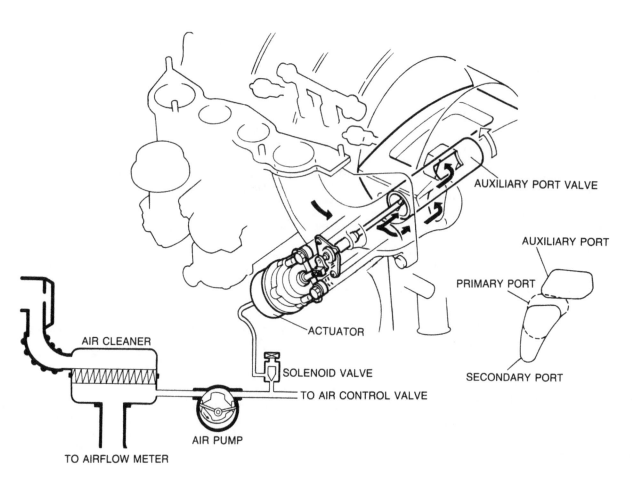

15.2   Cutaway of the auxiliary port valve system

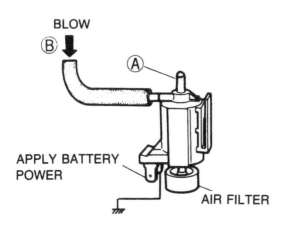

15.4   When no power is applied to the terminals, air should flow
out the air filter when you blow through port B – when you blow
through port B with battery power applied, air should pass
through the valve and out port A

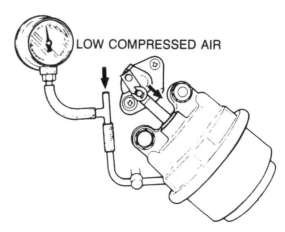

15.8   To check a port valve actuator, detach the air
hose, hook up a pressure gauge with a tee fitting and
apply low pressure compressed air

15.12   To remove a port valve actuator, unscrew the
mounting nuts and pry off the retaining clip (arrows),
then slide the lever off the shaft

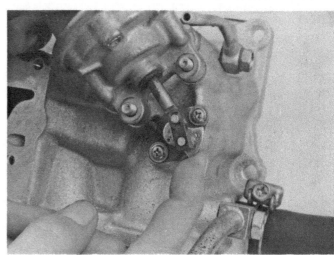

15.14   After you have installed a port valve actuator,
rotate the lever and make sure it moves smoothly

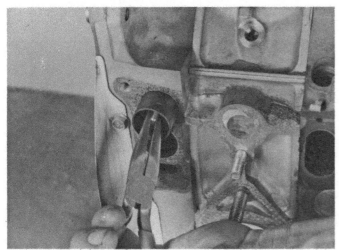

15.21   You may be able to remove the port valve(s) by
hand – if not, use a pair of needle-nose pliers – be
careful not to damage the shaft!

15.23   When you install the port valve(s), be sure to align the
thick part of the valve shaft with the notch on
the gasket (arrow)

16   Fuel pressure regulator – check and replacement

Refer to illustrations 16.3 and 16.4
Warning: *Gasoline is extremely flammable, so take extra precautions when you work on any part of the fuel system. Don't smoke or allow open flames or bare light bulbs near the work area. Also, don't work in a garage where a natural gas-type appliance with a pilot light is present. Finally, when you perform any kind of work on the fuel tank, wear safety glasses and have a Class B type fire extinguisher on hand. If you spill any fuel on your skin, clean it off immediately with soap and water.*

Check

1   Relieve the fuel system pressure (see Section 2).
2   Detach the cable from the negative battery terminal.
3   Detach the fuel hose from the fuel rail **(see illustration)**.
4   Using a Tee (three-way) joint, attach a pressure gauge between the fuel hose and fuel rail **(see illustration)**.
5   Reattach the cable to the negative battery terminal.
6   Start the engine and allow it to idle.
7   Detach the vacuum hose from the pressure regulator **(see illustration 16.3)**, note the fuel pressure on the gauge and compare your reading with the value listed in this Chapter's specifications.
8   Reattach the vacuum hose, note the new reading on the gauge and compare it with the value listed in this Chapter's specifications.

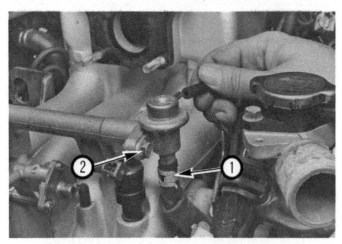

16.3   Using pliers, compress and slide down the hose clamp (1), then separate the fuel hose from the fuel rail – to detach the vacuum hose from the pressure regulator, pull it off as show – when removing the pressure regulator, unscrew the mounting bolts (2)

16.4   To check the fuel pressure regulator, detach the fuel hose and, using a tee fitting, hook up a fuel pressure gauge

9   If the pressure is not within specification for either of the above tests, replace the regulator.

Replacement

10   Relieve the system fuel pressure (see Section 2).
11   Detach the cable from the negative battery terminal.
12   Detach the vacuum hose and fuel hose from the pressure regulator, then unscrew the mounting bolts **(see illustration 16.3)**.
13   Remove the pressure regulator.
14   Installation is the reverse of removal. Be sure to use a new gasket.
15   Check for fuel leaks after installing the pressure regulator.

17   Pulsation damper – check and replacement

Refer to illustration 17.2
Warning: *Gasoline is extremely flammable, so take extra precautions when you work on any part of the fuel system. Don't smoke or allow open flames or bare light bulbs near the work area. Also, don't work in a garage where a natural gas-type appliance with a pilot light is present. Finally, when you perform any kind of work on the fuel tank, wear safety glasses and have a Class B type fire extinguisher on hand. If you spill any fuel on your skin, clean it off immediately with soap and water.*

1   Start the engine and run it at idle speed.
2   Locate the pulsation damper on the front end of the primary fuel rail. It's hard to see because it's buried beneath the extension manifold **(see illustration)**. Place your finger on the pulsation damper. It should pulsate.
3   If the pulsation damper is not functioning properly, relieve the system fuel pressure, remove the air cleaner, the throttle body and the dynamic chamber/surge tank. Also remove the extension manifold/VDI manifold or, if the vehicle is a turbo, the intake manifold. See Sections 2, 7, 12, 13, 14 and Chapter 2A for the proper procedures.
4   Using a backup wrench, remove the pulsation damper **(see illustration 17.2).**
5   Installation is the reverse of removal.

18   Fuel injectors – check and replacement

Warning: *Gasoline is extremely flammable, so take extra precautions when you work on any part of the fuel system. Don't smoke or allow open flames or bare light bulbs near the work area. Also, don't work in a garage where a natural gas-type appliance with a pilot light is present. Finally, when you perform any kind of work on the fuel tank, wear safety glasses and have a Class B type fire extinguisher on hand. If you spill any fuel on your skin, clean it off immediately with soap and water.*

17.2   The pulsation damper is located on the front end of the primary fuel rail (arrow) – when removing it, be sure to use a backup wrench

In-vehicle check

Refer to illustrations 18.1, 18.2 and 18.5

1   Using a mechanic's stethoscope (available at many auto parts stores), check for a clicking sound at each of the primary injectors while the engine is idling and while an assistant depresses the accelerator slightly **(see illustration)**.

2   To check the secondary injectors, detach the vacuum hose from the boost sensor **(see illustration)**.

3   Start the engine and have an assistant increase the engine speed above 3500 RPM.

4   Using a stethescope, check for a clicking sound from each of the secondary injectors.

5   If you can't hear the injectors operating:
   a) Check the resistance of the crank angle sensor (see Chapter 5).
   b) Check the wire from the crank angle sensor to the control unit for continuity **(see illustration)**.
   c) Check the resistance of the solenoid resistor (see Section 19).
   d) Check the EGI main fuse (see Section 20).
   e) Check the EGI main relay (see Section 21).

Resistance check

Refer to illustrations 18.6a and 18.6b

6   Unplug each injector connector and check the resistance of the injector **(see illustrations)**. Compare your measurement with the resis-

tance listed in this Chapter's Specifications. Replace the injector if the resistance is not within this range.

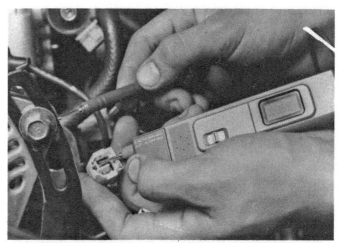

18.1   Use a stethoscope to listen for a clicking sound at the injectors – you can also use a long screwdriver if you don't have a stethoscope

18.2   Detach the vacuum hose (arrow) from the boost sensor

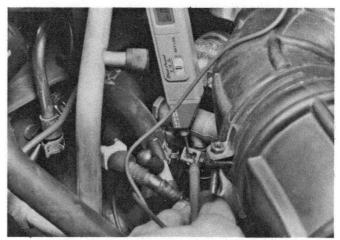

18.5   Unplug the wiring leading from the crank angle sensor, then check for continuity by attaching one ohmmeter probe to the terminal shown and grounding the other probe

18.6a   To unplug the injector connector, pry the lock spring away from the connector with a small screwdriver or a scribe, then pull the connector off

18.6b   Attach an ohmmeter as shown to check the injector resistance

Volume test

7   Because a special injection checker is required to test injector volume, this procedure is beyond the scope of the home mechanic. Have the injector volume test performed by a dealer service department or other repair shop.

Replacement

Refer to illustrations 18.11a, 18.11b, 18.13 and 18.14

8   If you are replacing the secondary injectors, remove the throttle body and the dynamic chamber/surge tank (see Sections 12 and 13). If you are replacing the primary injectors, remove the extension manifold/VDI manifold or, if the vehicle is a turbo, the intake manifold (see Section 14 or Chapter 2).

9   If you are replacing the secondary injectors, detach the vacuum hose from the fuel pressure regulator **(see illustration 16.3).**

10   Unplug the injector connectors **(see illustration 18.6a).**

11   Detach the fuel hoses from the fuel rail and remove the fuel rail mounting bolts **(see illustrations)**.

12   Detach the fuel rail/injector assembly from the engine.

13   Detach the injectors from the fuel rail **(see illustration)**.

14   Installation is the reverse of removal. Be sure to replace all O-rings with new ones **(see illustration)**. Coat them with a little fuel to prevent damage to the O-rings during installation. Before you install the dynamic chamber and intake duct, start the engine and check for fuel leaks.

19   Solenoid resistor – check and replacement

Refer to illustrations 19.1 and 19.2

1   Locate the solenoid resistor. It's at the right front corner of the engine compartment on most models **(see illustration)**. If the resistor is not at this location on your vehicle, check the illustrations in Section 1.

2   Unplug the electrical connector and check the resistance between the indicated terminals with an ohmmeter **(see illustration)**. It should be about 5 to 7 ohms.

3   Replace the solenoid resistor if necessary.

20   EGI main fuse – check and replacement

Refer to illustration 20.1

1   The EGI main fuse is located in a fuse panel adjacent to the left shock tower. Remove the cover and check it to see if it's blown **(see illustration)**.

2   Replace the fuse if necessary.

3   If the fuse is OK, but the fuel pump does not operate, check the EGI main relay (see Section 21).

18.11a   To remove the primary fuel rail, detach both fuel hoses and remove the mounting bolts (arrows)

18.11b   To remove the secondary fuel rail, detach both fuel hoses and remove the mounting bolts (arrows)

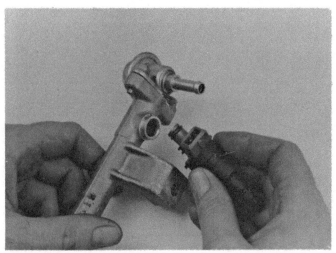

18.13   To remove an injector from the fuel rail, pull on it while simultaneously twisting it from side to side

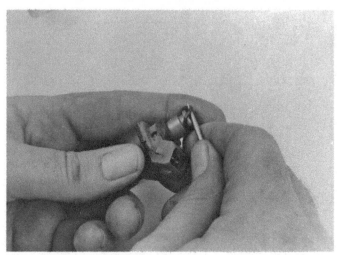

18.14   Be sure to replace the O-rings at each end of each injector whether the O-rings are leaking or not – be sure to coat the new O-rings with a little fuel before installing them

21   EGI main relay – check and replacement

Refer to illustrations 21.1 and 21.3

1   Locate the EGI main relay at the left rear corner of the engine compartment **(see illustration)**.

2   While turning the ignition switch on and off, listen for a clicking sound at the relay.

3   Apply battery voltage to the two-pin connector **(see illustration)**. Check for continuity at the indicated terminals with a test light, circuit tester or ohmmeter.

4   Replace the main relay if it fails either of the above checks.

22   Boost/pressure sensor – check and replacement

Refer to illustration 22.2

1   Locate the boost/pressure sensor at the front right corner of the engine compartment, just behind the air cleaner assembly (see the component location illustrations in Section 1).

19.1   The solenoid resistor is located in the engine compartment – it's usually on the right shock tower

19.2   To check the solenoid resistor, hook up an ohmmeter to these two terminals (arrows)

20.1   The EGI main fuse (arrow) is located in this fuse panel in the engine compartment – visually inspect the fuse to see if it's blown

21.1   The main relay is located at the left rear corner of the engine compartment

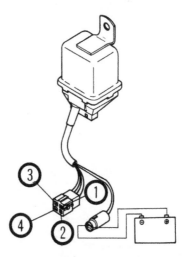

21.3   Apply battery voltage to the main relay connector and verify there is continuity between terminals 1 and 2 and terminals 3 and 4, then disconnect the battery and verify there is no continuity between terminals 1 and 2 and terminals 3 and 4

2   Detach the vacuum hose from the boost/pressure sensor, attach a hand vacuum pump in its place, then hook up a voltmeter to terminal D of the sensor's electrical connector **(see illustration)**.
3   Apply 3.9 in Hg of vacuum to terminal D of the boost/pressure sensor with the vacuum pump.
4   Turn on the ignition switch and check the voltmeter reading. With 3.9 in Hg of vacuum applied, it should indicate 3.5 to 4.5 volts.
5   Replace the boost/pressure sensor if the voltage is not correct or it does not hold vacuum.

23   Atmospheric pressure sensor – check and replacement

Refer to illustration 23.2

1   Locate the atmospheric pressure sensor at the right rear corner of the engine compartment (see the illustrations in Section 1).
2   Connect a voltmeter to terminal D of the atmospheric pressure sensor **(see illustration)**.
3   Turn the ignition switch to On and read the voltage. At sea level, the meter should read about 3.5 to 4.5 volts; at high altitude (6500 feet), it should read about 2.5 to 3.5 volts.
4   Replace the sensor if the voltage reading is not as specified.

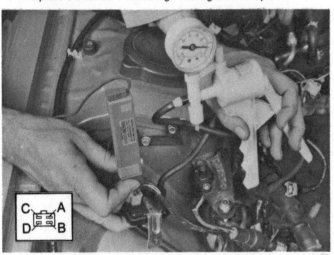

22.2   To check the boost/pressure sensor, detach the vacuum hose from the sensor, attach a vacuum pump/gauge in its place and hook up a voltmeter to terminal D; apply 3.9 in Hg of vacuum, turn on the ignition switch and check the voltmeter reading

24   Hot start assist system (1986 through 1988 models)

Refer to illustration 24.3

1   Locate the intake air temperature sensor on the dynamic chamber, just below the BAC valve or on the air intake between the intercooler and the throttle body **(see illustration 1.1c or 1.1f)**.
2   Warm the engine to its normal operating temperature.
3   Unplug the electrical connector from the sensor and connect a 2 to 3 k-ohm resistor (3.5 k-ohms on turbos) to the female side of the connector **(see illustration)**.
4   Start the engine and allow it to idle. Using the vehicle's tachometer, verify engine speed is about 800 rpm for the first 90 seconds after starting (about 850 rpm for turbos) and about 750 rpm after 90 seconds
5   Remove the resistor and reconnect the temperature sensor.

25   Turbocharger and control system – check and component replacement

General description

Refer to illustrations 25.1a and 25.1b

1   A turbocharger **(see illustrations)** harnesses the energy of escaping exhaust gases to create more engine power. The turbocharger itself is simply a pair of rotors on opposite ends of a common shaft. One rotor is in the exhaust stream and the other is in the intake air stream. The rotor in the exhaust stream is rotated by the force of escaping exhaust gasses. Since it is on the same shaft, the rotor in the intake stream also rotates and compresses the intake air, creating greater engine efficiency and producing more horsepower.

Control system check

Refer to illustrations 25.2 and 25.3

2   Warm the engine to its normal operating temperature. Turn off the engine and have an assistant restart it while you watch the control rod on the exhaust manifold **(see illustration)**. It should move when the engine starts. **Note:** *If the vehicle is equipped with ABS brakes, you may need to move an air hose out of the way to view the rod.*
3   Stop the engine, detach the green electrical connector from the turbocharger solenoid valve **(see illustration)** and verify the control rod returns to its original position.
4   Reattach the connector to the solenoid valve.
5   Have an assistant accelerate the engine. Verify the control rod starts to move when engine speed is above 2700 rpm.

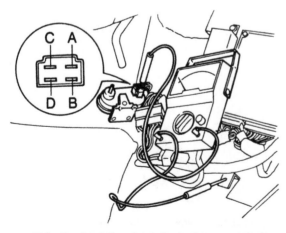

23.2   To check the atmospheric pressure sensor, connect a voltmeter to terminal D, then turn the ignition switch to On

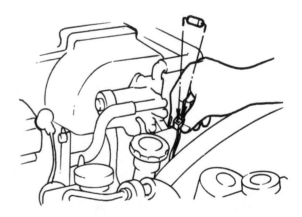

24.3   Unplug the connector from the intake air temperature sensor and attach a 2 to 3 k-ohm resistor to the female side of the connector

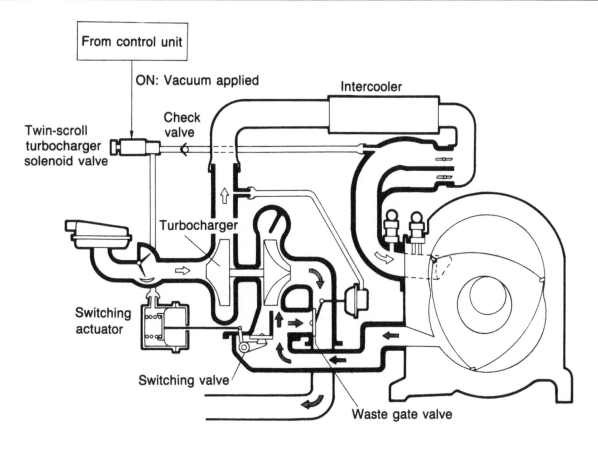

25.1a   Schematic of a typical turbocharger system

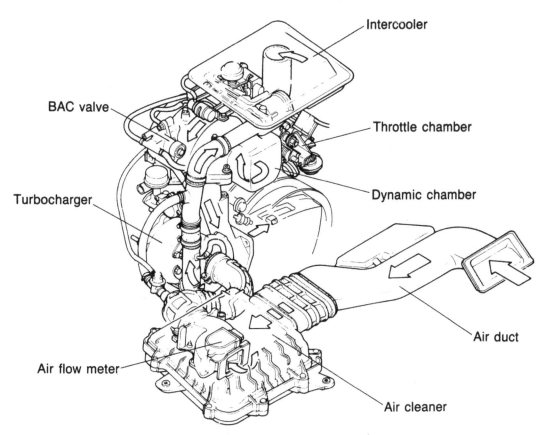

25.1b   Turbocharger system component locations

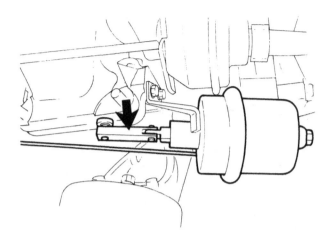

25.2   The control rod (arrow) should move when the engine starts

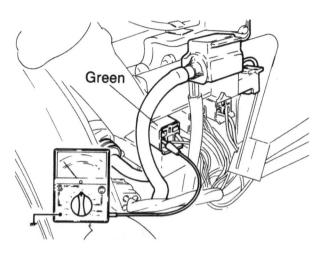

25.3   When checking the turbocharger control system, detach the green electrical connector – when checking the solenoid valve, attach a voltmeter to the LB terminal, as shown

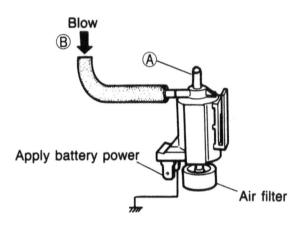

25.10   When no power is applied to the solenoid valve's electrical terminals, you should be able to blow through port B and air should flow out the air filter – when battery power is applied to the terminals, air should flow out port A when you blow through port B

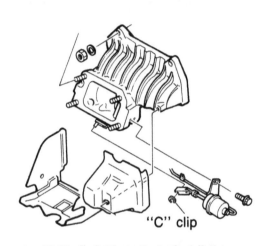

25.15   Switching actuator installation details – exploded view

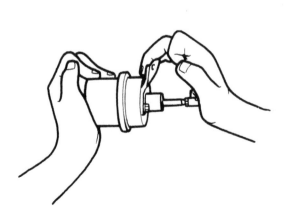

25.18   To check the switching actuator, push in on the rod – it should move smoothly

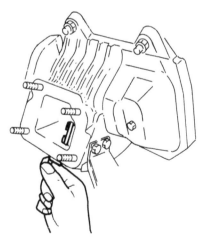

25.23   To check the switching valve, rotate it – it should move smoothly

Turbocharger solenoid valve check

Refer to illustration 25.10

6   Warm up the engine to its normal operating temperature.

7   Attach a voltmeter to the LB terminal of the solenoid valve **(see illustration 25.3).**

8   Increase the engine speed and check the voltmeter reading. Below 2700 rpm, it should be 2.0 volts; above 2700 rpm, it should be 12 volts.

9   Detach the vacuum hoses from the solenoid valve.

10   Blow through the solenoid valve at port B **(see illustration)** and verify air passes through the solenoid valve and flows from the air filter.

11   Detach the electrical connector from the solenoid valve and jumper the positive battery terminal to one of the solenoid's terminals. Ground the other terminal.

12   Blow through the solenoid at port B and verify air passes through the solenoid valve and flows from port A.

13   Replace the solenoid valve if it fails any of the above tests.

Switching actuator check

Refer to illustrations 25.15 and 25.18

14   Raise the vehicle and place it securely on jackstands.

15   Remove the actuator rod C-clip **(see illustration).**

16   Remove the actuator vacuum tube and mounting bolt(s).

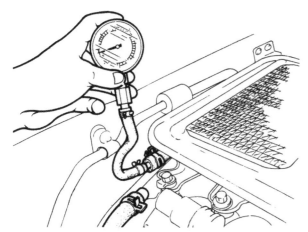

25.24   To check the boost pressure, detach the bypass air hose at the intercooler and attach a pressure gauge in its place

17   Remove the actuator.

18   Verify the rod moves smoothly when you push it **(see illustration).**

19   When the rod is pushed in all the way, put a finger over the vacuum port and verify air doesn't leak and the rod doesn't move until you remove your finger.

20   Replace the actuator if it fails the above checks.

21   Installation is the reverse of removal.

Switching valve check

Refer to illustration 25.23

22   Remove the C-clip and detach the switching actuator rod from the switching valve **(see illustration 25.15).**

23   Verify the switching valve moves smoothly **(see illustration).**

Boost pressure check

Refer to illustration 25.24

24   Detach the bypass valve air hose at the intercooler and attach a pressure gauge in its place **(see illustration).**

25   Warm up the engine to its normal operating temperature.

26   Have an assistant accelerate the engine and watch the tachometer while you watch the pressure gauge. Verify boost pressure begins at about 4000 rpm and attains 0.7 psi by 5000 rpm. If it doesn't, check the turbine rotor/compressor wheel and waste gate valve (see below).

Turbine rotor/compressor wheel check

Refer to illustration 25.29

27   Do not operate the vehicle for several hours to allow the engine to cool completely.

28   Remove the air intake duct from the turbocharger.

29   Verify the turbine rotor turns smoothly **(see illustration).** If it is noisy or drags when you turn it, replace the turbocharger.

30   Make sure the rotor does not touch its housing. If it does, replace the turbocharger.

Waste gate valve check

Refer to illustration 25.32

31   Do not operate the vehicle for several hours to allow the engine to cool completely.

32   Detach the air hose and hook up a pressure gauge/pump **(see illustration).**

33   Mark the rod on the waste gate valve with white paint.

34   Apply air pressure (not more than 14 psi) and verify the rod moves.

35   If the rod does not move, replace the valve.

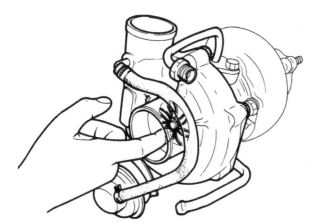

25.29   The turbine rotor should turn smoothly – if it makes a lot of noise or drags when you turn it, replace the turbocharger

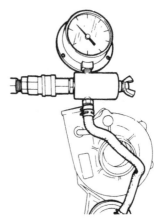

25.32   To check the waste gate valve, detach the air hose, attach a pressure gauge/pump, mark the valve rod with white paint and apply air pressure (no more than 14 psi) – the rod should move

Turbocharger replacement

Refer to illustration 25.37

36   Detach the cable from the negative battery terminal.
37   Detach the air hoses from the turbocharger **(see illustration)**.
38   Remove the air injection pump (see Chapter 6).
39   Detach the air funnel and air hose.
40   Remove the air control valve.

41   Detach the split air pipe.
42   Detach the water hose and water pipe. Position a drain pan under the hose and pipe to catch any coolant that may spill.
43   Detach the oil pipes.
44   Remove the bolts and nuts, then pull the insulator covers off the turbocharger.
45   Remove the front catalytic converter (see Section 26).

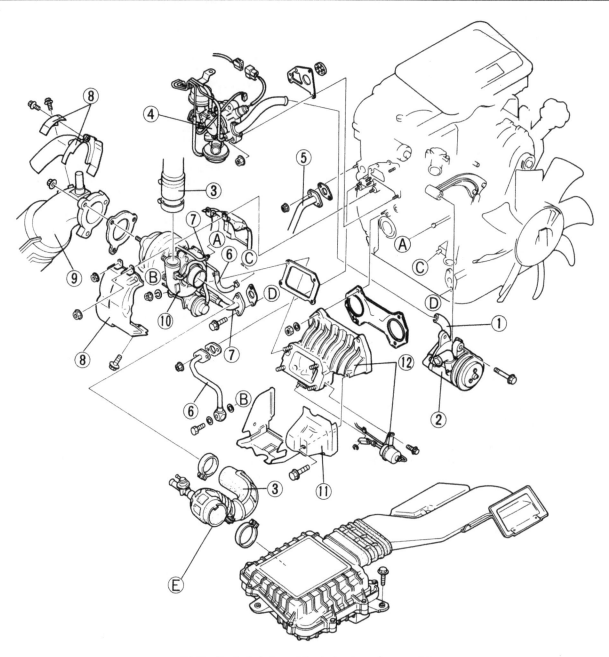

25.37   Exploded view of the turbocharger assembly

1	Air hoses	7	Oil pipes
2	Air pump	8	Insulator covers
3	Air funnel and air hose	9	Front catalytic converter
4	Air control valve	10	Turbocharger
5	Split air pipe	11	Insulator covers
6	Water hose and water pipe	12	Exhaust manifold and actuator

46 Lift off the turbocharger assembly.

47 Remove the insulator covers from the exhaust manifold.

48 Installation is the reverse of removal. Be sure to tighten the turbocharger and front converter fasteners to the torque listed in this Chapter's specifications. Tighten the exhaust manifold fasteners to the torque listed in Chapter 2A.

---

26 Exhaust system servicing – general information

Warning: *Inspect or repair exhaust system components only after enough time has elapsed after driving the vehicle to allow the system*

components to cool completely. Also, when working under the vehicle make sure it is securely supported by jackstands.

Muffler and pipes

Refer to illustrations 26.1a and 26.1b

1 The exhaust system **(see illustrations)** consists of the exhaust manifold, two or three catalytic converters, mufflers and all connecting pipes, brackets, hangers and clamps. The exhaust system is attached to the body with mounting brackets and rubber hangers. If any of the parts are improperly installed, excessive noise and vibration may be transmistted to the body.

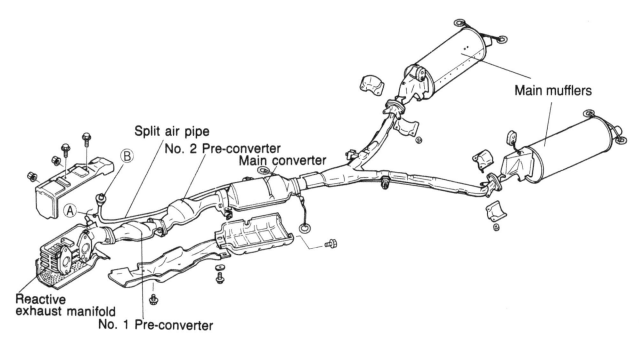

26.1a Exploded view of a typical non-turbo exhaust system

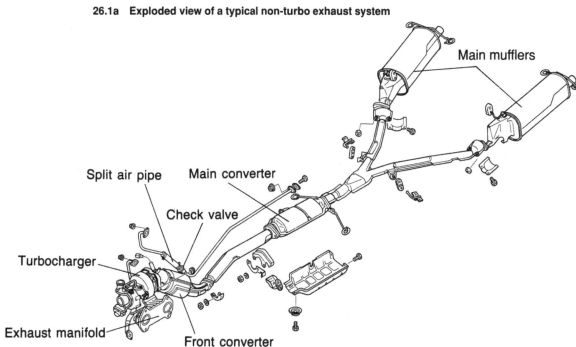

26.1b Exploded view of a typical turbo exhaust system

2   Inspect the exhaust system regularly to keep it safe and quiet. Look for any damaged or bent parts, open seams, holes, loose connections, excessive corrosion or other defects which could allow exhaust fumes to enter the vehicle. Deteriorated exhaust system components should not be repaired; they should be replaced with new parts.

3   If the exhaust system components are extremely corroded or rusted together, welding equipment will probably be required to remove them. The convenient way to accomplish this is to have a muffler repair shop remove the corroded sections with a cutting torch. If, however, you want to save money by doing it yourself (and you don't have a welding outfit with a cutting torch), cut off the old components with a hacksaw. If you have compressed air, a special pneumatic cutting chisel can also be used. If you decide to tackle the job at home, be sure to wear safety goggles to protect your eyes from metal chips and use work gloves to protect your hands.

4   Here are some simple guidelines to follow when repairing the exhaust system:

  a) Work from the back to the front of the vehicle when removing exhaust system components.
  b) Apply penetrating oil to the exhaust system fasteners to make them easier to remove.
  c) Use new gaskets, hangers and clamps when installing exhaust system components.
  d) Apply anti-seize compound to the threads of all exhaust system fasteners during reassembly.
  e) Be sure to allow sufficient clearance between newly installed parts and all points on the under body to avoid overheating the floor pan and possibly damaging the interior carpet and insulation. Pay particularly close attention to the catalytic converters and heat shields.

Catalytic converters

5   Although the catalytic converters are emissions-related components, they are discussed here because, physically, they're integral parts of the exhaust system. Always check the converters whenever you raise the vehicle to inspect or service the exhaust system.

6   Raise the vehicle and place it securely on jackstands.

7   Visually inspect all catalytic converters on the vehicle for cracks or damage.

8   Check all converters for tightness.

9   Check the insulation covers welded onto the catalytic converters for damage or a loose fit.

10   Start the engine and and run it at idle speed. Check all converter connections for exhaust gas leakage.

Chapter 5 Engine electrical systems

Contents

Alternator brushes – check and replacement 14
Alternator – removal and installation 12
Battery cables – check and replacement 4
Battery check and maintenance . . . . See Chapter 1
Battery – emergency jump starting 2
Battery – removal and installation 3
Charging system – check 11
Charging system – general information and precautions 10
Coil/igniter assembly – check and replacement 7
Crank angle sensor – check, removal and installation 8
Drivebelt check, adjustment and replacement . . . . See Chapter 1

General information 1
Ignition system – check 6
Ignition system – general information 5
Ignition timing – check and adjustment 9
Spark plug replacement . . . . See Chapter 1
Spark plug wire check and replacement . . . . See Chapter 1
Starter motor – in-vehicle check 16
Starter motor – removal and installation 17
Starter solenoid – removal and installation 18
Starting system – general information and precautions 15
Voltage regulator/rectifier – replacement 13

Specifications

General
Coil resistance . . . . 0.2 to 1 ohm
Crank angle sensor resistance
    Between terminals G1 and G2 . . . . 110 to 210 ohms
    Between terminals Ne1 and Ne2 . . . . 110 to 210 ohms

Torque specifications
Crank angle sensor locknuts . . . . 69.6 to 96 in-lbs

1 General information

The engine electrical systems include all ignition, charging and starting components. Because of their engine-related functions, these components are discussed separately from chassis electrical devices such as the lights, the instruments, etc. (which are included in Chapter 12).

Always observe the following precautions when working on the electrical systems:

a) Be extremely careful when servicing engine electrical components. They are easily damaged if checked, connected or handled improperly.

b) Never leave the ignition switch on for long periods of time with the engine off.

c) Don't disconnect the battery cables while the engine is running.

d) Maintain correct polarity when connecting a battery cable from another vehicle during jump starting.

e) Always disconnect the negative cable first and hook it up last or the battery may be shorted by the tool being used to loosen the cable clamps.

It's also a good idea to review the safety-related information regarding the engine electrical systems located in the *Safety First* section near the front of this manual before beginning any operation included in this Chapter.

2   Battery – emergency jump starting

Refer to the *Booster battery (jump) starting* procedure at the front of this manual.

3   Battery – removal and installation

Refer to illustration 3.2

1   Remove the battery cover by prying loose the snaps on the side.
2   **Caution:** *Always disconnect the negative cable first and hook it up last or the battery may be shorted by the tool being used to loosen the cable clamps.* Disconnect both cables from the battery terminals **(see illustration).**

3.2   Always detach the cable from the negative battery terminal first, then detach the positive cable – to remove the hold down strap, simply remove both nuts (arrows)

3   Remove the battery hold down strap.
4   Lift out the battery. Be careful – it's heavy.
5   While the battery is out, inspect the carrier (tray) for corrosion (see Chapter 1).
6   If you are replacing the battery, make sure that you get one that's identical, with the same dimensions, amperage rating, cold cranking rating, etc.
7   Installation is the reverse of removal.

4   Battery cables – check and replacement

1   Periodically inspect the entire length of each battery cable for damage, cracked or burned insulation and corrosion. Poor battery cable connections can cause starting problems and decreased engine performance.
2   Check the cable-to-terminal connections at the ends of the cables for cracks, loose wire strands and corrosion. The presence of white, fluffy deposits under the insulation at the cable terminal connection is a sign that the cable is corroded and should be replaced. Check the terminals for distortion, missing mounting bolts and corrosion.
3   When removing the cables, b\always disconnect the negative cable first and hook it up last\m or the battery may be shorted by the tool used to

loosen the cable clamps. Even if only the positive cable is being replaced, be sure to disconnect the negative cable from the battery first (see Chapter 1 for further information regarding battery cable removal).
4   Disconnect the old cables from the battery, then trace each of them to their opposite ends and detach them from the starter solenoid and ground terminals. Note the routing of each cable to ensure correct installation.
5   If you are replacing either or both of the old cables, take them with you when buying new cables. It is vitally important that you replace the cables with identical parts. Cables have characteristics that make them easy to identify: positive cables are usually red, larger in cross-section and have a larger diameter battery post clamp; ground cables are usually black, smaller in cross–section and have a slightly smaller diameter clamp for the negative post.
6   Clean the threads of the solenoid or ground connection with a wire brush to remove rust and corrosion. Apply a light coat of battery terminal corrosion inhibitor, or petroleum jelly, to the threads to prevent future corrosion.
7   Attach the cable to the solenoid or ground connection and tighten the mounting nut/bolt securely.
8   Before connecting a new cable to the battery, make sure that it reaches the battery post without having to be stretched.
9   Connect the positive cable first, followed by the negative cable.

5   Ignition system – general information

The ignition system includes the ignition switch, the battery, the crank angle sensor, the leading and trailing side coil/igniters, the primary (low voltage) and secondary (high voltage) wiring circuits, the spark plugs and the spark plug wires.
When working on the ignition system, take the following precautions:
a)   If the engine won't start, don't keep the ignition switch on for more than 10 seconds.
b)   Never allow an ignition coil terminal to contact ground. Grounding the ignition coil can damage the igniter and/or the coil itself.
c)   Don't disconnect the battery when the engine is running.
d)   Make sure the igniter is properly grounded.

6   Ignition system – check

1   Attach an inductive timing light to each plug wire, one at a time, and crank the engine.
a)   If the light flashes, voltage is reaching the plug.
b)   If the light does not flash, proceed to the next step.
2   Inspect the spark plug wire(s), and spark plug(s) (see Chapter 1).
3   If the engine still won't start, check the coil/igniter assemblies (see Section 7).

7   Coil/igniter assembly – check and replacement

Note: *Before performing the following test on either coil, make sure the battery is fully charged (see Section 11).*

Leading coil
Check
Refer to illustrations 7.2, 7.3 and 7.4
Note: *The leading coil/igniter assembly is actually two coils (one for each rotor) attached to a single igniter. The failure of either coil means both coils must be replaced.*

1   Detach the cable from the negative battery terminal.
2   Detach the high tension leads from the coil. Note that the leads are marked (white dot on high tension terminal No. 1 and white band on leading high tension lead No. 1) to insure proper reassembly **(see illustration).** If the leads on your vehicle are not marked, be sure that you mark them to prevent incorrect reassembly.

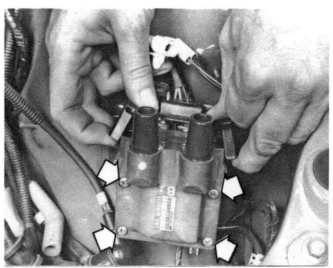

7.2   The coil high tension leads should already be marked – if they aren't, be sure to do so before you detach them to prevent switching them during reassembly

7.3   To remove the plastic cover from the primary terminals of the coil, spread the sides like this and lift up (if you need to replace the leading coil, remove the four phillips screws indicated by the arrows)

3   Remove the plastic cover from the primary terminals of the coil **(see illustration)**.
4   Using an ohmmeter, measure the resistance between the primary terminals of the coil **(see illustration)** and compare your measurement to the value listed in this Chapter's Specifications.
5   If the indicated resistance is not as specified, replace the leading coil.

Replacement
6   Label the primary leads, detach them from their respective terminals, remove the four phillips screws from the leading coil assembly **(see illustration 7.3)** and detach it from the igniter.
7   Installation is the reverse of removal. *When you reattach the high tension leads, be sure that you don't reverse them.*

Trailing coil
Check
Refer to illustration 7.11
Note: *the trailing coil assembly is actually two separate coils (one per*

rotor) attached to a common base housing the igniter. Either coil can therefore be replaced separately.
8   Detach the cable from the negative battery terminal.
9   Remove the plastic cover from the primary terminals of each coil **(see illustration 7.3)**.
10   Detach the high tension leads. The leads should be marked (a white dot on the No. 1 high tension terminal and a white band on the No. 1 high tension lead). If they're not marked on your vehicle, be sure that you mark them to insure proper reassembly.
11   Using an ohmmeter, measure the resistance between the primary terminals **(see illustration)** and compare your measurement with the value listed in this Chapter's Specifications.
12   Repeat this procedure for the other trailing coil.
13   If the indicated resistance of either unit is not within specification, replace it.

Replacement
Refer to illustrations 7.15a, 7.15b and 7.15c
14   Label the primary leads and detach them from their respective terminals.

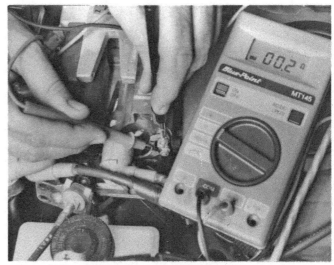

7.4   Using an ohmmeter, measure the resistance between the primary terminals of the leading coil

7.11   Using an ohmmeter, measure the resistance between the primary terminals of the trailing coil – it should have the same resistance value as the leading coil

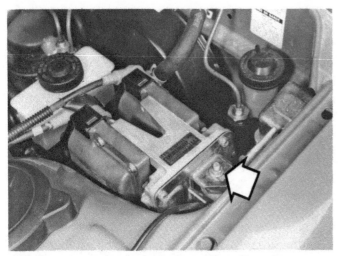

7.15a   To replace a defective trailing coil, you'll need to remove the trailing coil/igniter assembly from the engine compartment to get at the coil mounting screws – remove this mounting bracket nut (arrow), . . .

15   Unscrew the mounting bracket nut **(see illustrations)**, remove the assembly from the engine compartment and remove the four mounting screws from the defective coil(s) **(see illustration)**. Detach the coil(s) from the igniter base.

16   Installation is the reverse of removal. *Make sure that you don't reverse the high tension leads.*

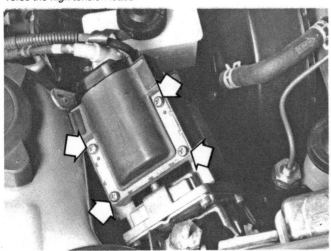

7.15c   Remove the four phillips screws (arrows) from the bad coil to separate it from the igniter assembly

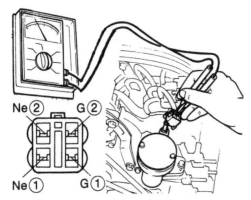

8.2   To check the crank angle sensor, measure the resistance between terminals G1 and G2 and between terminals Ne1 and Ne2

7.15b   . . . then remove these two mounting bracket nuts (arrows) and lift the assembly from the engine compartment

Igniter

17   Testing the igniter assemblies requires special equipment and is therefore beyond the scope of the home mechanic. Take the vehicle to a dealer service department or other qualified repair shop to have the igniters checked.

8   Crank angle sensor – check, removal and installation

Check

Refer to illustration 8.2

1   Unplug the electrical connector from the crank angle sensor.

2   Using an ohmmeter, check the resistance between terminals G1 and G2 and between terminals Ne1 and Ne2 **(see illustration)**. Compare your readings with the values listed in this Chapter's Specifications.

3   If the resistance is not as specified, replace the crank angle sensor.

Removal

Refer to illustrations 8.4 and 8.6

4   Rotate the eccentric shaft pulley clockwise until the leading (yellow) mark on the edge of the pulley is aligned with the pointer on the front cover **(see illustration)**.

8.4   Rotate the eccentric shaft pulley clockwise until the leading (yellow) mark on the edge of the pulley is aligned with the pointer on the front cover

8.6   Mark the base of the crank angle sensor and the front cover with paint or a scribe to assure proper alignment during reassembly

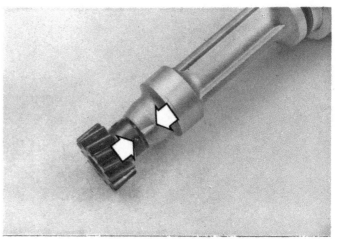

8.9   Align the matching marks on the sensor housing and driven gear before installing the sensor

5   Unplug the electrical connector from the sensor if you haven't already done so.
6   Mark the base of the sensor housing and the front cover to assure proper alignment during reassembly **(see illustration)**.
7   Remove the crank angle sensor locknut.
8   Lift the crank angle sensor straight up to remove it.

Installation

Refer to illustration 8.9

9   Align the matching marks on the sensor housing and driven gear **(see illustration)**.
10   Verify the leading (yellow) mark on the eccentric shaft pulley is still set to the pointer.
11   Lower the crank angle sensor into the front cover, making sure the marks on the housing base and the front cover are in alignment. Loosely install the locknut and plug in the electrical connector.
12   Check the ignition timing (see Section 9).
13   Tighten the locknut securely.

---

9   Ignition timing – check and adjustment

Note: *Self-powered timing lights may not function properly if used to check ignition timing on this vehicle. Use a vehicle-powered timing light for the following procedure*

Initial

1   Warm the engine up to its normal operating temperature.
2   Make sure all accessories are turned off.
3   Hook up a tachometer in accordance with the manufacturer's instructions.
4   Check and, if necessary, adjust the idle speed (see Chapter 1).
5   Hook up a timing light to the leading (L-1) high tension lead.
6   With the engine idling, verify that the leading (yellow) mark on the pulley is aligned with the pointer **(see illustration 8.4)**.
7   If they aren't aligned, loosen the crank angle sensor locknut and rotate the sensor until the marks are aligned.
8   Detach the timing light from the L-1 high tension lead and hook it up to the trailing (T-1) high tension lead.
9   Repeat the above procedure to check the trailing side, but note that the pointer should now be in alignment with the trailing (red) mark on the pulley.

Advance

10   Hook up a timing light to the L-1 high tension lead.

11   Increase the engine speed and verify that the ignition timing advances (the timing marks should move counterclockwise from the pointer). **Note:** *During deceleration, the ignition timing will drop to a certain point, momentarily level off, then return to normal.*

---

10   Charging system – general information and precautions

The charging system includes the alternator, an internal voltage regulator, a charge indicator, the battery, a fusible link and the wiring between all the components. The charging system supplies electrical power for the ignition system, the lights, the radio, etc. The alternator is driven by a drivebelt at the front of the engine.

The purpose of the voltage regulator is to limit the alternator's voltage to a preset value. This prevents power surges, circuit overloads, etc., during peak voltage output.

The fusible link is a short length of insulated wire integral with the engine compartment wiring harness. The link is four wire gauges smaller in diameter than the circuit it protects. Production fusible links and their identification flags are identified by the flag color. See Chapter 12 for additional information regarding fusible links.

The charging system doesn't ordinarily require periodic maintenance. However, the drivebelt, battery and wires and connections should be inspected at the intervals outlined in Chapter 1.

The dashboard warning light should come on when the ignition key is turned to Start, then go off immediately. If it remains on, there is a malfunction in the charging system (see Section 11). Some vehicles are also equipped with a voltmeter. If the voltmeter indicates abnormally high or low voltage, check the charging system (see Section 11).

Be very careful when making electrical circuit connections to a vehicle equipped with an alternator and note the following:

a)   When reconnecting wires to the alternator from the battery, be sure to note the polarity.
b)   Before using arc welding equipment to repair any part of the vehicle, disconnect the wires from the alternator and the battery terminals.
c)   Never start the engine with a battery charger connected.
d)   Always disconnect both battery leads before using a battery charger.
e)   The alternator is turned by an engine drivebelt which could cause serious injury if your hands, hair or clothes become entangled in it with the engine running.
f)   Because the alternator is connected directly to the battery, it could arc or cause a fire if overloaded or shorted out.
g)   Wrap a plastic bag over the alternator and secure it with rubber bands before steam cleaning the engine.

12.3   To remove the alternator, disconnect the electrical harness, loosen the pivot and adjustment bolts (arrows), remove the drivebelt from the pulley and remove the pivot and adjustment bolts

11   Charging system – check

1   If a malfunction occurs in the charging circuit, don't automatically assume that the alternator is causing the problem. First check the following items:

   a) Check the drivebelt tension and condition (Chapter 1). Replace it if it's worn or deteriorated.

   b) Make sure the alternator mounting and adjustment bolts are tight.

   c) Inspect the alternator wiring harness and the connectors at the alternator and voltage regulator. They must be in good condition and tight.

   d) Check the fusible link (if equipped) located between the starter solenoid and the alternator. If it's burned, determine the cause, repair the circuit and replace the link (the vehicle won't start and/or the accessories won't work if the fusible link blows). Sometimes a fusible link may look good, but still be bad. If in doubt, remove it and check for continuity.

   e) Start the engine and check the alternator for abnormal noises (a shrieking or squealing sound indicates a bad bearing).

   f) Check the specific gravity of the battery electrolyte. If it's low, charge the battery (doesn't apply to maintenance free batteries).

   g) Make sure the battery is fully charged (one bad cell in a battery can cause overcharging by the alternator).

   h) Disconnect the battery cables (negative first, then positive). Inspect the battery posts and the cable clamps for corrosion. Clean them thoroughly if necessary (see Chapter 1). Reconnect the cable to the negative terminal.

   i) With the key off, connect a test light between the negative battery post and the disconnected negative cable clamp.

     1) If the test light does not come on, reattach the clamp and proceed to Step 3.

     2) If the test light comes on, there is a short (drain) in the electrical system of the vehicle. The short must be repaired before the charging system can be checked.

     3) Disconnect the alternator wiring harness.

      a) If the light goes out, the alternator is bad.

      b) If the light stays on, pull each fuse until the light goes out (this will tell you which component is shorted).

2   Using a voltmeter, check the battery voltage with the engine off. If should be approximately 12-volts.

3   Start the engine and check the battery voltage again. It should now be approximately 14-to-15 volts.

4   Turn on the headlights. The voltage should drop, and then come back up, if the charging system is working properly.

5   If the voltage reading is more than the specified charging voltage, replace the voltage regulator (refer to Section 13). If the voltage is less, the alternator diode(s), stator or rectifier may be bad or the voltage regulator may be malfunctioning.

6   If the battery is constantly discharging, the alternator drivebelt is loose (see Chapter 1), the alternator brushes are worn, dirty or disconnected (see Section 14), the voltage regulator is malfunctioning (see Section 13) or the rectifier, stator coil or rotor coil is defective. Repairing or replacing the rectifier, stator coil or rotor coil is beyond the scope of the home mechanic. Replace the alternator.

12   Alternator – removal and installation

Refer to illustration 12.3

1   Detach the cable from the negative terminal of the battery.

2   Detach the electrical connectors from the alternator.

3   Loosen the alternator adjustment and pivot bolts **(see illustration)** and detach the drivebelt (see Chapter 1).

4   Remove the adjustment and pivot bolts and separate the alternator from the engine.

5   If you are replacing the alternator, take the old one with you when purchasing a replacement unit. Make sure the new/rebuilt unit looks identical to the old alternator. Look at the terminals – they should be the same in number, size and location as the terminals on the old alternator. Finally, look at the identification numbers – they will be stamped into the housing or printed on a tag attached to the housing. Make sure the numbers are the same on both alternators.

6   Many new/rebuilt alternators DO NOT have a pulley installed, so you may have to switch the pulley from the old unit to the new/rebuilt one. When buying an alternator, find out the shop's policy regarding pulleys – some shops will perform this service free of charge.

7   Installation is the reverse of removal.

8   After the alternator is installed, adjust the drivebelt tension (see Chapter 1).

9   Check the charging voltage to verify proper operation of the alternator (see Section 11).

13   Voltage regulator/rectifier – replacement

Refer to illustrations 13.2, 13.4, 13.6, 13.7, 13.8, 13.9 and 13.11

1   Remove the alternator (see Section 12).

2   Mark the alternator halves with paint or a scribe **(see illustration)** to ensure proper reassembly.

3   Remove the three through bolts. Don't attempt to pull the alternator apart until you have read the next step.

13.2   Mark the alternator halves with paint or a scribe to ensure that they are properly aligned when reassembled

4   The rotor bearing is pressed into the rear end frame. Place a 200 watt soldering iron on the rear end frame for three or four minutes **(see illustration)**. If you're using an iron with less output, keep it in contact a few minutes longer.

5   Pull the alternator halves apart. Pry them apart with a screwdriver if necessary, but don't use excessive force. If the two halves don't come apart fairly easily, the rotor bearing is still stuck in its bore in the end frame housing. You will damage the bearing or the end frame housing if you use excessive force. Put the soldering iron back on the end frame for a few more minutes.

6   Remove the B (battery) terminal nut and insulation bush **(see illustration)**.

7   Remove the rectifier and brush holder mounting screws **(see illustration)**.

8   Using a soldering iron, remove the solder from the rectifier and the stator lead **(see illustration)**. **Caution:** *Don't use the soldering iron for more than five seconds at a time – the rectifier may become damaged if it is overheated.*

9   Using a soldering iron, remove the solder from the lead between the voltage regulator and the rectifier **(see illustration)**.

10   Even if you are only planning to replace the regulator, check the brushes (see Section 14) while the alternator is disassembled.

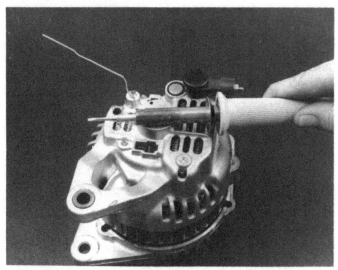

13.4   Heat the rear end frame with a 200 watt soldering iron to expand the rotor shaft bearing bore enough to pull the bearing loose

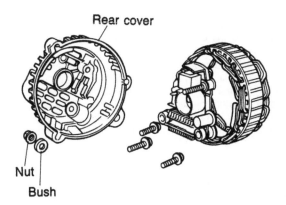

13.6   Exploded view of the rear cover (end frame), the B terminal nut and the insulation bush

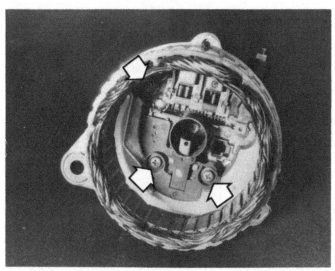

13.7   Remove the rectifier and brush holder mounting screws (arrows)

13.8   To replace the rectifier, remove the solder from the rectifier and stator leads (arrows) and from between the regulator and rectifier (shown) – if you're only replacing the regulator/brush holder assembly, it's not necessary to de-solder the rectifier leads, but you'll still have to de-solder the lead between the two components

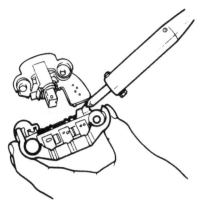

13.9   You may find it easier to remove the entire regulator/brush holder assembly, then de-solder the lead between the rectifier and the regulator/brush holder assembly to separate them

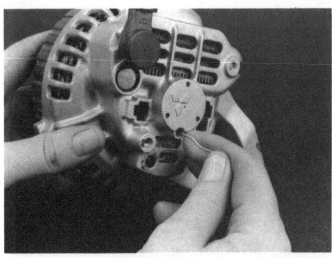

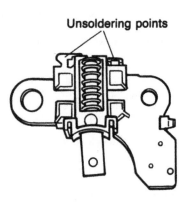

14.3   To remove the old brushes, de-solder the brush pigtails at the indicated points while pulling the brushes from the holder

13.11   Before assembling the alternator, push the brushes into the brush holder and pass a rigid wire through the hole

11   Before assembling the alternator, push the brushes into the brush holder and insert a rigid wire (a straightened-out paper clip will work) through the hole in the end frame to secure the brushes in position **(see illustration)**.
12   Installation is otherwise the reverse of removal. Be sure to heat the rear end frame before pushing the rear bearing into it.
13   Remove the wire securing the brushes when you have completed reassembly.

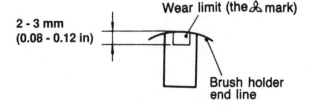

14.4   Solder the pigtail for the new brush so that the wear limit line of the brush projects 0.08 to 0.12-inch (2 to 3 mm) out from the end of the brush holder

14   Alternator brushes – check and replacement

Refer to illustrations 14.3 and 14.4

1   Remove the alternator (see Section 12).
2   Disassemble the alternator (see Section 13).
3   Remove the solder from the brush pigtail **(see illustration)**, then detach the brush from the holder.
4   Solder the pigtail for the new brush so that the wear limit line of the brush projects 0.08 to 0.12-inch (2 to 3 mm) out from the end of the brush holder **(see illustration)**.
5   Before assembling the alternator, push the brushes into the brush holder and pass a rigid wire through the indicated hole to secure the brushes in position **(see illustration 13.11)**.
6   Installation is otherwise the reverse of removal. Before you assemble the alternator halves, heat the rear end frame with a soldering iron (see Section 13).
7   Be sure to pull the wire out after you have reassembled the alternator.

15   Starting system – general information and precautions

The sole function of the starting system is to turn over the engine quickly enough to allow it to start.
The starting system consists of the battery, the starter motor, the starter solenoid and the wires connecting them. The solenoid is mounted directly on the starter motor.
The solenoid/starter motor assembly is installed on the lower part of the engine, next to the transmission bellhousing.
When the ignition key is turned to the Start position, the starter solenoid is actuated through the starter control circuit. The starter solenoid then connects the battery to the starter. The battery supplies the electrical energy to the starter motor, which does the actual work of cranking the engine.
The starter motor on a vehicle equipped with a manual transmission can only be operated when the clutch pedal is depressed; the starter on a vehicle equipped with an automatic transmission can only be operated when the transmission selector lever is in Park or Neutral.
Always observe the following precautions when working on the starting system:
  a) Excessive cranking of the starter motor can overheat it and cause serious damage. Never operate the starter motor for more than 30 seconds at a time without pausing to allow it to cool for at least two minutes.
  b) The starter is connected directly to the battery and could arc or cause a fire if mishandled, overloaded or shorted out.
  c) Always detach the cable from the negative terminal of the battery before working on the starting system.

16   Starter motor – in-vehicle check

Note: *Before diagnosing starter problems, make sure the battery is fully charged.*
1   If the starter motor does not turn at all when the switch is operated, make sure that the shift lever is in Neutral or Park (automatic transmission) or that the clutch pedal is depressed (manual transmission).
2   Make sure that the battery is charged and that all cables, both at the battery and starter solenoid terminals, are clean and secure.
3   If the starter motor spins but the engine is not cranking, the overrunning clutch in the starter motor is slipping and the starter motor must be replaced.
4   If, when the switch is actuated, the starter motor does not operate at all but the solenoid clicks, then the problem lies with either the battery, the main solenoid contacts or the starter motor itself (or the engine is seized).
5   If the solenoid plunger cannot be heard when the switch is actuated, the battery is bad, the fusible link is burned (the circuit is open) or the solenoid itself is defective.

17.4   To remove the starter/solenoid assembly, detach the electrical harness from the solenoid terminals (not visible in this photo), remove the starter nut and bolt (arrows) and detach the starter

6   To check the solenoid, connect a jumper lead between the battery (+) and the ignition switch wire terminal (the small terminal) on the solenoid. If the starter motor now operates, the solenoid is OK and the problem is in the ignition switch, neutral start switch or the wiring.

7   If the starter motor still does not operate, remove the starter/solenoid assembly for disassembly, testing and repair.

8   If the starter motor cranks the engine at an abnormally slow speed, first make sure that the battery is charged and that all terminal connections are tight. If the engine is partially seized, or has the wrong viscosity oil in it, it will crank slowly.

9   Run the engine until normal operating temperature is reached, then disconnect the coil wire from the distributor cap and ground it on the engine.

10   Connect a voltmeter positive lead to the positive battery post and connect the negative lead to the negative post.

11   Crank the engine and take the voltmeter readings as soon as a steady figure is indicated. Do not allow the starter motor to turn for more than 30 seconds at a time. A reading of 9 volts or more, with the starter motor turning at normal cranking speed, is normal. If the reading is 9 volts or more but the cranking speed is slow, the motor is faulty. If the reading is less than 9 volts and the cranking speed is slow, the solenoid contacts are probably burned, the starter motor is bad, the battery is discharged or there is a bad connection.

17   Starter motor – removal and installation

Refer to illustration 17.4

Note: *On some vehicles, it may be necessary to remove the exhaust pipe(s) or frame crossmember to gain access to the starter motor. In extreme cases it may even be necessary to unbolt the mounts and raise the engine slightly to get the starter out.*

1   Detach the cable from the negative terminal of the battery.

2   Raise the vehicle and support it securely on jackstands.

3   Clearly label, then disconnect the wires from the terminals on the starter motor and solenoid.

4   Remove the mounting bolts **(see illustration)** and detach the starter.

5   Installation is the reverse of removal.

18   Starter solenoid – removal and installation

Refer to illustration 18.3

1   Disconnect the cable from the negative terminal of the battery.

2   Remove the starter motor (see Section 17).

3   Remove the nut from switch terminal M **(see illustration)**.

4   Disconnect the strap from the solenoid to the starter motor terminal.

5   Remove the screws which secure the solenoid to the starter motor.

6   Detach the solenoid from the starter body **(see illustration 18.3)**.

7   Remove the plunger and plunger spring.

8   Installation is the reverse of removal.

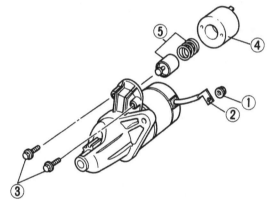

18.3   An exploded view of the starter solenoid assembly

1	*Nut for switch terminal "M"*	*4*	*Solenoid*
2	*Solenoid-to-starter motor strap*	*5*	*Spring and plunger*
3	*Solenoid-to-starter motor mounting screws*		

Chapter 6 Emissions control systems

Contents

Catalytic converter 5
Control system and trouble codes 7
Crankcase and evaporative emission control system 6
Deceleration control system 3
Evaporative emissions control system check .... See Chapter 1
Exhaust Gas Recirculation (EGR) system 4
General information 1
Secondary air injection system 2

Specifications

Throttle sensor resistance

Closed throttle .... 1 k-ohm
Wide open throttle .... 5 ± 1 k-ohm

---

1 General information

Refer to illustrations 1.6a, 1.6b, 1.6c, 1.6d and 1.6e

To prevent pollution of the atmosphere from incompletely burned or evaporating gases, and to maintain good driveability and fuel economy, a number of emission control systems are used on these vehicles. They include the:

    Secondary air injection system
    Deceleration control system
    Exhaust Gas Recirculation (EGR) system
    Catalytic converter
    Crankcase and evaporative emission control system

The Sections in this Chapter include general descriptions, checking procedures within the scope of the home mechanic and component replacement procedures (when possible) for each of the systems listed above.

Before assuming that an emissions control system is malfunctioning, check the fuel and ignition systems carefully. The diagnosis of some emission control devices requires specialized tools, equipment and training. If checking and servicing become too difficult or if a procedure is beyond your ability, consult a dealer service department. Remember – the most frequent cause of emissions problems is simply a loose or broken vacuum hose or wire, so always check the hose and wiring connections first.

This doesn't mean, however, that emission control systems are particularly difficult to maintain and repair. You can quickly and easily perform many checks and do most of the regular maintenance at home with common tune-up and hand tools. **Note:** *Because of a Federally mandated extended warranty which covers the emission control system components, check with your dealer about warranty coverage before working on any emissions-related systems. Once the warranty has expired, you may wish to perform some of the component checks and/or replacement procedures in this Chapter to save money.*

Pay close attention to any special precautions outlined in this Chapter. It should be noted that the illustrations of the various systems may not exactly match the system installed on your vehicle because of changes made by the manufacturer during production or from year to year.

A Vehicle Emissions Control Information label is located in the engine compartment **(see illustration)**. This label contains important emissions specifications and adjustment information. When servicing the engine or emissions systems, the VECI label in your particular vehicle should always be checked for up-to-date information. You will also find the accompanying vacuum hose diagrams helpful when you troubleshoot emissions problems **(see illustrations)**.

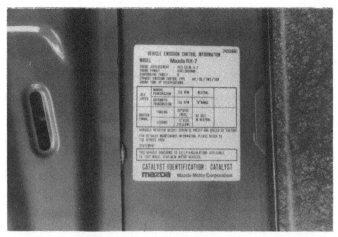

1.6a The Vehicle Emission Control Information (VECI) label contains such essential information as the types of emission control systems installed on the engine and the idle speed and ignition timing specifications

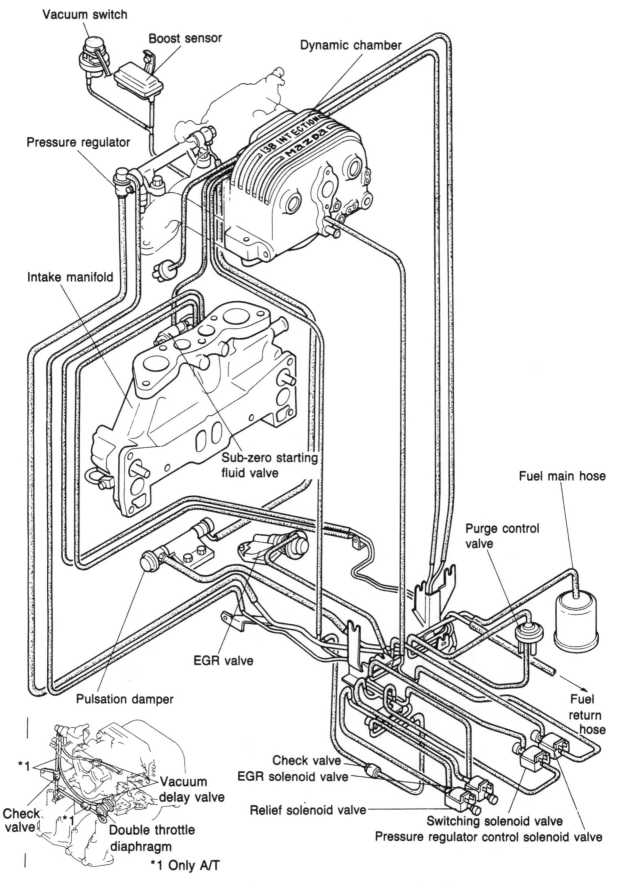

1.6b   Vacuum hose routing for 1986 through 1988 non-turbo models

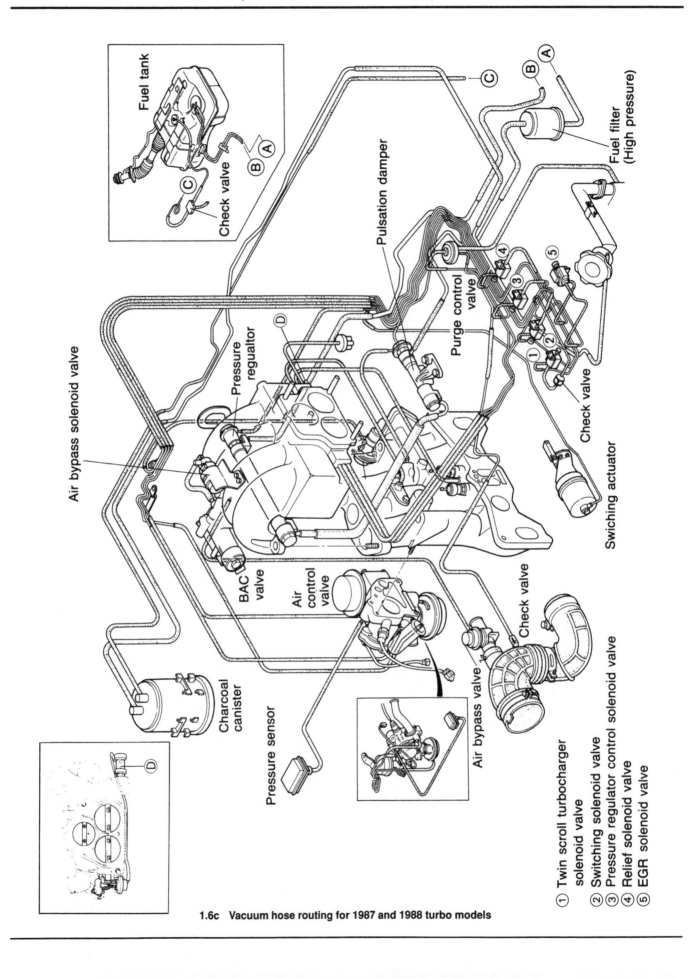

1.6c   Vacuum hose routing for 1987 and 1988 turbo models

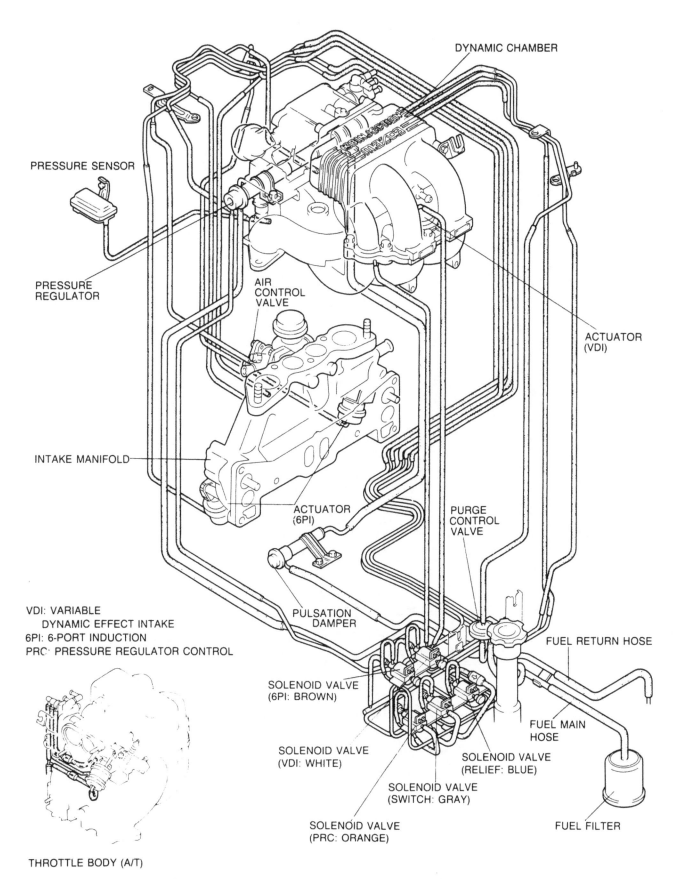

DYNAMIC CHAMBER

PRESSURE SENSOR

PRESSURE
REGULATOR

AIR
CONTROL
VALVE

ACTUATOR
(VDI)

INTAKE MANIFOLD

ACTUATOR
(6PI)

PURGE
CONTROL
VALVE

PULSATION
DAMPER

VDI: VARIABLE
    DYNAMIC EFFECT INTAKE
6PI: 6-PORT INDUCTION
PRC· PRESSURE REGULATOR CONTROL

FUEL RETURN HOSE

SOLENOID VALVE
(6PI: BROWN)

FUEL MAIN
HOSE

SOLENOID VALVE
(VDI: WHITE)

SOLENOID VALVE
(RELIEF: BLUE)

SOLENOID VALVE
(SWITCH: GRAY)

SOLENOID VALVE
(PRC: ORANGE)

FUEL FILTER

THROTTLE BODY (A/T)

1.6d   Vacuum hose routing for 1989 non-turbo models (later models similar)

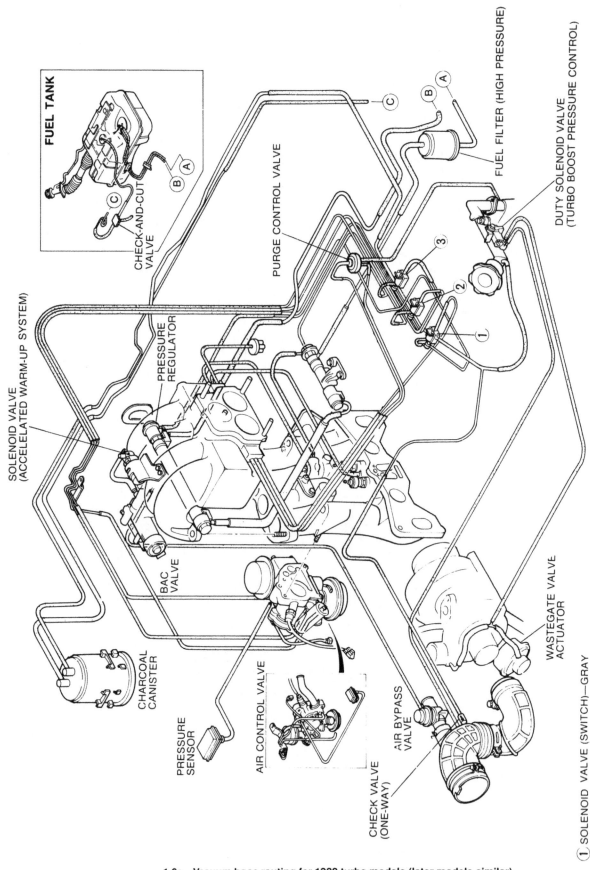

1.6e   Vacuum hose routing for 1989 turbo models (later models similar)

2   Secondary air injection system

General description

Refer to illustration 2.1

1   The secondary air injection system **(see illustration)** reduces un-burned hydrocarbons (HC) and carbon monoxide (CO) by introducing fresh air into the exhaust port and the main catalytic converter, which promotes further burning of the spent exhaust gases while they're in the exhaust system. If there is a problem with the system, which may be characterized by a failed emissions control test, rough idling, stalling, backfiring or overheating of the exhaust system, and the following procedures do not remedy the problem, take the vehicle to a dealer service department or other repair shop for further diagnosis.

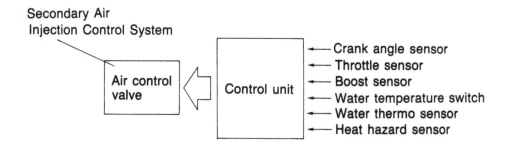

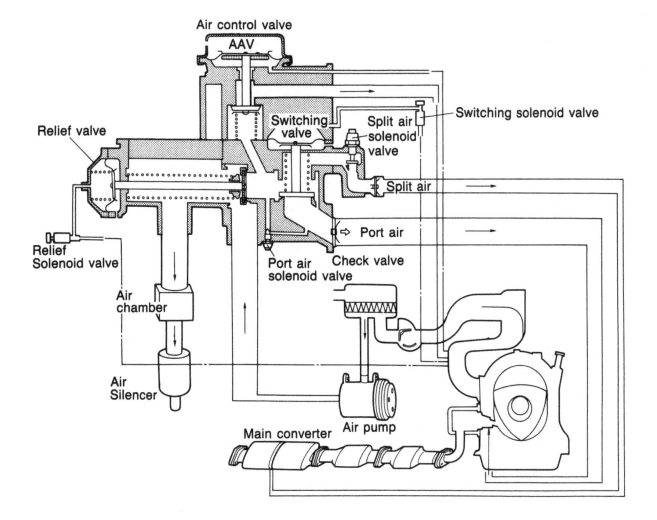

2.1   Schematic of a typical secondary air injection system (1987 non-turbo model shown, others similar)

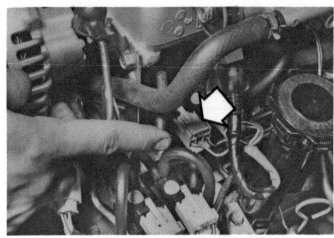

2.6　When checking the air pump or the intake manifold check valve, detach the air pump hose (1) from the air control valve (2) – when checking the air control valve, detach the air silencer hose (3) from the valve

2.11　Location of the switching solenoid valve

Check

Air pump

Refer to illustration 2.6

2　Warm up the engine to its normal operating temperature.
3　Check the air pump hoses and connections for leaks.
4　Check the air pump for noise. If it's noisy, replace it (see Step 61).
5　Check the tension of the air pump drivebelt and adjust it, if necessary (see Chapter 1).
6　Detach the air pump hose from the air control valve **(see illustration)**.
7　Start the engine and allow it to idle.
8　Hold your hand near the end of the hose, making sure air blows out.
9　If no air blows out from the hose, replace the pump (see Step 61).

Intake manifold check valve

Refer to illustration 2.11

10　Detach the air pump hose **(see illustration 2.6)**.
11　Start the engine and detach the electrical connector from the switching solenoid valve **(see illustration)**.
12　Increase the engine speed to about 1500 rpm.
13　Check for exhaust gas leakage at the hose end. To do this, hold a strip of paper over the end of the hose. **Warning:** *Don't use your finger to perform this test – the exhaust gas can be very hot.*

14　If exhaust gas is blowing out of the end of the hose, replace the check valve (see Step 66).

Catalytic converter check valve

15　Detach the catalytic converter air hose from the rear of the intake manifold.
16　Start the engine.
17　Hold a strip of paper over the end of the hose. **Warning:** *Don't use your finger to perform this test – the exhaust gas can be very hot.*
18　Increase the engine speed to about 1500 rpm.
19　Check for exhaust gas leakage from the air hose opening.
20　If there is exhaust gas leakage, replace the check valve (see Step 69).

Air control valve

Refer to illustrations 2.27 and 2.31

21　Warm the engine to its normal operating temperature.
22　Allow the engine to idle.
23　Detach the air silencer hose from the air control valve **(see illustration 2.6)**.
24　Place your finger over the air control valve outlet.
25　Increase the engine speed and verify air begins to flow out between 1500 and 2500 rpm.
26　Allow the engine to idle.
27　Detach the air control valve vacuum hose from the relief solenoid valve **(see illustration)**.

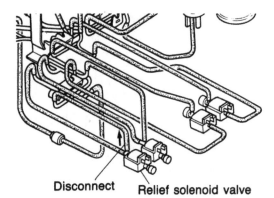

2.27　Disconnect the air control valve vacuum hose from the relief solenoid valve and verify air flows from the air control valve

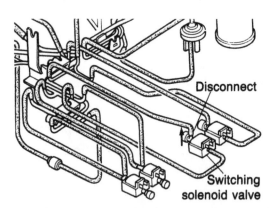

2.31　Detach the air control valve vacuum hose from the switching solenoid valve and verify that air flows from the air control valve

28   Verify that air flows from the air control valve outlet.

29   Reattach the vacuum hose and the air silencer hose.

30   Locate the large diameter hose at the rear of the intake manifold that leads to the catalytic converter check valve **(see illustration 2.69).** Detach the hose at the intake manifold and cover the port on the manifold with your finger.

31   Detach the air control valve vacuum hose from the switching solenoid valve **(see illustration).**

32   Verify air flows from the air control valve.

33   Reattach the vacuum hose and the catalytic converter air hose.

34   Replace the air control valve if it fails any of the above checks (see Step 72).

Switching solenoid valve

Refer to illustrations 2.37, 2.39 and 2.42

35   To check the switching solenoid valve signal, warm the engine and run it at idle speed.

36   Hook up a tachometer in accordance with the manufacturer's instructions.

37   Detach the switching solenoid valve hose from the vacuum pipe, then place your finger over the end of the hose **(see illustration).**

38   Gradually increase the engine speed and verify there is vacuum at the end of the hose.

39   Unplug the throttle sensor electrical connector **(see illustration).**

40   Gradually increase the engine speed and verify there is no vacuum when the engine speed is over 1200 rpm.

41   To check the switching solenoid valve itself, detach the vacuum hoses from the valve.

42   Blow through the solenoid from port A and verify air passes through the valve and flows from port B **(see illustration).**

43   Unplug the electrical connector from the solenoid valve and, using jumper wires connected to the battery, apply voltage to the terminals on the solenoid valve. **Caution:** *Apply voltage only long enough to perform the test described in the next Step.*

44   Blow through the solenoid valve from port A and verify air passes through the valve and flows from the air filter.

45   If the switching solenoid valve fails to perform as described, replace it.

Relief solenoid valve

Refer to illustrations 2.47, 2.52, 2.55 and 2.57

46   Warm up the engine and run it at idle speed.

47   Detach the air control vacuum hose from the relief solenoid valve **(see illustration),** place your finger over the hose end and increase the engine speed to over 1500 rpm.

48   Unplug the electrical connector from the throttle sensor **(see illustration 2.39).** You should feel vacuum at the hose end for two minutes, then it should stop.

49   Decrease the engine speed to idle and verify there is vacuum at the hose for 8 seconds.

50   Plug in the electrical connector to the throttle sensor.

51   Increase the engine speed and verify there is no vacuum when the engine speed is over 3400 to 3600 rpm.

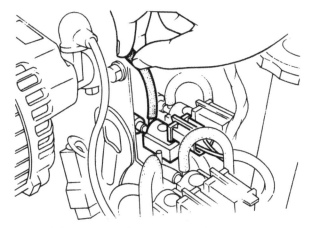

2.37   Detach the switching solenoid valve hose from the vacuum pipe and place your finger over the hose end

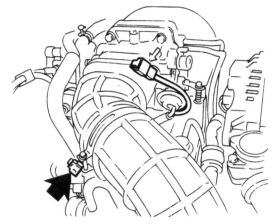

2.39   Unplug the electrical connector from the throttle sensor

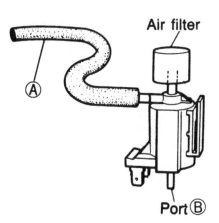

2.42   Blow into port A and verify air passes through the solenoid valve and flows from port B

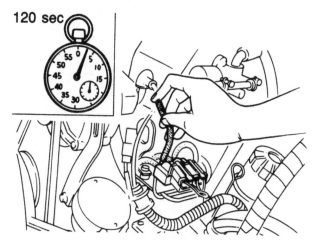

2.47   Detach the air control vacuum hose from the relief solenoid valve, place your finger over the hose end and increase the engine speed to over 1500 rpm – the vacuum should last for two minutes, then stop

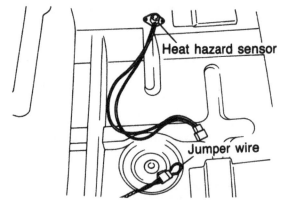

2.52   Unplug the electrical connector from the heat hazard sensor and attach a jumper wire across the connector terminals

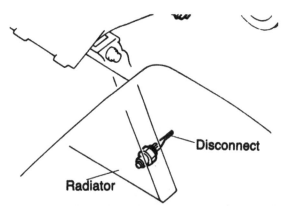

2.55   Disconnect the electrical connector from the water temperature switch, located in the lower left corner of the radiator

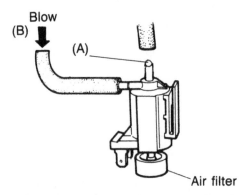

2.57   Blow through the solenoid valve from port B and verify that air passes through the valve and flows from the air filter

52   Unplug the electrical connector from the heat hazard sensor, located underneath the passenger seat, on the floorpan **(see illustration)**, and attach a jumper wire across the terminals in the connector.
53   Verify there is no vacuum at the hose at any engine speed.
54   Detach the jumper wire and plug in the electrical connector.
55   Stop the engine and unplug the electrical connector from the water temperature switch, which is screwed into the lower left corner of the radiator **(see illustration)**.

56   Start the engine, gradually increase the engine speed and verify there is no vacuum at the port opening when the engine speed is over 1200 rpm.
57   Detach the vacuum hose from the relief solenoid valve and blow through the valve from port B **(see illustration)**. Verify that air passes through the valve and flows from the air filter.
58   Unplug the electrical connector from the solenoid valve and, using jumper wires connected to the battery, apply voltage to the solenoid valve terminals. **Caution:** *Apply voltage only long enough to perform the test described in the next Step.*
59   Blow through the solenoid valve from port B. Verify that air passes through the valve and flows from port A.
60   If the valve fails either of the above tests, replace it.

Component replacement

Air pump
Refer to illustration 2.61

61   Detach the air hose **(see illustration)**.
62   Remove the air pump adjusting bolt.
63   Remove the air pump drivebelt.
64   Remove the air pump mounting bolt and remove the air pump.
65   Installation is the reverse of removal.

Intake manifold check valve
Refer to illustration 2.67

66   Remove the air control valve (see Step 72).
67   Remove the gasket and check valve **(see illustration)**.
68   Installation is the reverse of removal. Be sure to use a new gasket.

2.61   To remove the air pump:
1   *Detach the air hose*
2   *Remove the air pump adjusting bolt*
3   *Remove the drivebelt*
4   *Remove the air pump mounting bolt and lift the pump from its mounting bracket*

2.67   You'll have to remove the air control valve to replace the intake manifold check valve – note the way the valve is installed so you don't put it in backwards

2.69 Loosen the hose clamp and detach the air hose from the check valve, remove the split air pipe attaching bolts at the catalytic converter and remove the air pipe assembly

Catalytic converter check valve

Refer to illustration 2.69

69   Loosen the hose clamp and detach the air hose from the check valve **(see illustration)**.

70   Remove the bolts attaching the split air pipe to the catalytic converter and remove the air pipe and check valve assembly **(see illustration 5.1a or 5.1b)**.

71   Installation is the reverse of removal, but be sure to use a new gasket between the air pipe flange and the catalytic converter.

Air control valve

Refer to illustration 2.72

72   Detach the air hoses from the valve **(see illustration)**.

73   Unplug the electrical connectors from the split air solenoid and port air solenoid.

74   Remove the mounting bolts and nut and air control valve.

75   Installation is the reverse of removal. Be sure to use a new gasket between the valve and the manifold.

---

3   Deceleration control system

General description

1   The deceleration control system consists of a dashpot, an anti-afterburn valve and a fuel cut control system. The dashpot prevents the throttle valves from closing too abruptly. The anti-afterburn valve supplies air to the intake manifold during deceleration. The fuel cut control system improves fuel economy and prevents engine bucking during deceleration. On turbocharged models, an air bypass valve is used to bypass compressed air during deceleration from after the turbocharger to before the turbocharger to prevent noise. If there is a problem with the system, which may be characterized by a failed emissions control test, high idle speed, stalling, backfiring or overheating of the exhaust system, and the following procedures do not remedy the problem, take the vehicle to a dealer service department or other repair shop for further diagnosis.

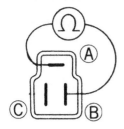

3.3 To check the throttle sensor, unplug the connector, touch the probes of an ohmmeter to the terminals of the connector and note the resistance readings at idle and full throttle – compare your readings with the values listed in this Chapter's specifications

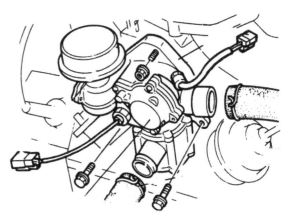

2.72 To remove the air control valve, detach the air hoses, unplug the electrical connectors from the split air solenoid valve and port air solenoid, then remove the mounting bolts and nut

Check

Throttle sensor

Refer to illustration 3.3

2   Unplug the electrical connector from the throttle sensor **(see illustration 2.39)**.

3   Touch the probes of an ohmmeter to the terminals of the sensor connector **(see illustration)**.

4   Check the resistance of the sensor with the throttle closed, then check it again with the throttle wide open. Compare your readings with the values listed in this Chapter's specifications.

5   If the sensor is out of adjustment, it must be adjusted before proceeding. Unfortunately, the throttle sensor cannot be adjusted without a special checker lamp. You will have to take the vehicle to a dealer service department or other qualified repair shop to have the throttle sensor adjusted or replaced.

Anti-afterburn valve

6   Warm the engine and allow it to idle.

7   Detach the hose from the air pump **(see illustration 2.61)**.

8   Place your finger over the end of the hose.

9   Verify there is no vacuum at the hose end at idle speed.

10   Increase the engine speed to over 3000 rpm, then decrease the engine speed abruptly (let the throttle snap shut).

11   Verify there is vacuum at the hose end for a few seconds during deceleration.

12   If there is no vacuum, replace the air control valve (the anti-afterburn valve is integral with the air control valve assembly).

Dashpot

Refer to illustration 3.14

13   If your vehicle is turbocharged, remove the intercooler (see Chapter 4).

14   Open the throttle valve fully, then push the dashpot rod **(see illustration)** with your finger and verify the rod slowly retracts into the dashpot.

15   Release the rod and verify it comes out quickly.

16   Replace the dashpot if it doesn't perform as described.

17   If the vehicle is turbocharged, install the intercooler (see Chapter 4).

Adjustment

Dashpot (non-turbo models)

18   Warm up the engine to its normal operating temperature and run it at idle speed.

19   Have an assistant watch the vehicle's tachometer.

20   Increase the engine speed to 3500 rpm.

21   Slowly decrease the engine speed and verify the dashpot rod contacts the lever at 2700 to 3100 rpm.

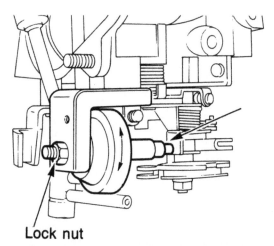

3.14   To check the dashpot, open the throttle valve fully, then push the dashpot rod (arrow) with your finger and verify the rod slowly retracts into the dashpot, release the rod and verify it comes out quickly – to adjust the dashpot, loosen the locknut and turn it

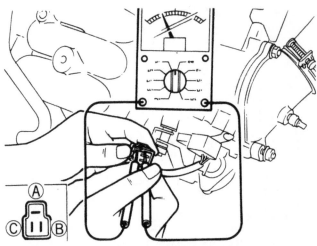

3.25   Unplug the electrical connector from the throttle sensor, connect an ohmmeter between sensor terminals A and B and check the resistance at the point where the dashpot rod separates from the lever

3.27   If the indicated resistance is incorrect, loosen the locknut (arrow) and turn the dashpot until the resistance is within specification

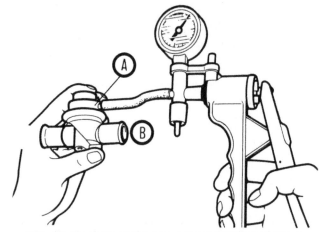

3.30   To check the air bypass valve on a turbo vehicle, remove the valve, attach a vacuum pump to port A, apply vacuum and blow into port B – air should flow through the valve

22   If necessary, loosen the lock nut and adjust the dashpot by turning it **(see illustration 3.14)**.

Dashpot (turbo models)

Refer to illustrations 3.25 and 3.27

23   Warm up the engine to its normal operating temperature, then turn it off.

24   Remove the intercooler (see Chapter 4).

25   Unplug the electrical connector from the throttle sensor and connect an ohmmeter between sensor terminals A and B **(see illustration)**.

26   Check the resistance at the point where the dash pot rod separates from the lever. It should be about 1.8 to 3.8 k-ohms.

27   If the resistance is incorrect, loosen the locknut and turn the dash pot until the resistance reading is within specification **(see illustration)**.

28   Install the intercooler (see Chapter 4).

Air bypass valve (turbo models only)

Refer to illustration 3.30

29   Remove the air bypass valve, which is located on the air intake duct between the intercooler and the turbocharger.

30   Attach a vacuum pump tester to port A of the valve **(see illustration)**.

31   Apply vacuum and blow into port B – air should flow through the valve.

32   Replace the air bypass valve if it doesn't operate as described.

---

4   Exhaust Gas Recirculation (EGR) system

Check

EGR valve (non-turbo models)

Refer to illustration 4.2

1   Warm the engine and run it at idle speed.

2   Detach the vacuum hose from the EGR solenoid valve **(see illustration)**.

3   Connect a hand-held vacuum pump to the hose and apply vacuum. The engine should either run roughly or stall.

4   If the engine doesn't run roughly or stall, replace the EGR valve.

EGR valve (turbo models)

Refer to illustration 4.6

5   Warm the engine and run it at idle speed.

6   Detach the vacuum hose from the EGR valve and attach a hand-held vacuum pump to the EGR valve **(see illustration)**.

7   Apply a vacuum of 3.9 in Hg. The engine speed should decrease. If it doesn't, replace the EGR valve.

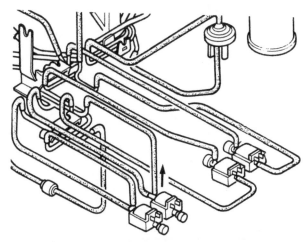

4.2   To check the EGR valve on a non–turbo model, start the engine, detach the vacuum hose from the EGR solenoid valve (arrow) and apply vacuum to the hose – the engine should run roughly or stall

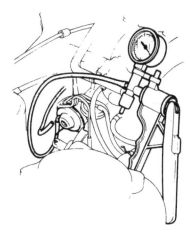

4.6   To check the EGR valve on a turbo model, start the engine, attach a vacuum pump to the EGR valve and apply 3.9 in Hg of vacuum – the engine speed should decrease

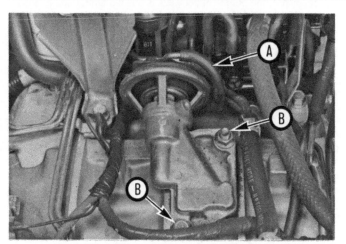

4.14   EGR valve mounting details (non-turbo model)

A   Vacuum hose   *B   Fasteners*

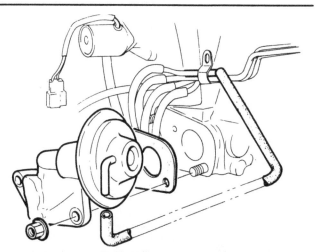

4.18   To remove the EGR valve on a turbo model, detach the vacuum hose and remove the mounting nuts

EGR solenoid valve

8   Detach the vacuum hose from the EGR solenoid valve **(see illustration 4.2)**.

9   Blow through the solenoid valve from port B. Verify air passes through the valve and flows from the air filter **(see illustration 2.57)**.

10   Unplug the electrical connector from the EGR solenoid valve and, using jumper wires connected to the battery, apply voltage to the solenoid valve terminals. **Caution:** *Only apply voltage long enough to perform the test described in the next Step.*

11   Blow through the solenoid valve from port B and verify air flows out port A.

12   If the solenoid doesn't operate as described, replace it.

Component replacement

EGR valve (non-turbo models)

Refer to illustration 4.14

13   Remove the throttle body, dynamic chamber and extension manifold/VDI manifold (see Chapter 4).

14   Detach the vacuum hose from the EGR valve **(see illustration)**.

15   Remove the EGR valve fasteners.

16   Remove the EGR valve.

17   Installation is the reverse of removal. Be sure to use a new gasket.

EGR valve (turbo models)

Refer to illustration 4.18

18   Detach the vacuum hose from the EGR valve **(see illustration)**.

19   Remove the EGR valve mounting nuts and the valve assembly.

20   Installation is the reverse of removal. Be sure to use a new gasket.

---

5   Catalytic converter

Note: *Because of a Federally mandated extended warranty which covers emissions-related components such as the catalytic converter, check with a dealer service department before replacing the converter at your own expense.*

General description

Refer to illustrations 5.1a and 5.1b

1   To reduce hydrocarbons (HC), carbon monoxide (CO) and oxides of nitrogen (NOx), the vehicles covered by this manual are equipped with multiple catalytic converters – a pair of pre-converters and a main converter on 1986 through 1988 models or two three-way converters – a front converter and main converter – on 1989 models **(see illustrations)**.

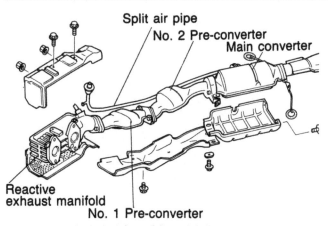

Split air pipe
No. 2 Pre-converter
Main converter
Reactive
exhaust manifold
No. 1 Pre-converter

5.1a   Exploded view of the catalytic converters on non-turbo models

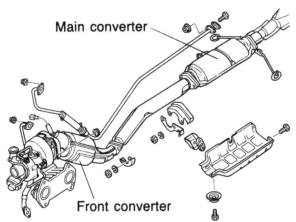

Main converter

Front converter

5.1b   Exploded view of the catalytic converters on turbo models

Check

2   Visually examine the converters for cracks or damage. Make sure all fasteners are tight.

3   Inspect the insulation covers (if equipped) welded onto the converters – they should be tight. **Caution:** *If an insulation cover is touching a converter housing, excessive heat at the floor may result.*

4   Start the engine and run it at idle speed.

5   Check for exhaust gas leakage from the converter flanges. Check the body of each converter for holes.

Component replacement

6   See Chapter 4 for removal and installation procedures.

---

6   Crankcase and evaporative emission control system

General description

Refer to illustrations 6.1a and 6.1b

1   The evaporative emission control system **(see illustrations)** stores fuel vapors generated in the fuel tank in a charcoal canister when the engine isn't running. When the engine is started, the fuel vapors are drawn

into the dynamic chamber and burned. The crankcase emission control system works like this: When the engine is running at idle, the purge control valve is opened slightly and a small amount of blow-by gas is drawn into the dynamic chamber and burned. At high engine speeds or heavy load conditions, the purge control valve is opened further and a larger amount of blow-by gas is drawn into the dynamic chamber.

Check

Evaporative line

Refer to illustration 6.2

2   Detach the fuel ventilation hose from the canister and connect a hand-held vacuum pump to the hose **(see illustration)**.

3   Gradually apply vacuum and verify no vacuum is held.

4   If vacuum is held, inspect the check and cut valve and the evaporation pipe for blockage (see Step 5 or 8).

Three-way check valve (1986 models)/check and cut valve (1987 models)

Refer to illustration 6.6

5   Remove the valve (see Step 23).

6   Blow through the valve from port A and verify air comes out port B **(see illustration)**. Block port B and verify air comes out port C. If it doesn't, replace the valve.

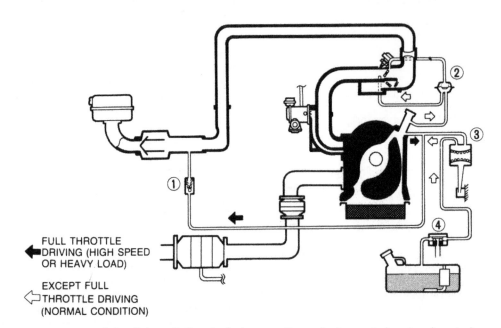

① CHECK VALVE

② PURGE CONTROL VALVE

③ CHARCOAL CANISTER

④ CHECK-AND-CUT VALVE

FULL THROTTLE DRIVING (HIGH SPEED OR HEAVY LOAD)

EXCEPT FULL THROTTLE DRIVING (NORMAL CONDITION)

6.1a   Schematic for a typical evaporative emission control system (non-turbo models)

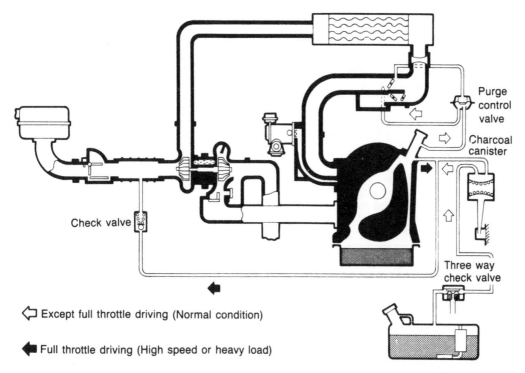

Except full throttle driving (Normal condition)

Full throttle driving (High speed or heavy load)

6.1b   Schematic for a typical evaporative emission control system (turbo models)

7   Block port B, attach a hand-held vacuum pump to port A, operate the pump and feel for vacuum at port C (the valve shouldn't hold vacuum unless ports B and C are plugged). If there is no vacuum at port C, replace the valve.

Check-and-cut valve (1988 and 1989 models)
Refer to illustration 6.9

8   Remove the check-and-cut valve (see Step 23).
9   Blow through the valve at port A and verify the valve opens with little resistance **(see illustration)**.
10   Blow through the valve at port B and verify the valve opens, but with slightly more resistance than in the previous check.
11   If the valve doesn't operate as described, replace it.

Purge valve
Refer to illustrations 6.14a and 6.14b

12   Detach the oil filler pipe hose from the port on the purge valve (the valve is located near the oil filter and the oil filler pipe).
13   Start the engine and let it idle.
14   Place your finger over the port on the valve **(see illustrations)** and verify there is no vacuum at the port. If there is, replace the valve.
15   Increase the engine speed to 2000 rpm and verify there is vacuum at the port. If there isn't, replace the valve.

Check valve (turbo models)
Refer to illustration 6.17

16   Remove the check valve **(see illustration 6.1b)**.

6.2   Detach the fuel tank ventilation hose from the canister, hook up a hand-held vacuum pump, gradually apply vacuum and verify no vacuum is held

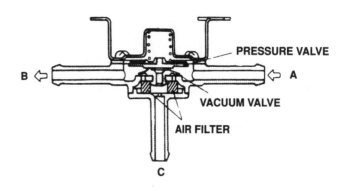

6.6 To test the three-way check valve (1986 models) or check-and-cut valve (1987 models), blow into port A and verify that air comes out port B; then block port B and verify that air comes out port C; then block port B, apply vacuum to port A and feel for vacuum at port C

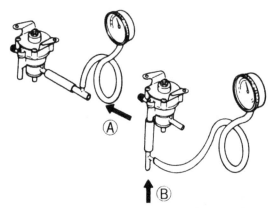

6.9   To test the check-and-cut valve on 1988 and 1989 models, blow into port A, then port B – air should pass through the valve in both directions

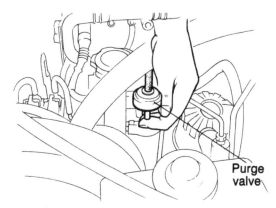

6.14a   At idle speed, there should be no vacuum at the purge valve, but at 2000 rpm, the valve should open and vacuum should be present (non-turbo model shown)

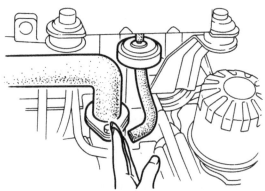

6.14b   Checking the purge valve on a turbo model

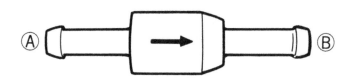

6.17   The check valve should only allow air to pass in the direction indicated by the arrow

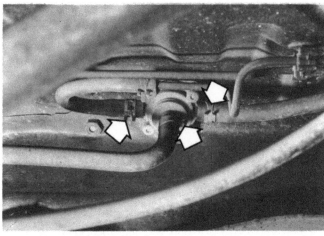

6.24   To remove the three-way/check-and-cut valve, loosen the hose clamps, detach the hoses from the valve and remove it

17   Blow through the check valve from port A and verify that air comes out port B (see illustration).
18   Blow through the check valve from port B and verify that air does not come out port A. If the check valve doesn't perform as described, replace it.

Canister

19   Label, then detach all hoses to the canister (see illustration 6.2).
20   Slide the canister out of its mounting clip.
21   Visually examine the canister for leakage or damage.
22   Replace the canister if you find evidence of damage or leakage.

Component replacement

Three-way check valve/check and cut valve

Refer to illustration 6.24

23   Raise the rear of the vehicle and support it securely with jackstands.
24   Loosen the hose clamps, detach the hoses from the check valve (see illustration) and remove it.
25   Installation is the reverse of removal. When installing the check valve, be sure to push the hoses onto the valve all the way and secure them with clamps or bands. Also, be sure to note the direction of the valve fittings when connecting the hoses to the valve.

7   Control system and trouble codes

1   The control system includes all the information sensors and computer controlled output devices that comprise the various emission control subsystems described in this Chapter. The control unit is the brain of the control system. It processes all incoming data from information sensors located throughout the engine compartment and controls a wide variety of output devices which alter engine operating conditions.
2   Due to the need for special tools and training, servicing or diagnosing the control unit is beyond the scope of the home mechanic. Take the vehicle to a dealer service department or other qualified repair shop.
3   Fortunately, the control unit and the system of which it is the central part are protected by a Federally-mandated, extended warranty that, at the time of publication, is good for five years or 50,000 miles, whichever comes first. However, by the time you read this information, the Federal warranty may have been extended significantly. We therefore don't recommend that you attempt to service, diagnose or repair the control unit or any device not specifically included in this Chapter.

Chapter 7 Part A Manual transmission

Contents

General information 1
Lubricant change .... See Chapter 1
Lubricant level check .... See Chapter 1
Manual transmission overhaul – general information 7
Manual transmission – removal and installation 6

Manual transmission shift lever – removal and installation 4
Oil seal replacement 2
Speedometer cable replacement 3
Starter safety switch check .... See Chapter 1
Transmission mount – check and replacement 5

Specifications

Torque specifications

	Ft-lbs
Transmission-to-engine bolts	
1989 and earlier	27 to 38
1990 on	37 to 52
Filler plug	
1989 and earlier	18 to 29
1990 on	25 to 39
Front cover bolts	
Non-turbocharged models	
1989 and earlier	14 to 19
1990 on	19 to 25
Turbocharged models	5 to 8
Drain plug	
1989 and earlier	29 to 43
1990 on	39 to 59
Shift lever-to-transmission bolts	5 to 8

---

1 General information

All vehicles covered in this manual come equipped with either a five-speed manual transmission or an automatic transmission. All information on the manual transmission is included in this Part of Chapter 7. Information on the automatic transmission can be found in Part B of this Chapter.

The manual transmission used in these models is a five-speed unit with the fifth gear being an overdrive.

Due to the complexity, unavailability of replacement parts and the special tools necessary, internal repair by the home mechanic is not recommended. The information in this Chapter is limited to general information and removal and installation of the transmission.

Depending on the expense involved in having a faulty transmission overhauled, it may be a good idea to replace the unit with either a new or rebuilt one. Your local dealer or transmission shop should be able to supply you with information concerning cost, availability and exchange policy.

Regardless of how you decide to remedy a transmission problem, you can still save a lot of money by removing and installing the unit yourself.

---

2 Oil seal replacement

Refer to illustrations 2.4, 2.6, 2.10 and 2.11

1 Oil leaks frequently occur due to wear of the extension housing oil seal and/or the speedometer drive gear O-ring. Replacement of these seals is relatively easy, since the repairs can usually be performed without removing the transmission from the vehicle.

2 The extension housing oil seal is located at the extreme rear of the transmission, where the driveshaft is attached. If leakage at the seal is suspected, raise the vehicle and support it securely on jackstands. If the seal is leaking, transmission lubricant will be built up on the front of the driveshaft and may be dripping from the rear of the transmission.

3 Refer to Chapter 8 and remove the driveshaft.

4   Using a screwdriver or pry bar, carefully pry the oil seal out of the rear of the transmission **(see illustration)**. Do not damage the splines on the transmission output shaft.

5   If the oil seal cannot be removed with a screwdriver or pry bar, a special oil seal removal tool (available at auto parts stores) will be required.

6   Using a large section of pipe or a very large deep socket as a drift, install the new oil seal **(see illustration)**. Drive it into the bore squarely and make sure it's completely seated.

7   Lubricate the splines of the transmission output shaft and the outside of the driveshaft sleeve yoke with lightweight grease, then install the driveshaft. Be careful not to damage the lip of the new seal.

8   The speedometer cable and driven gear housing is located on the side of the extension housing. Look for transmission oil around the cable housing to determine if the O-ring is leaking.

9   Disconnect the speedometer cable **(see illustration 3.5).**

10   Remove the driven gear housing **(see illustration)**.

11   Install a new O-ring in the driven gear housing and reinstall the driven gear housing and cable assembly on the extension housing **(see illustration)**.

3   Speedometer cable replacement

Refer to illustration 3.5

1   Disconnect the negative cable at the battery.

2.4   Use a screwdriver to pry the oil seal out of the transmission bore – be careful not to damage the output shaft splines

2.10   Remove the retaining bolt and withdraw the speedometer driven gear from the transmission

2   Inside the passenger compartment, remove the instrument cluster and pull it back for access (see Chapter 12). Reach behind the cluster, disconnect the speedometer cable by pressing the retaining lever and detaching it from the cluster (see Chapter 12).

3   Push the cable through the firewall into the engine compartment.

4   Raise the vehicle and support it securely on jackstands.

5   Under the vehicle, unscrew the speedometer cable collar and pull the cable from the driven gear housing **(see illustration)**.

6   Detach the cable from the retaining straps and remove it from the vehicle.

7   To install, push the cable through the firewall into the passenger compartment and seat the firewall grommet securely. Insert the cable into the cluster housing until it clicks in place. Install the cluster.

8   Insert the cable end into the driven gear in the transmission, install the retaining collar and tighten it securely. Secure the cable with the retaining straps.

4   Manual transmission shift lever – removal and installation

Refer to illustrations 4.6 and 4.7

1   Disconnect the negative cable at the battery.

2   Hold the locking collar of the shift knob with a wrench and unscrew the knob from the lever.

2.6   Tap the new seal evenly into the bore using a large socket and a hammer

2.11   Use a small screwdriver to remove the O-ring from the groove in the driven gear housing

3   Use a screwdriver to detach the four clips at the base of the shift boot of the console, then lift the boot up and off the shift lever.
4   Place the shift lever in Neutral.
5   Remove the three retaining bolts and lift the shift lever straight up and out of the transmission.
6   If the extension housing has been removed, refill it with the specified lubricant (see Chapter 1) before installing the shift lever **(see illustration)**.
7   Coat both sides of a new gasket with sealant, place it in position, lubricate the shift lever base and lower it into the transmission **(see illustration)**.
8   Install the retaining bolts. Tighten the bolts to the torque listed in this Chapter's Specifications.
9   Install the shift boot and knob.

---

5   Transmission mount – check and replacement

Refer to illustrations 5.2, 5.3 and 5.4

1   Insert a large screwdriver or prybar into the space between the transmission extension housing and the crossmember and try to pry the transmission up slightly.
2   The transmission should not move away from the crossmember much at all **(see illustration)**.

3   Support the transmission with a jack, unbolt the crossmember, then remove the nuts attaching the insulators to the crossmember and the bolts attaching the insulators to the transmission **(see illustration)**.

3.5   Unscrew the speedometer cable collar, then pull the cable from the driven gear housing

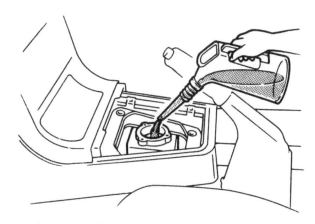

4.6   If the shift lever extension housing has been removed or drained, fill it with the specified lubricant before installing the shift lever

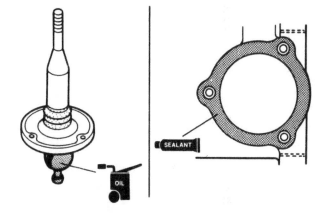

4.7   Lubricate the shift lever contact surfaces with the specified lubricant and coat the gasket with sealant prior to installation

5.2   Use a bar or large screwdriver to pry between the extension housing and the crossmember to check for excessive movement

5.3   With the transmission supported with a jack, remove the crossmember bolts and the mount and insulator nuts and bolts (arrows)

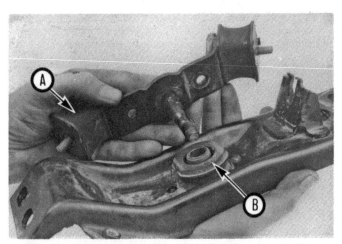

5.4   The engine mount insulators (A) can be replaced after removing the retaining nuts – the rubber mount in the crossmember (B) can be pressed out

4   Remove the mount from the crossmember. The insulators can be replaced after removing the nuts and the crossmember rubber mount can be pressed out **(see illustration).**
5   Installation is the reverse of the removal procedure. Be sure to tighten the nuts/bolts securely.

---

6   Manual transmission – removal and installation

Refer to illustration 6.5

Removal

1   Disconnect the negative cable from the battery.
2   Working inside the vehicle, remove the shift lever (see Section 4).
3   Raise the vehicle and support it securely on jackstands.
4   Remove the exhaust system components as necessary for clearance (see Chapter 4).
5   Disconnect the speedometer cable and wire harness connectors from the transmission **(see illustration).** Remove the starter (see Chapter 5) and the clutch release cylinder (see Chapter 8).

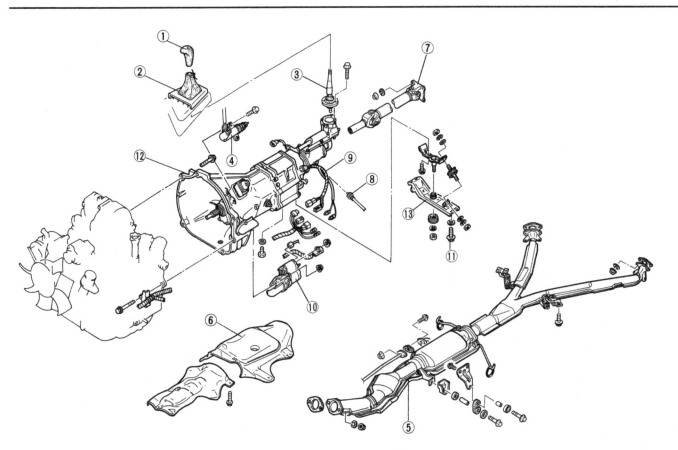

6.5   Typical transmission removal details

1	Shift knob	8	Speedometer cable
2	Shift boot	9	Electrical connectors
3	Shift lever assembly	10	Starter
4	Clutch release cylinder	11	Crossmember mounting bolts
5	Exhaust system	12	Transmission
6	Exhaust system heat insulator assembly	13	Crossmember
7	Driveshaft assembly		

6   Remove the driveshaft (see Chapter 8). Use a plastic bag to cover the end of the transmission to prevent fluid loss and contamination.

7   Support the transmission with a jack – preferably a special jack made for this purpose. Safety chains will help steady the transmission on the jack.

8   Remove the transmission rear crossmember bolts **(see illustration 5.3).**

9   Remove the bolts securing the transmission to the engine.

10   Make a final check that all wires and hoses have been disconnected from the transmission and then move the transmission and jack toward the rear of the vehicle until the transmission input shaft is clear of the clutch hub. Keep the transmission level as this is done.

11   Once the input shaft is clear, lower the transmission and remove it from under the vehicle. **Caution:** *Do not depress the clutch pedal while the transmission is out of the vehicle.*

12   The clutch components can be inspected at this time (see Chapter 8).

In most cases, new clutch components should be routinely installed if the transmission is removed.

Installation

13   If removed, install the clutch components (see Chapter 8).

14   With the transmission secured to the jack as on removal, raise the transmission into position behind the engine and then carefully slide it forward, engaging the input shaft with the clutch plate hub. Do not use excessive force to install the transmission – if the input shaft does not slide into place, readjust the angle of the transmission so it is level and/or turn the input shaft so the splines engage properly with the clutch.

15   Install the transmission–to–engine bolts. Tighten the bolts to the torque listed in this Chapter's Specifications.

16   Install the crossmember bolts. Tighten the bolts securely.

17   Remove the jack supporting the transmission.

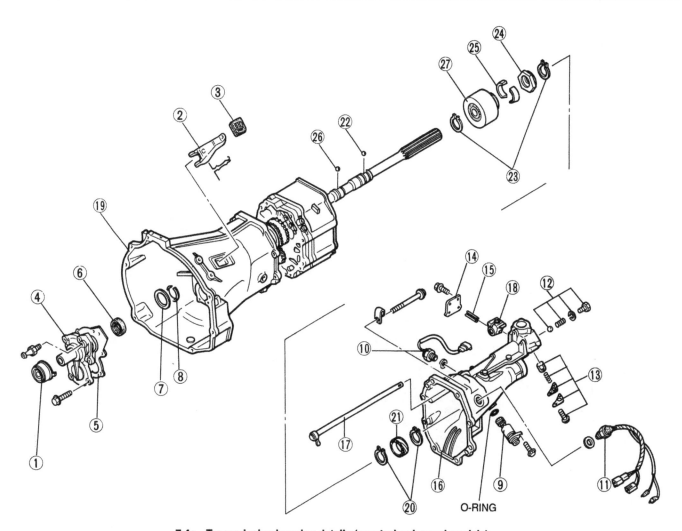

7.4a   Transmission housing details (non-turbocharged models)

1	Release bearing	10	Neutral switch	19	Transmission case
2	Release fork	11	Back-up light and fifth gear switch	20	Snap-rings
3	Boot	12	Steel ball, spring and spring cap	21	Speedometer driven gear
4	Front cover	13	Select-lock spindle, spring and spring cap	22	Steel ball
5	Gasket	14	Blind cover	23	Snap-rings
6	Oil seal	15	Roll pin	24	Locknut
7	Adjustment shim	16	Extension housing	25	Taper cotter
8	Snap-ring	17	Control lever	26	Steel ball
9	Speedometer drive gear	18	Control lever end	27	Dynamic damper

18   Install the various items removed previously, referring to Chapter 8 for the installation of the driveshaft and Chapter 4 for information regarding the exhaust system components.

19   Make a final check that all wires, hoses and the speedometer cable have been connected and the transmission has been filled with lubricant to the proper level (see Chapter 1). Lower the vehicle.

20   Working inside the vehicle, install the shift lever (see Section 4).

21   Connect the negative battery cable. Road test the vehicle for proper operation and check for leakage.

---

7   Manual transmission overhaul – general information

Refer to illustrations 7.4a through 7.4g

Overhauling a manual transmission is a difficult job for the do–it–yourselfer. It involves the disassembly and reassembly of many small parts. Numerous clearances must be precisely measured and, if necessary, changed with select fit spacers and snap-rings. As a result, if transmission problems arise, it can be removed and installed by a competent do-it-yourselfer, but overhaul should be left to a transmission repair shop. Rebuilt transmissions may be available – check with your dealer parts department and auto parts stores. At any rate, the time

and money involved in an overhaul is almost sure to exceed the cost of a rebuilt unit.

Nevertheless, it's not impossible for an inexperienced mechanic to rebuild a transmission if the special tools are available and the job is done in a deliberate step-by-step manner so nothing is overlooked.

The tools necessary for an overhaul include internal and external snap-ring pliers, a bearing puller, a slide hammer, a set of pin punches, a dial indicator and possibly a hydraulic press. In addition, a large, sturdy workbench and a vise or transmission stand will be required.

During disassembly of the transmission, make careful notes of how each piece comes off, where it fits in relation to other pieces and what holds it in place. Exploded views are included **(see illustrations)** to show where the parts go – but actually noting how they are installed when you remove the parts will make it much easier to get the transmission back together.

Before taking the transmission apart for repair, it will help if you have some idea what area of the transmission is malfunctioning. Certain problems can be closely tied to specific areas in the transmission, which can make component examination and replacement easier. Refer to the Troubleshooting section at the front of this manual for information regarding possible sources of trouble.

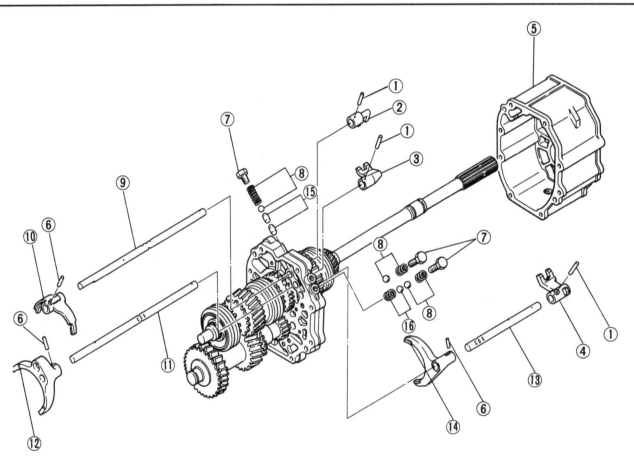

7.4b   Shift rod and fork assembly details (non-turbocharged models)

1	Roll pins	9	Shift rod (first/second)
2	Shift rod end (first/second)	10	Shift fork (first/second)
3	Shift rod end (third/fourth)	11	Shift rod (third/fourth)
4	Shift rod end (fifth/reverse)	12	Shift fork (third/fourth)
5	Intermediate housing	13	Shift rod (fifth/reverse)
6	Roll pins	14	Shift fork (fifth/reverse)
7	Cap plugs	15	Interlock pins
8	Springs and balls	16	Ball and spring

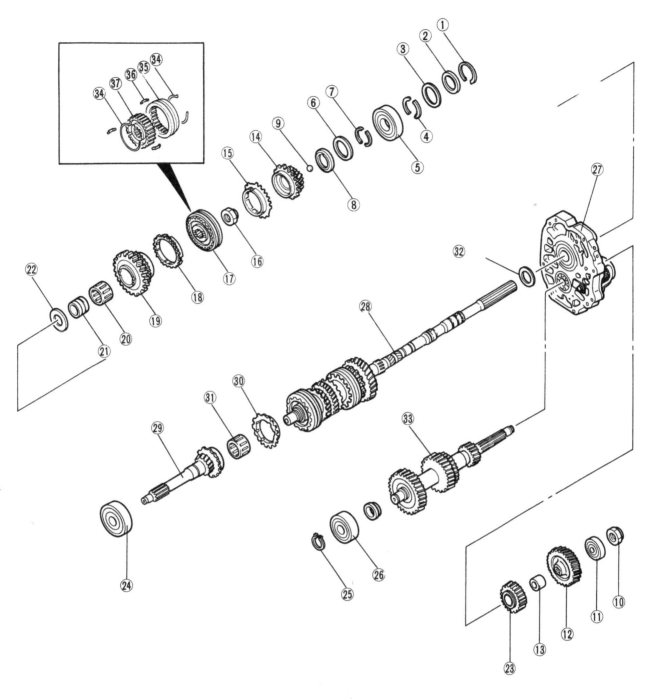

7.4c Mainshaft and control shaft details (non-turbocharged models)

1	Snap-ring	14	Fifth gear	27	Bearing housing assembly
2	Washer	15	Synchronizer ring (fifth)	28	Mainshaft gear assembly
3	Retaining ring	16	Locknut (mainshaft)	29	Main drive gear
4	C-washer (selective)	17	Clutch hub assembly (fifth/reverse)	30	Synchronizer ring (fourth)
5	Mainshaft rear bearing	18	Synchronizer ring (reverse)	31	Needle bearing
6	Retaining ring	19	Reverse gear	32	Washer (selective)
7	C-washer	20	Needle bearing	33	Countershaft
8	Thrust lock washer (selective)	21	Inner race	34	Synchronizer key spring
9	Steel ball	22	Washer	35	Clutch hub sleeve
10	Locknut (countershaft)	23	Counter reverse gear	36	Synchronizer key
11	Countershaft rear bearing	24	Main drive gear bearing	37	Clutch hub
12	Countergear	25	Snap-ring		
13	Spacer	26	Countershaft front bearing		

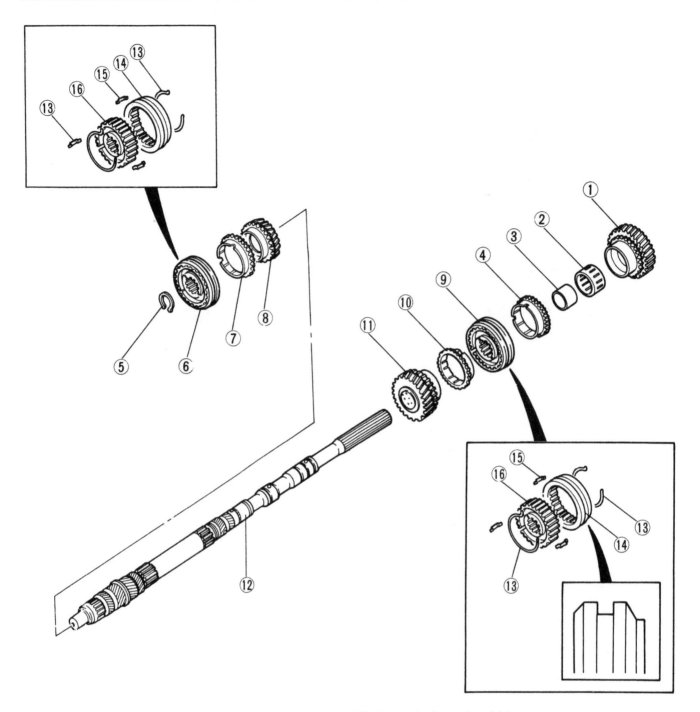

7.4d Mainshaft component details (non-turbocharged models)

1 First gear	9 Clutch hub assembly (first/second)
2 Needle bearing	10 Synchronizer ring (second)
3 Inner race	11 Second gear
4 Synchronizer ring (first)	12 Mainshaft
5 Snap-ring	13 Synchronizer key spring assembly
6 Clutch hub assembly (third/fourth)	14 Clutch hub sleeve
7 Synchronizer ring (third)	15 Synchronizer key
8 Third gear	16 Clutch hub

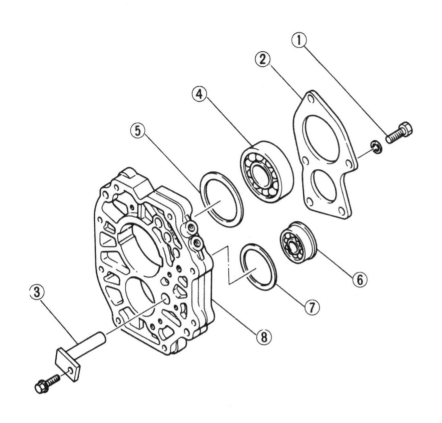

7.4e Bearing housing details (non-turbocharged models)

1 Bolt
2 Bearing cover
3 Reverse idler gear shaft
4 Ball bearing
5 Adjustment shim
6 Ball bearing
7 Adjustment shim
8 Bearing housing

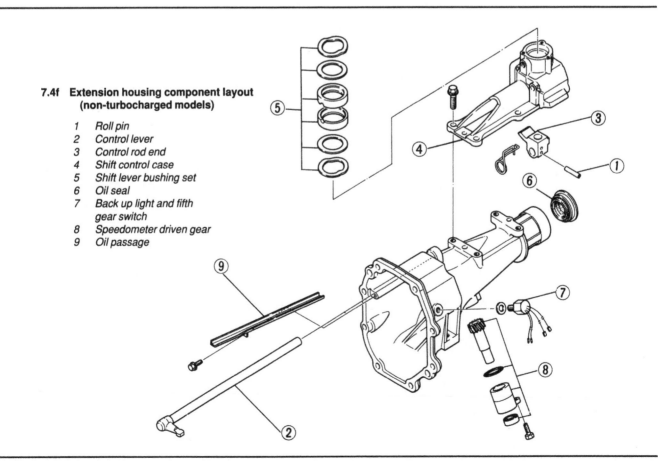

7.4f Extension housing component layout (non-turbocharged models)

1 Roll pin
2 Control lever
3 Control rod end
4 Shift control case
5 Shift lever bushing set
6 Oil seal
7 Back up light and fifth gear switch
8 Speedometer driven gear
9 Oil passage

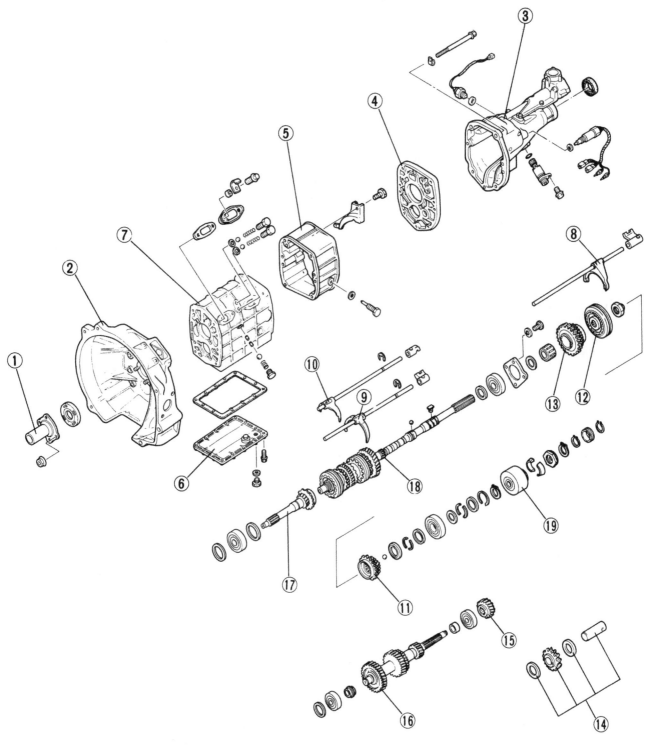

7.4g   Transmission (turbocharged models) – exploded view

1	Front cover	8	Shift fork and rod (fifth/reverse)	15	Counter reverse gear
2	Clutch housing	9	Shift fork and rod (first/second)	16	Countershaft
3	Extension housing	10	Shift fork and rod (third/fourth)	17	Main drive gear
4	Bearing housing	11	Fifth gear	18	Mainshaft assembly first gear, clutch
5	Center housing	12	Clutch hub assembly (fifth/reverse)		hub assembly (first/second), second gear,
6	Undercover	13	Reverse gear		third gear, clutch hub assembly (third/fourth)
7	Transmission case	14	Reverse idler gear assembly	19	Dynamic damper

Chapter 7 Part B Automatic transmission

Contents

Automatic transmission fluid and filter change .... See Chapter 1
Automatic transmission fluid level check .... See Chapter 1
Automatic transmission – removal and installation 5
Diagnosis – general 2
General information 1
Neutral safety switch – check, adjustment and replacement 4
Oil seal replacement .... See Chapter 7A
Shift linkage – check and adjustment 3
Speedometer cable replacement .... See Chapter 7A
Transmission mount – check and replacment ...... See Chapter 7A

Specifications

General

Torque converter end-to-transmission bellhousing (Dimension A in illustration 5.21)
    1986 through 1988 models .... 1.30 in (33 mm)
    1989 models .... 1.26 in (32 mm)

Torque specifications   Ft-lbs

Torque converter-to-driveplate bolts
    1986 through 1988 models 25
    1989 on .... 25 to 36
Fluid pan bolts .... See Chapter 1

---

1 General information

All vehicles covered in this manual come equipped with either a five-speed manual transmission or an automatic transmission. All information on the automatic transmission is included in this Part of Chapter 7. Information on the manual transmission can be found in Part A of this Chapter.

Due to the complexity of the automatic transmissions covered in this manual and the need for specialized equipment to perform most service operations, this Chapter contains only general diagnosis, routine maintenance, adjustment and removal and installation procedures.

If the transmission requires major repair work, it should be left to a dealer service department or an automotive or transmission repair shop. You can, however, remove and install the transmission yourself and save the expense, even if the repair work is done by a transmission shop.

---

2 Diagnosis – general

Note: *Automatic transmission malfunctions may be caused by five general conditions: poor engine performance, improper adjustments, hydraulic malfunctions, mechanical malfunctions or malfunctions in the* computer or its signal network. Diagnosis of these problems should always begin with a check of the easily repaired items: fluid level and condition (see Chapter 1), shift linkage adjustment and throttle linkage adjustment. Next, perform a road test to determine if the problem has been corrected or if more diagnosis is necessary. If the problem persists after the preliminary tests and corrections are completed, additional diagnosis should be done by a dealer service department or transmission repair shop. Refer to the Troubleshooting Section at the front of this manual for information on symptoms of transmission problems.

Preliminary checks

1   Drive the vehicle to warm the transmission to normal operating temperature.
2   Check the fluid level as described in Chapter 1:
   a) If the fluid level is unusually low, add enough fluid to bring the level within the designated area of the dipstick, then check for external leaks (see below).
   b) If the fluid level is abnormally high, drain off the excess, then check the drained fluid for contamination by coolant. The presence of engine coolant in the automatic transmission fluid indicates that a failure has occurred in the internal radiator walls that separate the coolant from the transmission fluid (see Chapter 3).
   c) If the fluid is foaming, drain it and refill the transmission, then check for coolant in the fluid or a high fluid level.
3   Check the engine idle speed. **Note:** If the engine is malfunctioning, do not proceed with the preliminary checks until it has been repaired and runs normally.
4   Inspect the shift linkage (see Section 3). Make sure that it's properly adjusted and that the linkage operates smoothly.

Fluid leak diagnosis

5   Most fluid leaks are easy to locate visually. Repair usually consists of replacing a seal or gasket. If a leak is difficult to find, the following procedure may help.
6   Identify the fluid. Make sure it's transmission fluid and not engine oil or brake fluid (automatic transmission fluid is a deep red color).
7   Try to pinpoint the source of the leak. Drive the vehicle several miles, then park it over a large sheet of cardboard. After a minute or two, you should be able to locate the leak by determining the source of the fluid dripping onto the cardboard.
8   Make a careful visual inspection of the suspected component and the area immediately around it. Pay particular attention to gasket mating surfaces. A mirror is often helpful for finding leaks in areas that are hard to see.
9   If the leak still cannot be found, clean the suspected area thoroughly with a degreaser or solvent, then dry it.
10   Drive the vehicle for several miles at normal operating temperature and varying speeds. After driving the vehicle, visually inspect the suspected component again.
11   Once the leak has been located, the cause must be determined before it can be properly repaired. If a gasket is replaced but the sealing flange is bent, the new gasket will not stop the leak. The bent flange must be straightened.
12   Before attempting to repair a leak, check to make sure that the following conditions are corrected or they may cause another leak. **Note:** Some of the following conditions cannot be fixed without highly specialized tools and expertise. Such problems must be referred to a transmission repair shop or a dealer service department.

Gasket leaks

13   Check the pan periodically. Make sure the bolts are tight, no bolts are missing, the gasket is in good condition and the pan is flat (dents in the pan may indicate damage to the valve body inside).
14   If the pan gasket is leaking, the fluid level or the fluid pressure may be too high, the vent may be plugged, the pan bolts may be too tight, the pan sealing flange may be warped, the sealing surface of the transmission housing may be damaged, the gasket may be damaged or the transmission casting may be cracked or porous. If sealant instead of gasket materi-

al has been used to form a seal between the pan and the transmission housing, it may be the wrong sealant.

Seal leaks

15   If a transmission seal is leaking, the fluid level or pressure may be too high, the vent may be plugged, the seal bore may be damaged, the seal itself may be damaged or improperly installed, the surface of the shaft protruding through the seal may be damaged or a loose bearing may be causing excessive shaft movement.
16   Make sure the dipstick tube seal is in good condition and the tube is properly seated. Periodically check the area around the speedometer gear for leakage. If transmission fluid is evident, check the O–ring for damage (see Chapter 7A).

Case leaks

17   If the case itself appears to be leaking, the casting is porous and will have to be repaired or replaced.
18   Make sure the oil cooler hose fittings are tight and in good condition.

Fluid comes out the vent pipe or fill tube

19   If this condition occurs, the transmission is overfilled, there is coolant in the fluid, the case is porous, the dipstick is incorrect, the vent is plugged or the drain back holes are plugged.

---

3   Shift linkage – check and adjustment

Check

1   Check the operation of the transmission in each shift lever position (try to start the engine in each gear – the starter should operate in Park and Neutral only). If the engine does not start or starts in any gear other than Park or Neutral, the shift linkage is in need of adjustment or the Neutral safety switch (see Section 4) is defective or in need of adjustment.

Adjustment

1986 through 1988 models
Refer to illustration 3.4
2   Remove the shift console.
3   Raise the vehicle and support it securely on jackstands.
4   Loosen the locknuts on the shift linkage and place the shift lever in Park **(see illustration)**.
5   Working under the vehicle, move the the shift lever on the transmission to Park.
6   Inside the vehicle, turn locknut B until locknut A is just lightly touching the adjusting lever **(see illustration 3.4)**. Back off locknut A one full turn and then tighten locknut B securely.
7   Check the operation of the shift lever to make sure there is a click when shifting from the Park to Low detents, the shifter button returns smoothly and the shift lever lines up with the indicator in each position.

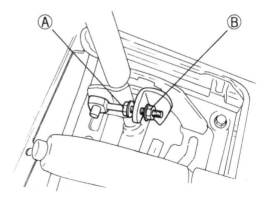

3.4   On 1986 through 1988 models, loosen the locknuts (A and B) prior to adjustment

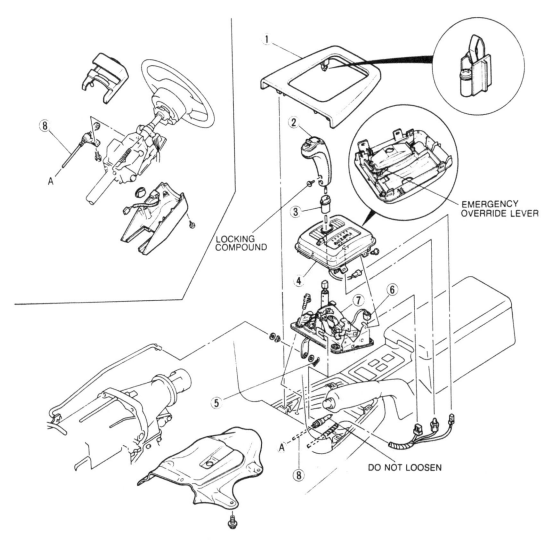

3.9 1989 and later model automatic transmission shift component details

1	Upper panel	5	Spring clip
2	Shift knob	6	Shift-lock actuator connector
3	Shift lever sleeve	7	Shift lever
4	Indicator panel	8	Interlock cable

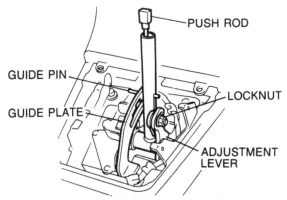

3.10 Loosen the adjustment lever locknut (1989 and later models)

1989 and later models

Refer to illustrations 3.9, 3.10, 3.12, 3.16 and 3.17

8   Disconnect the cable from the negative terminal of the battery.

9   Remove the console upper panel, shift knob, shift lever sleeve and indicator panel **(see illustration)**.

10   Loosen the adjustment lever locknut **(see illustration)**.

11   Push the shift lever forward, into Park.

12   Adjust the lever so the guide plate-to-guide pin clearance is as shown **(see illustration)**. Tighten the locknut securely.

13   Move the shift lever into the Neutral and Drive positions to verify that the guide plate-to-guide pin clearances are the same, loosening the locknut and adjusting, as necessary.

14   Install the indicator panel, shift sleeve and knob.

15   Check the operation of the shift lever to make sure there is a click when shifting from the Park to Low detents, the shifter button returns smoothly and the shift lever lines up with the indicator in each position.

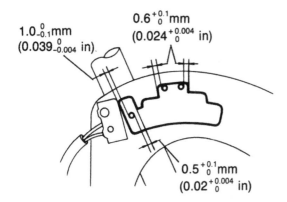

$1.0_{-0.1}^{0}$mm
$(0.039_{-0.004}^{0}$ in)

$0.6_{0}^{+0.1}$mm
$(0.024_{0}^{+0.004}$ in)

$0.5_{0}^{+0.1}$mm
$(0.02_{0}^{+0.004}$ in)

3.12   Shift linkage guide plate-to-guide pin clearance measurement details (1989 and later models)

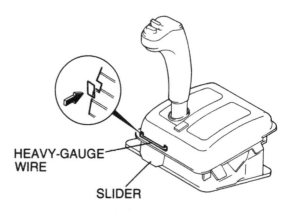

HEAVY-GAUGE WIRE

SLIDER

3.16   With the indicator retaining screws loose, insert a piece of heavy gauge wire into the alignment grooves (1989 and later models)

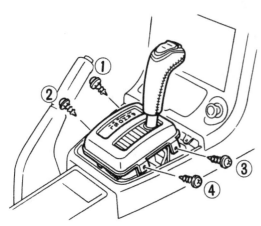

3.17   Tighten the retaining screws in the order shown and remove the piece of wire (1989 and later models)

16   If the shift lever is not properly aligned with the indicator, loosen the indicator retaining screws and insert a bent piece of heavy gauge wire into the alignment grooves (see illustration).

17   Tighten the screws in the order shown and remove the piece of wire (see illustration). Install the console upper panel.

All models

18   After adjustment check the operation of the transmission in each shift lever position (try to start the engine in each gear – the starter should operate in Park and Neutral only). Adjust the neutral safety switch if necessary (see Section 4).

---

4   Neutral safety switch – check, adjustment and replacement

1   The neutral safety switch, located on the side of the transmission, prevents the engine from starting with the transmission in gear.

Check

Refer to illustrations 4.4a through 4.4d

2   Make sure the engine will start only with the selector lever in Park and Neutral. With the key in the On position, make sure the backup lights function when the lever is in Reverse only.

3   If a malfunction is noted, raise the vehicle and support it on jackstands.

4   Disconnect the switch wire harness, attach the leads of an ohmmeter to the terminals and check for continuity (see illustrations).

5   Adjust the switch (see below) and then check that continuity is indicated between the switch terminals. If the switch does not operate properly after adjustment, replace it with a new one.

6   Disconnect the ohmmeter and reconnect the wire harness.

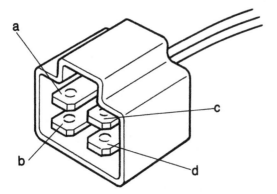

4.4a   Electrical connector terminals of the neutral safety switch (1986 through 1988 models)

Connection guide

Position	Connector terminal			
	a	b	c	d
P			○——○	
R	○——○			
N			○——○	
D, 1, 2				

○—○ : Indicates continuity

4.4b   Continuity should exist between the connector terminals shown when the switch is in the indicated position (1986 through 1988 models)

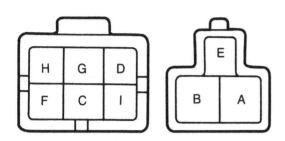

Position	Connector terminal								
	A	**B**	**C**	**D**	**E**	**F**	**G**	**H**	**I**
P	○——○		○——○						
R			○———————○						
N	○——○		○——————————○						
D			○———————————————○						
S			○——————————————————————○						
L			○——————————————————————————————○						

○———○: Indicates continuity

4.4c Electrical connector terminals of the 1989 and later model neutral safety switch

4.4d Check for continuity between the neutral safety switch terminals indicated (1989 and later models)

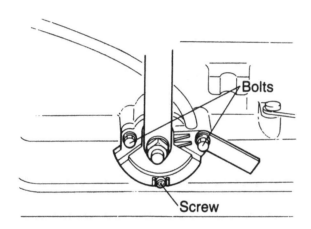

4.8 Mounting details of the neutral safety switch (1988 or earlier model shown, later models similar)

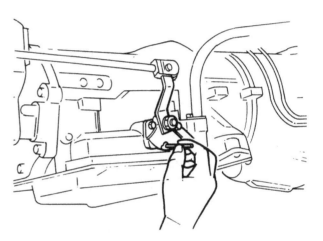

4.9 Insert an alignment pin (the shank of a 5/64-inch drill bit will work) into the hole in the Neutral safety switch – if the pin doesn't slide in fully, rotate the switch until it does

Adjustment

Refer to illustrations 4.8 and 4.9

7 Shift the transmission into Neutral.

8 Loosen the retaining bolts and remove the screw from the switch body **(see illustration)**.

9 Rotate the switch and insert a 5/64-inch (2.0 mm) diameter pin into the alignment hole and through the internal rotor **(see illustration)**.

10 Tighten the mounting bolts, then remove the pin and install the screw in the hole.

11 Recheck the switch operation as described in Step 17.

Replacement

12 Disconnect the cable from the negative terminal of the battery.

13 Remove the retaining nut that secures the shift lever to the lever shaft and separate the lever from the shaft.

14 Unplug the electrical connector, remove the screw and the two retaining bolts **(see illustration 4.8)** and lift the switch off.

15 Installation is the reverse of removal. Do not tighten the retaining bolts fully until the switch has been adjusted.

16 Connect the battery negative cable.

17 Start the engine in both Park and Neutral to verify that the switch is properly adjusted.

5 Automatic transmission – removal and installation

Refer to illustrations 5.11a, 5.11b and 5.21

Removal

1 Disconnect the negative cable from the battery.

2 Raise the vehicle and support it securely on jackstands.

3 Drain the transmission fluid (see Chapter 1), then reinstall the pan.

4 Remove any exhaust components which will interfere with transmission removal (see Chapter 4). On convertible models, remove the front crossmember.

5 Remove the torque converter cover.

6 Mark the torque converter and driveplate with white paint so they can be installed in the same position.

7 Remove the torque converter-to-driveplate bolts. Turn the crankshaft for access to each bolt. Turn the crankshaft in a clockwise direction only (as viewed from the front).

8 Remove the starter motor (see Chapter 5).

9 Remove the driveshaft (see Chapter 8).

10 Disconnect the speedometer cable.

11   Detach the wire harness connectors from the transmission **(see illustrations)**.
12   On models so equipped, disconnect the vacuum hoses.
13   Disconnect the shift linkage.
14   Support the engine with a jack. Use a block of wood under the oil pan to spread the load.
15   Support the transmission with a jack – preferably a jack made for this purpose. Safety chains will help steady the transmission on the jack.
16   Remove the rear crossmember bolts.
17   Remove the bolts securing the transmission to the engine.
18   Lower the transmission slightly and disconnect and plug the transmission fluid cooler lines.
19   Remove the transmission dipstick tube.
20   Move the transmission to the rear to disengage it from the engine block dowel pins and make sure the torque converter is detached from the driveplate. Secure the torque converter to the transmission so it won't fall out during removal. Lower the transmission slowly from the vehicle.

Installation

21   Prior to installation, make sure the torque converter hub is securely engaged in the pump **(see illustration)**.
22   With the transmission secured to the jack, raise it into position. Be sure to keep it level so the torque converter does not slide forward. Connect the transmission fluid cooler lines.
23   Turn the torque converter to line up the bolt holes with the holes in the driveplate. The white paint mark on the torque converter and the driveplate made in Step 6 must line up.
24   Move the transmission forward carefully until the dowel pins and the torque converter are engaged.
25   Install the transmission housing-to-engine bolts. Tighten them securely.
26   Install the torque converter-to-driveplate bolts. Tighten the bolts to the torque listed in this Chapter's Specifications.
27   Install the transmission mount crossmember and through-bolts. Tighten the bolts and nuts securely.
28   Remove the jacks supporting the transmission and the engine.
29   Install the dipstick tube, using a new O-ring.
30   Install the starter motor (see Chapter 5).
31   Connect the vacuum hose(s) (if equipped).
32   Connect the shift linkage.
33   Plug in the transmission wire harness connectors.
34   Install the torque converter cover.
35   Install the driveshaft.
36   Connect the speedometer cable.
37   Adjust the shift linkage.
38   Install any exhaust system components that were removed or disconnected. On convertible models, install the front crossmember.
39   Lower the vehicle.
40   Fill the transmission with the specified fluid (see Chapter 1), run the engine and check for fluid leaks.

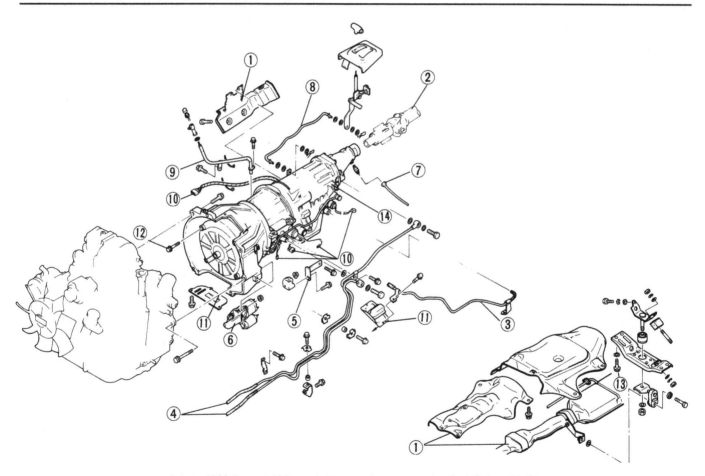

5.11a   1986 through 1988 model automatic transmission installation details

1	Exhaust system	6	Starter	11	Torque converter cover
2	Driveshaft	7	Speedometer cable	12	Bolt
3	Vacuum line	8	Shift linkage	13	Bolt
4	Fluid cooler lines	9	Fluid filler tube	14	Transmission
5	Starter bracket	10	Wiring harness		

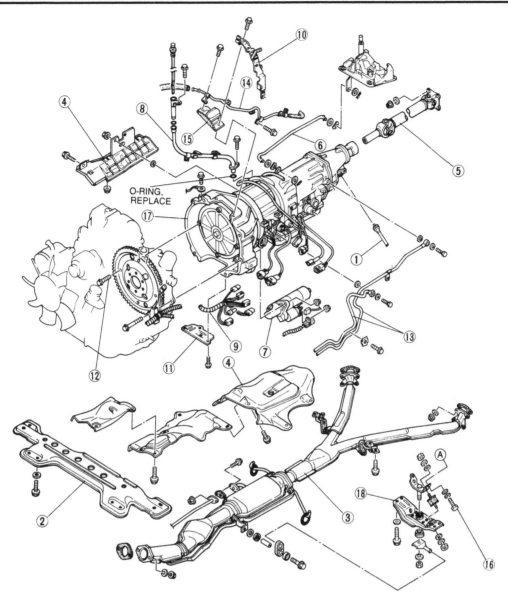

5.11b   1989 and later model automatic transmission installation details

1	Speedometer cable	7	Starter	
2	Front crossmember (convertible models)	8	Fluid filler tube	13 Fluid cooler lines
3	Exhaust system	9	Wiring harness	14 Vacuum line
4	Heat shield	10	Coupler bracket	15 Top cover
5	Driveshaft	11	Torque converter cover	16 Transmission mounting bolt
6	Shift linkage	12	Torque converter-to-driveplate bolt	17 Transmission
				18 Transmission mount

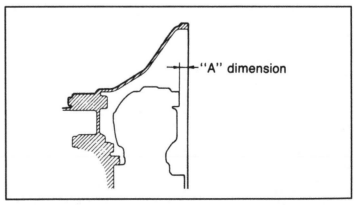

5.21   For the torque converter to be properly installed, the distance from the end of the torque converter to the end of the transmission housing (dimension A) must be as listed in the Specifications section at the front of this Chapter

Chapter 8 Clutch and drivetrain

Contents

Clutch components – removal, inspection and installation 3
Clutch – description and check 2
Clutch fluid level check . . . . See Chapter 1
Clutch hydraulic system – bleeding 8
Clutch master cylinder – removal, overhaul and installation 6
Clutch pedal freeplay and height check
  and adjustment . . . . See Chapter 1
Clutch pedal – removal, installation and adjustment 9
Clutch release bearing and lever – removal, inspection
  and installation 4
Clutch release cylinder – removal, overhaul and installation 7
Differential assembly – removal and installation 15

Differential lubricant level check . . . . See Chapter 1
Differential output shaft seal – replacement 17
Driveaxle boot replacement and constant velocity (CV)
  joint overhaul 14
Driveaxles – general information and check 12
Driveaxles – removal and installation 13
Driveline inspection 10
Driveshaft – removal and installation 11
Flywheel – removal and installation . . . . See Chapter 2
General information 1
Pilot bearing and seal – inspection and replacement 5
Pinion oil seal – replacement 16

Specifications

Clutch

Fluid type	See Chapter 1
Pedal height and freeplay	See Chapter 1

Drivetrain

Differential pinion shaft preload	11.3 to 15.6 in-lbs
Driveaxle standard length	
Turbo model	25.10 in (637.5 mm)
Non-turbo models	23.43 in (646.0 mm)

Torque specifications

	Ft-lbs
Pressure plate-to-flywheel bolts	
1989 and earlier	13 to 20
1990 on	18 to 26
Driveshaft-to-differential flange nuts	
1989 and earlier	36 to 43
1990 on	49 to 50
Driveaxle-to-differential output shaft	40 to 47
Driveaxle hub nut	174 to 231
Differential front mounting nuts	65 to 77
Differential rear mounting nuts	54 to 69

1   General information

The information in this Chapter deals with the components from the rear of the engine to the rear wheels, except for the transmission, which is dealt with in the previous Chapter. For the purposes of this Chapter, these components are grouped into three categories; clutch, driveshaft and rear axle. Separate Sections within this Chapter offer general descriptions and checking procedures for components in each of the three groups.

Since nearly all the procedures covered in this Chapter involve working under the vehicle, make sure it's securely supported on sturdy jackstands or on a hoist where the vehicle can be easily raised and lowered.

2   Clutch – description and check

Refer to illustration 2.1

1   All vehicles with a manual transmission use a single dry plate, diaphragm spring type clutch **(see illustration)**. The clutch disc has a splined hub which allows it to slide along the splines of the transmission input shaft. The clutch and pressure plate are held in contact by spring pressure exerted by the diaphragm in the pressure plate.

2   The clutch release system is operated by hydraulic pressure. The hydraulic release system consists of the clutch pedal, a master cylinder and fluid reservoir, the hydraulic line, a release (or slave) cylinder which actuates the clutch release lever and the clutch release (or throwout) bearing.

3   When pressure is applied to the clutch pedal to release the clutch, hydraulic or mechanical pressure is exerted against the outer end of the clutch release lever. As the lever pivots the shaft fingers push against the release bearing. The bearing pushes against the fingers of the diaphragm spring of the pressure plate assembly, which in turn releases the clutch plate.

4   Terminology can be a problem when discussing the clutch components because common names are in some cases different from those used by the manufacturer. For example, the driven plate is also called the clutch plate or disc, the clutch release bearing is sometimes called a throwout bearing, the release cylinder is sometimes called the operating or slave cylinder.

5   Other than to replace components with obvious damage, some preliminary checks should be performed to diagnose clutch problems. These checks assume the transmission is in good working condition.

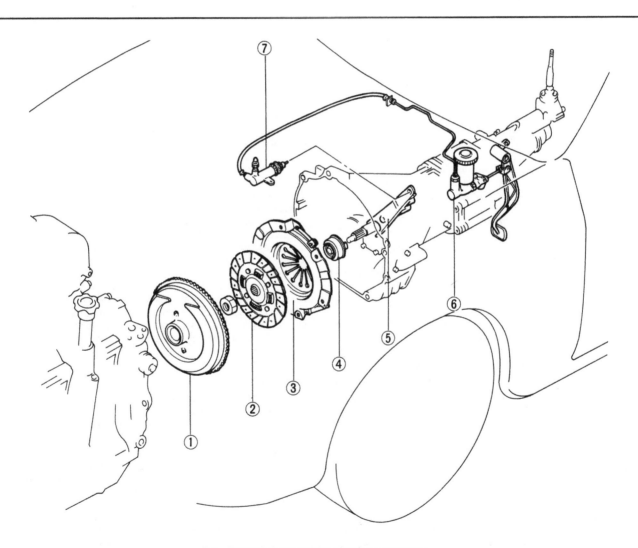

2.1   Exploded view of the clutch components

1	Flywheel				
2	Clutch disc	4	Release bearing	6	Master cylinder
3	Pressure plate	5	Release fork	7	Release cylinder

3.6   Mark the relationship of the pressure plate to the flywheel (in case you are going to re-use the same pressure plate)

a) The first check should be of the fluid level in the clutch master cylinder. If the fluid level is low, add fluid as necessary and inspect the hydraulic system for leaks. If the master cylinder reservoir has run dry, bleed the system as described in Section 8 and retest the clutch operation.

b) To check "clutch spin down time," run the engine at normal idle speed with the transmission in Neutral (clutch pedal up – engaged). Disengage the clutch (pedal down), wait several seconds and shift the transmission into Reverse. No grinding noise should be heard. A grinding noise would most likely indicate a problem in the pressure plate or the clutch disc.

c) To check for complete clutch release, run the engine (with the parking brake applied to prevent movement) and hold the clutch pedal approximately 1/2-inch from the floor. Shift the transmission between 1first gear and Reverse several times. If the shift is rough, component failure is indicated. Check the release cylinder pushrod travel. With the clutch pedal depressed completely, the release cylinder pushrod should extend substantially. If it doesn't, check the fluid level in the clutch master cylinder.

d) Visually inspect the pivot bushing at the top of the clutch pedal to make sure there is no binding or excessive play.

e) Wiggle the clutch release lever and make sure it is solidly mounted on the ball stud.

---

3   Clutch components – removal, inspection and installation

Warning: *Dust produced by clutch wear and deposited on clutch components may contain asbestos, which is hazardous to your health. DO NOT blow it out with compressed air and DO NOT inhale it. DO NOT use gasoline or petroleum-based solvents to remove the dust. Brake system cleaner should be used to flush the dust into a drain pan. After the clutch components are wiped clean with a rag, dispose of the contaminated rags and cleaner in a covered, marked container.*

Removal

Refer to illustration 3.6

1   ¯Access to the clutch components is normally accomplished by removing the transmission, leaving the engine in the vehicle. If, of course, the engine is being removed for major overhaul, then check the clutch for wear and replace worn components as necessary. However, the relatively low cost of the clutch components compared to the time and trouble spent gaining access to them warrants their replacement anytime the engine or transmission is removed, unless they are new or in near perfect condition. The following procedures are based on the assumption the engine will stay in place.

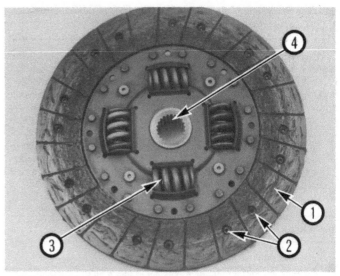

3.11   Examine the clutch disc for evidence of excessive wear, such as a thin, smeared or glazed lining, loose rivets, worn hub splines and distorted damper springs

1	Lining	3	Damper springs
2	Rivets	4	Hub splines

2   Referring to Chapter 7 Part A, remove the transmission from the vehicle. Support the engine while the transmission is out. Preferably, an engine hoist should be used to support it from above. However, if a jack is used underneath the engine, make sure a piece of wood is positioned between the jack and oil pan to spread the load. **Caution:** *The pickup for the oil pump is very close to the bottom of the oil pan. If the pan is bent or distorted in any way, engine oil starvation could occur.*

3   Remove the release cylinder (see Section 7).

4   The clutch fork and release bearing can remain attached to the transmission for the time being.

5   To support the clutch disc during removal, install a clutch alignment tool through the clutch disc hub.

6   Carefully inspect the flywheel and pressure plate for indexing marks. The marks are usually an X, an O or a white letter. If they cannot be found, apply marks yourself so the pressure plate and the flywheel will be in the same alignment during installation **(see illustration)**.

7   Turning each bolt a little at a time, loosen the pressure plate-to-flywheel bolts. Work in a criss-cross pattern until all spring pressure is relieved. Then hold the pressure plate securely and completely remove the bolts, followed by the pressure plate and clutch disc.

Inspection

Refer to illustrations 3.11 and 3.13

8   Ordinarily, when a problem occurs in the clutch, it can be attributed to wear of the clutch driven plate assembly (clutch disc). However, all components should be inspected at this time.

9   Inspect the flywheel for cracks, heat checking, grooves and other obvious defects. If the imperfections are slight, a machine shop can machine the surface flat and smooth, which is highly recommended regardless of the surface appearance. Refer to Chapter 2 for the flywheel removal and installation procedure.

10   Inspect the pilot bearing (see Section 5).

11   Inspect the lining on the clutch disc. There should be at least 1/16-inch of lining above the rivet heads. Check for loose rivets, distortion, cracks, broken springs and other obvious damage **(see illustration)**. As mentioned above, ordinarily the clutch disc is routinely replaced, so if in doubt about the condition, replace it with a new one.

12   The release bearing should also be replaced along with the clutch disc (see Section 4).

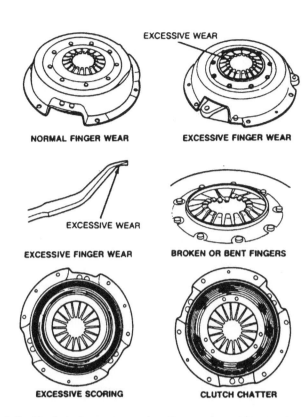

NORMAL FINGER WEAR   EXCESSIVE FINGER WEAR

EXCESSIVE FINGER WEAR   BROKEN OR BENT FINGERS

EXCESSIVE SCORING   CLUTCH CHATTER

3.13   Replace the pressure plate if excessive or abnormal wear is noted

13   Check the machined surfaces and the diaphragm spring fingers of the pressure plate **(see illustration)**. If the surface is grooved or otherwise damaged, replace the pressure plate. Also check for obvious damage, distortion, cracking, etc. Light glazing can be removed with medium grit emery cloth. If a new pressure plate is required, new and factory-rebuilt units are available.

Installation

Refer to illustration 3.15

14   Before installation, clean the flywheel and pressure plate machined surfaces with lacquer thinner or acetone. It's important that no oil or grease is on these surfaces or the lining of the clutch disc. Handle the parts only with clean hands.

15   Position the clutch disc and pressure plate against the flywheel with the clutch held in place with an alignment tool **(see illustration)**. Make sure it's installed properly (most replacement clutch plates will be marked "flywheel side" or something similar – if not marked, install the clutch disc with the damper springs toward the transmission).

16   Tighten the pressure plate-to-flywheel bolts only finger tight, working around the pressure plate.

17   Center the clutch disc by ensuring the alignment tool extends through the splined hub and into the pilot bearing in the crankshaft. Wiggle the tool up, down or side-to-side as needed to bottom the tool in the pilot bearing. Tighten the pressure plate-to-flywheel bolts a little at a time, working in a criss-cross pattern to prevent distorting the cover. After all of the bolts are snug, tighten them to the torque listed in this Chapter's specifications. Remove the alignment tool.

18   Using high temperature grease, lubricate the inner groove of the release bearing (see Section 4). Also place grease on the release lever contact areas and the transmission input shaft bearing retainer.

19   Install the clutch release bearing as described in Section 4.

20   Install the transmission, slave cylinder and all components removed previously. Tighten all fasteners to the proper torque specifications.

3.15   Center the clutch disc in the pressure plate with a clutch alignment tool

4.3   To remove the release bearing, slide it forward until the release lever is at its maximum travel, then disengage the release lever ends from the tangs on the release bearing (arrows)

4   Clutch release bearing and lever – removal, inspection and installation

Refer to illustrations 4.3 and 4.5

Warning: *Dust produced by clutch wear and deposited on clutch components may contain asbestos, which is hazardous to your health. DO NOT blow it out with compressed air and DO NOT inhale it. DO NOT use gasoline or petroleum-based solvents to remove the dust. Brake system cleaner should be used to flush the dust into a drain pan. After the clutch components are wiped clean with a rag, dispose of the contaminated rags and cleaner in a covered, marked container.*

Removal

1   Disconnect the negative cable from the battery.

2   Remove the transmission (see Chapter 7).

3   The release bearing slides on a sleeve located around the transmission input shaft **(see illustration)**. Slide the bearing forward, to its maximum travel on the sleeve, disengage the tangs on the bearing from the release lever ends and slide the bearing off the input shaft. Give the release lever a sharp tug to pull it off its ball stud.

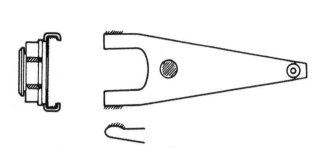

4.5   Apply a light coat of high-temperature grease to the shaded areas of the bearing and release fork

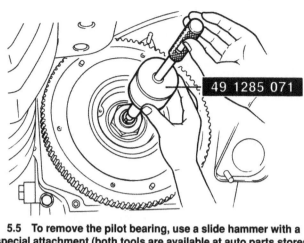

5.5   To remove the pilot bearing, use a slide hammer with a special attachment (both tools are available at auto parts stores)

Inspection

4   Hold the center of the bearing and rotate the outer portion while applying pressure. If the bearing doesn't turn smoothly or if it's noisy, replace it with a new one. Wipe the bearing with a clean rag and inspect it for damage, wear and cracks. Don't immerse the bearing in solvent – it's sealed for life and to do so would ruin it.

Installation

5   Lightly lubricate the clutch lever ends and spring retention crown where they contact the bearing with high-temperature grease. Fill the inner groove of the bearing with the same grease **(see illustration)**.

6   Snap the release lever back into place on its ball stud. Guide the release bearing onto the input shaft sleeve, pull the release lever out to its maximum travel and engage the lever ends with the tangs on the bearing.

7   Apply a light coat of high-temperature grease to the face of the release bearing, where it contacts the pressure plate diaphragm fingers.

8   Prior to installing the transmission, apply a light coat of grease to the input shaft sleeve.

9   The remainder of installation is the reverse of the removal procedure. Tighten all bolts to the specified torque.

---

5   Pilot bearing and seal – inspection and replacement

Refer to illustration 5.5

1   The clutch pilot bearing is a needle roller type bearing which is pressed into the rear of the eccentric shaft. It is greased at the factory and does not require additional lubrication. Its primary purpose is to support the front of the transmission input shaft. The pilot bearing should be inspected whenever the clutch components are removed from the engine. Due to its inaccessibility, if you are in doubt as to its condition, replace it with a new one. **Note:** *If the engine has been removed from the vehicle, disregard the following steps which do not apply.*

2   Remove the transmission (see Chapter 7 Part A).

3   Remove the clutch components (see Section 3).

4   Inspect for any excessive wear, scoring, lack of grease, dryness or obvious damage. If any of these conditions are noted, the bearing should be replaced. A flashlight will be helpful to direct light into the recess.

5   You will need a slide hammer and a special attachment to remove the bearing **(see illustration)**. These tools are available from most auto parts stores.

6   Insert the attachment into the pilot bearing and tighten it to expand the end behind the bearing. A couple of sharp blows with the slide hammer should be all that is necessary to pull the bearing and seal from the recess in the eccentric shaft.

7   To install the new bearing, lightly lubricate the outside surface with lithium-base grease, then drive it into the recess with a socket that is slightly smaller in diameter than the bearing.

8   Tap the new seal into the bore using the same socket. The seal must bottom against the bearing.

9   Lubricate the bearing with lithium-based grease.

10   Install the clutch components, transmission and all other components removed previously. Tighten all fasteners properly.

---

6   Clutch master cylinder – removal, overhaul and installation

---

Refer to illustrations 6.1, 6.2, 6.3, 6.4, 6.5a, 6.5b and 6.6

Caution: *Do not allow brake fluid to contact any painted surfaces of the vehicle, as damage to the finish may result.*

Removal

1   Disconnect the hydraulic line from the master cylinder and plug the line **(see illustration)**.

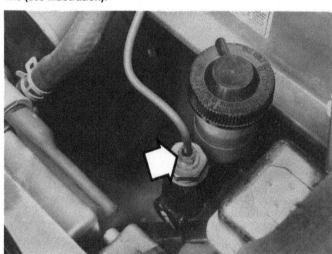

6.1   Unscrew the fitting (arrow) from the master cylinder using a flare nut wrench, if available, to prevent rounding off the corners of the fitting.

2   Remove the master cylinder mounting nuts from under the dash **(see illustration)** and withdraw the unit from the engine compartment. Be careful not to spill any of the fluid on the paint.

Overhaul

3   Pry the reservoir off the master cylinder with a screwdriver **(see illustration)**.

4   Push the piston in with a phillips screwdriver. Remove the snap-ring with a pair of snap-ring pliers or a small screwdriver **(see illustration)**.

5   Pull out the piston assembly and spring **(see illustrations)**.

6.2   Unscrew the two mounting nuts (arrows) from under the dash, then remove the master cylinder from the engine compartment – it's not necessary to disconnect the pushrod from the pedal

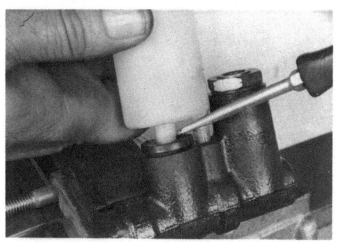

6.3   When detaching the reservoir from the master cylinder body, pry it straight up to avoid cracking the reservoir outlets

6.4   Depress the piston with a phillips screwdriver, then remove the snap-ring: if the cylinder is equipped with a snap-ring like the one shown, remove it with snap-ring pliers – if it has a triangular snap-ring, remove it with a small screwdriver

6.5a   After removing the piston assembly, pull out the return spring and primary cup – note the translucent cup protector on the back side of the cup

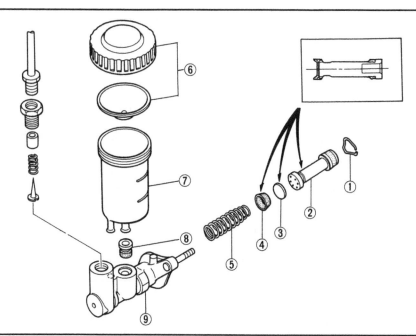

6.5b   Exploded view of the clutch master cylinder

1   Snap-ring
2   Piston and secondary cup assembly
3   Protector
4   Primary cup
5   Return spring
6   Reservoir cap and baffle
7   Reservoir
8   Reservoir seal
9   Master cylinder body

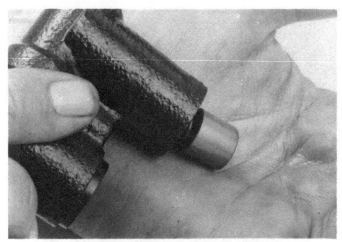

6.6   After unscrewing the outlet fitting, the one-way fluid valve piston and spring can be removed by tapping the cylinder against the palm of your hand – do not attempt to remove the pin at the bottom of the bore

7.2   To disconnect the hydraulic line fitting at the bracket on the firewall, hold the hose end (1) with an open end wrench, loosen the tube nut (2) with a flare-nut wrench, then pull out the clip (3) that secures the hose to the bracket

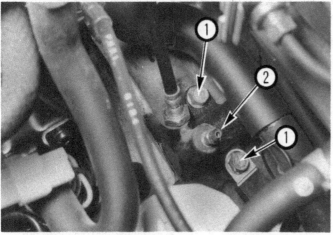

7.3   The clutch release cylinder is mounted to the top of the clutch housing with two bolts (1) – when bleeding the hydraulic system, use the bleeder valve (2) (bleeder valve cap shown removed for clarity)

7.5a   Peel the dust boot from the release cylinder body and remove it along with the pushrod

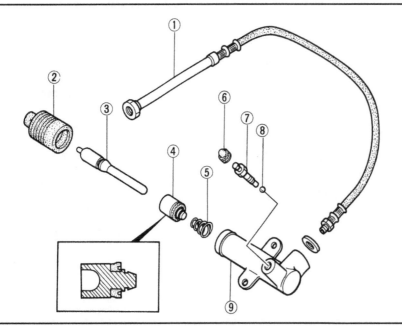

7.5b   Exploded view of the clutch release cylinder

1   Fluid hose
2   Boot
3   Pushrod
4   Piston and cup assembly
5   Return spring
6   Bleeder valve cap
7   Bleeder valve
8   Steel ball

7.6   Tap the cylinder sharply against a block of wood to remove the piston – if this doesn't work, apply compressed air to the fluid feed hole while pointing the open end of the cylinder into a pile of rags – use only enough pressure to ease the piston out

6   Some models have a one-way fluid valve under the outlet fitting. Unscrew the fitting and remove the piston one-way valve and spring **(see illustration)**.
7   Examine the inner surface of the cylinder bore. If it is scored or exhibits bright wear areas, the entire master cylinder should be replaced.
8   If the cylinder bore is in good condition, obtain a clutch master cylinder rebuild kit, which will contain all of the necessary replacement parts.
9   Prior to installing any parts, first dip them in brake fluid to lubricate them.
10   Install the new parts in the reverse order of removal.

Installation

11   Position the clutch master cylinder against the firewall, inserting the pedal pushrod into the piston. Install the nuts, tightening them securely.
12   Bleed the clutch hydraulic system following the procedure in Section 8, then check the pedal height and freeplay as described in Chapter 1.

---

7   Clutch release cylinder – removal, overhaul and installation

---

Note: *Before beginning this procedure, contact local parts stores and dealer service departments concerning the purchase of a rebuild kit or a new release cylinder. Availability and cost of the necessary parts may dictate whether the cylinder is rebuilt or replaced with a new one. If it's decided to rebuild the cylinder, inspect the bore as described in Step 8 before purchasing parts.*

Removal

Refer to illustrations 7.2 and 7.3

1   Disconnect the negative cable from the battery.
2   Disconnect the hydraulic line at the firewall **(see illustration)**. If available, use a flare nut wrench on the fitting, which will prevent the fitting from being rounded off. Have some rags handy, as some fluid will be spilled as the line is removed.
3   Remove the two release cylinder mounting bolts **(see illustration)**.
4   Remove the release cylinder.

Overhaul

Refer to illustrations 7.5a, 7.5b and 7.6

5   Remove the pushrod and the boot **(see illustrations)**.
6   Tap the cylinder on a block of wood to eject the piston and seal **(see illustration)**. Also remove the spring from inside the cylinder.
7   Carefully inspect the bore of the cylinder. Check for deep scratches, score marks and ridges. The bore must be smooth to the touch. If any imperfections are found, the release cylinder must be replaced with a new one.

8   Using the new parts in the rebuild kit, assemble the components using plenty of fresh brake fluid for lubrication. Note that the lip on the piston cup faces away from the piston **(see illustration 7.5b)**.

Installation

9   Install the release cylinder on the clutch housing. Make sure the push-rod is seated in the release fork pocket.
10   Reconnect the hydraulic line. Tighten the fitting securely.
11   Fill the clutch master cylinder with brake fluid conforming to DOT 3 specifications.
12   Bleed the system as described in Section 8.
13   Connect the negative battery cable.

---

8   Clutch hydraulic system – bleeding

---

1   The hydraulic system should be bled to remove all air whenever any part of the system has been removed or if the fluid level has fallen so low that air has been drawn into the master cylinder. The procedure is very similar to bleeding a brake system.
2   Fill the master cylinder with new brake fluid conforming to DOT 3 specifications. **Caution:** *Don't re-use any of the fluid coming from the system during the bleeding operation. Also, don't use fluid which has been inside an open container for an extended period of time.*
3   Remove the dust cap which fits over the bleeder valve **(see illustration 7.3)** and push a length of plastic hose over the valve. Place the other end of the hose in a clear container with about two inches of brake fluid. The hose end must be in the fluid at the bottom of the container.
4   Have an assistant depress the clutch pedal and hold it. Open the bleeder valve, allowing fluid to flow through the hose. Close the bleeder valve when the flow of fluid and bubbles ceases. Once closed, have your assistant release the pedal.
5   Continue this process until all air is evacuated from the system, indicated by a solid stream of fluid being ejected from the bleeder valve each time with no air bubbles in the hose or container. Keep a close watch on the fluid level inside the master cylinder – if the level drops too low, air will be sucked back into the system and the process will have to be started all over again.
6   Install the dust cap and lower the vehicle. Check carefully for proper operation before placing the vehicle in normal service.

---

9   Clutch pedal – removal, installation and adjustment

Refer to illustrations 9.2 and 9.3

1   Disconnect the cable from the negative terminal of the battery.
2   Working under the dash, disconnect the master cylinder pushrod from the clutch pedal by removing the C-clip from the clevis pin and pushing the clevis pin out **(see illustration)**.

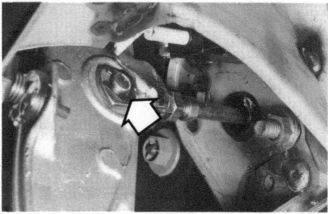

9.2   Remove the C-clip (arrow) from the clevis pin, then push the clevis pin out to disconnect the pushrod from the pedal

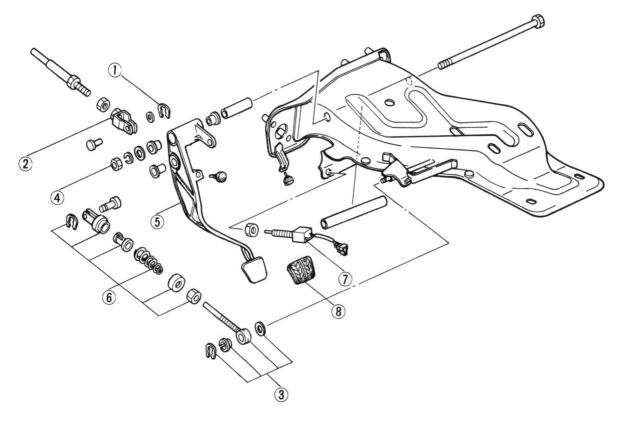

9.3   Clutch pedal mounting details

1	C-clip	4	Pivot shaft nut, bushing and washer	6	Clutch assist lever assembly
2	Pushrod clevis	5	Clutch pedal	7	Clutch switch
3	Assist lever clip, bushing and washer			8	Pedal pad

3   Disconnect the clutch assist lever assembly from the pedal by removing the C-clip and pushing out the clevis pin **(see illustration)**.
4   Unscrew the pivot shaft nut and slide the shaft to the right. Hold the pedal as this is done to keep it from falling.
5   Inspect the bushings in the pedal for wear and deterioration, replacing them if necessary. You can remove the bushings by prying them out with a screwdriver. Apply a light coat of multi-purpose grease to the bushings before installing the pedal.
6   Installation is the reverse of removal. Adjust the clutch pedal height and freeplay following the procedure in Chapter 1.

10   Driveline inspection

1   Raise the rear of the vehicle and support it securely on jackstands.
2   Crawl under the vehicle and visually inspect the driveshaft. Look for any dents or cracks in the tubing. If any are found, the driveshaft must be replaced.
3   Check for any oil leakage at the front and rear of the driveshaft. Leakage where the driveshaft enters the transmission indicates a defective rear transmission seal. Leakage where the driveshaft enters the differential indicates a defective pinion seal. For these repair operations refer to Chapters 7 and 8 respectively.
4   While under the vehicle, have an assistant turn the rear wheel so the driveshaft will rotate. As it does, make sure the U-joints are operating properly without binding, noise or looseness.
5   The U-joints can also be checked with the driveshaft motionless, by gripping your hands on either side of the joint and attempting to twist the

joint. Any movement at all in the joint is a sign of considerable wear. Lifting up on the shaft will also indicate movement in the U-joints. If the U-joints show wear, the entire driveshaft must be replaced.
6   Check the driveshaft mounting bolts at the rear to make sure they are tight.
7   Check for looseness in the joints of the driveaxles. Also check for grease or oil leakage from around the driveaxles by inspecting the rubber boots and both ends of each axle. Oil leakage at the differential junction indicates a defective side oil seal. Leakage at the wheel side indicates a defective front hub seal, while leakage at the boots means a damaged rubber boot. For servicing of these components, see the appropriate Sections.

11   Driveshaft – removal and installation

Refer to illustrations 11.4 and 11.5

Removal

1   Disconnect the negative cable from the battery.
2   Raise the rear of vehicle and support it securely on jackstands. Place the transmission in Neutral with the parking brake off. Block the front wheels.
3   Remove the rear half of the exhaust system (see Chapter 4).
4   Using a scribe, white paint or a hammer and punch, place marks on the driveshaft and the differential flange in line with each other **(see illustration)**. This is to make sure the driveshaft is reinstalled in the same position to preserve the balance.

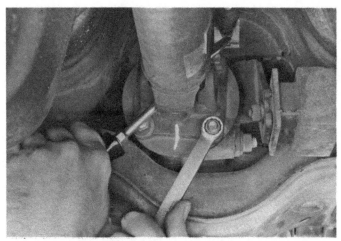

11.4   Mark the relationship of the U-joint flange to the pinion flange, then remove the nuts – to prevent the driveshaft from turning, use a screwdriver, as shown here

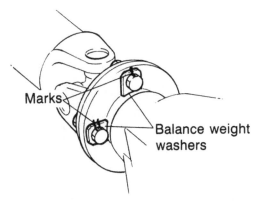

11.5   If any balance weights are on the rear of the pinion flange, mark their positions before removing the bolts

5   Remove the rear universal joint nuts, bolts and washers. Turn the driveshaft (or tires) as necessary to bring the bolts into the most accessible position. If any balance weights are present on the rear of the pinion flange, mark their positions with a scribe or white paint **(see illustration)**.

6   Lower the rear of the driveshaft, then slide the front out of the transmission.

7   To prevent loss of fluid and protect against contamination while the driveshaft is out, wrap a plastic bag over the transmission housing and hold it in place with a rubber band.

Installation

8   Remove the plastic bag from the transmission and wipe the area clean. Inspect the oil seal carefully. Procedures for replacement of this seal can be found in Chapter 7.

9   Slide the front of the driveshaft into the transmission.

10   Raise the rear of the driveshaft into position, checking to be sure the marks are in alignment. If not, turn the rear wheels to match the pinion flange and the driveshaft.

11   Install the bolts, washers and nuts (and balance weights if any were present). Tighten the nuts to the torque listed in this Chapter's specifications.

12   Install the rear of the exhaust system and reconnect the battery cable.

---

12   Driveaxles – general information and check

Power is transmitted from the transmission to the wheels through a pair of driveaxles. The inner end of each driveaxle is connected to the differential by an output shaft (flanged stub axle) splined to the differential side gear. The output shafts are lightly press fitted and can be easily pried out if it becomes necessary to replace the output shaft oil seals (see Section 17). The outer ends of the driveaxles are splined to the axle hubs and locked in place by an axle nut.

The inner ends of the driveaxles are equipped with sliding constant velocity (CV) joints , which are capable of both angular and axial motion. Each inner joint assembly consists of an inner race, bearings, cage and a housing in which the joint is free to slide in and out as the driveaxle moves up and down with the wheel. The inner joints are rebuildable (see Section 14).

Each outer joint, which consists of ball bearings running between an inner race and an outer cage, is capable of angular but not axial movement. The outer joints are neither rebuildable nor removable. Should one of them fail, a new driveaxle/outer joint assembly must be installed.

The boots should be periodically inspected for damage, leaking lubricant and cuts. Damaged CV joint boots must be replaced immediately or the joints can be damaged. Boot replacement involves removal of the driveaxle (see Section 13). **Note:** *Some auto parts stores carry "split" type replacement boots, which can be installed without removing the driveaxle from the vehicle. This is a convenient alternative; however, it's recommended that the driveaxle be removed and the CV joint disassembled and cleaned to ensure that the joint is free from contaminants such as moisture and dirt, which will accelerate CV joint wear.* The most common symptom of worn or damaged CV joints, besides lubricant leaks, is a clicking noise in turns, a clunk when accelerating from a coasting condition or vibration at highway speeds.

To check for wear in the CV joints and driveaxle shafts, grasp each axle (one at a time) and rotate it in both directions while holding the CV joint housings, inspecting for movement, indicating worn splines or sloppy CV joints. Also check the driveaxle shafts for cracks, dents, twisting and bending.

---

13   Driveaxles – removal and installation

Refer to illustrations 13.2a, 13.2b, 13.4 and 13.5

Removal

1   Loosen the rear wheel lug nuts, raise the rear of the vehicle and support it securely on jackstands. Remove the wheel.

2   Use a hammer and punch to knock the staked portion of the driveaxle hub nut out of the groove in the driveaxle **(see illustration)**, then remove the nut. To prevent the hub from turning, place a prybar between two of the wheel studs, then loosen the nut **(see illustration)**.

13.2a   Use a hammer and punch to knock the staked portion of the hub nut out of the groove in the driveaxle end

13.2b   To prevent the hub from turning while loosening the hub nut, brace a large pry bar across two of the wheel studs and allow it to come into contact with the ground

13.4   Mark the relationship of the driveaxle inner CV joint to the differential output shaft, then remove the nuts and washers – to prevent the driveaxle from turning, insert a screwdriver between a nut and the CV joint housing

13.5   Use a puller to force the splined portion of the driveaxle out of the hub

14.3   Pry the clamp retaining tabs up with a small screwdriver and slide the clamps off the boot

3   Remove the brake caliper, caliper mounting bracket and disc. Support the caliper out of the way with a piece of wire (see Chapter 9).

4   Mark the relationship of the driveaxle to the differential flange, then remove the nuts **(see illustration)**. Separate the driveaxle from the flange and hang it with a piece of wire from the underbody.

5   Push the driveaxle out of the hub with a puller **(see illustration)** and carefully remove the driveaxle from the vehicle.

Installation

6   Apply a light coat of multi-purpose grease to the outer CV joint splines and install the stub axle into the hub.

7   Connect the inner end of the driveaxle to the differential flange, aligning the previously applied matchmarks. Install the washers and nuts, tightening them to the torque listed in this Chapter's specifications.

8   Install the brake disc, caliper mounting bracket and caliper (see Chapter 9 if necessary).

9   Install a new hub nut. Lock the disc so it cannot turn as described in Step 2, then tighten the hub nut to the torque listed in this Chapter's specifications. Stake the collar of the nut into the groove in the driveaxle using a hammer and punch.

10   Install the wheel and lower the vehicle. Tighten the lug nuts to the torque specified in Chapter 1.

---

14   Driveaxle boot replacement and constant velocity (CV) joint overhaul

---

Inner CV joint and boot
Disassembly
Refer to illustrations 14.3, 14.4, 14.5a, 14.5b, 14.6, 14.7, 14.9, 14.10a and 14.10b

1   Remove the driveaxle from the vehicle (see Section 13).

2   Mount the driveaxle in a vise. The jaw of the vise should be lined with wood or rags to prevent damage to the axleshaft.

3   Pry the boot clamp retaining tabs up with a small screwdriver and slide the clamps off the boot **(see illustration)**.

4   Slide the boot back on the axleshaft and pry the wire ring ball retainer from the outer race **(see illustration)**.

5   Mark the relationship of the outer race to the axleshaft and pull the outer race off the inner bearing assembly **(see illustrations)**.

6   Mark the inner race, cage and axleshaft end to ensure that they are reassembled in the same position **(see illustration)**.

7   Remove the snap-ring from the groove in the axleshaft with a pair of snap-ring pliers **(see illustration)**.

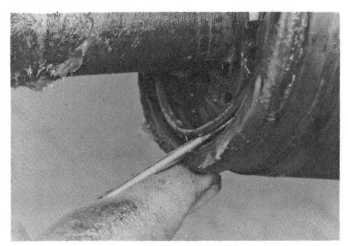

14.4   Pry the wire ring ball retainer out of the outer race, then slide the outer race (housing) off the bearing assembly

14.5a   Use paint or a felt–tip marker to mark the outer race and axleshaft – DO NOT use a punch or scribe

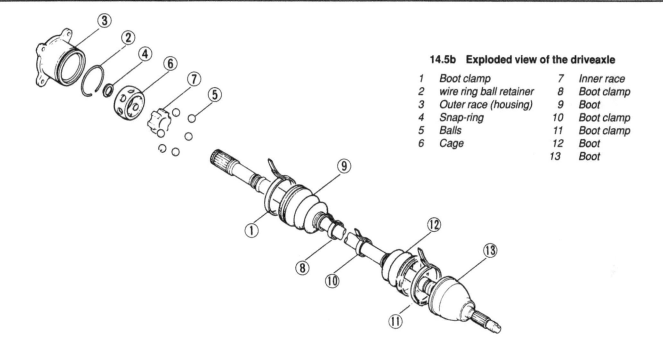

14.5b   Exploded view of the driveaxle

1	Boot clamp	7	Inner race
2	wire ring ball retainer	8	Boot clamp
3	Outer race (housing)	9	Boot
4	Snap-ring	10	Boot clamp
5	Balls	11	Boot clamp
6	Cage	12	Boot
		13	Boot

14.6   Apply marks to the inner race, cage and axleshaft . . .

14.7   . . . then remove the outer snap-ring

14.9   Pry the balls out of the cage, but be careful not to nick or scratch them

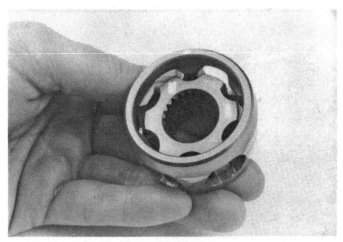

14.10a   Align the lands of the inner race with the window of the cage . . .

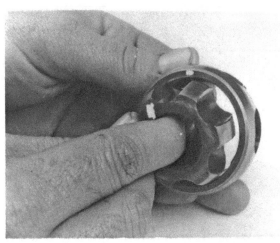

14.10b   . . . then remove the inner race from the cage

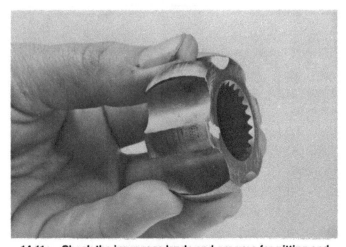

14.11a   Check the inner race lands and grooves for pitting and score marks

8   Slide the inner bearing assembly off the axleshaft.

9   Using a small screwdriver or a piece of wood, pry the balls from the cage **(see illustration)**. Be careful not to scratch the inner race, the balls or the cage.

10   Align the inner race lands with the cage windows and pull the race out of the cage **(see illustrations)**.

Inspection

Refer to illustrations 14.11a and 14.11b

11   Clean the components with solvent to remove all traces of grease. Inspect the cage and races for pitting, score marks, cracks and other signs of wear and damage. Shiny, polished spots are normal and will not adversely affect CV joint performance **(see illustrations)**.

14.11b   Check the cage for cracks, pitting and score marks (shiny spots are normal and don't affect operation)

14.13   Press the balls into the cage through the windows using thumb pressure only

14.14 Wrap the splined area of the axle with tape to prevent damage to the boot when installing it

Reassembly

Refer to illustrations 14.13, 14.14, 14.17, 14.19, 14.20, 14.21a and 14.21b

12   Insert the inner race into the cage and align the matchmarks.

13   Press the balls into the cage windows with your thumbs **(see illustration)**.

14   Wrap the axleshaft splines with tape to avoid damaging the boot **(see illustration)**. Slide the small boot clamp and boot onto the axleshaft, then remove the tape.

15   Install the inner race and cage assembly on the axleshaft with the larger diameter side or bulge of the cage (and the previously applied marks) facing the axleshaft end.

16   Install the snap-ring in the groove. Make sure it's completely seated by pushing on the inner race and cage assembly.

17   Fill the outer race and boot with the specified type and quantity of CV joint grease (normally included with the new boot kit). Pack the inner race and cage assembly with grease, by hand, until grease is worked completely into the assembly **(see illustration)**.

18   Slide the outer race down onto the inner race, aligning the matchmarks and install the wire ring retainer.

19   Wipe any excess grease from the axle boot groove on the outer race. Seat the small diameter of the boot in the recessed area on the axleshaft. Push the other end of the boot onto the outer race and move the race in or out to adjust the driveaxle to the length listed in this Chapter's specifications **(see illustration)**.

14.17 Pack the inner race and cage assembly full of CV joint grease (also note that the larger diameter side, or bulge, is facing the axleshaft end)

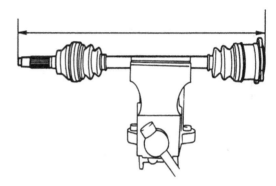

14.19 Before tightening the boot clamps, adjust the driveaxle to the proper length (see this Chapter's specifications)

20   With the axle set to the proper length, equalize the pressure in the boot by inserting a dull screwdriver between the boot and the outer race **(see illustration)**. Don't damage the boot with the tool.

21   Install the boot clamps **(see illustrations)**

22   Install the driveaxle as described in Section 13.

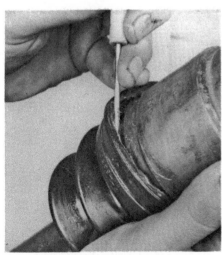

14.20 Also before tightening the clamps, equalize the pressure inside the boot by inserting a small, dull screwdriver between the boot and the outer race

14.21a To tighten a new clamp, bend the tang down and . . .

14.21b . . . fold the tabs over to hold it in place

14.26   After the old grease has been rinsed away and the solvent blown out with compressed air, rotate the outer joint housing through its full range of motion and inspect the bearing surfaces for wear and damage – if any of the balls, the race or the cage look damaged, replace the driveaxle and outer joint assembly

Outer CV joint and boot

Disassembly

Refer to illustration 14.26

23   Following Steps 1 through 10, remove the inner CV joint from the axleshaft and disassemble it.

24   Remove the outer CV joint boot clamps, using the technique described in Step 3. Slide the boot off the axleshaft.

Inspection

25   Thoroughly wash the inner and outer CV joints in clean solvent and blow them dry with compressed air, if available. **Note:** *Because the outer joint cannot be disassembled, it is difficult to wash away all the old grease and to rid the bearing of solvent once it's clean. But it's imperative the job be done thoroughly, so take your time and do it right.*

26   Bend the outer CV joint housing at an angle to the driveaxle to expose the bearings, inner race and cage **(see illustration)**. inspect the bearing surfaces for signs of wear. If the bearings are damaged or worn, replace the driveaxle.

Reassembly

27   Slide the new outer boot onto the driveaxle. It's a good idea to wrap vinyl tape around the spline of the shaft to prevent damage to the boot **(see illustration 14.14)**. When the boot is in position, add the specified amount of grease (included in the boot replacement kit) to the outer joint and the boot (pack the joint with as much grease as it will hold and put the rest into the boot). Slide the boot on the rest of the way and install the new clamps **(see illustrations 14.21a and 14.21b)**.

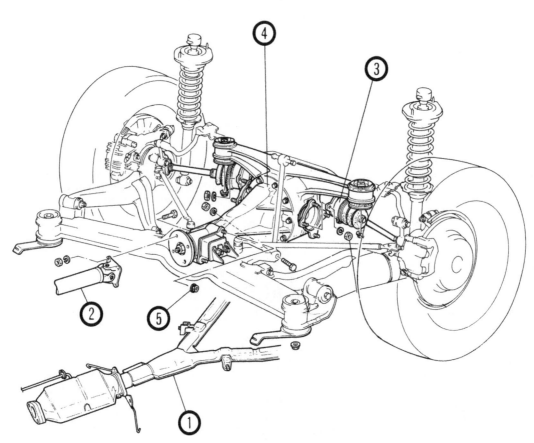

15.5   Differential mounting details

1	Exhaust pipe	4	Differential assembly
2	Driveshaft	5	Differential front
3	Driveaxle		mounting nuts

28 Clean and reassemble the inner CV joint by following Steps 11 through 21, then install the driveaxle as described in Section 13.

15 Differential assembly – removal and installation

Refer to illustrations 15.5 and 15.6

Removal

1 Raise the rear of the vehicle and support it securely on jackstands. Disconnect the cable from the negative battery terminal.
2 Drain the differential lubricant (see Chapter 1).
3 Unbolt the driveshaft from the differential flange (see Section 11). Slide the driveshaft towards the front of the vehicle as far as possible.
4 Disconnect the driveaxles from the differential (see Section 13) and hang them from the underbody with pieces of wire.
5 Remove the differential front mounting nuts **(see illustration)**.
6 Support the differential assembly with a floor jack. Remove the left rear mounting nut **(see illustration)** and slowly lower the jack to allow the differential to hang down a few inches.
7 Disconnect the rear suspension sub-link from the differential housing (see Chapter 10).
8 Remove the right rear mounting nut, then lower the differential and slide it to the rear, guiding it out between the subframe and body.

Installation

9 Place the assembly on the jack and carefully raise it up as far as possible. Guide the nose (pinion end) of the differential up above the subframe then slide the entire assembly forward until the two rear mounting holes are aligned. Connect the sub-link to the differential housing, raise the unit into position and install the two rear mounting nuts. Don't tighten the nuts or the sub-link fasteners completely at this time.
10 Install the front mounting nuts, tightening them to the torque listed in this Chapter's specifications.
11 Tighten the rear mounting nuts to the torque listed in this Chapter's specifications.
12 Tighten the sub-link fasteners to the torque listed in the Chapter 10 specifications.
13 Connect the driveaxles to the differential, tightening the nuts to the torque listed in this Chapter's specifications.
14 Connect the driveshaft to the differential flange and tighten the nuts to the torque listed in this Chapter's specifications.
15 Fill the differential with the proper type and quantity of lubricant (see Chapter 1).
16 Lower the vehicle and connect the negative battery cable.

15.6   The differential housing is fastened at the rear by two mounting nuts (arrow) (the left side is shown here)

16 Pinion oil seal – replacement

Refer to illustrations 16.5 and 16.7

1 A pinion shaft oil seal failure results in the leakage of differential gear lubricant past the seal and onto the driveshaft companion flange. The seal is replaceable without removing or disassembling the differential.
2 Raise the rear of the vehicle and place it on jackstands. Remove the rear half of the exhaust system (see Chapter 4).
3 Remove the drain plug from the differential housing and allow the differential lubricant to drain into a container (see Chapter 1, if necessary). When the draining is complete, install the drain plug.
4 Disconnect the driveshaft from the differential flange (see Section 11).
5 Using an inch-pound torque wrench, slowly turn the pinion shaft nut and measure the amount of torque required to start the pinion shaft turning **(see illustration)**. Record this figure.
6 Remove the pinion shaft nut, using a chain wrench or holding tool to prevent the differential flange from turning.
7 Using a puller, remove the differential flange **(see illustration)**.
8 After noting what the visible side of the oil seal looks like, carefully pry it out of the differential with a screwdriver or pry bar. Be careful not to damage the splines on the pinion shaft or disturb the position of the shaft.

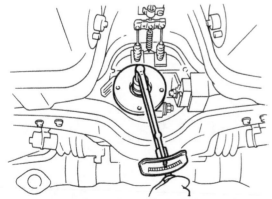

16.5   Turn the pinion shaft with an inch-pound torque wrench to measure the torque at which it starts to turn – a beam-type torque wrench works best for this

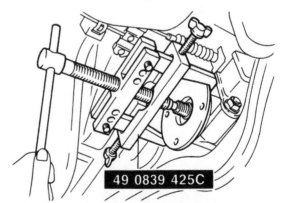

49 0839 425C

16.7   If the pinion flange is stuck, a gear puller may be needed to pull it from the shaft – do not attempt to knock it off with a hammer

17.4   Two large pry bars can be used to remove the output shaft from the differential, but be careful where you pry and how hard – you might break the aluminum differential housing

17.5   The output shaft seal can be pried out with a screwdriver

9   Lubricate the new seal lip with moly-base grease and carefully install it in position in the differential. Using a short section of pipe or a socket of the proper circumference and a hammer, carefully drive the seal in until it bottoms.

10   Clean the seal contact surface of the differential flange. Apply a thin coat of moly-base grease to the seal contact surface and the shaft spines and, using a plastic hammer, tap the flange onto the shaft.

11   Coat the threads of a new pinion shaft nut with multi-purpose grease and, using the holder or chain wrench to hold the flange, tighten the nut in small increments until the torque required to start the pinion shaft turning is the same as that recorded in Step 5. When doing this, be careful not to overtighten the nut, which will increase the pinion shaft preload. If, however, you do overtighten the nut (indicated by a higher torque required to start the pinion shaft turning), do not loosen the nut in an attempt to reduce the starting torque. Instead, unbolt the driveaxles from the output shafts and measure the pinion shaft preload, comparing your reading with that listed in this Chapter's specifications.

12   If the drive pinion preload is within the specified range, reinstall the

driveaxles and driveshaft. If the preload is greater than specified, the differential must be removed and the collapsible spacer must be replaced (this must be done by a dealer service department or other repair shop, as special tools and expertise are required to properly set up the differential).

13   Fill the differential housing to the proper level with the recommended gear lubricant (see Chapter 1). Install the filler plug and tighten it securely.

14   Lower the vehicle to the ground, test drive it and check around the pinion flange for evidence of leakage.

17   Differential output shaft seal – replacement

Refer to illustrations 17.4, 17.5, 17.6 and 17.7

1   Raise the rear of the vehicle and support it on jackstands.

2   Drain the differential lubricant (see Chapter 1).

3   Separate the driveaxle from the differential (see Section 13) and suspend it out of the way.

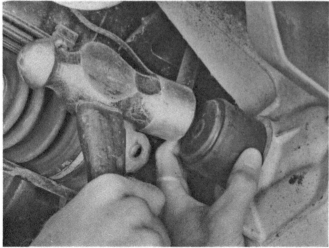

17.6   If you don't have a seal driver, a large socket or a piece of pipe with a diameter slightly less than that of the seal can be used to drive the seal into place

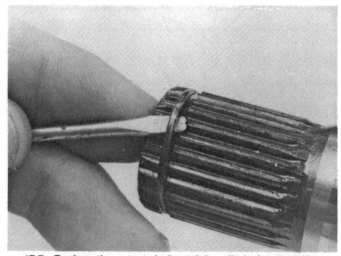

17.7   Replace the output shaft retaining clip before installing the shaft

4   Using two pry bars, gently pry the differential output shaft out of the differential **(see illustration)**. **Note:** *Be ready to catch the shaft as it comes out.*

5   Use a screwdriver to pry the seal out **(see illustration)**.

6   Use a hammer and a seal driver, large socket or section of pipe to install the new seal **(see illustration)**.

7   Before installing the output shaft, pry the circlip from the splined end and install a new one **(see illustration)**.

8   Apply a film of grease to the lips of the seal, insert the shaft and tap it into position. Use only enough force to overcome the resistance of the circlip.

9   Connect the driveaxle to the output shaft, tightening the nuts to the torque listed in this Chapter's specifications.

10   Fill the differential with the proper type and quantity of lubricant (see Chapter 1).

Chapter 9 Brakes

Contents

Anti-lock brake system (ABS) – general information 2
Brake check .... See Chapter 1
Brake disc – inspection, removal and installation 5
Brake fluid level check .... See Chapter 1
Brake hoses and lines – inspection and replacement 10
Brake hydraulic system – bleeding 11
Brake light switch – removal, installation and adjustment 16
Brake pedal – removal, installation and adjustment 15
Front brake caliper – removal, overhaul and installation 4

Front brake pads – replacement 3
General information and precautions 1
Master cylinder – removal, overhaul and installation 8
Parking brake – adjustment 13
Parking brake cables – replacement 14
Power brake booster – check, removal and installation 12
Proportioning bypass valve – removal and installation 9
Rear brake caliper – removal and installation 7
Rear brake pads – replacement 6

Specifications

General

Brake fluid type	See Chapter 1
Brake pedal	
Height	
1986 through 1988	8 in (205 mm)
1989	7-1/4 to 7-1/2 in (184 to 189 mm)
Freeplay	0.16 to 0.28 in (4 to 7 mm)
Pedal-to-floor clearance (minimum)	4 in (100 mm)
Power brake booster-to-master cylinder	
pushrod clearance (@ 20 in-Hg vacuum)	0.004 to 0.012 in (0.1 to 0.3 mm)

Front brakes

Minimum brake pad thickness	See Chapter 1
Brake disc	
Standard thickness	0.87 in (22 mm)
Minimum thickness*	0.79 in (20 mm)
Runout limit	0.004 in (0.1 mm)

Rear brakes

Minimum brake pad thickness	See Chapter 1.
Brake disc	
Standard thickness	
Non-ventilated	0.40 in (10 mm)
Ventilated	0.79 in (20 mm)
Minimum thickness*	
Non-ventilated	0.31 in (8 mm)
Ventilated	0.71 in (18 mm)
Runout limit	0.004 in (0.1 mm)

Refer to the marks stamped on the disc (they supersede information printed here)

Torque specifications

	Ft-lbs (unless otherwise indicated)
Master cylinder mounting nuts	144 in-lbs
Power brake booster mounting nuts	14 to 19
Front caliper lock pin bolt (single-piston caliper)	22 to 30
Front caliper mounting bracket bolts	58 to 72
Front caliper mounting bolts (four-piston caliper)	58 to 72
Rear caliper lock pin bolt	
1986 through 1988	22 to 30
1989	12 to 17
Rear caliper mounting bracket bolt	33 to 40
Rear brake hose-to-caliper union bolt	16 to 22

---

1   General information and precautions

Refer to illustration 1.2

The vehicles covered by this manual are equipped with hydraulically operated front and rear disc brakes. GXL and turbo models employ four-piston calipers with ventilated discs on the front and single-piston calipers with ventilated discs in the rear. Other models utilize single-piston calipers and ventilated discs on the front and single-piston calipers and solid (non ventilated) discs in the rear.

Hydraulic system

The hydraulic system consists of two separate circuits, which are split front-to-rear **(see illustration)**. The master cylinder has separate pistons for the two circuits and, in the event of a leak or failure in one hydraulic circuit, the other circuit will remain operative. A proportioning bypass valve limits pressure to the rear wheels during heavy braking to prevent lockup of the rear wheels. Some models are equipped with an anti-lock brake system (ABS) (see Section 2).

Power brake booster

The effort required of the driver to operate the brakes is reduced by the power brake booster, which utilizes engine vacuum to help activate the master cylinder. The booster is mounted on the firewall in the engine compartment, directly behind the master cylinder.

Parking brake

The parking brake operates the rear brakes only, through cables. The parking brake is operated by a handle mounted in the center console. The cables pull on levers that are attached to screw-type actuators in the caliper housings, which apply force to the caliper pistons, clamping the brake pads against the brake disc.

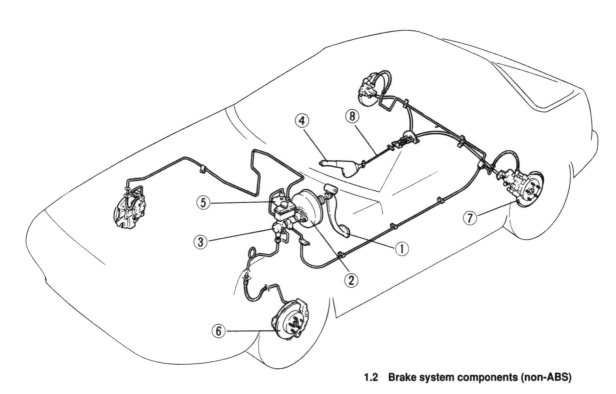

1.2   Brake system components (non-ABS)

1	Brake pedal	5	Proportioning bypass valve
2	Power brake booster	6	Front brake disc
3	Brake master cylinder	7	Rear brake disc
4	Parking brake lever	8	Parking brake cable

Precautions

a) Use only the recommended brake fluid (see Chapter 1)

b) The brake pads may contain asbestos fibers, which are hazardous to your health if inhaled. Whenever you work on brake system components, clean all parts with brake system cleaner. Do not allow the fine dust to become airborne.

c) Safety should be paramount whenever any servicing of the brake components is performed. Do not use parts or fasteners which are not in perfect condition, and be sure that all clearances and torque specifications are adhered to. If you are at all unsure about a certain procedure, seek professional advice. Upon completion of any brake system work, test the brakes carefully in an isolated area before putting the vehicle into normal service.

d) If a problem is suspected in the brake system, don't drive the vehicle until it's fixed.

2　Anti-lock brake system (ABS) – general information

Refer to illustrations 2.2, 2.4 and 2.5

The anti-lock brake system was introduced in 1987 and is designed to maintain vehicle steerablility, directional stability and optimum deceleration under severe braking conditions and on most road surfaces. It does so by monitoring the rotational speed of each wheel and controlling the brake line pressure to each wheel during braking. This prevents the wheels from locking-up and provides maximum vehicle controllabiltiy.

Components

Hydraulic Unit

The hydraulic unit consists of a hydraulic pump and a solenoid valve body assembly **(see illustration)**.

a) The electric pump provides hydraulic pressure for the system.

b) The solenoid valve body modulates brake line pressure during ABS operation. The valve body contains three valves – one for each front wheel and one for both of the rear wheels.

Wheel sensors

These sensors are located at each wheel and generate small electrical pulsations when the toothed rotors are turning, sending a signal to the electronic controller indicating wheel rotational speed.

The front wheel sensors are mounted on the steering knuckles in close relationship to the toothed rotors, which are mounted on the inside of the wheel hubs **(see illustration)**.

The rear wheel sensors bolt to the toe control hubs **(see illustration)**. These rotors are also mounted to the inside of the wheel hubs.

ABS control unit

The electronic controller is mounted under the right side of the dash and is the brain for the ABS system. The function of the control module – consisting of microprocessors and the related circuits needed for their operation – is to accept and process information received from the wheel sensors to control the hydraulic line pressure, avoiding wheel lock-up. The controller also constantly monitors the system, even under normal driving conditions, to find faults within the system.

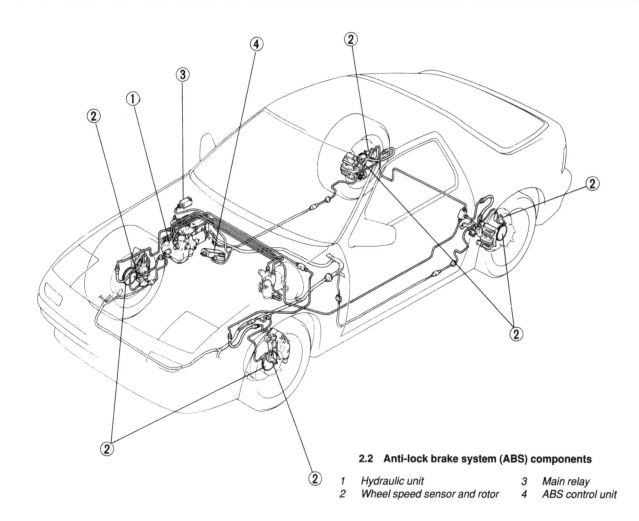

2.2　Anti-lock brake system (ABS) components

1	Hydraulic unit	3	Main relay
2	Wheel speed sensor and rotor	4	ABS control unit

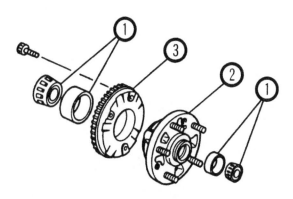

2.4 Mounting arrangement of the ABS front wheel rotors

1   Wheel bearing and race   3   Rotor
2   Wheel hub

2.5 The ABS rear wheel rotors bolt to the toe control hubs

If a problem develops within the system, an ABS indicator light will glow on the dashboard. A diagnostic code will also be stored in the controller, which, when retrieved by a service technician, will indicate the problem area or component.

Diagnosis and repair

If the dashboard warning light comes on and stays on while the vehicle is in operation, the ABS system requires attention. Although a special electronic ABS diagnostic tester is necessary to properly diagnose the system, the home mechanic can perform a few preliminary checks before taking the vehicle to a dealer who is equipped with this tester.

a) Check the brake fluid level in the master cylinder reservoir.
b) Check that the control unit electrical connector is securely connected.
c) Check the electrical connectors at the hydraulic unit.
d) Check the fuses.
e) Follow the wiring harness to each wheel and check that all connections are secure and that the wiring is not damaged.

If the above preliminary checks do not rectify the problem, the vehicle should be diagnosed by a dealer service department. Due to the rather complex nature of this system, all actual repair work must be done by a dealer.

Note: *Due to the mounting location of the ABS hydraulic unit, it may be necessary to remove it to perform certain procedures on the fuel system, turbocharger and engine. This can be accomplished by the home mechanic, provided everything is kept spotlessly clean. The lines must be disconnected using a flare-nut wrench to prevent rounding off the corners of the fittings. Once all of the lines are disconnected and plugged, unplug the electrical connectors and unbolt the unit from its mounts. Be careful not to drip any brake fluid onto the paint when lifting it out of the engine compartment. Store the unit in a sealed plastic bag. After the unit has been installed, be sure to bleed the brake system as described in Section 11.*

---

3   Front brake pads – replacement

Warning: *Disc brake pads must be replaced on both front wheels at the same time – never replace the pads on only one wheel. Also, the dust created by the brake pads may contain asbestos, which is harmful to your health. Never blow it out with compressed air and don't inhale any of it. An approved filtering mask should be worn when working on the brakes. Do not, under any circumstances, use petroleum-based solvents to clean brake parts. Use brake cleaner only!*

Note: *When servicing the brakes, use only high quality, nationally recognized name brand pads.*

1   Remove the cap from the brake fluid reservoir and siphon off about half of the fluid (see Chapter 1).
2   Loosen the wheel lug nuts, raise the front of the vehicle and support it securely on jackstands.
3   Remove the front wheels. Work on one brake assembly at a time, using the assembled brake for reference, if necessary.
4   While the caliper is off, inspect the brake disc as described in Section 5. If machining is necessary, follow the information in that Section to remove the disc. **Note:** *The pad replacement procedure varies, depending on whether you have single-piston or four-piston calipers. Illustration 3.5 shows a single-piston caliper and illustration 3.16 shows a four-piston caliper.*

Single piston caliper

Refer to illustrations 3.5, 3.6, 3.7, 3.8, 3.9, 3.10, 3.11, 3.12 and 3.13

5   Before beginning work, clean the caliper and brake pads off with a brake system cleaner. The kind in an aerosol can works best **(see illustration)**.

3.5   Before removing anything, clean the caliper and pads with brake cleaner and allow it to dry – position a drain pan under the brake to catch the residue – DO NOT USE COMPRESSED AIR TO BLOW THE DUST FROM THE PARTS!

3.6　Using a large C-clamp, push the piston back into the caliper bore – note that one end of the clamp is on the flat area near the brake hose fitting and the other end (screw end) is pressing against the outer brake pad

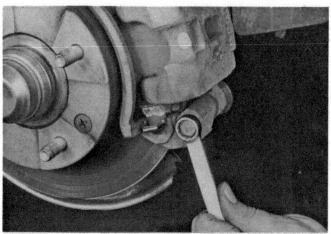

3.7　Unscrew the lock pin bolt from the bottom of the caliper – it isn't necessary to remove the top one

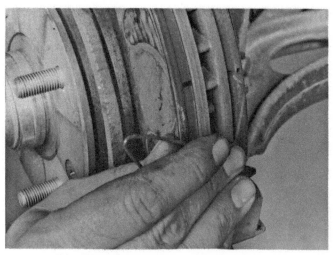

3.8　The pad spring seats in the inner pad only

3.9　To remove the brake pads from the caliper mounting bracket, slide them straight out away from the brake disc

3.10　Unclip the anti-squeal shims from the brake pads – if the retaining tabs are weak, they can be bent in so they grip better

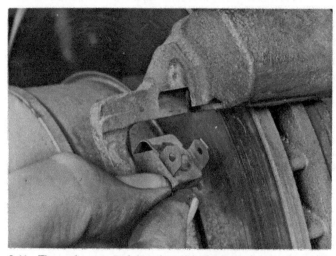

3.11　The pad support plates should be inspected and replaced if there are any obvious defects

3.12 There are two types of disc brake anti-squeal compound – aerosol (shown) and semi liquid type – whichever you use, apply only enough to form a thin film, and make sure you apply it to the backing plate, not the friction surface

3.13 Press the pad spring into the hole in the inner pad, hold the pads against the brake disc and compress the pad spring with your fingers while rotating the caliper down into position

6   Using a large C-clamp, compress the caliper piston back into its bore **(see illustration)**.
7   Remove the lock pin bolt at the bottom of the caliper **(see illustration)** and rotate the caliper up to expose the brake pads. The caliper can be held in this position with a piece of wire.
8   Remove the pad spring from the inner pad **(see illustration)**.
9   Remove the brake pads from the caliper mounting bracket **(see illustration)**.
10   Remove the anti-squeal shims from the pads **(see illustration)**.
11   Remove the pad support plates from the caliper mounting bracket and inspect them for cracks, replacing them if necessary **(see illustration)**.
12   Before installing the new pads, apply a thin coat of disc brake anti-squeal compound to the pad backing plates **(see illustration)**.
13   Insert the new pads into the caliper mounting bracket and install the pad spring into the hole in the inner pad. Squeeze the spring together with your fingers **(see illustration)**, then rotate the caliper down over the pads. Install the lock pin bolt and tighten it to the torque listed in this Chapter's specifications.
14   Depress the brake pedal a few times to bring the pads into contact with the disc, then check the brake fluid level, adding some if necessary (see Chapter 1).

Four-piston caliper

Refer to illustration 3.16

15   Clean the pads and caliper with brake cleaner, as described in Step 5.
16   Remove the retaining clip and drive out the pad pins **(see illustration)**. Drive out the upper pin first, then hold your hand over the opening in the caliper when removing the lower pin so the pad spring doesn't fly out.
17   Force the pistons back into their bores to make room for the thicker new pads. This can be accomplished by pulling the pads away from the disc with a pair of large adjustable pliers, squeezing them against the caliper body.
18   Pull the pads straight out of the caliper.
19   Before installing the new pads, apply a thin coat of anti-squeal compound to the backing plates of the pads **(see illustration 3.12)**.
20   Slide the new pads into the caliper and install the pad pins, retaining clip and spring.
21   Depress the brake pedal a few times to bring the pads into contact with the disc, then check the brake fluid level, adding some if necessary (see Chapter 1).

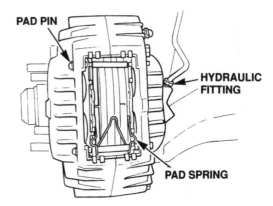

PAD PIN

HYDRAULIC FITTING

PAD SPRING

3.16 On a four-piston caliper, remove the retaining clips from the pad pins, drive the pad pins out of the caliper with a drift punch and a hammer, then remove the pad spring – unscrew the hydraulic fitting only when removing the caliper for overhaul

4   Front brake caliper – removal, overhaul and installation

Warning: *Dust created by the brake system may contain asbestos, which is harmful to your health. Never blow it out with compressed air and don't inhale any of it. An approved filtering mask should be worn when working on the brakes. Do not, under any circumstances, use petroleum-based solvents to clean brake parts. Use brake cleaner only!*
Note: *If an overhaul is indicated (usually because of fluid leakage) explore all options before beginning the job. New and factory rebuilt calipers are available from auto parts stores on an exchange basis, which makes this job quite easy. If it's decided to overhaul the calipers, make sure an overhaul kit is available before proceeding. Always rebuild the calipers in pairs – never rebuild just one of them.*

Removal

Refer to illustrations 4.2 and 4.5
Note: *If you are only relocating the caliper so other components can be removed (you are not removing the caliper for overhaul), do not disconnect the brake hose or line from the caliper body (Steps 3 and 4).*
1   Loosen the wheel lug nuts, raise the front of the vehicle and support it securely on jackstands. Remove the wheel.

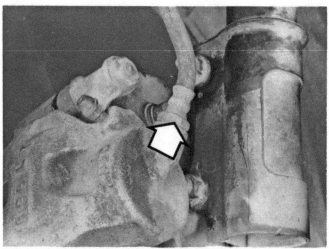

4.2   The brake hose screws directly into the caliper body – be sure to use a new sealing washer when installing it

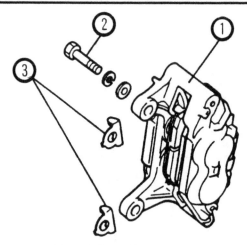

4.5   Four-piston caliper mounting details

1   Caliper   3   Guard plates
2   Mounting bolts

4.7a   Using a screwdriver, remove the boot retaining ring

2   On vehicles equipped with single-piston calipers, loosen the brake hose at the bracket on the inner fender panel and remove the retaining clip at the bracket on the strut assembly. Unscrew the hose fitting from the caliper body **(see illustration)**. Cap the hose end with a piece of appropriately sized rubber hose with a bolt screwed into the end of it. This will prevent excessive fluid loss and the entry of contaminants.

3   On vehicles with four-piston calipers, unscrew the hydraulic fitting **(see illustration 3.16)** from the caliper body using a flare-nut wrench to avoid rounding off the corners of the fitting. Cap the end of the line using the technique described in Step 2.

4   On vehicles with single-piston calipers, remove the lock pin bolt **(see illustration 3.7)**, swing the caliper up then slide the caliper toward the center of the vehicle, off the mounting bracket pin.

5   On vehicles with four-piston calipers, remove the brake pads as described in Section 3, then remove the two caliper mounting bolts **(see illustration)** and lift the caliper from the steering knuckle. Don't confuse the mounting bolts with the bridge bolts that connect the two halves of the caliper together. The bridge bolts should never be removed. Be careful not to lose the two guard plates from between the caliper and steering knuckle.

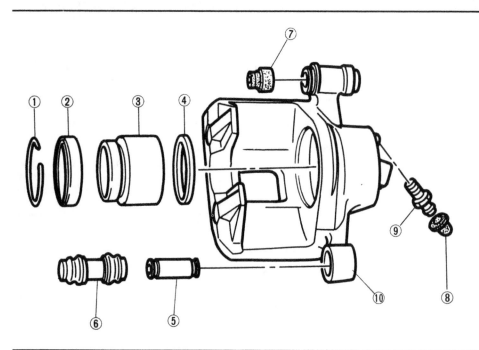

4.7b   Exploded view of the single-piston brake caliper

1   Retaining ring
2   Dust boots
3   Piston
4   Piston seal
5   Sleeve
6   Boot
7   Boot
8   Cap
9   Bleeder screw
10   Caliper body

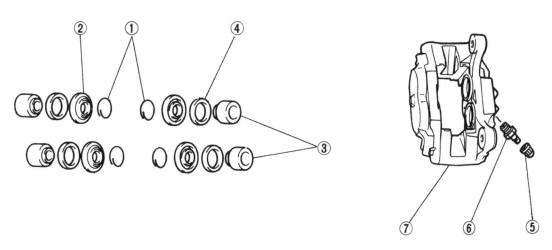

4.7c Exploded view of the four-piston brake caliper

1	Retaining rings	4	Piston seals	6	Bleeder screw
2	Dust boot	5	Cap	7	Caliper body
3	Pistons				

Overhaul

Refer to illustrations 4.7a, 4.7b, 4.7c, 4.8 and 4.9

6   Clean the exterior of the caliper with brake cleaner. Never use gasoline, kerosene or petroleum-based cleaning solvents. Place the caliper on a clean working surface.

7   Pry the retaining ring(s) from the dust boot(s) and remove the boot(s) **(see illustrations)**.

8   Position a wooden block or several shop rags in the caliper as a cushion, then use compressed air at the brake line port to remove the piston(s) **(see illustration)**. Use only enough air pressure to ease the piston(s) out of the bore(s), otherwise damage may occur. On vehicles with four-piston calipers, all pistons will probably not come out at the same time, so, to keep the air pressure from escaping through a bore where a piston has already come out, place the piston back into the bore far enough to seal off the bore, then hold it in place with a piece of wood. **Warning:** *When applying compressed air, never place your fingers in front of a piston in an attempt to catch, protect or hold it. Serious injury could result.*

9   Using a wood or plastic tool, remove the piston seal from the groove in the caliper bore **(see illustration)**. Metal tools may cause bore damage.

10   Remove the caliper bleeder screw, then remove the mounting pin boots and sleeve from the caliper ears (single-piston caliper only). Discard all rubber parts.

11   Clean the remaining parts with brake system cleaner, then blow them dry with compressed air, if available.

12   Carefully examine the piston(s) for nicks, burrs and loss of plating. If surface defects are present, the parts must be replaced.

13   Check the caliper bore in the same way. Light polishing with crocus cloth is permissible to remove light corrosion and stains. Check the mounting bolts for corrosion or damage. Discard them if any is found.

14   To begin assembly, lubricate the piston seal(s) with brake fluid and position the seal(s) in the groove(s) in the caliper bore(s). Some rebuild kits may come with a packet of silicone grease, in which case this should be smeared on the seal(s) instead.

15   Lubricate the piston(s) with clean brake fluid and insert it squarely into the caliper bore, applying moderate force to bottom it.

16   Stretch the new dust boot(s) over the piston(s) and install the retaining ring(s).

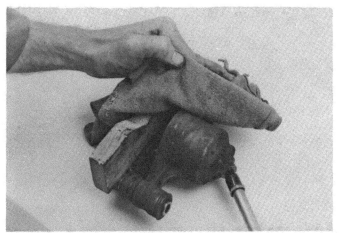

4.8   With the caliper padded to catch the piston(s), use compressed air to force the piston(s) out of the bore(s) – make sure your hands or fingers are not between the piston(s) and the caliper frame (single-piston caliper shown)

4.9   The piston seal should be removed with a plastic or wooden tool to avoid damage to the bore and seal groove – a pencil will do the job

4.18   Before installing a single-piston caliper, smear silicone grease on the upper mounting pin

5.2   Once the brake caliper has been removed, hang it from a piece of wire – DON'T let it hang by the brake hose!

17   Install the bleeder screw. On single-piston calipers, lubricate the mounting pin boots and sleeve with silicone grease and insert them into the caliper ears.

Installation

Refer to illustration 4.18

18   When installing a single-piston caliper, lubricate the upper mounting pin with silicone grease **(see illustration)**, slide the caliper onto the pin and rotate it down into position. Install the lock pin bolt, tightening it to the torque listed in this Chapter's specifications.

19   When installing a four-piston caliper, lower the caliper down over the brake disc and align the mounting bolt holes. Install the guard plates and mounting bolts, tightening them to the torque listed in this Chapter's specifications. Install the brake pads as described in Section 3.

20   On single-piston calipers, connect the brake hose to the caliper using a new sealing washer and tighten it securely. Route the hose through the bracket on the strut and install the securing clip, making sure there are no twists or kinks in the hose. Connect the hose end to the line at the bracket on the inner fender panel, tightening the fitting securely. Install the clip.

21   On four-piston calipers, connect the brake line and tighten it securely using a flare-nut wrench.

22   Bleed the brakes as described in Section 11.

23   Install the wheels and lug nuts. Lower the vehicle and tighten the lug nuts to the torque specified in Chapter 1.

24   After the job has been completed, firmly depress the brake pedal several times to bring the pads into contact with the disc.

25   Check the brake fluid level and test the operation of the brakes before driving the vehicle in traffic.

---

5   Brake disc – inspection, removal and installation

Inspection

Refer to illustrations 5.2, 5.3, 5.4a, 5.4b, 5.5a, 5.5b and 5.5c

1   Loosen the wheel lug nuts, raise the vehicle and support it securely on jackstands. Remove the wheel.

2   Remove the brake caliper as described in Section 3 or 7. It's not necessary to disconnect the brake hose. After removing the bolt, suspend the caliper out of the way with a piece of wire **(see illustration)**. Don't let the caliper hang by the hose and don't stretch or twist the hose.

3   Visually check the disc surface for score marks and other damage. Light scratches and shallow grooves are normal after use and may not always be detrimental to brake operation, but deep score marks – over 0.015-inch (0.38 mm) – require disc removal and refinishing by an automotive machine shop **(see illustration)**. Be sure to check both sides of the disc. If pulsating has been noticed during application of the brakes, suspect disc runout. Be sure to check the wheel bearings to make sure they're properly adjusted.

5.3   The brake pads on this vehicle were obviously neglected, as they wore down to the rivets and cut deep grooves into the disc – wear this severe will require replacement of the disc

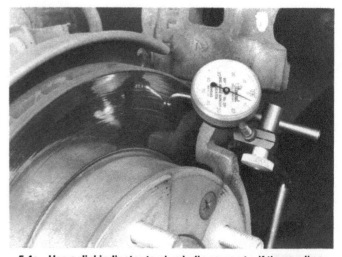

5.4a   Use a dial indicator to check disc runout – if the reading exceeds the maximum allowable runout limit, the disc will have to be machined or replaced

5.4b Using a swirling motion, remove the glaze from the disc surface with sandpaper or emery cloth

5.5a The minimum wear dimension for the front brake disc is stamped onto the hub of the disc

4   To check disc runout, place a dial indicator at a point about 1/2-inch from the outer edge of the disc **(see illustration)**. Set the indicator to zero and turn the disc. The indicator reading should not exceed the specified allowable runout limit. If it does, the disc should be refinished by an automotive machine shop. **Note:** *Professionals recommend resurfacing of brake discs regardless of the dial indicator reading (to produce a smooth, flat surface that will eliminate brake pedal pulsations and other undesirable symptoms related to questionable discs). At the very least, if you elect not to have the discs resurfaced, deglaze them with sandpaper or emery cloth (use a swirling motion to ensure a nondirectional finish)* **(see illustration)**.

5   The disc must not be machined to a thickness less than the specified minimum refinish thickness. The minimum wear (or discard) thickness is stamped into the hub of the disc (front) or the edge of the disc (rear) **(see illustrations)**. The disc thickness can be checked with a micrometer **(see illustration)**.

Removal

Refer to illustrations 5.6 and 5.9

6   Loosen the two screws that secure the disc to the hub. The disc can be immobilized by inserting a screwdriver into the cooling vanes (if equipped) and bracing it against the caliper mounting bracket **(see illustration)** or by bracing a prybar across two of the wheel studs **(see illustration 13.2b** in Chapter 8).

5.5b The minimum wear dimension for the rear brake disc is stamped onto the edge of the disc

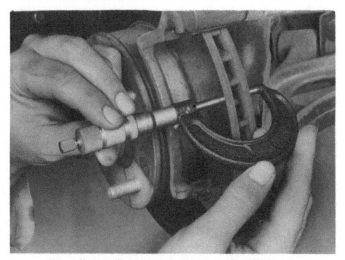

5.5c Use a micrometer to measure disc thickness

5.6 While removing the disc-to-hub screws, wedge a screwdriver in the cooling vanes (shown) or position a prybar between two wheel studs to prevent the disc from turning

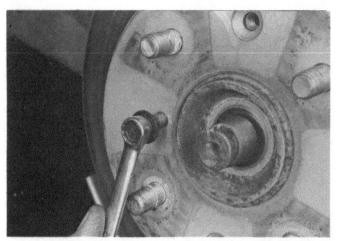

5.9   If the rear disc will not come off, install a bolt of the proper size and thread pitch into the threaded hole – when the bolt is tightened, the disc will pop off

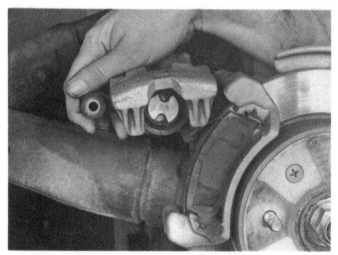

6.4b   Rotate the caliper up, then slide it off of the upper mounting pin

6.4c   Place the caliper assembly on the trailing arm carefully so it will not fall off

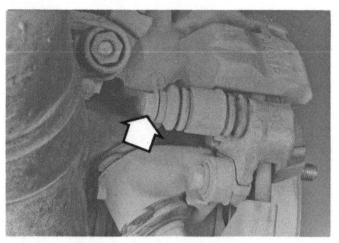

6.4a   Remove the lock pin bolt (arrow)

7   Unscrew the two bolts that retain the caliper mounting bracket to the steering knuckle and remove the mounting bracket (single piston calipers).
8   Remove the disc retaining screws and pull the disc from the hub.
9   If a rear disc is being removed, it may be necessary to screw a bolt of the proper size into the threaded hole in the disc **(see illustration)**. When tightened, the bolt will force the disc away from the hub.

Installation

10   Place the disc on the hub and install the retaining screws.
11   On single-piston calipers, install the caliper mounting bracket and brake pads, then install the caliper (see Section 3 or 7 for the caliper installation procedure, if necessary). Tighten the mounting bracket bolts and lock pin bolt to the torque figures listed in this Chapter's specifications.
12   On four-piston calipers, install the caliper (see Section 4) then the brake pads (see Section 3).
13   Install the wheel, then lower the vehicle to the ground. Depress the brake pedal a few times to bring the brake pads into contact with the disc. Bleeding of the system will not be necessary unless the brake hose was disconnected from the caliper. Check the operation of the brakes carefully before placing the vehicle into normal service.

---

6   Rear brake pads – replacement

Refer to illustrations 6.4a, 6.4b, 6.4c, 6.5, 6.6, 6.11a and 6.11b
Warning: *Dust created by the brake system may contain asbestos, which is harmful to your health. Never blow it out with compressed air and don't inhale any of it. An approved filtering mask should be worn when working on the brakes. Disc brake pads must be replaced on both rear wheels at the same time – never replace the pads on only one wheel. Do not, under any circumstances, use petroleum-based solvents to clean brake parts. Use brake cleaner only!*

1   Remove the cap from the brake master cylinder fluid reservoir. Siphon off about one-third of the fluid, as the level will rise when the caliper pistons are retracted to make room for the new pads. Be careful not to spill any of the fluid onto the vehicle's paint.
2   Loosen the wheel lug nuts, raise the rear of the vehicle and support it securely on jackstands. Remove the wheel. Work on one brake assembly at a time, using the assembled brake for reference, if necessary.
3   Remove the lock pin bolt, swing the caliper up then slide it off the caliper mounting bracket pin **(see illustrations)**. Set the caliper on the top of the trailing arm (don't allow it to hang by the brake hose or parking brake cable) **(see illustration)**.
4   While the caliper is off, inspect the brake disc as described in Section 5. If machining is necessary, follow the information in that Section to remove the disc. Before removing the caliper, clean it and the pads with brake system cleaner to remove as much of the brake dust as possible.

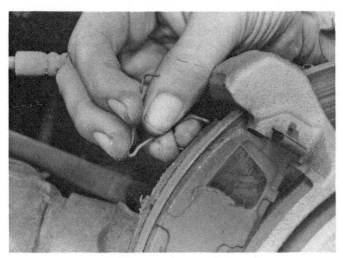

6.5 Pull the V-spring off of the pads

6.6 The brake pads can be removed from the caliper bracket by pulling them away from the disc, out of their mounting slots

5   Remove the V-spring from the pads **(see illustration)**.
6   Slide the pads away from the disc and out of the mounting bracket **(see illustration)**.
7   Separate the anti-squeal shims from the pad backing plate **(see illustration 3.10)**.
8   Remove the pad support plates from the caliper mounting bracket **(see illustration 3.11)** and inspect them for cracks, replacing them if necessary.
9   Apply a thin coat of disc brake anti-squeal compound to the backing plate of the brake pads **(see illustration 3.12)**. Allow the pads to dry, then clip the anti-squeal shims to the backing plates.
10   Position the pads in the caliper mounting bracket and install the V-spring.
11   Before installing the caliper, the caliper piston must be retracted in its bore. Using a pair of needle-nose pliers, turn the piston clockwise until the caliper can be lowered over the brake pads **(see illustration)**. When doing this, one of the cutouts in the piston face must be positioned to engage with the pin on the inner brake pad backing plate **(see illustration)**.
12   Place the caliper onto the top mounting pin of the caliper bracket and rotate it down over the pads. Install the lock pin bolt and tighten it to the torque listed in this Chapter's specifications.
13   Install the wheel and lug nuts. Lower the vehicle and tighten the lug nuts to the torque specified in Chapter 1.
14   When the job has been completed, firmly depress the brake pedal several times to bring the pads into contact with the disc. Check the brake fluid level in the master cylinder reservoir and add fluid, if necessary (see Chapter 1).
15   Test the operation of the brakes in an isolated area before returning the vehicle to normal use.

6.11a Rotate the caliper piston clockwise to retract it

---

7   Rear brake caliper – removal and installation

Refer to illustration 7.3
Warning: *Dust created by the brake system may contain asbestos, which is harmful to your health. Never blow it out with compressed air and don't inhale any of it. An approved filtering mask should be worn when working on the brakes. Do not, under any circumstances, use petroleum-based solvents to clean brake parts. Use brake cleaner only!*

Note: *Due to the relatively complex design of the rear brake caliper/parking brake actuator assembly, all service procedures requiring disassembly and reassembly should be left to a professional mechanic. The home mechanic can, however, remove the caliper and take it to a repair shop or dealer service department for repair, thereby saving the cost of removal and installation.*

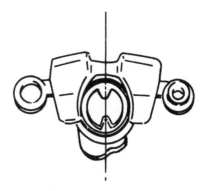

6.11b The cutouts in the caliper piston must be as shown so the caliper can be swung down over the brake pads

1   Loosen the wheel lug nuts, raise the rear of the vehicle and support it securely on jackstands. Remove the wheel.
2   Disconnect the parking brake cable from the caliper, referring to Section 14 for the correct procedure. It is not necessary to disconnect the parking brake cable if the caliper is being repositioned so another component – such as the brake disc – can be removed.

3   Disconnect the brake hydraulic hose from the caliper by removing the union bolt **(see illustration)**. Wrap a plastic bag tightly around the end of the hose to prevent excessive fluid leakage and the entry of contaminants. Just like the parking brake cable, it isn't necessary to disconnect the hydraulic hose if the caliper is just being repositioned.

7.3   The rear brake hose is connected to the caliper by a union ·bolt (arrow) – be sure to use new sealing washers when reconnecting the fitting

8.4   Remove the three hydraulic lines (two on turbo models) (1), then remove the master cylinder mounting nuts (2)

8.9   Using a phillips screwdriver, depress the pistons, then remove the stop screw – be sure to replace the sealing washer on the stop screw when reassembling the cylinder

4   Proceed to Section 6, Step 4, for the remainder of the removal procedure, as it is part of the brake pad replacement procedure.
5   To install the caliper, refer to Section 6, Step 12. If new pads have been installed, it will also be necessary to perform Step 11.

---

8   Master cylinder – removal, overhaul and installation

Note: *Before deciding to overhaul the master cylinder, check on the availability and cost of a new or factory rebuilt unit and also the availability of a rebuild kit.*

Removal

Refer to illustration 8.4

1   The master cylinder is located in the engine compartment, mounted on the power brake booster. Unplug the wire harness connector for the fluid level sensor.
2   Remove as much fluid as you can from the reservoir with a suction gun or syringe.
3   Place rags under the fluid fitting and prepare caps or plastic bags to cover the ends of the lines once they're disconnected. **Caution:** *Brake fluid will damage paint. Cover all body parts and be careful not to spill fluid during this procedure.*
4   Loosen the tube nuts at the ends of the brake lines where they enter the master cylinder **(see illustration)**. To prevent rounding off the flats on these nuts, use of a flare-nut wrench which wraps around the nut.

8.8   To remove the reservoir on earlier models, rock it back and forth while pulling straight up – the reservoir on later models is secured by a screw

8.10   Depress the pistons again and remove the snap-ring with a pair of snap-ring pliers

5   Pull the brake lines slightly away from the master cylinder and plug the ends to prevent contamination. It may be necessary to loosen the right master cylinder mounting nut (the one that also secures the proportioning valve) before you can do this **(see illustration 8.4)**.

6   Disconnect the electrical connector at the master cylinder, then remove the two nuts attaching the master cylinder to the power booster **(see illustration 8.4)**. Pull the master cylinder off the studs and out of the engine compartment. Again, be careful not to spill fluid as this is done.

Overhaul

Refer to illustrations 8.8, 8.9, 8.10, 8.11a, 8.11b, 8.11c, 8.11d, 8.11e, 8.11f, 8.11g, 8.11h and 8.15

7   Before attempting the overhaul of the master cylinder, obtain the proper rebuild kit, which will contain the necessary replacement parts and also any instructions which may be specific to your model.

8   Inspect the reservoir grommets for indications of leakage near the base of the reservoir. Remove the reservoir **(see illustration)**. **Note:** *Later models use a screw to attach the reservoir to the cylinder.*

9   Place the cylinder in a vise and use a punch or Phillips screwdriver to depress the pistons until they bottom against the other end of the master cylinder. Hold the pistons in this position and remove the stop screw on the bottom of the master cylinder **(see illustration)**.

10   While still holding the pistons in the bottomed position, carefully remove the snap-ring at the end of the master cylinder **(see illustration)**.

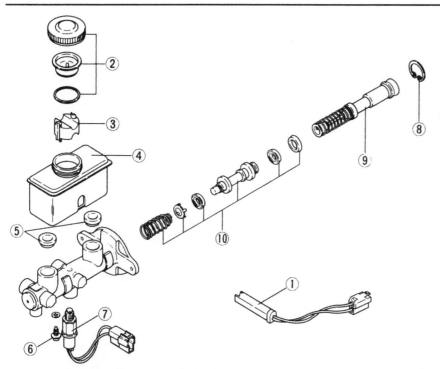

8.11a   Exploded view of the master cylinder (1986 through 1988 models)

1   Fluid level sensor
2   Reservoir cap assembly
3   Float
4   Reservoir
5   Bushings
6   Stop screw
7   Brake fluid pressure switch
8   Snap-ring
9   Primary piston assembly
10   Secondary piston assembly

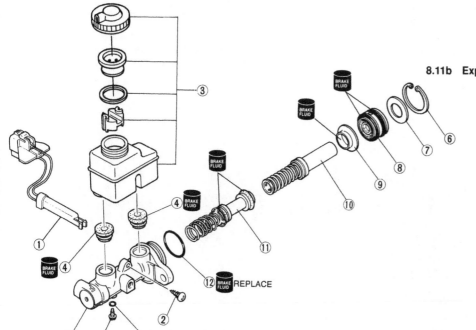

8.11b   Exploded view of the master cylinder (1989 and later models)

1   Fluid level sensor
2   Reservoir securing screw
3   Reservoir
4   Bushing
5   Stop screw and sealing washer
6   Snap-ring
7   Spacer
8   Piston guide assembly
9   Stopper
10   Primary piston assembly
11   Secondary piston assembly
12   O-ring
13   Master cylinder body

11   The internal components can now be removed from the cylinder bore **(see illustrations)**. Make a note of the proper order of the components so they can be returned to their original locations. **Note:** *The two springs are of different tension, so pay particular attention to their order. Also, do not disassemble the primary piston components – they are serviced as an assembly. The secondary piston components on 1986 through 1988 models are replaceable* **(see illustrations)**.

12   Carefully inspect the bore of the master cylinder. Any deep scoring or other damage will mean a new master cylinder is required.

13   Replace all parts included in the rebuild kit, following any instructions in the kit. Clean all reused parts with clean brake fluid or brake cleaner. Do not use any petroleum-based solvents. During assembly, lubricate all parts liberally with clean brake fluid.

8.11c   Invert the master cylinder and tap it against a block of wood to expel the secondary piston assembly

8.11d   Begin overhaul of the secondary piston assembly by removing the spring, which can be pulled straight off

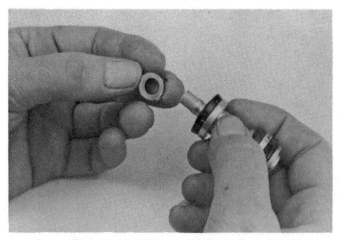

8.11e   Remove the piston cup retainer, followed by the rubber cup

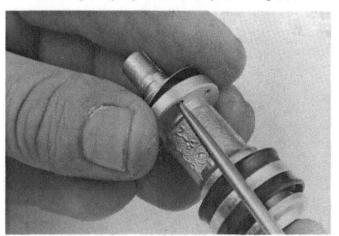

8.11f   Remove the cup protector by inserting a thin instrument through one of the holes in the piston

8.11g   Pry the remaining piston cups off the piston – when installing them, use your fingers only, or you may damage the cups

8.11h   When assembled, the cups on the secondary piston must be positioned like this

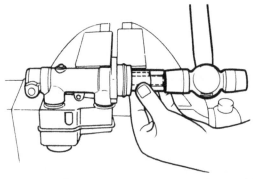

8.15 On 1989 and later models, it may be necessary to gently tap the piston guide into place with a socket and a hammer

14 Push the assembled components into the bore, bottoming them against the end of the master cylinder, then install the stop screw. Be sure to install a new sealing washer on the stop screw.
15 When installing the piston guide on later models, use a hammer and socket to tap it into place **(see illustration)**.
16 Install the new snap-ring, making sure it is seated properly in the groove, then install the brake fluid reservoir.
17 Before installing the master cylinder it should be bench bled. Because it will be necessary to apply pressure to the master cylinder piston and, at the same time, control flow from the brake line outlets, it is recommended that the master cylinder be mounted in a vise, with the jaws of the vise clamping on the mounting flange.
18 Insert threaded plugs into the brake line outlet holes and snug them down so that there will be no air leakage past them, but not so tight that they cannot be easily loosened.
19 Fill the reservoir with brake fluid of the recommended type (see Chapter 1).
20 Remove one plug and push the piston assembly into the master cylinder bore to expel the air from the master cylinder. A large phillips screwdriver can be used to push on the piston assembly.
21 To prevent air from being drawn back into the master cylinder the plug must be replaced and snugged down before releasing the pressure on the piston assembly.
22 Repeat the procedure until only brake fluid is expelled from the brake line outlet hole. When only brake fluid is expelled, repeat the procedure with the other outlet holes and plugs. Be sure to keep the master cylinder reservoir filled with brake fluid to prevent the introduction of air into the system.
23 Since high pressure is not involved in the bench bleeding procedure, an alternate to the removal and replacement of the plugs with each stroke of the piston assembly is available. Before pushing in on the piston assembly, remove the plug as described in Step 20. Before releasing the piston, however, instead of replacing the plug, simply put your finger tightly over the hole to keep air from being drawn back into the master cylinder. Wait several seconds for brake fluid to be drawn from the reservoir into the piston bore, then depress the piston again, removing your finger as brake fluid is expelled. Be sure to put your finger back over the hole each time before releasing the piston, and when the bleeding procedure is complete for that outlet, replace the plug and snug it before going on to the other ports.

Installation

24 Install the master cylinder over the studs on the power brake booster and tighten the attaching nuts only finger tight at this time.
25 Thread the brake line fittings into the master cylinder. Since the master cylinder is still a bit loose, it can be moved slightly for the fitting to thread in easily. Do not cross-thread the fittings as they are started.
26 Fully tighten the mounting nuts and the brake fittings.
27 Fill the master cylinder reservoir with fluid, then bleed the master cylinder (only if the cylinder has not been bench bled) and the brake system as described in Section 11. To bleed the cylinder on the vehicle, have an assistant pump the brake pedal several times, then hold the pedal to the

floor. Loosen the fitting nut to allow air and fluid to escape. Repeat this procedure until the fluid is clear of air bubbles. Test the operation of the brake system carefully before placing the vehicle into normal service.

9   Proportioning bypass valve – removal and installation

Removal

1 Although special test equipment is necessary to properly diagnose a proportioning bypass valve malfunction, the home mechanic can remove and install it if it has been diagnosed as faulty.
2 The proportioning bypass valve is located to the right side of the master cylinder. Using a flare-nut wrench to avoid rounding off the tube nuts, unscrew the tube nuts at the ends of the brake lines where they enter the valve. Gently pull the lines away from the valve and plug the ends of the lines or wrap plastic bags tightly around them to prevent excessive leakage and brake system contamination.
3 Remove the mounting nut or bolt from the center of the valve and maneuver the valve out from the brake lines.

Installation

4 Position the valve on the bracket and insert the brake lines into the holes. Screw all of the tube nuts into the valve by hand, being careful not to cross thread them. Install the mounting nut or bolt and tighten it securely.
5 Tighten the tube nuts securely, again using the flare-nut wrench.
6 Bleed the entire brake system as described in Section 11. If the ends of the lines were not capped securely and all of the fluid in the master cylinder reservoir has drained out, the master cylinder will have to be bled first. The master cylinder bleeding procedure (on vehicle) can be found in Section 8, Step 27.

10   Brake hoses and lines – inspection and replacement

Inspection

1 About every six months, with the vehicle raised and supported securely on jackstands, the rubber hoses which connect the steel brake lines with the front and rear brake assemblies should be inspected for cracks, chafing of the outer cover, leaks, blisters and other damage. These are important and vulnerable parts of the brake system and inspection should be complete. A light and mirror will be helpful for a thorough check. If a hose exhibits any of the above conditions, replace it with a new one.

Replacement
Front brake hose
Refer to illustrations 10.2 and 10.3
2 At the hose bracket on the inner fender panel, hold the hose fitting with an open end wrench and unscrew the tube nut from the hose **(see illustration)**. Use a flare-nut wrench to prevent rounding off the corners.

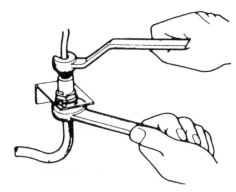

10.2 Hold the hose fitting with a wrench so you don't twist the line, then loosen the tube nut with a flare-nut wrench

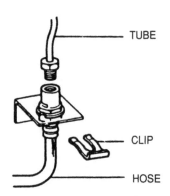

TUBE

CLIP

HOSE

10.3   Once the nut has been completeley loosened, remove the clip with a pair of pliers

3   Use a pair of pliers to remove the clip from the fitting at the bracket **(see ilustration)**, then slide the hose female end out of the bracket.
4   Also using a pair of pliers, remove the clip from the hose bracket on the strut and slide the hose center mount out of the bracket.
5   Unscrew the brake hose from the caliper.
6   To install the hose, place a new sealing washer on the end of the hose (single-piston calipers only) and thread it into the caliper, tightening it securely.
7   Route the hose center mount into the bracket on the strut, making sure it isn't twisted. Install the clip.
8   Without twisting the hose, install the female hose end in the hose bracket on the inner fender panel. Install the clip retaining the fitting to the bracket.
9   Using a back-up wrench, attach the brake line to the hose fitting.
10   When the brake hose installation is complete, there should be no kinks in the hose. Make sure the hose doesn't contact any part of the suspension. Check this by turning the wheels to the extreme left and right positions. If the hose makes contact, remove it and correct the installation as necessary. Bleed the system (Section 11).

Rear brake hose

11   Using a back-up wrench on the hose end and a flare nut wrench on the fitting, disconnect the hose at the frame bracket, being careful not to bend the bracket or brake line **(see illustration 10.2)**.
12   Remove the hose clip with a pair of pliers and separate the hose end from the bracket **(see illustration 10.3)**.
13   Remove the union bolt from the hose end at the caliper, then remove the hose.
14   Connect the hose to the caliper, using new sealing washers on each side of the union fitting. Tighten the union bolt to the torque listed in this Chapter's specifications.
15   Install the clip retaining the hose female fitting to the bracket. Make sure the hose is not twisted.
16   Using a back-up wrench, attach the brake line fitting to the female fitting. Be careful not to bend the bracket or steel line.
17   Make sure the hose installation did not loosen the frame bracket. Tighten the bracket if necessary.
18   Fill the master cylinder reservoir and bleed the system (refer to Section 11).

Metal brake lines

19   When replacing brake lines, be sure to use the correct parts. Don't use copper tubing for any brake system components. Purchase steel brake lines from a dealer or auto parts store.
20   Prefabricated brake line, with the tube ends already flared and fittings installed, is available at auto parts stores and dealers. These lines are also bent to the proper shapes.
21   When installing the new line, make sure it's securely supported in the brackets and has plenty of clearance between moving or hot components.

22   After installation, check the master cylinder fluid level and add fluid as necessary. Bleed the brake system as described in the next Section and test the brakes carefully before driving the vehicle in traffic.

---

11   Brake hydraulic system – bleeding

Refer to illustrations 11.8 and 11.12
Warning: *Wear eye protection when bleeding the brake system. If the fluid comes in contact with your eyes, immediately rinse them with water and seek medical attention.*
Note: *Bleeding the hydraulic system is necessary to remove any air that manages to find its way into the system when it's been opened during removal and installation of a hose, line, caliper or master cylinder.*
1   It will probably be necessary to bleed the system at all four brakes if air has entered the system due to low fluid level, or if the brake lines have been disconnected at the master cylinder.
2   If a brake line was disconnected only at a wheel, then only that caliper must be bled.
3   If a brake line is disconnected at a fitting located between the master cylinder and any of the brakes, that part of the system served by the disconnected line must be bled.
4   Remove any residual vacuum from the brake power booster by applying the brake several times with the engine off.
5   Remove the master cylinder reservoir cover and fill the reservoir with brake fluid. Reinstall the cover. **Note:** *Check the fluid level often during the bleeding operation and add fluid as necessary to prevent the fluid level from falling low enough to allow air bubbles into the master cylinder.*
6   Have an assistant on hand, as well as a supply of new brake fluid, a clear container partially filled with clean brake fluid, a length of 3/16-inch plastic, rubber or vinyl tubing to fit over the bleeder valve and a wrench to open and close the bleeder valve.
7   Beginning at the right rear wheel, loosen the bleeder valve slightly, then tighten it to a point where it is snug but can still be loosened quickly and easily. **Note:** *The rear brake calipers have two bleeder valves each. Use the upper valve if only the hose has been disconnected or the brake fluid is being replaced. Use the bottom valve is the caliper has been overhauled or removed from the vehicle.*
8   Place one end of the tubing over the bleeder valve and submerge the other end in brake fluid in the container **(see illustration)**.

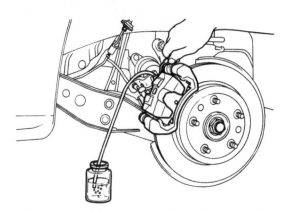

11.8   When bleeding the brakes, a hose is connected to the bleeder valve at the caliper and then submerged in brake fluid – air will be seen as bubbles in the tube and container (all air must be expelled before moving to the next wheel)

9   Have the assistant pump the brakes slowly a few times to get pressure in the system, then hold the pedal firmly depressed.
10   While the pedal is held depressed, open the bleeder valve just enough to allow a flow of fluid to leave the valve. Watch for air bubbles to exit the submerged end of the tube. When the fluid flow slows after a couple of seconds, close the valve and have your assistant release the pedal.

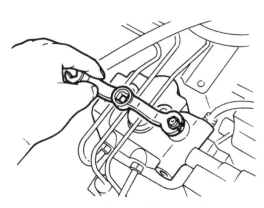

11.12 The bleeder valve for the ABS hydraulic unit is located at the top

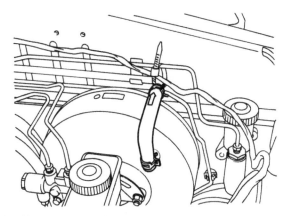

12.5 When testing the booster check valve, make sure air flows away from the booster only

11   Repeat Steps 9 and 10 until no more air is seen leaving the tube, then tighten the bleeder valve and proceed to the left rear wheel, the right front wheel and the left front wheel, in that order, and perform the same procedure. Be sure to check the fluid in the master cylinder reservoir frequently.
12   After all of the calipers have been bled, bleed the ABS hydraulic unit, if the vehicle is so equipped. This is done in the same manner as bleeding a caliper, but the bleeder valve is located on the top of the hydraulic unit **(see illustration)**.
13   Never use old brake fluid. It contains moisture which will deteriorate the brake system components.
14   Refill the master cylinder with fluid at the end of the operation.
15   Check the operation of the brakes. The pedal should feel solid when depressed, with no sponginess. If necessary, repeat the entire process.
Warning: *Do not operate the vehicle if you are in doubt about the effectiveness of the brake system.*

---

12   Power brake booster – check, removal and installation

Operating check

1   Depress the brake pedal several times with the engine off and make sure there is no change in the pedal reserve distance.
2   Depress the pedal and start the engine. If the pedal goes down slightly, operation is normal.

Air tightness check

3   Start the engine and turn it off after one or two minutes. Depress the brake pedal several times slowly. If the pedal goes down farther the first time but gradually rises after the second or third depression, the booster is air tight.
4   Depress the brake pedal while the engine is running, then stop the engine with the pedal depressed. If there is no change in the pedal reserve travel after holding the pedal for 30 seconds, the booster is air tight.

Check valve inspection

Refer to illustration 12.5

5   Disconnect the power brake booster hose where it enters the metal pipe on the firewall **(see illustration)**.
6   Apply pressure and suction to the end of the hose, making sure air flows away from the booster only. If it flows in both directions or if there is no airflow at all, replace the valve and hose assembly (the valve is inside the hose).
7   When installing the hose, make sure the arrow on the hose points toward the metal pipe on the firewall (away from the booster). Inspect the clamps before reinstalling them, replacing them if they appear distorted or weak.

Removal

Refer to illustration 12.10

8   Power brake booster units should not be disassembled. They require special tools not normally found in most service stations or shops. They are fairly complex and because of their critical relationship to brake performance it is best to replace a defective booster unit with a new or rebuilt one.
9   To remove the booster, first remove the brake master cylinder, as described in Section 8.
10   Locate the pushrod clevis pin connecting the booster to the brake pedal **(see illustration)**. This is accessible from under the dash, above the brake pedal.
11   Remove the retaining clip with pliers and pull out the clevis pin.
12   Disconnect the hose leading from the firewall to the booster. Be careful not to damage the hose when removing it from the booster fitting.
13   Remove the four nuts and washers holding the brake booster to the firewall. You may need a light to see these, as they are up under the dash area **(see illustration 12.10)**.
14   Slide the booster straight out from the firewall until the studs clear the holes and pull the booster from the engine compartment.

Installation

Refer to illustrations 12.16a and 12.16b

15   Installation procedures are basically the reverse of those for removal. Tighten the booster mounting nuts to the torque listed in this Chapter's specifications.

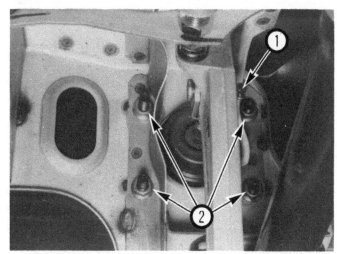

12.10   Remove the clevis pin clip (1), pull out the clevis pin, then remove the four nuts securing the booster to the firewall (2)

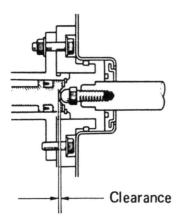

**12.16a   The booster pushrod-to-master cylinder piston clearance
must be as specified – if there's interference between the two, the
brakes may drag; if there's too much clearance, there will be
excessive brake pedal travel**

16   If the power booster unit is being replaced, the clearance between the
master cylinder piston and the pushrod in the vacuum booster must be
measured. Using a depth micrometer or vernier calipers, measure the distance from the seat (recessed area) in the master cylinder to the master
cylinder mounting flange. Next, using a hand vacuum pump, apply 20 in-
Hg of vacuum and measure the distance from the end of the vacuum
booster pushrod to the mounting face of the booster (including any gaskets or brackets) where the master cylinder mounting flange seats. Subtract the two measurements to get the clearance **(see illustration)**. If the
clearance is more or less than specified, turn the adjusting screw on the
end of the power booster pushrod until the clearance is within the limit
listed in this Chapter's specifications **(see illustration)**.
17   After the final installation of the master cylinder and brake lines, the
brake pedal height and freeplay must be adjusted and the system must be
bled. See the appropriate Sections of this Chapter for the procedures.

---

13   Parking brake – adjustment

Refer to illustration 13.4

1   The parking brake lever, when properly adjusted, should travel four to
five clicks when you pull with moderate force on the parking brake lever. If
it travels less than five clicks, there is a chance the parking brake might not
be releasing completely and might be dragging on the drum. If the lever
can be pulled up more than eight clicks, the parking brake may not hold
adequately on an incline, allowing the car to roll.
2   Raise the rear of the vehicle and support it securely on jackstands.
Place the transmission in Neutral and block the front wheels.

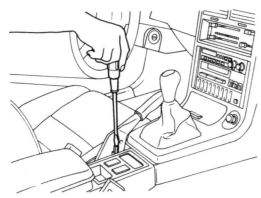

**13.4   Once the parking brake lever trim has been removed, the
cable adjuster nut can be turned**

**12.16b   To adjust the length of the booster pushrod, hold the
serrated portion of the rod with a pair of pliers and turn the
adjusting screw in or out, as necessary, to achieve the
desired setting**

3   To gain access to the parking brake adjuster, remove the parking
brake lever trim. It is held to the lever by a single screw on the left inside of
the lever.
4   Loosen or tighten the adjusting nut until the desired travel is attained
(see illustration). With the parking brake lever in the released position,
rotate the rear wheels to ensure they move freely. If the brakes drag, the
adjusting nut must be loosened.
5   Install the parking brake lever trim.

---

14   Parking brake cables – replacement

Refer to illustrations 14.3a, 14.3b, 14.8 and 14.9

Front cable

1   Refer to Section 13 and remove the parking brake lever trim, then unscrew the adjuster nut from the front cable.
2   Raise the vehicle and support it securely on jackstands. Remove the
rear half of the exhaust system (see Chapter 4) and the driveshaft (see
Chapter 8).
3   Unbolt the two cable guides from the underbody, pry the grommet
from the hole in the floorpan and pull the cable through **(see illustrations)**.
Disconnect the spring and the two rear cables from the equalizer.

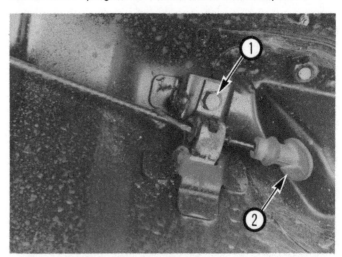

**14.3a   Unscrew the bolt (1) from the cable guide, unhook the
guide's strap from the mount, then pry the grommet (2) from the
hole in the floorpan**

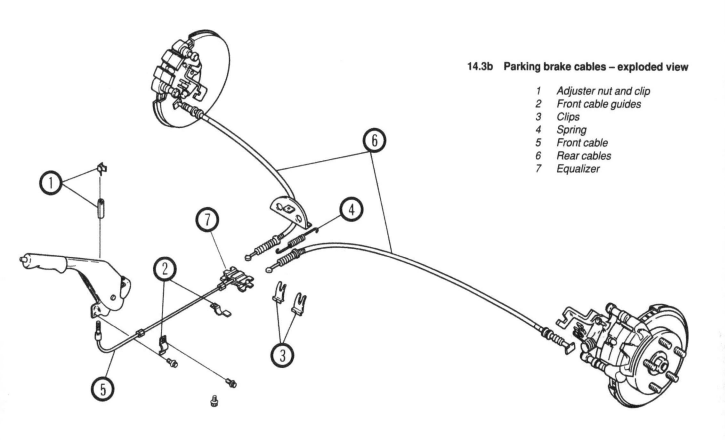

14.3b Parking brake cables – exploded view

1 Adjuster nut and clip
2 Front cable guides
3 Clips
4 Spring
5 Front cable
6 Rear cables
7 Equalizer

4   Installation is the reverse of the removal procedure, but be sure to adjust the cable as described in the previous Section.

Rear cable(s)

5   Referring to Section 13, remove the parking brake lever trim and loosen the adjuster nut to provide slack in the cable.

6   Loosen the rear wheel lug nuts, raise the rear of the vehicle and support it securely on jackstands. Remove the rear wheels and block the front wheels.

7   Remove the rear half of the exhaust system (see Chapter 4) and the driveshaft (see Chapter 8).

8   At the brake caliper, loosen the cable-to-bracket nut (**see illustration**), lift the cable out of the bracket and unhook the cable end from the lever on the caliper.

9   Remove the clip that secures the cable to the floorpan (**see illustration**). At the equalizer, rotate the cable end 90-degrees, aligning the cable with the slot, then disconnect the cable from the equalizer.

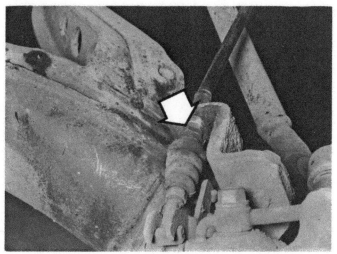

14.8 Loosen the nut (arrow) on the cable to free it from its bracket

14.9 Remove the clip (1), then slide the cable through the slot in the equalizer (2)

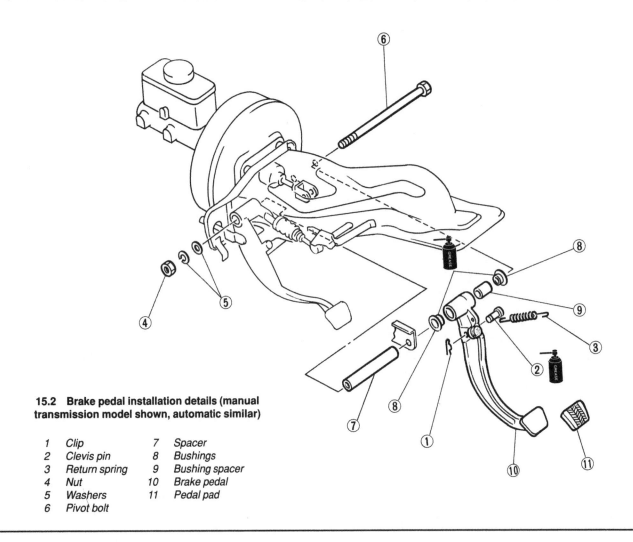

15.2   Brake pedal installation details (manual transmission model shown, automatic similar)

1	Clip	7	Spacer
2	Clevis pin	8	Bushings
3	Return spring	9	Bushing spacer
4	Nut	10	Brake pedal
5	Washers	11	Pedal pad
6	Pivot bolt		

10   Pull the forward end of the cable from its mounting hole and remove the cable from the vehicle.

11   Installation is the reverse of the removal procedure. When the job is complete, adjust the cable as described in Section 13.

15   Brake pedal – removal, installation and adjustment

Refer to illustrations 15.2 and 15.10

Removal

1   Disconnect the cable from the negative terminal of the battery.

2   Remove the clip from the clevis pin and pull out the pin, disconnecting the power brake booster pushrod from the pedal **(see illustration)**.

3   Disconnect the return spring from the pedal.

4   Unscrew the nut from the end of the pivot bolt **(see illustration 15.2)**. Pull out the bolt from the right and remove the pedal. **Note:** *On models with a manual transmission, insert a long bolt or dowel from the left as the pivot bolt is being removed. This will prevent the clutch pedal from falling.*

5   Remove the bushings and spacer from the top of the pedal and inspect them for wear, replacing them if necessary.

Installation

6   Apply a thin coat of multi-purpose grease to the pedal bushings and spacer and insert them into the top of the pedal.

7   Position the pedal and spacer in the pedal bracket, then insert the pivot bolt. Install the washers and pivot bolt nut, tightening it securely.

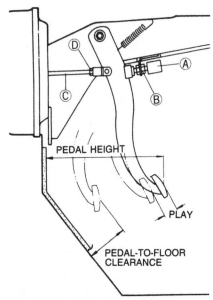

15.10   The brake light switch must be backed-out so it doesn't contact the pedal, then the pedal height and freeplay can be set

A	Brake light switch	C	Booster pushrod
B	Brake light switch locknut	D	Booster pushrod locknut

8   Connect the booster pushrod to the pedal, lubricate and install the clevis pin and insert the clip. Attach the return spring to the pedal.

Adjustment

9   After the pedal has been installed, there are two adjustments that need to be made – pedal height and pedal freeplay. The pedal-to-floor clearance will also have to be checked.

10   To adjust the brake pedal height, disconnect the brake light switch electrical connector and loosen the switch locknut **(see illustration)**. Unscrew the switch until it does not contact the pedal.

11   Loosen the booster pushrod locknut and turn the pushrod until the desired pedal height (listed in this Chapter's specifications) is attained.

12   Now that the pedal height is set, turn the pushrod until the freeplay is within the range listed in this Chapter's specifications **(see illustration 15.10)**. Freeplay is the distance the pedal moves before resistance is felt.

13   With the freeplay now set, tighten the booster pushrod locknut. Turn the brake light switch until it contacts the pedal, then give it an additional 1/2-turn and tighten the locknut. Reconnect the electrical connector.

14   Measure the distance from the pedal pad to the floor **(see illustration 15.10)** while an assistant pushes heavily on the pedal. Compare your measurement with the figure listed in the this Chapter's specifications. If your measurement is less than specified, check for worn brake pads or a malfunction of the automatic adjuster on one of the rear calipers (indicated by excessive clearance between the brake pads and the brake disc). If neither of these conditions are found, bleed the brake system (see Section 11).

---

16   Brake light switch – removal, installation and adjustment

---

Refer to illustration 16.1

Removal and installation

1   The brake light switch is located on a bracket at the top of the brake pedal, under the dash **(see illustration)**. The switch activates the brake lights at the rear of the vehicle whenever the pedal is depressed.

2   Disconnect the negative battery cable and secure it out of the way so it cannot come into contact with the battery post.

3   Disconnect the electrical connector from the brake light switch.
4   Loosen the locknut and unscrew the switch from the pedal bracket.
5   Installation is the reverse of removal.

Adjustment

6   Loosen the locknut, screw the switch in so the end of the switch contacts the pedal stopper, then give it another 1/2-turn. Tighten the locknut.
7   Connect electrical connector at the switch and reconnect the battery. With the help of an assistant, check that the brake lights are functioning properly.

16.1   Brake light switch mounting details

1	*Switch*	*3*	*Electrical connector (the tang*
2	*Locknut*		*on the side of the connector must*
			be depressed before unplugging it)

Chapter 10 Suspension and steering systems

Contents

Balljoint – check and replacement   4
Control link – removal and installation   11
Front stabilizer bar and bushings – removal and installation   2
Front strut/shock absorber and coil spring
   assembly – removal, overhaul and installation   5
Front suspension control arm – removal and installation   3
General information   1
Intermediate shaft – removal and installation   16
Lateral link – removal and installation   10
Power steering fluid level check . . . .   See Chapter 1
Power steering pump – removal and installation   20
Power steering system – bleeding   21
Rear shock absorber and coil spring
   assembly – removal, overhaul and installation   8
Rear stabilizer bar and bushings – removal and installation   7
Rear trailing arm – removal and installation   9
Steering gear boots – replacement   19
Steering gear – removal and installation   17
Steering knuckle and hub – removal and installation   6
Steering wheel – removal and installation   15
Subframe – removal and installation   13
Sublink – removal and installation   12
Suspension and steering checks . . . .   See Chapter 1
Tie-rod ends – removal and installation   18
Tire and tire pressure checks . . . .   See Chapter 1
Tire rotation . . . .   See Chapter 1
Toe control hub and bearing assembly – removal and installation .   14
Wheel alignment – general information   23
Wheels and tires – general information   22

Specifications

Torque specifications

Front suspension

	Ft–lbs
Strut-to-strut tower nuts	22 to 27
Strut-to-steering knuckle bolts/nuts	69 to 86
Strut damper shaft nut	47 to 59
Balljoint-to-steering knuckle pinch bolt	27 to 40
Control arm pivot bolt nut	46 to 69
Control arm bushing clamp bolts	43 to 54

Rear suspension

Rear shock absorber upper mounting nuts	17 to 22
Rear shock absorber lower mounting bolt	46 to 69
Rear shock absorber damper shaft nut	47 to 59
Rear trailing arm pivot bolt nut	46 to 70
Lateral link nuts	
Subframe end	33 to 43
Trailing arm end	22 to 33
Control link nuts	27 to 40
Sublink nuts	54 to 69
Subframe-to-body nuts	72 to 87
Toe control hub-to-trailing arm bolts/nuts	
Upper	46 to 69
Front lower	82 to 111
Rear lower	46 to 69

Steering

Steering wheel nut	29 to 36
Intermediate shaft pinch bolts	13 to 17
Steering gear mounting bolts	22 to 33
Tie-rod end-to-steering knuckle nut	22 to 33
Wheel lug nuts	See Chapter 1

---

1   General information

Description

Refer to illustrations 1.1 and 1.2

The vehicles covered by this manual utilize a Macpherson strut style front suspension **(see illustration)**. A telescopic shock absorber is encased within the body of the strut. A mount on the outside of the strut body supports the lower end of the coil spring – the upper end of the spring rides in the upper spring seat, which is fastened to the shock absorber rod. The control arm is a single-piece aluminum forging. On the inner end, the arm pivots on two bushings, while at the outer end, a detachable balljoint connects the arm with the steering knuckle. A stabilizer bar prevents excessive body roll when cornering.

The unique rear suspension, called the Dynamic Tracking Suspension System (DTSS) or Multilink, is a bit more complex than the front. Its main components include a trailing arm and hub assembly, a diagonal-lateral locating link, stabilizer bar and telescopic shock absorbers **(see illustration)**. This arrangement allows the hub (which can shift its position in three axial directions in the trailing arm) to alter the toe-in, toe-out and camber settings during different driving conditions to provide better roadholding capability.

Some models are equipped with an Auto Adjusting Suspension (AAS) feature, which incorporates an actuator mounted atop each shock absorber. When activated (by the driver moving the switch from Normal to Sport) the actuators change the dampening capability of the shocks, firming the ride to enhance cornering feel.

The rack-and-pinion steering gear is mounted on the front of the subframe, underneath the engine. Manual steering is provided on the base models, while some models are equipped with power-assisted steering, which is comprised of the steering gear, pump and hydraulic hoses. As an option, some later models may be equipped with one of two variable assist power steering systems – the Engine Speed Sensing Power Steering (ESPS) or the Electronically Controlled Power Steering (ECPS). Due to the technical complexities of these systems, only the removal and installation procedures for the major components will be covered in this Chapter.

Servicing techniques

Frequently, when working on the suspension or steering system components, you may come across fasteners which seem impossible to loosen. These fasteners on the underside of the vehicle are continually subjected to water, road grime, mud, etc., and can become rusted or "frozen," making them extremely difficult to remove. To unscrew these stubborn fasteners without damaging them (or other components), be sure to use lots of penetrating oil and allow it to soak in for a while. Using a wire brush to clean exposed threads will also ease removal of the nut or bolt and prevent damage to the threads. Sometimes a sharp blow with a hammer and punch is effective in breaking the bond between nut and bolt threads, but care must be taken to prevent the punch from slipping off the fastener and ruining the threads. Heating the stuck fastener and surrounding area with a torch sometimes helps too, but isn't recommended because of the obvious dangers associated with fire. Long breaker bars and extension, or "cheater", pipes will increase leverage, but never use an extension pipe on a ratchet – the ratcheting mechanism could be damaged. Sometimes, turning the nut or bolt in the tightening (clockwise) direction first will help to break it loose. Fasteners that require drastic measures to unscrew should always be replaced with new ones.

Since most of the procedures that are dealt with in this Chapter involve jacking up the vehicle and working underneath it, a good pair of jackstands will be needed. A hydraulic floor jack is the preferred type of jack to lift the vehicle, and it can also be used to support certain components during various operations. **Warning:** *Never, under any circumstances, rely on a jack to support the vehicle while working on it. Whenever any of the suspension or steering fasteners are loosened or removed they must be inspected and, if necessary, replaced with new ones of the same part number or of original equipment quality and design. Torque specifications must be followed for proper reassembly and component retention. Never attempt to heat or straighten any suspension or steering components. Instead, replace bent or damaged parts with new ones.*

---

2   Front stabilizer bar and bushings – removal and installation

Refer to illustrations 2.2 and 2.3

Removal

1   Apply the parking brake. Raise the front of the vehicle and support it securely on jackstands. Remove the lower splash pan.

2   Remove the stabilizer bar-to-link nut (and bolt, on some models) **(see illustration)**. If necessary, remove the nut and disconnect the link from the control arm.

3   Remove the bracket bolts and detach the stabilizer bar from the vehicle **(see illustration)**.

4   Pull the brackets off the stabilizer bar and inspect the bushings for cracks, hardness and other signs of deterioration. If the bushings are damaged, replace them.

1.1   Front suspension and steering components

1 Stabilizer bar	4 Front strut/shock absorber	6 Steering gear boot
2 Control arm	and coil spring assembly	7 Tie-rod end
3 Balljoint	5 Steering gear	8 Subframe

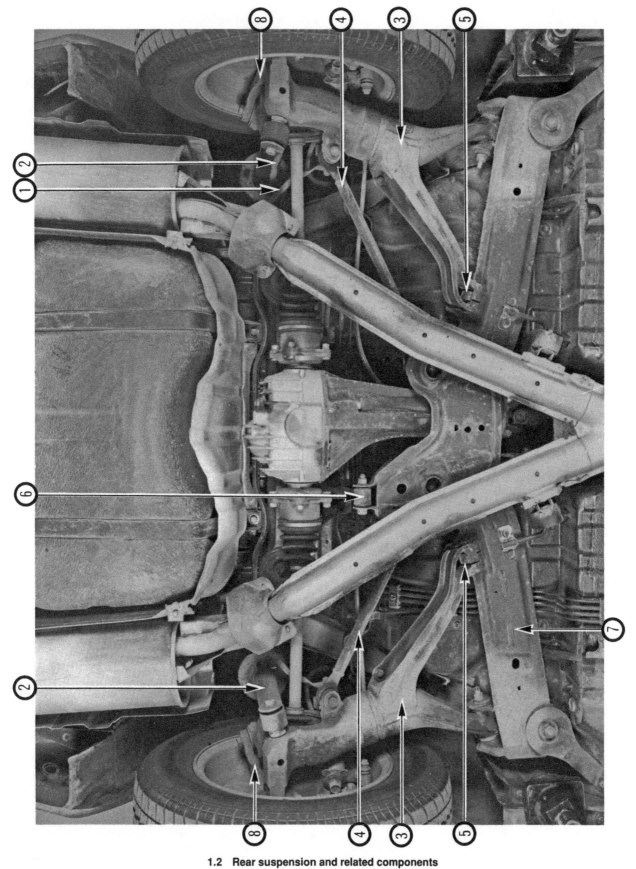

1.2   Rear suspension and related components

1	Stabilizer bar	3	Trailing arm	6	Sublink
2	Rear shock absorber and coil spring assembly	4	Lateral link	7	Subframe
		5	Control link	8	Toe control hub

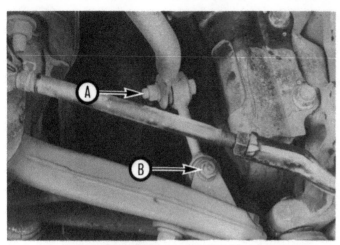

2.2   Remove the stabilizer-to-link bolt (A) – remove the lower bolt (B) if it's necessary to separate the stabilizer link from the control arm

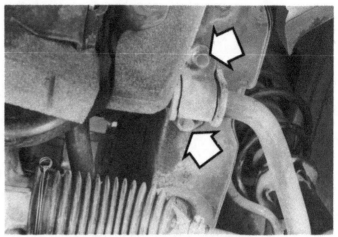

2.3   There's a stabilizer bar U-bracket like this on each side of the bar – remove the bolts (arrows)

Installation

5   Position the stabilizer bar bushings on the bar with the slits facing the front of the vehicle. The inner edge of the bushing must be aligned with the white line (1988 and earlier models) or must contact the rubber collar (1989 models).

6   Push the brackets over the bushings and raise the bar up to the frame. Install the bracket bolts, but don't tighten them completely at this time.

7   Install the stabilizer bar-to-link nut (and bolt, if equipped) and tighten them securely.

8   Lower the vehicle and tighten the bracket bolts. Install the lower splash pan.

---

3   Front suspension control arm – removal and installation

Refer to illustrations 3.3, 3.4 and 3.5

Warning: *Whenever any of the suspension or steering fasteners are loosened or removed, they must be inspected and, if necessary, replaced with new ones of the same part number or of original equipment quality and design. Torque specifications must be followed for proper reassembly and component retention.*

Removal

1   Loosen the wheel lug nuts, raise the front of the vehicle and support it securely on jackstands. Remove the wheel.

2   Disconnect the stabilizer bar link from the control arm **(see illustration 2.2).**

3   Remove the balljoint stud pinch bolt from the bottom of the steering knuckle **(see illustration)**, then pry the control arm down, separating it from the knuckle.

4   Remove the two bolts that secure the rear bushing clamp to the subframe **(see illustration)**.

5   Unscrew the nut from the control arm inner pivot bolt **(see illustration)**, then remove the bolt. It may be necessary to drive the bolt out with a hammer and drift.

6   Inspect the bushings in the arm for hardness, cracking and general deterioration. If they appear to be in need of replacement, take the arm to a dealer service department or other qualified repair shop to have them replaced. Special tools are required to perform the job.

7   Check the arm for distortion and cracks, replacing it if necessary. Inspect the balljoint as described in Section 4.

Installation

8   Position the control arm on the subframe and install the inner pivot bolt, washer and nut. Do not tighten the nut fully at this time.

9   Install the two rear bushing clamp bolts, but don't tighten them completely.

10   Insert the balljoint stud into the steering knuckle and install the pinch bolt, tightening it to the torque listed in this Chapter's specifications.

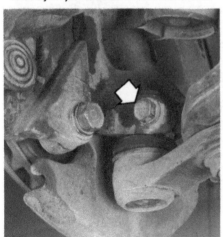

3.3   The balljoint stud is secured to the steering knuckle by a pinch bolt (arrow)

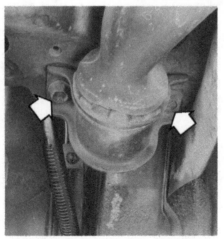

3.4   The rear bushing clamp is fastened to the body with two bolts (arrows)

3.5   Support the control arm and remove the nut (arrow) and pivot bolt – use a hammer and punch to drive the bolt out, if necessary

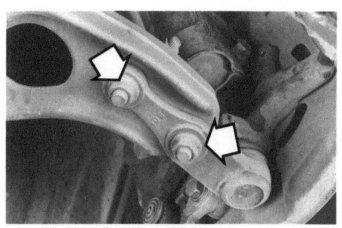

4.6 The balljoint is fastened to the control arm with two nuts (arrows)

11 Using a floor jack with a block of wood on the jack head to act as a cushion, raise the outer end of the control arm to simulate normal ride height. Tighten the pivot bolt nut and the rear bushing clamp bolts to the torque figures listed in this Chapter's specifications.

12 Connect the stabilizer bar link to the lower arm.

13 Install the wheel and lug nuts. Lower the vehicle and tighten the lug nuts to the torque specified in Chapter 1.

4 Balljoint – check and replacement

Refer to illustration 4.6

Warning: *Whenever any of the suspension or steering fasteners are loosened or removed, they must be inspected and, if necessary, replaced with new ones of the same part number or of original equipment quality and design. Torque specifications must be followed for proper reassembly and component retention.*

Check

1 Raise the vehicle and support it securely on jackstands.

2 Visually inspect the rubber dust boot for cuts, tears or leaking grease. If any of these conditions are noted, the balljoint should be replaced.

3 Using a floor jack positioned under the wheel, raise the wheel a couple of inches to take the weight off of the balljoint. Place a large pry bar under the balljoint and attempt to push the balljoint up. Next, position the prybar between the steering knuckle and the lower arm and apply downward pressure. If any movement is seen or felt during either of these checks, the balljoint is worn out.

5.2 The brake hose is supported by a bracket on the strut – use a screwdriver to remove the spring clip, then slide the hose out of the bracket

4 Following the procedure in Section 3, disconnect the control arm from the steering knuckle. Using your fingers, try to twist the balljoint stud in its socket. If the stud turns easily, replace the balljoint.

Replacement

5 If the control arm has not yet been disconnected from the steering knuckle, do so now (see Section 3).

6 Remove the nuts that secure the balljoint to the control arm **(see illustration)** and separate the balljoint from the arm. If it's stuck, tap it off with a hammer.

7 If the dust boot is not installed on the new balljoint, coat the inside of the new boot with a liberal amount of chassis grease and set it into position on the balljoint. Place a large socket or piece of pipe with a diameter equal to that of the boot over the balljoint stud. Clamp the joint and socket (or pipe) in a vise and tighten the vise until the collar on the boot is seated.

8 Position the new balljoint on the control arm and install the nuts, tightening them securely.

9 Insert the balljoint stud into the bottom of the steering knuckle and tighten the pinch bolt to the torque listed in this Chapter's specifications.

10 Install the wheel and lug nuts. Lower the vehicle and tighten the lug nuts to the torque specified in Chapter 1.

5 Front strut/shock absorber and coil spring assembly – removal, overhaul and installation

Warning: *Whenever any of the suspension or steering fasteners are loosened or removed, they must be inspected and, if necessary, replaced with new ones of the same part number or of original equipment quality and design. Torque specifications must be followed for proper reassembly and component retention.*

Note: *If the struts or coil springs exhibit the telltale signs of wear (leaking fluid, loss of damping capability, chipped, sagging or cracked coil springs), explore all options before beginning any work. The strut/shock absorber assemblies are not serviceable and must be replaced if a prolem develops. However, strut assemblies complete with springs may be available on an exchange basis, which eliminates much time and work. Whichever route you choose to take, check on the cost and availability of parts before disassembling anything.*

Removal

Refer to illustrations 5.2, 5.3 and 5.5

1 Loosen the wheel lug nuts, raise the front of the vehicle and support it securely on jackstands. Remove the wheel.

2 Remove the clip that secures the brake hose to the strut **(see illustration)**. Slide the hose out of the strut bracket.

3 Remove the strut-to-steering knuckle nuts and bolts **(see illustration)**. It may be necessary to drive the bolts out with a hammer and drift.

5.3 Remove the two bolts and nuts that hold the strut to the steering knuckle (caliper and brake disc shown removed for clarity)

5.5   The strut assembly is fastened to the body with four nuts (arrows) – DON'T UNSCREW THE NUT IN THE CENTER!

5.7a   Install the spring compressor according to the tool manufacturer's instructions and compress the spring until all pressure is relieved from the upper seat

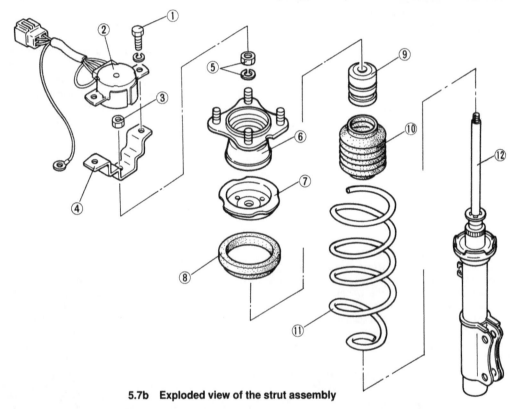

5.7b   Exploded view of the strut assembly

1	Bolt	5	Nut and washer	9	Rubber bumper
2	AAS actuator (not on all models)	6	Mounting block	10	Dust boot
3	Nut	7	Spring upper seat	11	Coil spring
4	Actuator bracket	8	Insulator	12	Strut/shock absorber

4   Pull out on the steering knuckle while pushing in on the strut to separate the two. On vehicles equipped with AAS, unplug the electrical connector from the actuator located on the top of the strut.

5   Support the strut assembly with one hand (to keep it from falling) and remove the four strut-to-tower nuts **(see illustration)**. Remove the assembly from the fenderwell.

Overhaul

Refer to illustrations 5.7a, 5.7b, 5.8, 5.9a, 5.9b, 5.9c, 5.11 and 5.13

Warning: *Disassembling a strut is a potentially dangerous job – pay close attention to what you're doing or you could get hurt! Use only a high quality*

spring compressor and carefully follow the manufacturer's instructions furnished with the tool. After removing the coil spring from the strut assembly, set it aside in a safe, isolated area (a steel cabinet is preferred).

6   Mount the strut assembly in a vise. Line the vise jaws with wood or rags to prevent damage to the unit and don't tighten the vise excessively.

7   Following the tool manufacturer's instructions, install the spring compressor (which can be obtained at most auto parts stores or equipment yards on a daily rental basis) on the spring and compress it sufficiently to relieve all pressure from the upper seat **(see illustrations)**. This can be verified by wiggling the spring.

5.8   Remove the damper shaft nut – to prevent the mounting block from turning, brace a screwdriver or prybar across two of the mounting studs

5.9a   Remove the mounting block . . .

5.9b   . . . followed by the spring upper seat

5.9c   The bearing in the mounting block should turn smoothly – if it doesn't, replace the mounting block

8   On models equipped with AAS, remove the actuator from the top of the strut **(see illustration 5.7b)**. On all models, loosen the damper shaft nut with a socket wrench **(see illustration)**. To prevent the mounting block and damper shaft from turning, wedge a prybar between two of the mounting studs.

9   Remove the nut, mounting block and upper seat **(see illustrations)**. Inspect the bearing in the mounting block for smooth operation **(see illustration)**. If it doesn't turn smoothly, replace the mounting block. Check the rubber portion of the mounting block for cracking, separation from the block and general deterioration. If any of these conditions are present, replace the mounting block.

10   Check the rubber insert in the upper seat for cracking and hardness, replacing it if necessary.

11   Slide the rubber bumper and dust boot off the damper shaft **(see illustration)**.

12   Carefully lift the compressed spring from the assembly and set it in a safe place, such as a steel cabinet. **Warning:** *Keep the ends of the spring facing away from your body!*

13   To begin assembly, carefully place the coil spring onto the lower seat, with the end of the spring resting in the lowest part of the seat **(see illustration)**.

14   Install the dust boot and rubber bumper – extend the damper rod as far as it will go and slide the boot and bumper down to the strut body.

15   Install the rubber insert into the upper spring seat. Install the upper seat and mounting block, making sure the flat in the D-shaped hole in the mounting block matches up with the flat on the damper shaft.

5.11   Slide the dust boot and the rubber bumper (located inside the dust boot) off the damper shaft

16   Install the damper shaft nut and tighten it to the torque listed in this Chapter's specifications. Use the technique described in Step 8 to prevent the shaft from turning. On models equipped with AAS, reinstall the actuator.

5.13   When installing the spring, make sure the end of the lower coil seats in the recessed portion of the lower seat

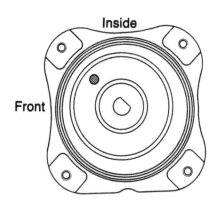

5.17   The white dot on the mounting block should be situated at the front inside hole when the strut assembly is installed

Installation

Refer to illustration 5.17

17   Guide the strut assembly up into the fenderwell. The white mark on the top of the mounting block must be situated at the front inside mounting hole **(see illustration)**. Insert the mounting studs through the holes and install the nuts, but don't tighten them completely yet.

18   Insert the top of the steering knuckle into the strut mounting flanges, install the bolts and nuts and tighten them to the torque listed in this Chapter's specifications. On models equipped with AAS, reconnect the electrical connector for the actuator.

19   Slide the brake hose into the bracket on the strut and install the clip.

20   Install the wheel and lug nuts. Lower the vehicle and tighten the lug nuts to the torque listed in this Chapter's specifications.

---

6   Steering knuckle and hub – removal and installation

Refer to illustration 6.7

Warning: *Whenever any of the suspension or steering fasteners are loosened or removed they must be inspected and, if necessary, replaced with new ones of the same part number or of original equipment quality and design. Torque specifications must be followed for proper reassembly and component retention. Dust created by the brake system may contain asbestos, which is harmful to your health. Never blow it out with compressed air and don't inhale any of it. Do not, under any circumstances, use petroleum-based solvents to clean brake parts. Use brake cleaner or denatured alcohol only.*

6.7   Pry the pinch joint open with a large screwdriver to ease separation from the balljoint stud

Removal

1   Loosen the wheel lug nuts, raise the vehicle and support it securely on jackstands. Remove the wheel.

2   Remove the brake caliper and support it with a piece of wire as described in Chapter 9. Also remove the caliper mounting bracket.

3   Remove the brake disc and hub assembly (see Chapter 1, "Front wheel bearing check, repack and adjustment").

4   Loosen, but do not remove the strut-to-steering knuckle nuts **(see illustration 5.3)**.

5   Separate the tie-rod end from the steering knuckle arm as described in Section 18.

6   Remove the balljoint-to-steering knuckle pinch bolt **(see illustration 3.3)**. The strut-to-steering knuckle nuts and bolts can now be removed. It may be necessary to knock the bolts out with a hammer and drift.

7   Pull the top of the knuckle out of the strut flange. To separate the knuckle from the balljoint stud, insert a screwdriver into the pinch joint gap and pry it apart slightly **(see illustration)**, then pull the knuckle from the balljoint stud.

Installation

8   Set the steering knuckle onto the balljoint stud and install the pinch bolt. Tighten the bolt to the torque listed in this Chapter's specifications.

9   Push the knuckle into the strut flange and install the bolts, tightening them to the torque listed in this Chapter's specifications.

10   Attach the tie-rod end to the steering knuckle arm as described in Section 18. Tighten the tie-rod nut to the torque listed in this Chapter's specifications.

11   Install the brake disc and hub assembly (see Chapter 1), then install the caliper and mounting bracket (see Chapter 9).

12   Install the wheel and lug nuts. Lower the vehicle and tighten the lug nuts to the torque specified in Chapter 1.

---

7   Rear stabilizer bar and bushings – removal and installation

---

Refer to illustrations 7.2 and 7.3

Warning: *Whenever any of the suspension or steering fasteners are loosened or removed, they must be inspected and, if necessary, replaced with new ones of the same part number or of original equipment quality and design. Torque specifications must be followed for proper reassembly and component retention.*

1   Raise the rear of the vehicle and support it securely on jackstands.

2   Unbolt the stabilizer bar from the stabilizer bar link **(see illustration)**. If necessary, the link can be unbolted from the trailing arm.

3   On earlier models, unscrew the nut from each stabilizer bar bracket and unhook the brackets from the undercarriage **(see illustration)**. On later models, each bracket is retained by two nuts.

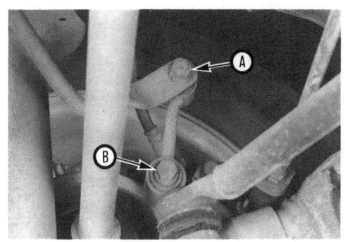

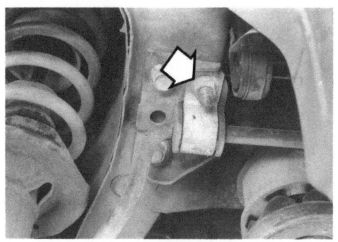

7.2   When removing the rear stabilizer bar, the bar can be unbolted from the link (A) or the link can be unbolted from the trailing arm (B)

7.3   The stabilizer bar brackets on some models have only one nut (arrow) retaining them – the other side of the bracket is hooked to the frame

4   Remove the bar from the vehicle. Pull the rubber bushings from the bar and inspect them for cracking, hardness and general deterioration. They should be replaced if any of these conditions are noted.
5   Installation is the reverse of removal.

---

8   Rear shock absorber and coil spring assembly – removal, overhaul and installation

---

Refer to illustrations 8.2, 8.3 and 8.5
Warning: *Whenever any of the suspension or steering fasteners are loosened or removed, they must be inspected and, if necessary, replaced with new ones of the same part number or of original equipment quality and design. Torque specifications must be followed for proper reassembly and component retention.*

Removal

Note: *If the shock absorbers or coil springs exhibit the telltale signs of wear (leaking fluid, loss of damping capability, chipped, sagging or cracked coil springs), explore all options before beginning any work. The shock absorber assemblies are not serviceable and must be replaced if a problem develops. However, strut assemblies complete with springs may be available on an exchange basis, which eliminates much time and work.*

Whichever route you choose to take, check on the cost and availability of parts before disassembling the vehicle.
1   Loosen the rear wheel lug nuts, raise the rear of the vehicle and support it securely on jackstands. Remove the wheel.
2   Position a floor jack under the trailing arm and raise it just enough to take the weight off the shock absorber. Remove the shock absorber lower mounting bolt **(see illustration)**.
3   Open the rear hatch and remove the speaker (see Chapter 12) to gain access to the shock absorber upper mounting nuts **(see illustration)**.
4   Hold onto the shock absorber with one hand (to keep it from falling) while unscrewing the mounting nuts. Lower the assembly and remove it from the fenderwell.

Overhaul

5   Follow the procedure in Section 5 for the basic overhaul sequence, but refer to the accompanying exploded view drawing for the proper positioning of parts **(see illustration)**.

Installation

6   Guide the shock absorber up into the shock tower and slide the mounting studs through their holes. Install the nuts to prevent the shock from falling back through, but don't tighten them completely yet.
7   Connect the lower end of the shock absorber to its mounting point on the trailing arm and tighten the bolt to the torque listed in this Chapter's specifications.

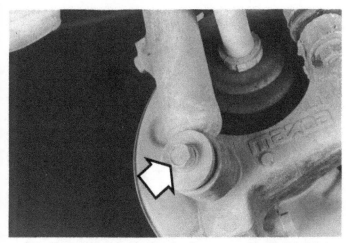

8.2   Remove the shock absorber lower mounting bolt (arrow)

8.3   The upper end of the rear shock absorber is attached to the body with two nuts (arrows) – DON'T UNSCREW THE NUT IN THE CENTER!

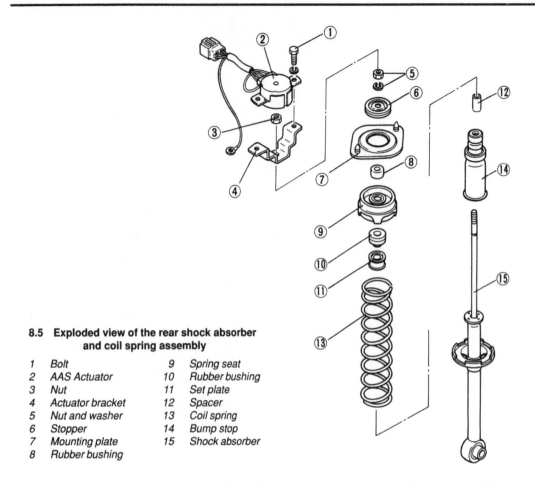

8.5　Exploded view of the rear shock absorber and coil spring assembly

1	Bolt	9	Spring seat
2	AAS Actuator	10	Rubber bushing
3	Nut	11	Set plate
4	Actuator bracket	12	Spacer
5	Nut and washer	13	Coil spring
6	Stopper	14	Bump stop
7	Mounting plate	15	Shock absorber
8	Rubber bushing		

8　Install the wheel and lug nuts. Lower the vehicle and tighten the lug nuts to the torque specified in Chapter 1.

9　Tighten the upper mounting nuts to the torque listed in this Chapter's specifications, then install the speaker (see Chapter 12).

9　Rear trailing arm – removal and installation

Refer to illustrations 9.11 and 9.13

Warning: *Whenever any of the suspension or steering fasteners are loosened or removed, they must be inspected and, if necessary, replaced with new ones of the same part number or of original equipment quality and design. Torque specifications must be followed for proper reassembly and component retention.*

Removal

1　Loosen the rear wheel lug nuts, raise the rear of the vehicle and support it securely on jackstands. Remove the wheel.

2　Remove the rear half of the exhaust system (see Chapter 4).

3　Remove the driveshaft (see Chapter 8).

4　Remove the rear stabilizer bar (see Section 7).

5　Remove the rear shock absorber/coil spring assembly (see Section 8).

6　Remove the driveaxle (see Chapter 8).

7　Remove the toe control hub from the trailing arm, following the procedure in Section 14.

8　Remove the lateral link (see Section 10).

9　Remove the mounting bolts from the front of the differential (see Chapter 8).

10　Unbolt the sublink from the subframe (see Section 12).

11　Mark the relationship of the toe adjuster cam to the subframe **(see il**

lustration). Remove the nut.

12　Unbolt the control link from the trailing arm (see Section 11).

13　Remove the subframe-to-body nuts and brackets **(see illustration)** and lower the subframe sufficiently to allow removal of the toe adjuster bolt. Support the trailing arm and remove the bolt. It may be necessary to tap the bolt through the bushing using a hammer and a long drift.

14　Remove the trailing arm from the vehicle. Check it carefully for cracks and distortion and replace it, if necessary. If the bushings exhibit signs of deterioration, have them replaced by a dealer service department or other qualified repair shop, as special tools are required for the job.

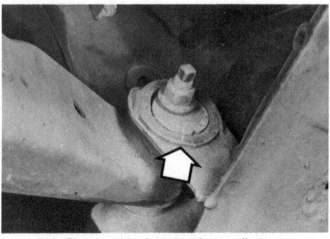

9.11　Place matchmarks across the toe adjuster cam and its bracket (arrow)

**9.13   There's a bracket like this on each end of the subframe –
unscrew the small nut that retains the bracket to the body, then
remove the large mounting nut (arrows)**

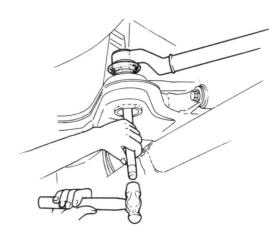

**10.4   The inner end of the lateral link must be driven out
with a hammer and a brass punch**

Installation

15   Installation is the reverse of removal. Be sure to tighten all of the fasteners to the torque figures listed in this Chapter's specifications. It would be a good idea to drive the vehicle to an alignment shop to have the rear wheel alignment checked and, if necessary, adjusted.

---

10   Lateral link – removal and installation

Refer to illustration 10.4

Warning: *Whenever any of the suspension or steering fasteners are loosened or removed, they must be inspected and, if necessary, replaced with new ones of the same part number or of original equipment quality and design. Torque specifications must be followed for proper reassembly and component retention.*

1   Raise the rear of the vehicle and support it securely on jackstands.
2   Locate the lateral link **(see illustration 1.2)** and remove the nuts from the balljoint studs at each end of the link.
3   Separate the link from the trailing arm using a balljoint separator or a two-jaw puller.
4   Separate the link from the subframe by tapping on the end of the balljoint stud with a hammer and a brass punch **(see illustration)**.
5   If the balljoints feel loose or if the link is bent, replace it. If the balljoints don't feel excessively loose but the balljoint boots are torn, remove the boots with a hammer and chisel and install new ones following the procedure in Section 4.
6   Installation of the link is the reverse of removal. Tighten the nuts to the torque listed in this Chapter's specifications.

---

11   Control link – removal and installation

Refer to illustration 11.2

Warning: *Whenever any of the suspension or steering fasteners are loosened or removed, they must be inspected and, if necessary, replaced with new ones of the same part number or of original equipment quality and design. Torque specifications must be followed for proper reassembly and component retention.*

1   Raise the rear of the vehicle and support it securely on jackstands.
2   Remove the nuts and bolts securing the control link to the trailing arm **(see illustration)** and remove the arm from the vehicle.
3   Inspect the control link for damage or bending. Check the spherical bearings at each end of the link for excessive looseness or sticky movement. Replace the link if any of these conditions are found.

**11.2   The control link is retained by a bolt and nut at
each end (arrows)**

4   Install the link by reversing the removal procedure, then tighten the fasteners to the torque listed in this Chapter's specifications.

---

12   Sublink – removal and installation

Refer to illustration 12.2

Warning: *Whenever any of the suspension or steering fasteners are loosened or removed, they must be inspected and, if necessary, replaced with new ones of the same part number or of original equipment quality and design. Torque specifications must be followed for proper reassembly and component retention.*

1   Raise the rear of the vehicle and support it securely on jackstands.
2   Remove the nuts and bolts at the top and bottom of the sublink, then remove the link from the vehicle **(see illustration)**.
3   Check the link for bending and worn-out bushings, replacing it if either of these conditions is noted.
4   Installation of the sublink is the reverse of the removal procedure. Tighten the fasteners to the torque listed in this Chapter's specifications.

---

13   Subframe – removal and installation

Refer to illustration 13.7

Warning: *Whenever any of the suspension or steering fasteners are loosened or removed, they must be inspected and, if necessary, replaced*

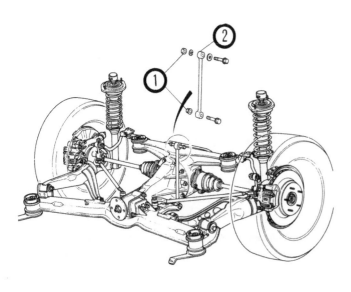

new ones of the same part number or of original equipment quality and design. Torque specifications must be followed for proper reassembly and component retention.

1   Loosen the rear wheel lug nuts, raise the rear of the vehicle and support it securely on jackstands (the jackstands must not be placed under the subframe). Remove the rear wheels.
2   Remove the rear half of the exhaust system (see Chapter 4).
3   Remove the driveshaft (see Chapter 8).
4   Disconnect the driveaxles from the differential output shafts and hang them from the underbody with pieces of wire (see Chapter 8).
5   Remove the differential front mounting nuts (see Chapter 8).
6   Disconnect the lateral links from the subframe (see Section 10).
7   Place a floor jack under the center of the subframe. Detach the trailing arms from the subframe by referring to Section 9 and performing Steps 11 through 13, then lower the subframe **(see illustration)** from the vehicle with the jack.
8   To install the subframe, reverse the removal procedure. After the job has been completed, drive the vehicle to an alignment shop to have the rear wheel alignment checked and, if necessary, adjusted.

12.2   Sublink installation details

1	Bolts and nuts	2	Sublink

14   Toe control hub and bearing assembly – removal and installation

Refer to illustrations 14.4a, 14.4b and 14.4c
Warning: Whenever any of the suspension or steering fasteners are loosened or removed, they must be inspected and, if necessary, replaced with new ones of the same part number or of original equipment quality and design. Torque specifications must be followed for proper reassembly and component retention.

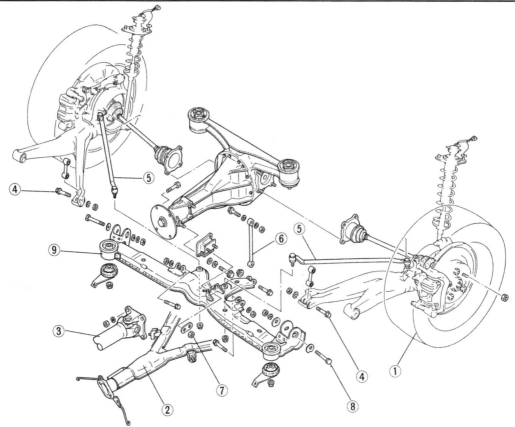

13.7   Exploded view of the subframe and associated components

1	Wheel	4	Bolt	7	Nut
2	Exhaust pipe	5	Lateral link	8	Bolt
3	Driveshaft	6	Sublink	9	Subframe

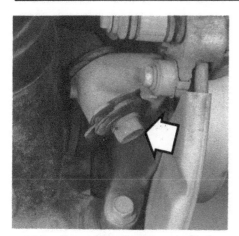

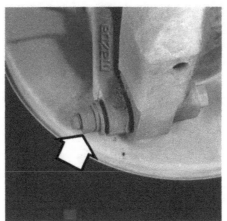

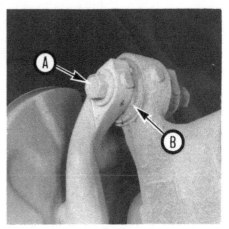

14.4a To separate the toe control hub from the trailing arm, first remove the front bolt (arrow) . . .

14.4b . . . next, remove the lower bolt (arrow) . . .

14.4c . . . and finally, remove the upper bolt (A) – when reinstalling the hub, be sure the stopper (B) is positioned on the rear of the bushing

Removal

1   Loosen the rear wheel lug nuts, raise the rear of the vehicle and support it securely on jackstands. Remove the wheel.

2   Remove the brake caliper and disc, referring to the procedures in Chapter 9. If the vehicle is equipped with ABS, also unbolt the sensor from the hub.

3   Unscrew the driveaxle hub nut (see Chapter 8).

4   Remove the three bolts that retain the toe control hub to the trailing arm **(see illustrations)**. Once the bolts are out, use a two-jaw puller to push the driveaxle out of the hub (see Chapter 8, illustration 13.5) while simultaneously withdrawing the assembly from the trailing arm. Take note of how the various fasteners, washers and spacers are situated. Allow the driveaxle to rest on the bottom of the trailing arm opening.

5   Inspect the toe control hub for damage and worn bushings. Individual parts are no longer available, so the entire assembly must be replaced as a unit if any of the bushings are worn out.

Installation

6   Support the driveaxle and position the toe control hub against the trailing arm, guiding the driveaxle into the hub splines as you go.

7   Install the toe control hub-to-trailing arm bolts, washers and nuts. Before installing the upper bolt, make sure the stopper (large washer) is positioned on the rear of the bushing (this can be seen in illustration 14.4c). Tighten all the fasteners to the torque listed in this Chapter's specifications.

8   Install the driveaxle hub nut (see Chapter 8) and tighten it to the torque specified in Chapter 8.

9   Install the brake disc and caliper (see Chapter 9). If the vehicle is equipped with ABS, don't forget to install the wheel speed sensor.

10   Install the wheel and lug nuts. Lower the vehicle and tighten the lug nuts to the torque specified in Chapter 1.

11   Drive the vehicle to an alignment shop to have the rear wheel alignment checked and, if necessary, adjusted.

---

15   Steering wheel – removal and installation

Refer to illustrations 15.3 and 15.4

Warning: *If the vehicle you are working on is equipped with an airbag, DO NOT attempt to remove the steering wheel. Have it removed by a dealer service department or other qualified repair shop.*

1   Disconnect the cable from the negative terminal of the battery.

2   Detach the horn pad from the steering wheel and disconnect the wire to the horn switch. The horn pad is secured by a screw under the plastic cover in the center of the wheel (pry the cover off for access) and two screws on the backside of the steering wheel spokes.

3   Remove the steering wheel retaining nut, then mark the relationship of the steering shaft to the hub (if marks don't already exist or don't line up) to simplify installation and ensure steering wheel alignment **(see illustration)**.

4   Use a puller to detach the steering wheel from the shaft **(see illustration)**. Don't hammer on the shaft to dislodge the steering wheel.

15.3 Paint or scribe alignment marks from the steering wheel hub to the steering shaft

15.4 Use a steering wheel puller to separate the steering wheel from the shaft – DON'T attempt to remove the wheel with a hammer!

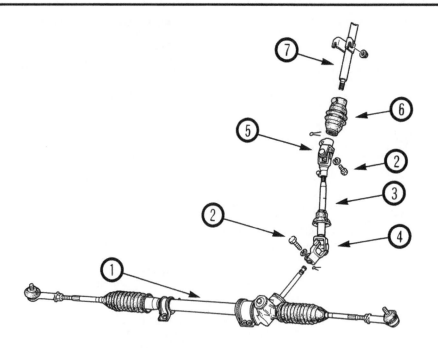

16.2　Steering intermediate shaft installation details

1　Steering gear
2　Pinch bolts
3　Intermediate shaft
4　Lower universal joint
5　Upper universal joint
6　Dust boot
7　Steering column shaft

5　To install the wheel, align the mark on the steering wheel hub with the mark on the shaft and slip the wheel onto the shaft. Install the nut and tighten it to the torque listed in this Chapter's specifications.
6　Connect the horn wire and install the horn pad.
7　Connect the negative battery cable.

16　Intermediate shaft – removal and installation

Refer to illustration 16.2
1　Turn the front wheels to the straight ahead position.
2　Working in the engine compartment, pull back the dust boot to expose the upper universal joint, then, using white paint, place alignment marks on the upper universal joint, the steering column shaft, the lower universal joint and the steering gear input shaft **(see illustration)**.
3　Remove the upper and lower universal joint pinch bolts **(see illustration 16.2)**. Some designs require the steering gear to be loosened (bolts removed) and repositioned to allow shaft removal.
4　Pry the intermediate shaft out of the steering shaft universal joint with a large screwdriver, then pull the shaft from the steering gear.

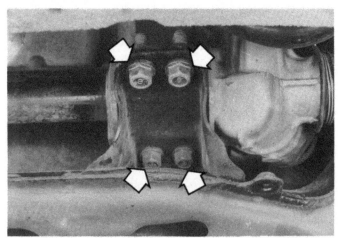

17.6　The steering gear is held to the frame on each end by a bracket such as this – remove the four bolts (arrows)

5　Installation is the reverse of removal. Be sure to align the marks and tighten the pinch bolts to the torque listed in this Chapter's specifications.

17　Steering gear – removal and installation

Refer to illustration 17.6
Warning: *Whenever any of the suspension or steering system components are loosened or removed, they must be inspected and, if necessary, replaced with new ones with the same part number or of original equipment quality and design*
Note: *This procedure applies to both power and manual steering gear assemblies. When working on a vehicle equipped with a manual steering gear, simply ignore any references made to the power steering system.*

Removal

1　Raise the front of the vehicle and support it securely on jackstands. Apply the parking brake.
2　Remove the stabilizer bar (see Section 2).
3　On vehicles equipped with power steering, place a drain pan under the steering gear, remove the hoses/lines and cap the ends to prevent excessive fluid loss and contamination.
4　Mark the relationship of the intermediate shaft lower universal joint to the steering gear input shaft **(see illustration 16.2)**. Remove the lower intermediate shaft pinch bolt.
5　Separate the tie-rod ends from the steering knuckle arms (see Section 18).
6　Support the steering gear and remove the mounting bolts **(see illustration)**. Lower the unit, separate the intermediate shaft from the steering gear input shaft and remove the steering gear from the vehicle.

Installation

7　Raise the steering gear into position and connect the intermediate shaft, aligning the marks you made previously.
8　Install the mounting bolts and washers and tighten them to the torque listed in this Chapter's specifications.
9　Connect the tie-rod ends to the steering knuckle arms (see Section 18).
10　Install the lower intermediate shaft pinch bolt and tighten it to the torque listed in this Chapter's specifications.

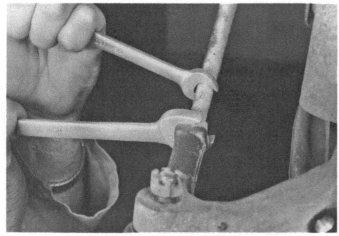

18.2a Loosen the jam nut while holding the tie-rod with a wrench to prevent it from turning

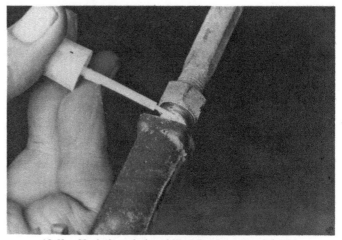

18.2b Mark the relationship of the tie-rod end to the tie-rod with white paint

18.4 A two-jaw puller works well for separating the tie-rod end from the steering knuckle arm – note that the nut hasn't been removed – it will prevent the two components from separating violently

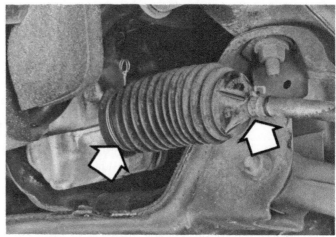

19.3 The steering gear boots are retained by a small clamp at one end and a twisted wire at the other (arrows)

11 Connect the power steering hoses/lines to the steering gear and fill the power steering pump reservoir with the recommended fluid (see Chapter 1).
12 Install the stabilizer bar.
13 Lower the vehicle and bleed the power steering system as described in Section 21.

18 Tie-rod ends – removal and installation

Refer to illustrations 18.2a, 18.2b and 18.4

Warning: *Whenever any of the suspension or steering system components are loosened or removed, they must be inspected and, if necessary, replaced with new ones with the same part number or of original equipment quality and design.*

Removal

1 Loosen the wheel lug nuts. Raise the front of the vehicle, support it securely on jackstands, block the rear wheels and set the parking brake. Remove the front wheel.
2 Hold the tie-rod with a wrench and loosen the jam nut enough to mark the position of the tie-rod end in relation to the threads **(see illustrations)**.
3 Remove the cotter pin and loosen the nut on the tie-rod end stud. Don't completely remove the nut.

4 Separate the tie-rod from the steering knuckle arm with a puller **(see illustration)**. Remove the nut and detach the tie-rod.
5 Unscrew the tie-rod end from the tie-rod.

Installation

6 Thread the tie-rod end on to the marked position and insert the tie-rod stud into the steering knuckle arm. Tighten the jam nut securely.
7 Install the castellated nut on the stud and tighten it to the torque listed in this Chapter's specifications. Install a new cotter pin.
8 Install the wheel and lug nuts. Lower the vehicle and tighten the lug nuts to the torque specified in Chapter 1.
9 Have the alignment checked by a dealer service department or an alignment shop.

19 Steering gear boots – replacement

Refer to illustration 19.3

1 Loosen the lug nuts, raise the front of the vehicle and support it securely on jackstands. Apply the parking brake. Remove the wheel.
2 Refer to Section 18 and remove the tie-rod end and jam nut.
3 Remove the steering gear boot clamps and slide the boot off **(see illustration)**.
4 Before installing the new boot, wrap the threads and serrations on the end of the steering rod with a layer of tape so the small end of the new boot isn't damaged.
5 Slide the new boot into position on the steering gear until it seats in the groove in the steering rod and install new clamps.

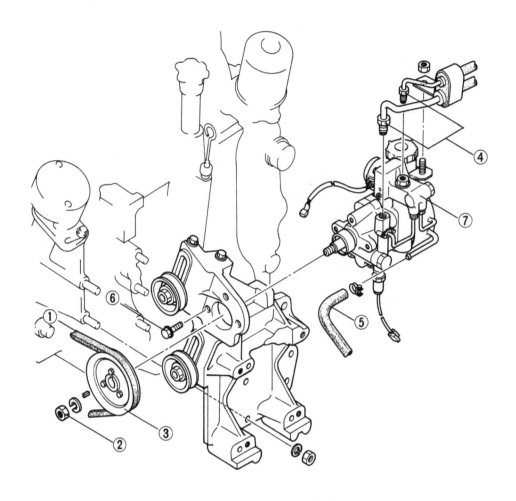

20.5   Power steering pump installation details

1	Drivebelt	5	Return hose
2	Pulley nut	6	Pump-to-bracket bolt
3	Pulley	7	Pump
4	Pressure lines		

6   Remove the tape and install the tie-rod end (see Section 18).

7   Install the wheel and lug nuts. Lower the vehicle and tighten the lug nuts to the torque specified in Chapter 1.

20   Power steering pump – removal and installation

Refer to illustration 20.5

Warning: *Whenever any of the suspension or steering fasteners are loosened or removed, they must be inspected and, if necessary, replaced with new ones of the same part number or of original equipment quality and design. Torque specifications must be followed for proper reassembly and component retention.*

Removal

1   Disconnect the cable from the negative battery terminal.

2   Loosen the tension on the pump drivebelt and remove the belt (see

Chapter 1).

3   Remove the nut in the center of the power steering pump pulley. Prevent the pulley from turning by bracing a large screwdriver across two of the three bolt heads on the front of the pulley. Slide the pulley from the pump shaft.

4   Using a suction gun, suck out as much fluid from the power steering reservoir as possible. Place a drain pan under the vehicle to catch any fluid that may spill out when the hoses are disconnected.

5   Disconnect the pressure and return lines from the pump **(see illustration)**. Also disconnect any hoses and electrical connectors that may be attached to the pump.

6   Unbolt the pump from its bracket and remove it from the vehicle.

Installation

7   Installation is the reverse of removal. Be sure to adjust the drivebelt tension and add fluid to the power steering pump reservoir (see Chapter 1).

8   Bleed the power steering system as described in Section 21.

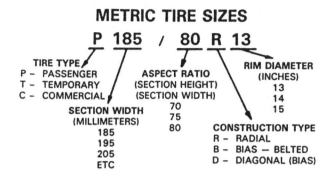

METRIC TIRE SIZES

P 185 / 80 R 13

TIRE TYPE
P – PASSENGER
T – TEMPORARY
C – COMMERCIAL

SECTION WIDTH
(MILLIMETERS)
185
195
205
ETC

ASPECT RATIO
(SECTION HEIGHT)
(SECTION WIDTH)
70
75
80

CONSTRUCTION TYPE
R – RADIAL
B – BIAS — BELTED
D – DIAGONAL (BIAS)

RIM DIAMETER
(INCHES)
13
14
15

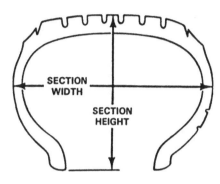

22.1   Metric tire size code

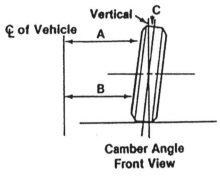

Camber Angle
Front View

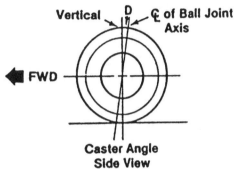

Caster Angle
Side View

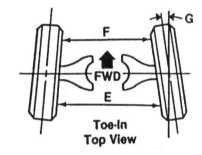

Toe-In
Top View

23.1   Typical front end alignment details

A minus B = C (degrees camber)
D = caster (measured in degrees)
E minus F = toe–in (measured in inches)
G = toe–in (expressed in degrees)

---

21   Power steering system – bleeding

1   Following any operation in which the power steering fluid lines have been disconnected, the power steering system must be bled to remove all air and obtain proper steering performance.
2   With the front wheels in the straight ahead position, check the power steering fluid level and, if low, add fluid until it reaches the lower mark on the dipstick.
3   Start the engine and allow it to run at fast idle. Recheck the fluid level and add more, if necessary, to reach the lower mark on the dipstick.
4   Bleed the system by turning the wheels from side-to-side, without hitting the stops. This will work the air out of the system. Keep the reservoir full of fluid as this is done.
5   When the air is worked out of the system, return the wheels to the straight ahead position and leave the vehicle running for several more minutes before shutting it off.
6   Road test the vehicle to be sure the steering system is functioning normally and noise free.
7   Recheck the fluid level to be sure it is up to the upper mark on the dipstick while the engine is at normal operating temperature. Add fluid if necessary (see Chapter 1).

---

22   Wheels and tires – general information

Refer to illustration 22.1

All vehicles covered by this manual are equipped with metric-sized fiberglass or steel belted radial tires (**see illustration**). Use of other size or type of tires may affect the ride and handling of the vehicle. Don't mix different types of tires, such as radials and bias belted, on the same vehicle as handling may be seriously affected. It's recommended that tires be replaced in pairs on the same axle, but if only one tire is being replaced, be sure it's the same size, structure and tread design as the other.

Because tire pressure has a substantial effect on handling and wear, the pressure on all tires should be checked at least once a month or before any extended trips (see Chapter 1).

Wheels must be replaced if they are bent, dented, leak air, have elongated bolt holes, are heavily rusted, out of vertical symmetry or if the lug nuts won't stay tight. Wheel repairs that use welding or peening are not recommended.

Tire and wheel balance is important to the overall handling, braking and performance of the vehicle. Unbalanced wheels can adversely affect handling and ride characteristics as well as tire life. Whenever a tire is installed on a wheel, the tire and wheel should be balanced by a shop with the proper equipment.

---

23   Wheel alignment – general information

Refer to illustration 23.1

A wheel alignment refers to the adjustments made to the wheels so they are in proper angular relationship to the suspension and the ground. Wheels that are out of proper alignment not only affect steering control, but also increase tire wear. The adjustments normally required are camber, caster and toe-in (**see illustration**).

Getting the proper wheel alignment is a very exacting process, one in which complicated and expensive machines are necessary to perform the job properly. Because of this, you should have a technician with the proper equipment perform these tasks. We will, however, use this space to give you a basic idea of what is involved with wheel alignment so you can better understand the process and deal intelligently with the shop that does the work.

Toe-in is the turning in of the wheels. The purpose of a toe specification is to ensure parallel rolling of the wheels. In a vehicle with zero toe-in, the distance between the front edges of the wheels will be the same as the distance between the rear edges of the wheels. The actual amount of toe-in is normally only a fraction of an inch. Toe-in adjustment on the front wheels is controlled by the tie-rod end position on the tie-rod. On the rear wheels, toe-in is adjusted by turning a cam bolt at the front of the trailing arm. Incorrect toe-in will cause the tires to wear improperly by making them scrub against the road surface.

Camber is the tilting of the front wheels from vertical when viewed from the front of the vehicle. When the wheels tilt out at the top, the camber is said to be positive (+). When the wheels tilt in at the top the camber is negative (-). The amount of tilt is measured in degrees from vertical and this measurement is called the camber angle. This angle affects the amount of tire tread which contacts the road and compensates for changes in the suspension geometry when the vehicle is cornering or travelling over an undulating surface.

Caster is the tilting of the top of the front steering axis from vertical. A tilt toward the rear is positive caster and a tilt toward the front is negative caster.

Camber and caster are adjusted by changing the position of the strut upper mounting block in the four mounting stud holes.

Chapter 11   Body

Contents

Body – maintenance 2
Body repair – major damage 6
Body repair – minor damage 5
Bumpers – removal and installation 10
Center console – removal and installation 13
Dashboard trim panels – removal and installation 12
Door latch, lock cylinder and handles – removal
   and installation 18
Door – removal, installation and adjustment 14
Door trim panel – removal and installation 11
Door window glass and regulator – removal and installation 19
Exterior mirror – removal and installation 20
Fixed glass – replacement 8

General information 1
Headlight door – adjustment 15
Headlight retractor motor – manual operation ...... See Chapter 12
Hinges and locks – maintenance 7
Hood – removal, installation and adjustment 9
Rear hatch – removal, installation and adjustment 17
Seats – removal and installation 21
Seat belt check 22
Trunk lid (convertible models) – removal, installation
   and adjustment 16
Upholstery and carpets – maintenance 4
Vinyl trim – maintenance 3

Specifications

Torque specifications

	Ft-lbs
Seat bolt	28 to 38

1   General information

These models feature a "unibody" layout, using a floor pan with front and rear frame side rails which support the body components, front and rear suspension systems and other mechanical components.

Certain components are particularly vulnerable to accident damage and can be unbolted and repaired or replaced. Among these parts are the body moldings, bumpers, the hood and trunk lids and all glass.

Only general body maintenance practices and body panel repair procedures within the scope of the do-it-yourselfer are included in this Chapter.

2   Body – maintenance

1   The condition of your vehicle's body is very important, because the resale value depends a great deal on it. It's much more difficult to repair a neglected or damaged body than it is to repair mechanical components. The hidden areas of the body, such as the wheel wells, the frame and the engine compartment, are equally important, although they don't require as frequent attention as the rest of the body.

2   Once a year, or every 12,000 miles, it's a good idea to have the underside of the body steam cleaned. All traces of dirt and oil will be removed and the area can then be inspected carefully for rust, damaged brake lines, frayed electrical wires, damaged cables and other problems.

3   At the same time, clean the engine and the engine compartment with a steam cleaner or water soluble degreaser.

4   The wheel wells should be given close attention, since undercoating can peel away and stones and dirt thrown up by the tires can cause the paint to chip and flake, allowing rust to set in. If rust is found, clean down to the bare metal and apply an anti-rust paint.

5   The body should be washed about once a week. Wet the vehicle thoroughly to soften the dirt, then wash it down with a soft sponge and plenty of clean soapy water. If the surplus dirt is not washed off very carefully, it can wear down the paint.

6   Spots of tar or asphalt thrown up from the road should be removed with a cloth soaked in solvent.

7   Once every six months, wax the body and chrome trim. If a chrome cleaner is used to remove rust from any of the vehicle's plated parts, remember that the cleaner also removes part of the chrome, so use it sparingly.

3   Vinyl trim – maintenance

Don't clean vinyl trim with detergents, caustic soap or petroleum based cleaners. Plain soap and water works just fine, with a soft brush to clean dirt that may be ingrained. Wash the vinyl as frequently as the rest of the vehicle.

After cleaning, application of a high quality rubber and vinyl protectant will help prevent oxidation and cracks. The protectant can also be applied to weatherstripping, vacuum lines and rubber hoses, which often fail as a result of chemical degradation, and to the tires.

4   Upholstery and carpets – maintenance

1   Every three months remove the carpets or mats and clean the interior of the vehicle (more frequently if necessary). Vacuum the upholstery and carpets to remove loose dirt and dust.

2   Leather upholstery requires special care. Stains should be removed with warm water and a very mild soap solution. Use a clean, damp cloth to remove the soap, then wipe again with a dry cloth. Never use alcohol, gasoline, nail polish remover or thinner to clean leather upholstery.

3   After cleaning, regularly treat leather upholstery with a leather wax. Never use car wax on leather upholstery.

4   In areas where the interior of the vehicle is subject to bright sunlight, cover leather seats with a sheet if the vehicle is to be left out for any length of time.

5   Body repair – minor damage

See photo sequence

Repair of scratches

1   If the scratch is superficial and does not penetrate to the metal of the body, repair is very simple. Lightly rub the scratched area with a fine rubbing compound to remove loose paint and built up wax. Rinse the area with clean water.

2   Apply touch-up paint to the scratch, using a small brush. Continue to apply thin layers of paint until the surface of the paint in the scratch is level with the surrounding paint. Allow the new paint at least two weeks to harden, then blend it into the surrounding paint by rubbing with a very fine rubbing compound. Finally, apply a coat of wax to the scratch area.

3   If the scratch has penetrated the paint and exposed the metal of the body, causing the metal to rust, a different repair technique is required. Remove all loose rust from the bottom of the scratch with a pocket knife, then apply rust inhibiting paint to prevent the formation of rust in the future. Using a rubber or nylon applicator, coat the scratched area with glaze-type filler. If required, the filler can be mixed with thinner to provide a very thin paste, which is ideal for filling narrow scratches. Before the glaze filler in the scratch hardens, wrap a piece of smooth cotton cloth around the tip of a finger. Dip the cloth in thinner and then quickly wipe it along the surface of the scratch. This will ensure that the surface of the filler is slightly hollow. The scratch can now be painted over as described earlier in this section.

Repair of dents

4   When repairing dents, the first job is to pull the dent out until the affected area is as close as possible to its original shape. There is no point in trying to restore the original shape completely as the metal in the damaged area will have stretched on impact and cannot be restored to its original contours. It is better to bring the level of the dent up to a point which is about 1/8-inch below the level of the surrounding metal. In cases where the dent is very shallow, it is not worth trying to pull it out at all.

5   If the back side of the dent is accessible, it can be hammered out gently from behind using a soft-face hammer. While doing this, hold a block of wood firmly against the opposite side of the metal to absorb the hammer blows and prevent the metal from being stretched.

6   If the dent is in a section of the body which has double layers, or some other factor makes it inaccessible from behind, a different technique is required. Drill several small holes through the metal inside the damaged area, particularly in the deeper sections. Screw long, self tapping screws into the holes just enough for them to get a good grip in the metal. Now the dent can be pulled out by pulling on the protruding heads of the screws with locking pliers.

7   The next stage of repair is the removal of paint from the damaged area and from an inch or so of the surrounding metal. This is easily done with a wire brush or sanding disk in a drill motor, although it can be done just as effectively by hand with sandpaper. To complete the preparation for filling, score the surface of the bare metal with a screwdriver or the tang of a file or drill small holes in the affected area. This will provide a good grip for the filler material. To complete the repair, see the Section on filling and painting.

Repair of rust holes or gashes

8   Remove all paint from the affected area and from an inch or so of the surrounding metal using a sanding disk or wire brush mounted in a drill motor. If these are not available, a few sheets of sandpaper will do the job just as effectively.

9   With the paint removed, you will be able to determine the severity of the corrosion and decide whether to replace the whole panel, if possible, or repair the affected area. New body panels are not as expensive as most people think and it is often quicker to install a new panel than to repair large areas of rust.

10   Remove all trim pieces from the affected area except those which will act as a guide to the original shape of the damaged body, such as headlight shells, etc. Using metal snips or a hacksaw blade, remove all loose metal and any other metal that is badly affected by rust. Hammer the edges of the hole inward to create a slight depression for the filler material.

11   Wire brush the affected area to remove the powdery rust from the surface of the metal. If the back of the rusted area is accessible, treat it with rust inhibiting paint.

12   Before filling is done, block the hole in some way. This can be done with sheet metal riveted or screwed into place, or by stuffing the hole with wire mesh.

13   Once the hole is blocked off, the affected area can be filled and painted. See the following subsection on filling and painting.

Filling and painting

14 Many types of body fillers are available, but generally speaking, body repair kits which contain filler paste and a tube of resin hardener are best for this type of repair work. A wide, flexible plastic or nylon applicator will be necessary for imparting a smooth and contoured finish to the surface of the filler material. Mix up a small amount of filler on a clean piece of wood or cardboard (use the hardener sparingly). Follow the manufacturer's instructions on the package, otherwise the filler will set incorrectly.

15 Using the applicator, apply the filler paste to the prepared area. Draw the applicator across the surface of the filler to achieve the desired contour and to level the filler surface. As soon as a contour that approximates the original one is achieved, stop working the paste. If you continue, the paste will begin to stick to the applicator. Continue to add thin layers of paste at 20-minute intervals until the level of the filler is just above the surrounding metal.

16 Once the filler has hardened, the excess can be removed with a body file. From then on, progressively finer grades of sandpaper should be used, starting with a 180-grit paper and finishing with 600-grit wet-or-dry paper. Always wrap the sandpaper around a flat rubber or wooden block, otherwise the surface of the filler will not be completely flat. During the sanding of the filler surface, the wet-or-dry paper should be periodically rinsed in water. This will ensure that a very smooth finish is produced in the final stage.

17 At this point, the repair area should be surrounded by a ring of bare metal, which in turn should be encircled by the finely feathered edge of good paint. Rinse the repair area with clean water until all of the dust produced by the sanding operation is gone.

18 Spray the entire area with a light coat of primer. This will reveal any imperfections in the surface of the filler. Repair the imperfections with fresh filler paste or glaze filler and once more smooth the surface with sandpaper. Repeat this spray-and-repair procedure until you are satisfied that the surface of the filler and the feathered edge of the paint are perfect. Rinse the area with clean water and allow it to dry completely.

19 The repair area is now ready for painting. Spray painting must be carried out in a warm, dry, windless and dust free atmosphere. These conditions can be created if you have access to a large indoor work area, but if you are forced to work in the open, you will have to pick the day very carefully. If you are working indoors, dousing the floor in the work area with water will help settle the dust which would otherwise be in the air. If the repair area is confined to one body panel, mask off the surrounding panels. This will help minimize the effects of a slight mismatch in paint color. Trim pieces such as chrome strips, door handles, etc., will also need to be masked off or removed. Use masking tape and several thicknesses of newspaper for the masking operations.

20 Before spraying, shake the paint can thoroughly, then spray a test area until the spray painting technique is mastered. Cover the repair area with a thick coat of primer. The thickness should be built up using several thin layers of primer rather than one thick one. Using 600-grit wet-or-dry sandpaper, rub down the surface of the primer until it is very smooth. While doing this, the work area should be thoroughly rinsed with water and the wet-or-dry sandpaper periodically rinsed as well. Allow the primer to dry before spraying additional coats.

21 Spray on the top coat, again building up the thickness by using several thin layers of paint. Begin spraying in the center of the repair area and then, using a circular motion, work out until the whole repair area and about two inches of the surrounding original paint is covered. Remove all masking material 10 to 15 minutes after spraying on the final coat of paint. Allow the new paint at least two weeks to harden, then use a very fine rubbing compound to blend the edges of the new paint into the existing paint. Finally, apply a coat of wax.

6   Body repair – major damage

1 Major damage must be repaired by an auto body shop specifically equipped to perform unibody repairs. These shops have the specialized equipment required to do the job properly.

2 If the damage is extensive, the body must be checked for proper alignment or the vehicle's handling characteristics may be adversely affected and other components may wear at an accelerated rate.

3 Due to the fact that all of the major body components (hood, fenders, etc.) are separate and replaceable units, any seriously damaged components should be replaced rather than repaired. Sometimes the components can be found in a wrecking yard that specializes in used vehicle components, often at considerable savings over the cost of new parts.

7   Hinges and locks – maintenance

Once every 3000 miles, or every three months, the hinges and latch assemblies on the doors, hood and rear hatch should be given a few drops of light oil or lock lubricant. The door latch strikers should also be lubricated with a thin coat of grease to reduce wear and ensure free movement. Lubricate the door and hatch locks with spray-on graphite lubricant.

8   Fixed glass – replacement

Replacement of the windshield and fixed glass requires the use of special fast-setting adhesive/caulk materials and some specialized tools and techniques. These operations should be left to a dealer service department or a shop specializing in glass work.

9   Hood – removal, installation and adjustment

Refer to illustrations 9.2 and 9.10
Note: *The hood is heavy and somewhat awkward to remove and install – at least two people should perform this procedure. Some models are equipped with aluminum hoods which are more susceptible to damage, so extra care must be taken when handling them. The way to determine if your hood is aluminum is to check the area of the latch loop. If there are pop rivets retaining the inner panel, the hood is aluminum – if there are spot welds, it is steel.*

Removal and installation

1 Use blankets or pads to cover the cowl area of the body and the fenders. This will protect the body and paint as the hood is lifted off.

2 Scribe or paint alignment marks around the bolt heads to insure proper alignment during installation **(see illustration)**.

3 Disconnect any cables or wire harnesses which will interfere with removal.

4 Have an assistant support the weight of the hood. Remove the hinge-to-hood nuts or bolts.

9.2   Use white paint or a felt-tip marker to outline the hood bolt locations

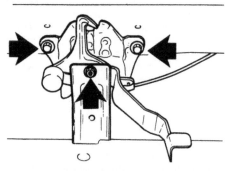

9.10   Loosen the bolts and nut (arrows), position the latch and retighten the bolts before checking the hood closing position

5   Lift off the hood.
6   Installation is the reverse of removal.

Adjustment

7   Fore-and-aft and side-to-side adjustment of the hood is done by moving the hood in relation to the hinge plate after loosening the bolts or nuts.
8   Scribe a line around the entire hinge plate so you can judge the amount of movement **(see illustration 9.2)**.
9   Loosen the bolts or nuts and move the hood into correct alignment. Move it only a little at a time. Tighten the hinge bolts or nuts and carefully lower the hood to check the alignment.
10   If necessary after installation, the entire hood latch assembly can be adjusted up-and-down as well as from side-to-side on the radiator support so the hood closes securely and is flush with the fenders. To do this, scribe a line around the hood latch mounting bolts and nut to provide a reference point. Then loosen the bolts and nut and reposition the latch assembly as

necessary. Following adjustment, retighten the mounting bolts and nut **(see illustration)**.
11   The hood latch assembly, as well as the hinges, should be periodically lubricated with white lithium-base grease to prevent sticking and wear.

10   Bumpers – removal and installation

Refer to illustrations 10.1a and 10.1b
Warning: *On models equipped with airbags, disconnect the cable from the negative terminal of the battery.*
1   Detach the bumper cover **(see illustrations)**.
2   Disconnect any wiring or other components that would interfere with bumper removal.
3   Support the bumper with a jack or jackstand. Alternatively, have an assistant support the bumper as the bolts are removed.
4   Remove the retaining bolts and detach the bumper.
5   Installation is the reverse of removal.
6   Tighten the retaining bolts securely.
7   Install the bumper cover and any other components that were removed.

11   Door trim panel – removal and installation

Refer to illustrations 11.2, 11.3, 11.5, 11.8a and 11.8b
1   Disconnect the negative cable from the battery.
2   Remove the outside mirror (see Section 20), all door trim panel retaining screws and door pull/armrest assemblies **(see illustration)**.
3   On models equipped with manual window regulators, remove the window crank **(see illustration)**. On power regulator models, pry out the control switch assembly and unplug it.

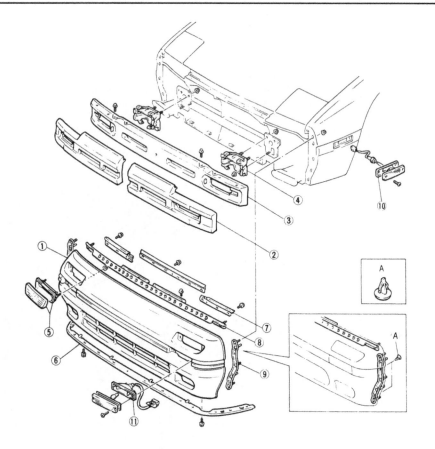

10.1a   Typical front bumper installation details

1   *Cover*
2   *Energy-absorbing foam*
3   *Bumper reinforcement assembly*
4   *Bumper mounting bracket*
5   *Passing port window cover*
6   *Front air dam skirt*
7   *Upper set plate*
8   *Retainer*
9   *Side set plate*
10   *Front side marker light*
11   *Combination light*

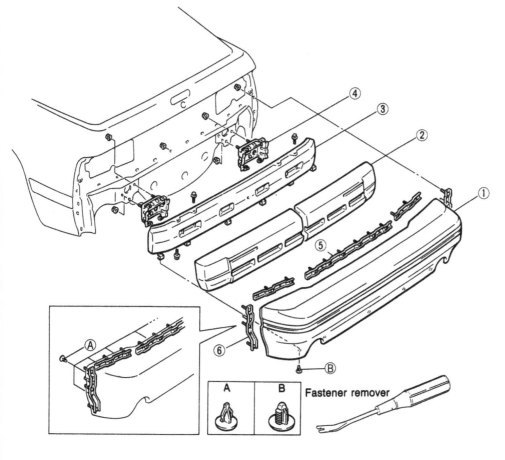

10.1b   Typical rear bumper installation details

1   Cover
2   Energy-absorbing foam
3   Bumper reinforcement assembly
4   Bumper mounting bracket
5   Retainer
6   Side set plate

Fastener remover

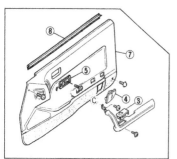

11.2   Typical door trim panel details

1   Manual window crank handle
2   Armrest
3   Power window switch
4   Courtesy light lens
5   Inner handle cover
7   Door trim panel
8   Weatherstrip

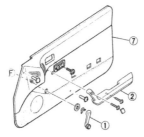

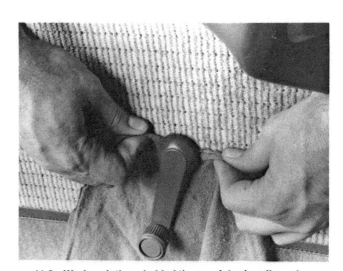

11.3   Work a cloth up behind the regulator handle and move it back and forth until the clip is dislodged

11.5 Pull the bottom of the trim panel out, then rotate the top of the panel up and out of the door

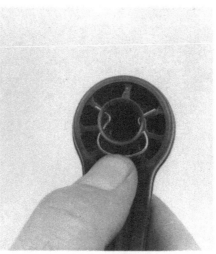

11.8a Snap the clip back into the window crank . . .

11.8b . . . and install the plastic cover – the crank can now be reinstalled by pushing it onto the regulator shaft

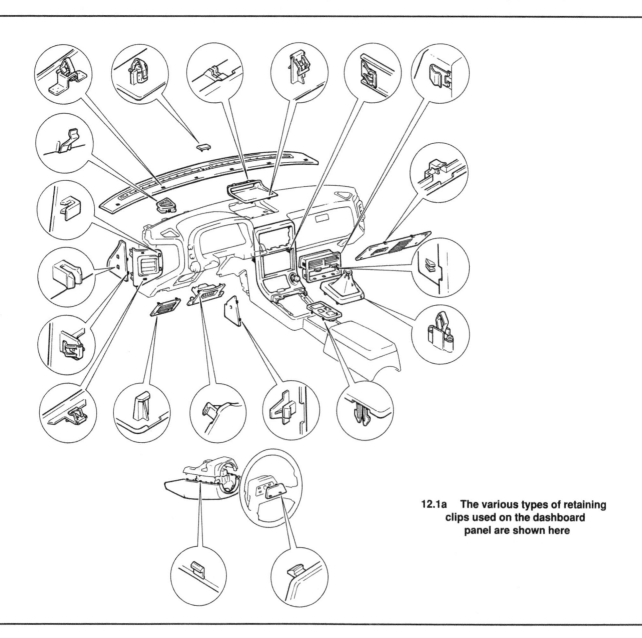

12.1a The various types of retaining clips used on the dashboard panel are shown here

4   Insert a putty knife between the trim panel and the door and disengage the retaining clips. Work around the outer edge until the panel is free.
5   Once all of the clips are disengaged, detach the trim panel, unplug any wire harness connectors and remove the trim panel from the vehicle **(see illustration)**.
6   For access to the inner door, carefully peel back the plastic watershield.
7   Prior to installation of the door panel, be sure to reinstall any clips in the panel which may have come out during the removal procedure and remain in the door itself.
8   Plug in the wire harness connectors and place the panel in position in the door. Press the door panel into place until the clips are seated and install the armrest/door pulls. Install the manual regulator window crank or power window switch assembly **(see illustrations)**.

12   Dashboard trim panels – removal and installation

Refer to illustrations 12.1a and 12.1b
1   The dashboard panels are held in place by a combination of screws and clips **(see illustrations)**.

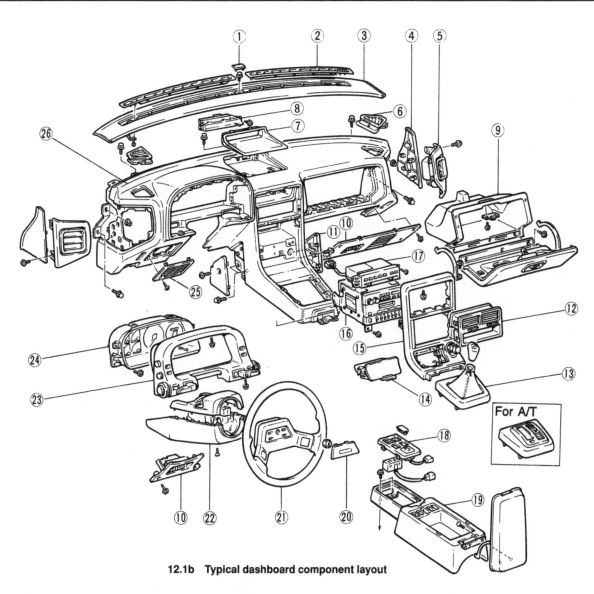

12.1b   Typical dashboard component layout

1	Center cap	10	Lower panel	18	Switch panel
2	Defroster grille	11	Side wall	19	Center console
3	Instrument panel garnish	12	Center louver	20	Steering wheel cap
4	Side cover	13	Shift boot	21	Steering wheel
5	Side panel	14	Ashtray	22	Steering column cover
6	Demister grille	15	Center panel	23	Instrument cluster switch housing
7	Clock and warning light center panel	16	Radio	24	Instrument cluster
8	Clock and warning light assembly	17	Air conditioning control panel	25	Speaker grille
9	Glove box			26	Instrument panel

These photos illustrate a method of repairing simple dents. They are intended to supplement *Body repair - minor damage* in this Chapter and should not be used as the sole instructions for body repair on these vehicles.

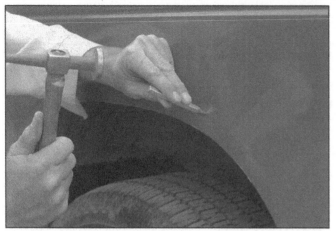

1   If you can't access the backside of the body panel to hammer out the dent, pull it out with a slide-hammer-type dent puller. In the deepest portion of the dent or along the crease line, drill or punch hole(s) at least one inch apart . . .

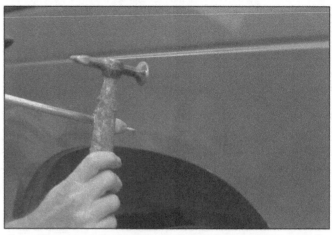

2   . . . then screw the slide-hammer into the hole and operate it. Tap with a hammer near the edge of the dent to help 'pop' the metal back to its original shape. When you're finished, the dent area should be close to its original contour and about 1/8-inch below the surface of the surrounding metal

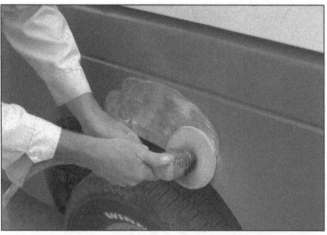

3   Using coarse-grit sandpaper, remove the paint down to the bare metal. Hand sanding works fine, but the disc sander shown here makes the job faster. Use finer (about 320-grit) sandpaper to feather-edge the paint at least one inch around the dent area

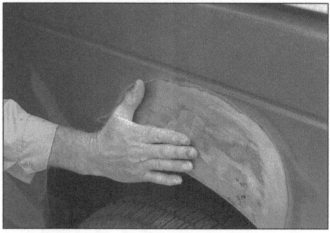

4   When the paint is removed, touch will probably be more helpful than sight for telling if the metal is straight. Hammer down the high spots or raise the low spots as necessary. Clean the repair area with wax/silicone remover

5   Following label instructions, mix up a batch of plastic filler and hardener. The ratio of filler to hardener is critical, and, if you mix it incorrectly, it will either not cure properly or cure too quickly (you won't have time to file and sand it into shape)

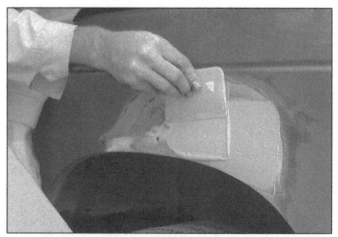

6   Working quickly so the filler doesn't harden, use a plastic applicator to press the body filler firmly into the metal, assuring it bonds completely. Work the filler until it matches the original contour and is slightly above the surrounding metal

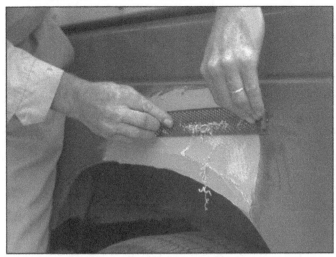

7   Let the filler harden until you can just dent it with your fingernail. Use a body file or Surform tool (shown here) to rough-shape the filler

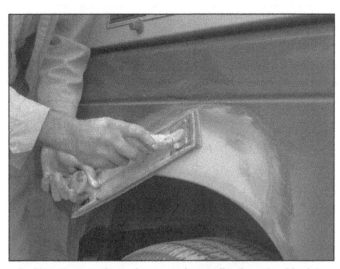

8   Use coarse-grit sandpaper and a sanding board or block to work the filler down until it's smooth and even. Work down to finer grits of sandpaper - always using a board or block - ending up with 360 or 400 grit

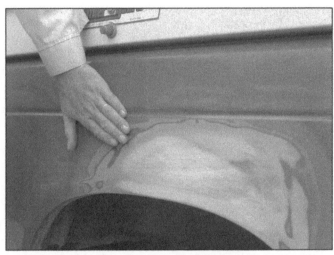

9   You shouldn't be able to feel any ridge at the transition from the filler to the bare metal or from the bare metal to the old paint. As soon as the repair is flat and uniform, remove the dust and mask off the adjacent panels or trim pieces

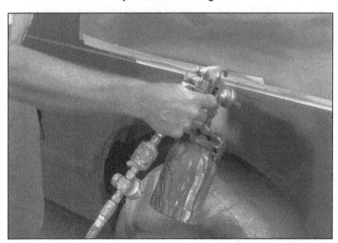

10   Apply several layers of primer to the area. Don't spray the primer on too heavy, so it sags or runs, and make sure each coat is dry before you spray on the next one. A professional-type spray gun is being used here, but aerosol spray primer is available inexpensively from auto parts stores

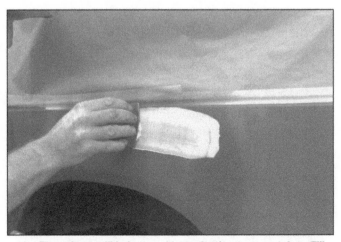

11   The primer will help reveal imperfections or scratches. Fill these with glazing compound. Follow the label instructions and sand it with 360 or 400-grit sandpaper until it's smooth. Repeat the glazing, sanding and respraying until the primer reveals a perfectly smooth surface

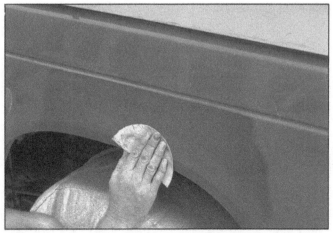

12   Finish sand the primer with very fine sandpaper (400 or 600-grit) to remove the primer overspray. Clean the area with water and allow it to dry. Use a tack rag to remove any dust, then apply the finish coat. Don't attempt to rub out or wax the repair area until the paint has dried completely (at least two weeks)

COUPE

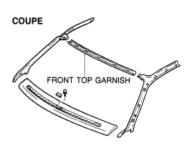

FRONT TOP GARNISH

CONVERTIBLE

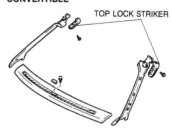

TOP LOCK STRIKER

12.3   Before the instrument panel garnish can be lifted out, the front top garnish (coupe) or lock striker (convertible models) must be removed

Side panel

2   Use a screwdriver pry the side cover off, then remove the screws and detach the side cover from the dashboard. Installation is the reverse of removal.

Instrument panel garnish

Refer to illustration 12.3

3   Remove the front top garnish (coupe) or top lock strikers (convertible), remove the center cap and screw from the instrument panel then lift the garnish panel with defroster grille assembly off **(see illustration)**.
4   Installation is the reverse of removal.

Steering column cover

5   Remove the steering wheel (see Chapter 10).
6   Remove the instrument cluster switch housing (see Chapter 12).
7   Pry the garnish ring off the ignition switch.
8   Remove the screws and separate the cover halves.
9   Installation is the reverse of removal.

Center panel

Refer to illustrations 12.11, 12.12 and 12.13

10   Use a screwdriver to detach the shift boot or selector panel and pull it up the shift lever and out of the way.
11   Remove the cigarette lighter. Open the ashtray, grasp the cover and pull the ashtray assembly out of the center panel. Remove the screws at the base of the center panel **(see illustration)**.
12   Detach the four retaining clips by prying with a screwdriver and then remove the center louver **(see illustration)**.
13   Remove the screws at the top edge and lift the center panel out of the dashboard **(see illustration)**.
14   Installation is the reverse of removal.

Clock and warning light center panel

Refer to illustration 12.15

15   Use a small screwdriver to pry up the front edge of the panel, then lift it from the dashboard **(see illustration)**.
16   Place the panel in position and press it in until it snaps in place.

Glove box

Refer to illustration 12.18

17   Remove the three hinge-to-glove box screws, then remove the glove box door.
18   Remove the retaining screws and lift the glove box out of the dashboard **(see illustration)**.
19   Installation is the reverse of removal.

Lower panel

Refer to illustration 12.21

20   Remove the five retaining screws.
21   Detach the panel, pull it out, unplug any electrical connectors and disconnect the heater ducts. Lower the panel and remove it from the dashboard **(see illustration)**.
22   Installation is the reverse of removal.

---

13   Center console – removal and installation

Refer to illustration 13.3

1   Disconnect the negative cable at the battery.
2   Pry out the switch panel (if equipped) and unplug the electrical connectors.
3   Open the lid and remove the small piece of carpeting in the bottom of the console to expose the screws **(see illustration)**.
4   Remove the screws or bolts and lift the console from the vehicle.
5   Installation is the reverse of removal.

12.11   The lower two center panel retaining screws are accessible after removing the ashtray

12.12   After working around the edge with a screwdriver to detach the clips, the center louver can be lifted out

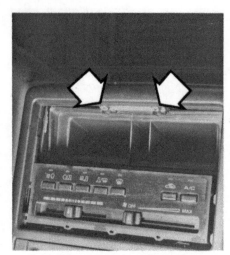

12.13   The center panel is retained at the upper edge by two screws

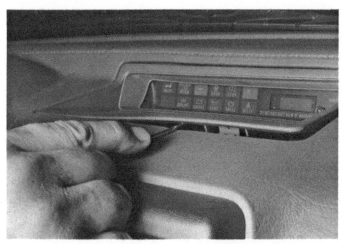

12.15 Pry up at the front edge to detach the panel

14 Door – removal, installation and adjustment

1   Remove the door trim panel (see Section 11). Disconnect any wire harness connectors and push them through the door opening so they won't interfere with door removal.

2   Place a jack or jackstand under the door or have an assistant on hand to support it when the hinge bolts are removed. **Note:** *If a jack or jackstand is used, place a rag between it and the door to protect the door's painted surfaces.*
3   Scribe around the door hinges.
4   Disconnect the check strap **(see illustration 18.2)** by tapping the retaining pin up with a small hammer.
5   Remove the hinge-to-door bolts or drive out the pins and carefully lift off the door.
6   Installation is the reverse of removal.
7   Following installation of the door, check the alignment and adjust it if necessary as follows:
   a) Up-and-down and forward-and-backward adjustments are made by loosening the hinge-to-body bolts and moving the door as necessary.
   b) The door lock striker can also be adjusted both up-and-down and sideways to provide positive engagement with the lock mechanism. This is done by loosening the mounting bolts and moving the striker as necessary.

15 Headlight door – adjustment

Refer to illustrations 15.3. 15.4 and 15.5
1   Raise the headlights.
2   Disconnect the negative cable at the battery.
3   Remove the nut and disconnect the motor operating link **(see illustration)**.

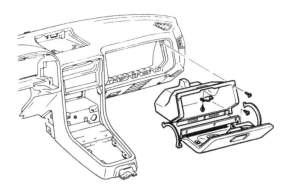

12.18 Remove the screws and detach the glove box from the dashboard

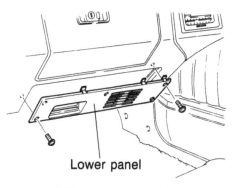

Lower panel

12.21 Lower panel details

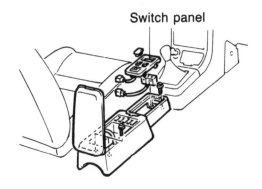

Switch panel

13.3 Pry out the switch panel for access to the front center console bolts

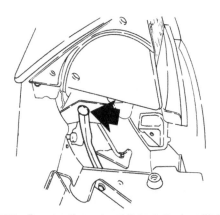

15.3 Remove the nut and detach the headlight retractor motor operating link (arrow)

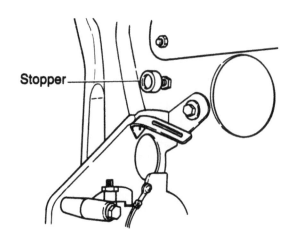

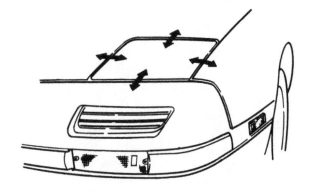

15.4   Hinge stopper location

15.5   Adjust the stopper position until the door is flush with the body

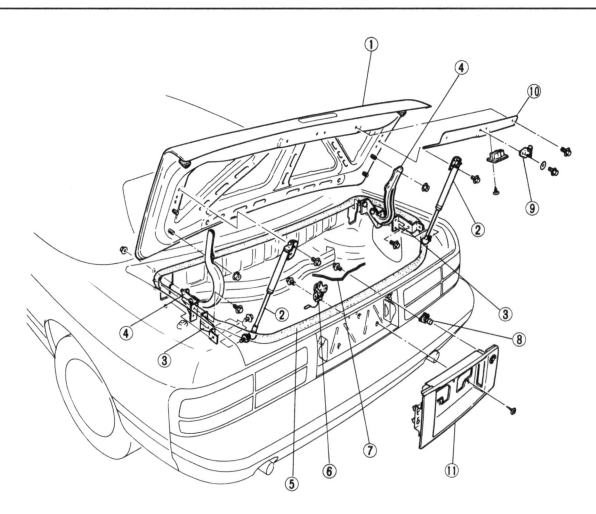

16.5   Trunk lid installation details

1	Trunk lid	5	Weatherstripping	8	Lock cylinder
2	Support struts	6	Trunk latch	9	Striker
3	Bracket	7	Opening rod	10	Reinforcement
4	Hinge			11	Finish panel

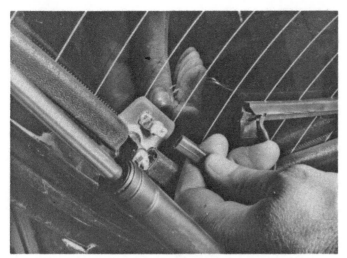

17.2   Pry the rear window defroster wiring holder out of the glass frame and unplug the connector

17.4   Use an open end wrench to unscrew the support strut mount from the hatch

4   Lower the retractor hinge until it rests on the stopper **(see illustration)**.
5   Use the stopper to adjust the headlight door position until it is flush with the surrounding body panels **(see illustration)**.
6   Connect the operating link

---

16   Trunk lid (convertible models) – removal, installation and adjustment

---

Refer to illustration 16.5
1   Open the trunk lid and cover the edges of the trunk compartment with pads or cloths to protect the painted surfaces when the lid is removed.
2   Disconnect any cables or wire harness connectors attached to the trunk lid that would interfere with removal.
3   Scribe or paint alignment marks around the hinge mounting flanges.
4   Unbolt the support struts from the trunk lid and swing them back out of the way.
5   While an assistant supports the trunk lid, remove the hinge nuts from both sides and lift it off **(see illustration)**.
6   Installation is the reverse of removal. **Note:** *When reinstalling the trunk lid, align the hinge flanges with the marks made during removal.*
7   After installation, close the lid and see if it's in proper alignment with the surrounding panels. Fore-and-aft and side-to-side adjustments of the lid are controlled by the position of the hinge nuts in the slots. To adjust it, loosen the hinge nuts, reposition the lid and retighten the nuts.
8   The height of the lid in relation to the surrounding body panels when closed can be adjusted by loosening the lock striker bolts, repositioning the striker and retightening the bolts.

---

17   Rear hatch – removal, installation and adjustment

Refer to illustrations 17.2, 17.4 and 17.5
1   Open the rear hatch and cover the upper body area around the opening with pads or cloths to protect the painted surfaces when the hatch is removed.
2   Disconnect all cables and wire harness connectors that would interfere with removal of the hatch **(see illustration)**.
3   Pull down the headliner for access and paint or scribe around the hinge flanges.
4   While an assistant supports the hatch, detach the support struts **(see illustration)**.

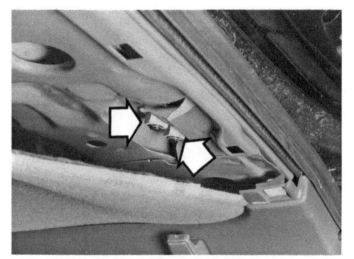

17.5   The nuts retaining the hatch hinge to the body (arrows) are located under the headliner

5   Remove the hinge nuts and detach the hatch from the vehicle **(see illustration)**.
6   Installation is the reverse of removal.
7   After installation, close the hatch and make sure it's in proper alignment with the surrounding body panels. Adjustments are made by moving the position of the hinge studs in the slots. To adjust it, loosen the hinge nuts and reposition the hinges either side-to-side or fore-and-aft the desired amount and retighten the nuts.
8   The engagement of the hatch can be adjusted by loosening the lock striker bolts, repositioning the striker and retightening the bolts.

---

18   Door latch, lock cylinder and handles – removal and installation

---

Refer to illustrations 18.2, 18.3, 18.9 and 18.10
1   Remove the door trim panel and plastic shield (see Section 11).

Latch

2   Disconnect the operating rods from the latch **(see illustration)**.
3   Remove the three latch retaining screws located in the end of the door **(see illustration)**.
4   Detach the latch assembly and lift it from the door.
5   Installation is the reverse of removal.

Lock cylinder

6   Remove the outside door handle (see Step 13).
7   Detach the lock cylinder from the handle assembly.
8   Installation is the reverse of removal.

Inside handle

9   Disconnect the operating rod from the handle **(see illustration)**
10   Remove the three retaining screws and lift the handle from the door **(see illustration)**.
11   Installation is the reverse of removal.

Outside handle

12   Disconnect the operating rods, remove the two retaining nuts and lift the handle off the door.
13   Installation is the reverse of removal.

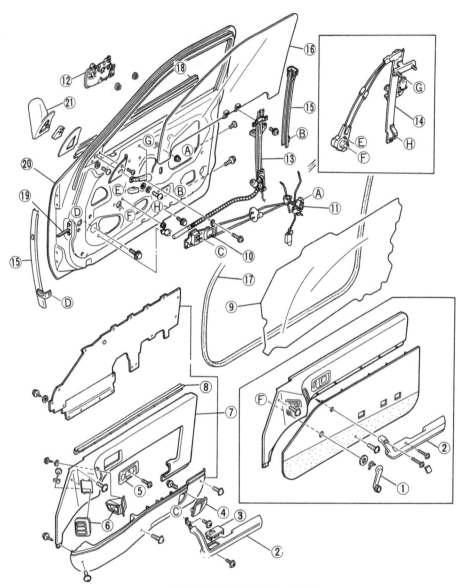

18.2   Door component layout

1	Window crank	8	Inner weatherstrip	15	Glass guide
2	Armrest	9	Plastic water shield	16	Door glass
3	Power window switch	10	Inside door handle	17	Weatherstrip
4	Courtesy light lens	11	Door latch assembly	18	Outer weatherstrip
5	Inside door handle cover	12	Outside handle	19	Door check strap
6	Door ventilation grille	13	Power window regulator	20	Door
7	Door trim panel	14	Manual window regulator	21	Exterior mirror

18.3   The three latch retaining screws are located in the end of the door

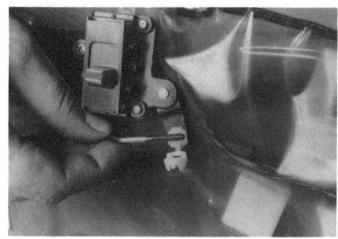

18.9   After prying the plastic connector open with a screwdriver, disconnect the operating rod

19   Door window glass and regulator– removal and installation

1   Disconnect the cable from the negative terminal of the battery.
2   Remove the door trim panel and the plastic water shield (see Section 11).
3   Remove the door outer weatherstrip **(see illustration 18.2).**

Window glass

4   Lower the window so that the mounting bolts can be reached through the access hole. On power windows, temporarily reconnect the battery cable to accomplish this.
5   Remove the retaining bolts **(see illustration 18.2).**
6   Lift the window glass up and out of the door window slot, then tilt it and remove it from the door.
7   Installation is the reverse of removal. To adjust the position of the regulator and glass guides so the glass runs smoothly, loosen the attaching bolts, check the window operation, then retighten.

Regulator

8   Remove the attaching bolts and lift the window regulator assembly out of the door (withdraw the regulator mechanism through the access hole) **(see illustration 18.2).** On power window models, unplug the electrical connector.
9   Installation is the reverse of removal. To adjust the position of the regulator and glass guides so the glass runs smoothly, loosen the attaching bolts, check the window operation, then retighten.

20   Exterior mirror – removal and installation

Refer to illustrations 20.2, 20.3 and 20.4
1   Remove the door trim panel (see Section 11).
2   Remove the control knob **(see illustration).**
3   Pry off the cover panel **(see illustration).**

18.10   The inside door handle is held in place by three screws

20.2   Detach the knob cover with a screwdriver, remove the retaining screw and pull the knob off the post

20.3   Use a screwdriver to pry the cover panel off

20.4   The mirror is held in place by three screws

4   Remove the retaining screws and lift the mirror off **(see illustration)**. On power models, unplug the electrical connector.
5   Installation is the reverse of removal.

21   Seats – removal and installation

Refer to illustration 21.1
1   Remove the retaining bolts, unplug any electrical connectors and lift the seats from the vehicle **(see illustration)**.
2   Installation is the reverse of removal.

22   Seat belt check

1   Check the seat belts, buckles, latch plates and guide loops for obvious damage and signs of wear.
2   Check that the seat belt reminder light comes on when the key is turned to the Run or Start positions. A chime should also sound.
3   The seat belts are designed to lock up during a sudden stop or impact, yet allow free movement during normal driving. Check that the retractors return the belt against your chest while driving and rewind the belt fully when the buckle is unlatched.
4   If any of the above checks reveal problems with the seat belt system, replace parts as necessary.

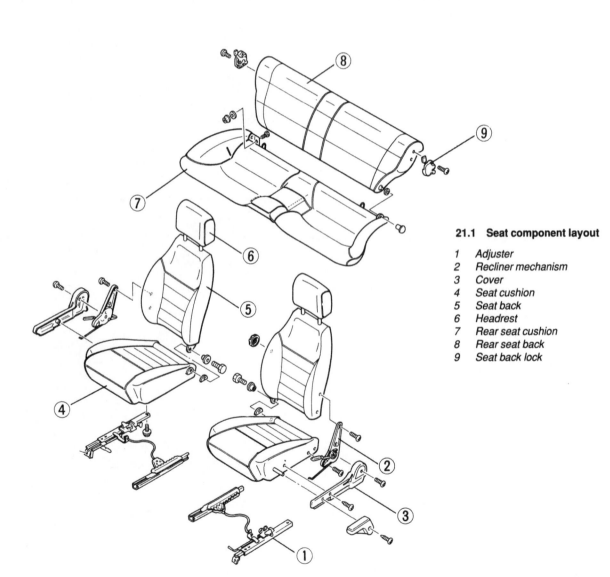

21.1   Seat component layout

1   *Adjuster*
2   *Recliner mechanism*
3   *Cover*
4   *Seat cushion*
5   *Seat back*
6   *Headrest*
7   *Rear seat cushion*
8   *Rear seat back*
9   *Seat back lock*

Chapter 12   Chassis electrical system

Contents

Antenna – removal and installation 15
Battery check and maintenance .... See Chapter 1
Battery – removal and installation .... See Chapter 5
Bulb replacement 19
Central Processing Unit (CPU) – general information 4
Circuit breakers – general information 5
Clock and warning light assembly.– removal and installation 17
Cruise control system – description and check 20
Electrical troubleshooting – general information 2
Fuses – general information 3
General information 1
Headlights – adjustment 12
Headlights – removal and installation 11
Headlight retractor motor – manual operation 10
Ignition switch – removal and installation 9

Instrument cluster housing and cluster – removal
  and installation 16
Instrument cluster housing switches – replacement 7
Instrument panel – removal and installation 18
Neutral safety switch – check, adjustment
  and replacement .... See Chapter 7B
Power door lock system – description and check 21
Power window system – description and check 22
Radio and speakers – removal and installation 14
Relays – general information 6
Turn signal cancelling cam and angle sensor switch – removal
  and installation 8
Wiper motor – removal and installation 13
Wiring diagrams – general information 23

Specifications

Light bulb application   Type

Front
Headlight
  Halogen ....   H6054 or HP6054
  Standard   6052
Front park/turn signal light   1157
Front side marker light   194

Interior
Map light   168
Dome light ....   10 watt
Cargo area or trunk light ....   5 watt

Rear
License plate light   89
Backup light   1156
Brake/tail light   1157
High mounted brake light   1156
Rear turn signal light   1156
Rear side marker light   194

1   General information

The electrical system is a 12-volt, negative ground type. Power for the lights and all electrical accessories is supplied by a lead/acid-type battery which is charged by the alternator.

This Chapter covers repair and service procedures for the various electrical components not associated with the engine. Information on the battery, alternator, distributor and starter motor can be found in Chapter 5.

It should be noted that when portions of the electrical system are serviced, the negative battery cable should be disconnected from the battery to prevent electrical shorts and/or fires.

2   Electrical troubleshooting – general information

A typical electrical circuit consists of an electrical component, any switches, relays, motors, fuses, fusible links or circuit breakers related to that component and the wiring and connectors that link the component to both the battery and the chassis. To help you pinpoint an electrical circuit problem, wiring diagrams are included at the end of this book.

Before tackling any troublesome electrical circuit, first study the appropriate wiring diagrams to get a complete understanding of what makes up that individual circuit. Trouble spots, for instance, can often be narrowed down by noting if other components related to the circuit are operating properly. If several components or circuits fail at one time, chances are the problem is in a fuse or ground connection, because several circuits are often routed through the same fuse and ground connections.

Electrical problems usually stem from simple causes, such as loose or corroded connections, a blown fuse, a melted fusible link or a bad relay. Visually inspect the condition of all fuses, wires and connections in a problem circuit before troubleshooting it.

If testing instruments are going to be utilized, use the diagrams to plan ahead of time where you will make the necessary connections in order to accurately pinpoint the trouble spot.

The basic tools needed for electrical troubleshooting include a circuit tester or voltmeter (a 12-volt bulb with a set of test leads can also be used), a continuity tester, which includes a bulb, battery and set of test leads, and a jumper wire, preferably with a circuit breaker incorporated, which can be used to bypass electrical components. Before attempting to locate a problem with test instruments, use the wiring diagram(s) to decide where to make the connections.

Voltage checks

Voltage checks should be performed if a circuit is not functioning properly. Connect one lead of a circuit tester to either the negative battery terminal or a known good ground. Connect the other lead to a connector in the circuit being tested, preferably nearest to the battery or fuse. If the bulb of the tester lights, voltage is present, which means that the part of the circuit between the connector and the battery is problem free. Continue checking the rest of the circuit in the same fashion. When you reach a point at which no voltage is present, the problem lies between that point and the last test point with voltage. Most of the time the problem can be traced to a loose connection. **Note:** *Keep in mind that some circuits receive voltage only when the ignition key is in the Accessory or Run position.*

Finding a short

One method of finding shorts in a circuit is to remove the fuse and connect a test light or voltmeter in its place to the fuse terminals. There should be no voltage present in the circuit. Move the wiring harness from side-to-side while watching the test light. If the bulb goes on, there is a short to ground somewhere in that area, probably where the insulation has rubbed through. The same test can be performed on each component in the circuit, even a switch.

Ground check

Perform a ground test to check whether a component is properly grounded. Disconnect the battery and connect one lead of a self-powered test light, known as a continuity tester, to a known good ground. Connect the other lead to the wire or ground connection being tested. If the bulb goes on, the ground is good. If the bulb does not go on, the ground is not good.

Continuity check

A continuity check is done to determine if there are any breaks in a circuit – if it is passing electricity properly. With the circuit off (no power in the circuit), a self-powered continuity tester can be used to check the circuit. Connect the test leads to both ends of the circuit (or to the "power" end and a good ground), and if the test light comes on the circuit is passing current properly. If the light doesn't come on, there is a break somewhere in the circuit. The same procedure can be used to test a switch, by connecting the continuity tester to the switch terminals. With the switch turned On, the test light should come on.

Finding an open circuit

When diagnosing for possible open circuits, it is often difficult to locate them by sight because oxidation or terminal misalignment are hidden by the connectors. Merely wiggling a connector on a sensor or in the wiring harness may correct the open circuit condition. Remember this when an open circuit is indicated when troubleshooting a circuit. Intermittent problems may also be caused by oxidized or loose connections.

Electrical troubleshooting is simple if you keep in mind that all electrical circuits are basically electricity running from the battery, through the wires, switches, relays, fuses and fusible links to each electrical component (light bulb, motor, etc.) and to ground, from which it is passed back to the battery. Any electrical problem is an interruption in the flow of electricity to and from the battery.

3   Fuses – general information

Refer to illustration 3.1

The electrical circuits of the vehicle are protected by a combination of fuses and circuit breakers. The fuse boxes are located under the instrument panel on the left side of the dashboard and in the engine compartment **(see illustration)**.

Each of the fuses is designed to protect a specific circuit, and the various circuits are identified on the fuse panel itself.

Miniaturized fuses are employed in the fuse boxes. These compact fuses, with blade terminal design, allow fingertip removal and replacement. If an electrical component fails, always check the fuse first. A blown fuse is easily identified through the clear plastic body. Visually inspect the element for evidence of damage. If a continuity check is called for, the blade terminal tips are exposed in the fuse body.

Be sure to replace blown fuses with the correct type. Fuses of different ratings are physically interchangeable, but only fuses of the proper rating should be used. Replacing a fuse with one of a higher or lower value than specified is not recommended. Each electrical circuit needs a specific amount of protection. The amperage value of each fuse is molded into the fuse body.

If the replacement fuse immediately fails, don't replace it again until the cause of the problem is isolated and corrected. In most cases, the cause will be a short circuit in the wiring caused by a broken or deteriorated wire.

4   Central Processing Unit (CPU) – general information

Refer to illustration 4.1

1   These models are equipped with a Central Processing Unit (CPU) located behind the driver's side kick panel, next to the fuse box **(see illustration)**. The CPU is a compact unit which performs many functions that are normally controlled by relays and other electronic devices.

2   Special equipment is required to check the CPU, so if a fault is suspected take the vehicle to a dealer.

**3.1   The fuse boxes are located under the left side of the
instrument panel and in the engine compartment**

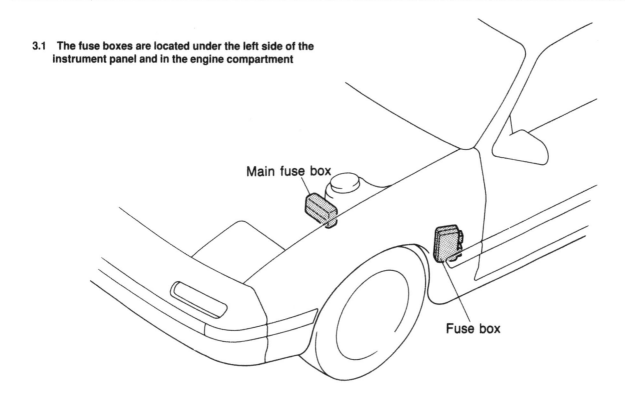

**4.1   The CPU is located next to the passenger compartment fuse box
and contains circuit boards which perform a variety of functions**

A   Turn signal and hazard
     warning unit
B   Brake light warning relay

C   Light Off reminder buzzer
     Key illumination timer
     Seat belt timer and buzzer
     Horn relay
     Alternator warning light relay
     Key reminder buzzer

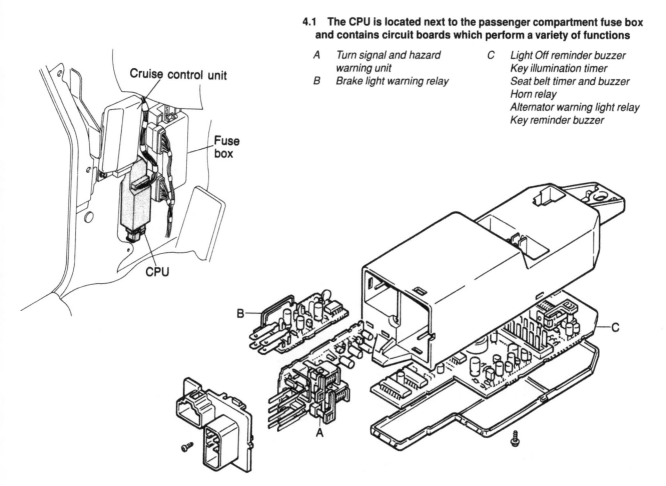

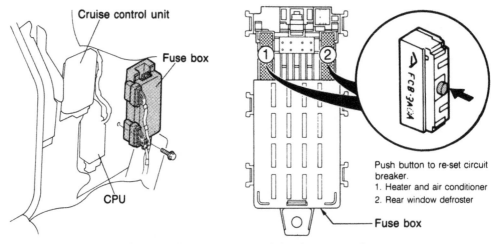

5.2   Press the button on the circuit breaker to reset it

1   *Heater and air conditioner*   2   *Rear window defroster*

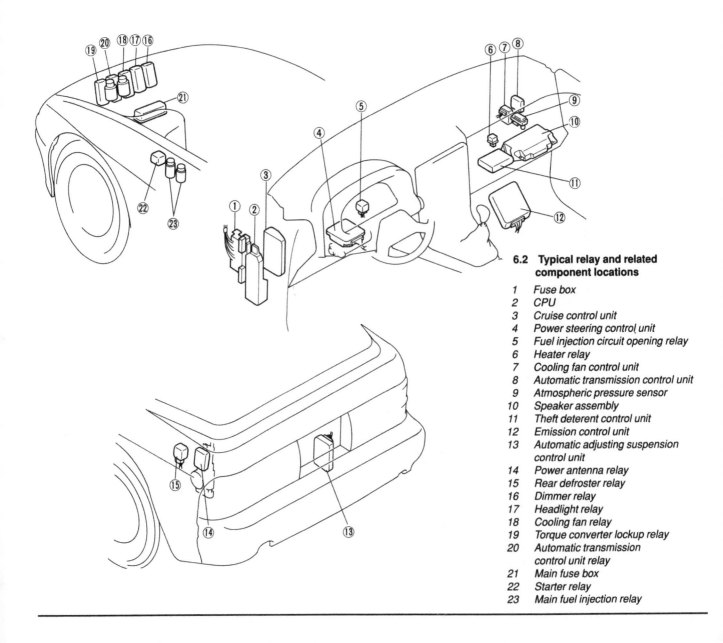

6.2   Typical relay and related component locations

1   Fuse box
2   CPU
3   Cruise control unit
4   Power steering control unit
5   Fuel injection circuit opening relay
6   Heater relay
7   Cooling fan control unit
8   Automatic transmission control unit
9   Atmospheric pressure sensor
10   Speaker assembly
11   Theft deterent control unit
12   Emission control unit
13   Automatic adjusting suspension control unit
14   Power antenna relay
15   Rear defroster relay
16   Dimmer relay
17   Headlight relay
18   Cooling fan relay
19   Torque converter lockup relay
20   Automatic transmission control unit relay
21   Main fuse box
22   Starter relay
23   Main fuel injection relay

5 Circuit breakers – general information

Refer to illustration 5.2

Circuit breakers protect components such the heater, air conditioner and rear window defroster. The circuit breakers are located in the passenger compartment fuse box and can be reset by pressing the button **(see illustration)**.

6 Relays – general information

Refer to illustration 6.2

Several electrical accessories in the vehicle use relays to transmit the electrical signal to the component. If the relay is defective, that component will not operate properly.

The various relays are grouped together in several locations **(see illustration)**.

If a faulty relay is suspected, it can be removed and tested by a dealer service department or a repair shop. Defective relays must be replaced as a unit.

7 Instrument cluster housing switches – replacement

Refer to illustrations 7.3, 7.4a and 7.4b

1 Disconnect the cable from the negative terminal of the battery.

2 Remove the instrument cluster housing assembly (see Section 16).
3 To remove the switch knob(s), pry gently at the base with a small screwdriver while pulling the knob off the shaft **(see illustration)**. To install, align the knob with the tab on the shaft and press it into place. The turn signal switch handle is held in place by a screw.
4 To replace a switch, remove the retaining screws and lift the switch from the housing **(see illustrations)**.
5 Installation is the reverse of removal.

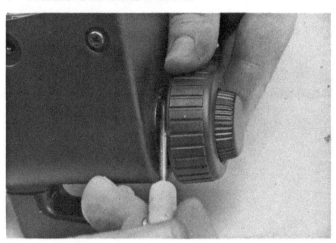

7.3 To detach the control knob, pull out while prying at the base with a small screwdriver

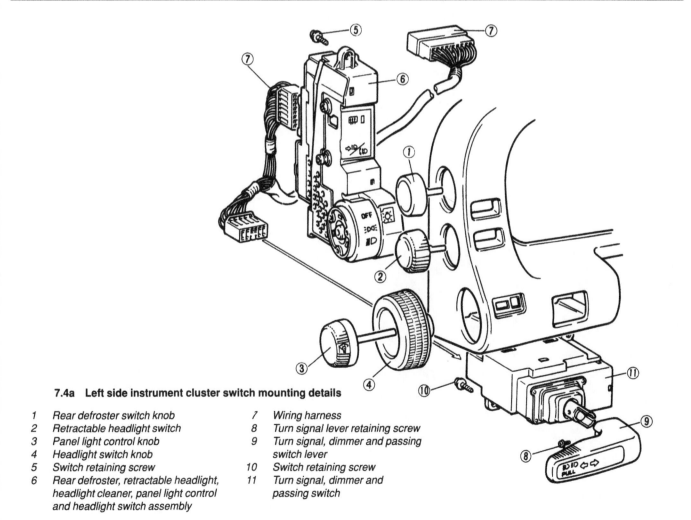

7.4a Left side instrument cluster switch mounting details

1	Rear defroster switch knob	7	Wiring harness
2	Retractable headlight switch	8	Turn signal lever retaining screw
3	Panel light control knob	9	Turn signal, dimmer and passing
4	Headlight switch knob		switch lever
5	Switch retaining screw	10	Switch retaining screw
6	Rear defroster, retractable headlight,	11	Turn signal, dimmer and
	headlight cleaner, panel light control		passing switch
	and headlight switch assembly		

7.4b   Right side instrument cluster switch mounting details

1 Hazard warning switch knob
2 Rear wiper and washer switch
   knob,convertible top switch
3 Front washer switch knob
4 Front wiper switch knob
5 Switch retaining screw
6 Hazard warning, rear wiper and
   washer and front wiper and
   washer switch assembly

7 Wiring harness
8 Cruise control switch
   retaining screw
9 Cruise control switch cover
10 Cruise control switch

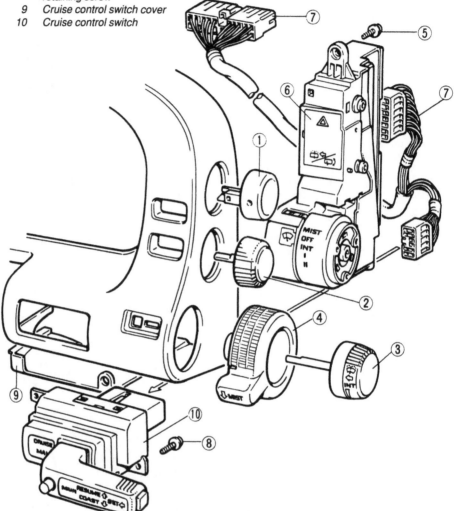

**8.4   The turn signal cancelling cam and angle sensor
switch is retained by two screws (arrows)**

8   Turn signal cancelling cam and angle sensor switch – removal and installation

Refer to illustration 8.4

1   Disconnect the cable from the negative terminal of the battery.
2   Remove the steering wheel (see Chapter 10).
3   Remove the steering column cover (see Chapter 11).
4   Unplug the electrical connector, remove the two retaining screws and
lift the switch off the steering column **(see illustration)**.
5   Installation is the reverse of removal.

9   Ignition switch – removal and installation

Refer to illustration 9.5

1   Disconnect the negative cable from the battery.
2   Remove the steering wheel (see Chapter 10).
3   Remove the steering column cover (see Chapter 11).
4   Unplug the electrical connector.

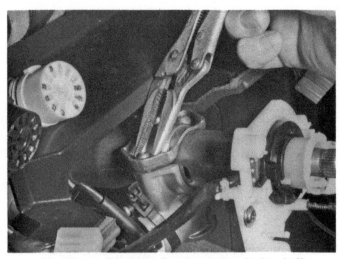

9.5   Use small locking pliers to unscrew the breakoff
head bolts retaining the ignition switch

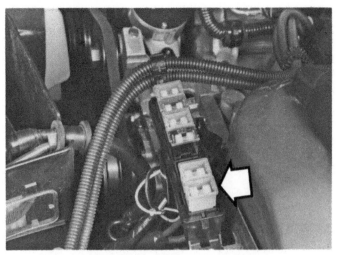

10.1   Remove the the headlight motor retractor fuse
(arrow) before operating the motor manually

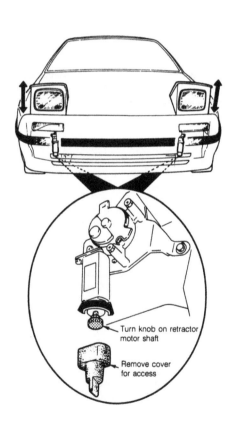

10.2   With the fuse removed or the negative cable of the
battery disconnected, pull off the cover and turn the
retractor motor knob to raise or lower the headlight

5   Use a small pair of locking pliers to unscrew the two breakoff head
bolts and remove the switch and retaining plate from the steering column
(see illustration).
6   To install, place the switch and retaining plate in position and install
new breakoff head retaining bolts. Tighten the bolts until the heads break
off.
7   Plug in the electrical connector and install the column cover and
steering wheel.

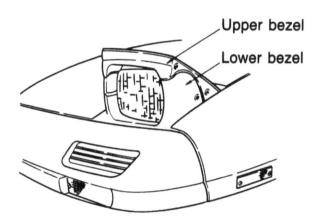

11.2   Remove the screws and detach the headlight bezels

---

10   Headlight retractor motor – manual operation

Refer to illustrations 10.1 and 10.2
1   Either disconnect the cable from the negative terminal of the battery
or remove the fuse for the headlight retractor motor from the engine compartment fuse block **(see illustration)**. **Caution:** *Never operate the headlight retractor motor manually unless the battery negative cable is
disconnected or the retractor fuse is removed, or personal injury could result.*
2   Reach up under the front bumper, remove the rubber cover then turn
the retractor motor knob to raise or lower the headlight **(see illustration)**.

---

11   Headlights – removal and installation

Refer to illustrations 11.2 and 11.3
1   Turn the headlight switch on to raise the lights, then disconnect the
negative cable from the battery.
2   Remove the retaining screws and detach the headlight bezels **(see
illustration)**.
3   Remove the headlight retainer screws, taking care not to disturb the
adjustment screws **(see illustration)**.
4   Remove the retainer and pull the headlight out enough to allow the
connector to be unplugged.
5   Remove the headlight.

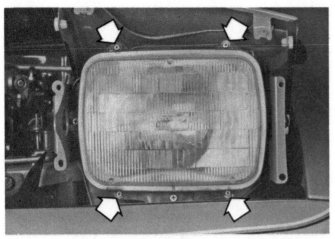

11.3 Remove only the headlight retaining screws (arrows); don't touch the adjusting screws

6   To install the headlight, plug the connector in, place the headlight in position and install the retainer and screws. Tighten the screws securely.
7   Place the headlight bezels in position and install the retaining screws.
8   Reconnect the cable to the battery.

---

12 Headlights – adjustment

Refer to illustration 12.1
Note: *The headlights must be aimed correctly. If adjusted incorrectly they could blind the driver of an oncoming vehicle and cause a serious accident or seriously reduce your ability to see the road. The headlights should be checked for proper aim every 12 months and any time a new headlight is installed or front end body work is performed. It should be emphasized that the following procedure is only an interim step which will provide temporary adjustment until the headlights can be adjusted by a properly equipped shop.*

1   Headlights have two spring loaded adjusting screws, one on the top controlling up-and-down movement and one on the side controlling left-and-right movement **(see illustration)**.
2   There are several methods of adjusting the headlights. The simplest method requires a blank wall 25 feet in front of the vehicle and a level floor.
3   Position masking tape vertically on the wall in reference to the vehicle centerline and the centerlines of both headlights.
4   Position a horizontal tape line in reference to the centerline of all the headlights. **Note:** *It may be easier to position the tape on the wall with the vehicle parked only a few inches away.*
5   Adjustment should be made with the vehicle sitting level, the gas tank half-full and no unusually heavy load in the vehicle.
6   Starting with the low beam adjustment, position the high intensity zone so it is two inches below the horizontal line and two inches to the right of the headlight vertical line. Adjustment is made by turning the top adjusting screw *clockwise* to raise the beam and *counterclockwise* to lower the beam. The adjusting screw on the side should be used in the same manner to move the beam left or right.
7   With the high beams on, the high intensity zone should be vertically centered with the exact center just below the horizontal line. **Note:** *It may not be possible to position the headlight aim exactly for both high and low beams. If a compromise must be made, keep in mind that the low beams are the most used and have the greatest effect on driver safety.*
8   Have the headlights adjusted by a dealer service department or service station at the earliest opportunity.

---

13 Wiper motor – removal and installation

Refer to illustrations 13.2, 13.6 and 13.7
1   Disconnect the negative cable at the battery.

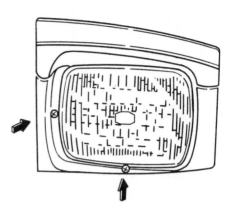

12.1 Headlight adjustment screw locations (arrows)

Windshield wiper motor

2   Remove the retaining nuts and detach the wiper arms **(see illustration)**.
3   Remove the retaining screws, then detach the cowl grille for access to the wiper link assembly.
4   Detach the wiper link from the motor shaft by prying carefully with a screwdriver.
5   Remove the three retaining bolts, unplug the electrical connector and remove the wiper motor from the vehicle.
6   Installation is the reverse of removal. When installing the wiper arms, note that they are not interchangeable and are marked PL (passenger) and DL (driver) side **(see illustration)**.

Rear wiper motor

7   Flip up the cover, remove the wiper arm retaining nut and remove the wiper arm **(see illustration)**.
8   Remove the nut and washers from the wiper arm shaft. Note the order in which they are arranged for ease of installation.
9   Open the rear hatch.
10   Unplug the electrical connector, remove the retaining bolts and lower the motor from the rear hatch **(see illustration 13.7)**.
11   Installation is the reverse of removal.

---

14 Radio and speakers – removal and installation

1   Disconnect the negative cable at the battery.

Radio

Refer to illustration 14.3
2   Remove the dashboard center panel (see Chapter 11).
3   Remove the radio retaining screws **(see illustration)**.
4   Pull the radio out, unplug the electrical connector and remove the assembly from the vehicle.
5   Installation is the reverse of removal.

Speakers

Driver side speaker
Refer to illustration 14.6
6   Remove the screws and detach the grille **(see illustration)**.
7   Remove the screws, pull the speaker out, unplug the electrical connector and remove the speaker.
8   Installation is the reverse of removal.

Passenger side speaker
Refer to illustrations 14.9a and 14.9b
9   Remove the lower panel from the dashboard **(see illustrations)**.

13.2 Windshield wiper motor installation details

1 Driver side wiper arm
2 Passenger side wiper arm
3 Wiper blade assembly
4 Cowl grille
5 Service hole cover
6 Washer nozzle
7 Washer hose
8 Linkage
9 Wiper motor assembly
10 Washer tank
11 Optional 5.5 liter washer tank

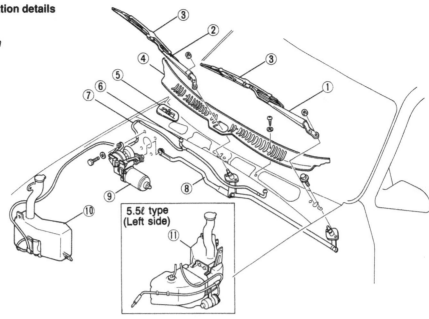

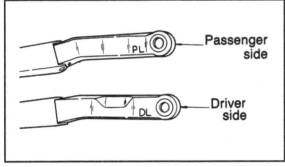

13.6 The wiper arms are not interchangeable – they are marked for the side they must be installed on

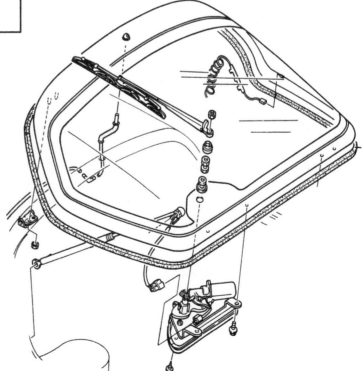

13.7 Rear wiper motor installation details

14.3   Locations of the radio retaining screws (arrows)

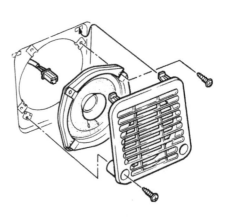

14.6   Driver side speaker installation details

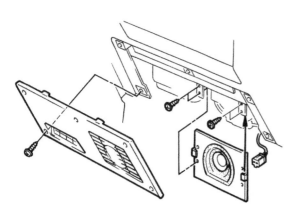

14.9a   Passenger side speaker details (coupe models)

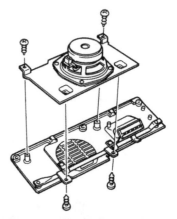

**14.9b   Passenger side speaker installation details
(passive seat belt equipped and convertible models)**

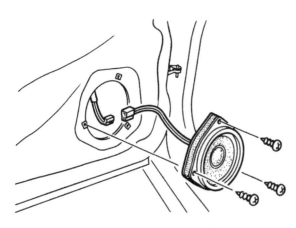

14.13   Door mounted speaker details

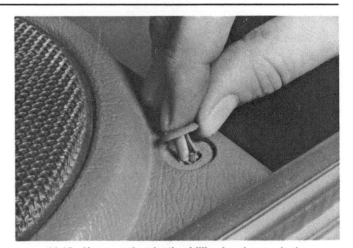

**14.15   Unscrew the plastic phillips head screw in the
center, then pry out the retainer**

10   Remove the screws, pull the speaker out, unplug the electrical connector and remove the speaker.
11   Installation is the reverse of removal.

Door speaker
Refer to illustration 14.13
12   Remove the door trim panel
13   Remove the screws, pull the speaker out, unplug the electrical connector and remove the speaker **(see illustration)**.

14   Installation is the reverse of removal.

Rear speaker
Refer to illustrations 14.15, 14.17 and 14.18
15   Use a phillips head screwdriver to remove the plastic screw in the center, then pry out the speaker cover retainer **(see illustration)**.
16   Detach the speaker cover.
17   Remove the retaining screws and lift the speaker up **(see illustration)**.

14.17   Remove the rear speaker retaining screws (arrows)

14.18   Press the retaining tab and unplug the speaker connector

15.2   Unscrew the antenna mounting nut with snap-ring pliers

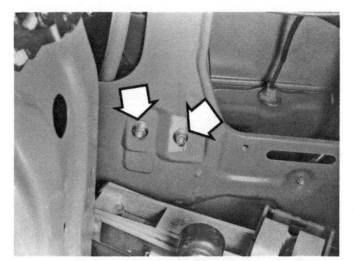

15.4   Remove the two mounting nuts (arrows) and guide the motor assembly out through the access hole

18   Unplug the electrical connector and remove the speaker **(see illustration)**.
19   Installation is the reverse of removal.

15   Antenna – removal and installation

Refer to illustrations 15.2 and 15.4

1   Disconnect the negative cable at the battery.
2   Use snap-ring pliers to unscrew the antenna-to-fender mounting nut **(see illustration)**.
3   Open the rear hatch or trunk and remove the left side trim panel.
4   Unplug the antenna power and radio lead connectors, remove the two retaining nuts and remove the antenna and motor assembly through the access hole **(see illustration)**.
5   Installation is the reverse of removal.

16   Instrument cluster housing and cluster – removal and installation

Refer to illustrations 16.4, 16.7a, 16.7b and 16.7c
1   Disconnect the negative cable at the battery.

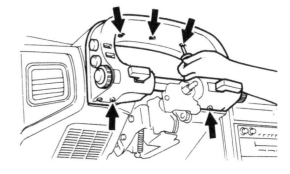

16.4   Use a phillips screwdriver to remove the instrument cluster housing screws (arrows)

Instrument cluster housing

2   Remove the steering wheel (see Chapter 10).
3   Remove the steering column cover (see Chapter 11).
4   Remove the five retaining screws, pull the housing out, unplug the electrical connectors and remove the assembly from the instrument panel **(see illustration)**.

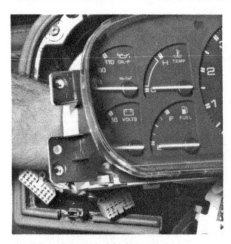

16.7a   Reach behind the cluster . . .

16.7b   . . . and disconnect the
speedometer cable by pressing
on the plastic lever

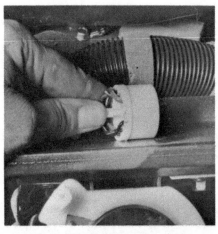

16.7c   To unplug the electrical
connectors, press the lever and pull the
connector from the cluster

5   To install, plug in the electrical connectors, place the housing in position and install the retaining screws.

Cluster

6   Remove the screws attaching the instrument cluster to the instrument
panel.
7   Pull the cluster out, reach behind it and disconnect the speedometer
cable and the electrical connectors **(see illustrations).**

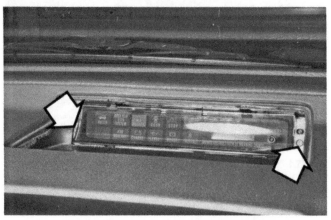

17.3   The clock and warning light assembly is retained
by two screws (arrows)

8   Detach the cluster from the instrument panel.
9   Installation is the reverse of removal.

---

17   Clock and warning light assembly – removal and installation

Refer to illustration 17.3
1   Disconnect the cable from the negative battery terminal.
2   Remove the clock and warning light center panel from the dashboard
(see Chapter 11).
3   Remove the two retaining screws, pull the assembly out, unplug the
connectors and remove the assembly from the vehicle **(see illustration).**
4   Installation is the reverse of removal.

---

18   Instrument panel – removal and installation

Refer to illustrations 18.5, 18.6 and 18.7
1   Disconnect the negative cable at the battery.
2   Remove the dashboard panels (see Chapter 11).
3   Remove the radio and the dashboard mounted speakers (see Section 14).
4   Remove instrument cluster housing and the cluster (see
Section 16).
5   Remove the tilt steering column bolts **(see illustration).**
6   Remove the hood release handle **(see illustration).**

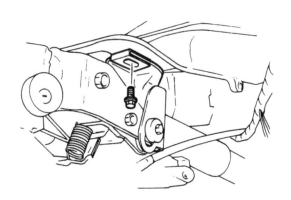

18.5   Remove the tilt steering column bolts

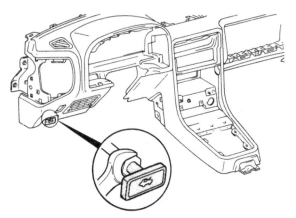

18.6   Unscrew the retaining nut and detach the hood
release handle

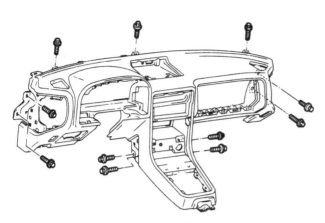

18.7 Remove the mounting bolts, pull the instrument panel back, disconnect the electrical harnesses and other connections and remove the panel

7   Remove the attaching bolts and carefully lift the instrument panel back for access to the electrical connectors **(see illustration)**.
8   Unplug the electrical connectors and disconnect any component which would interfere with removal. Lift the instrument panel from the vehicle.
9   Installation is the reverse of removal. Make sure none of the wiring is crimped when the instrument panel is rotated back into position.

19 Bulb replacement

Refer to illustrations 19.1, 19.3a, 19.3b, 19.3c and 19.4
1   The lenses of many lights are held in place by screws, which makes it a simple procedure to gain access to the bulbs **(see illustration)**.
2   On some lights the lenses are held in place by clips. The lenses can be removed either by unsnapping them or by using a small screwdriver to pry them off.

19.1 The turn signal/parking light bulb can be replaced after removing the screws and detaching the lens

3   Several types of bulbs are used **(see illustrations)**. Some are removed by pushing in and turning them counterclockwise **(see illustration)**. Others can simply be unclipped from the terminals or pulled straight out of the socket.
4   To gain access to the instrument panel lights, the instrument cluster will have to be removed first **(see illustration)**.

20 Cruise control system – description and check

The cruise control system maintains vehicle speed with a vacuum actuated servo motor located in the engine compartment, which is connected to the throttle linkage by a cable. The system consists of the servo motor, clutch switch, brake switch, control switches, a relay and associated vacuum hoses.

19.3a Typical front bulb replacement details

1	Headlight	4	Interior dome light bulb
2	Parking/turn signal light bulb	5	Map light bulb
3	Side marker light bulb		

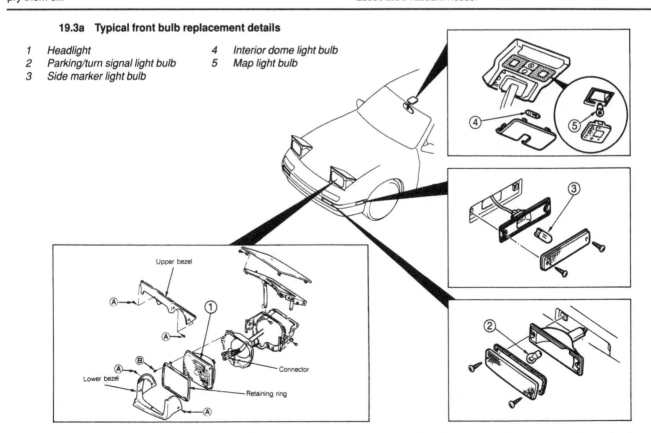

19.3b   Typical rear bulb replacement details

1   Turn signal light bulb
2   Brake and turn signal light bulb
3   Backup light bulb
4   License plate light bulb
5   Side marker light bulb
6   Cargo light bulb
7   Convertible model high-mounted brake light bulb
8   Convertible model trunk light bulb

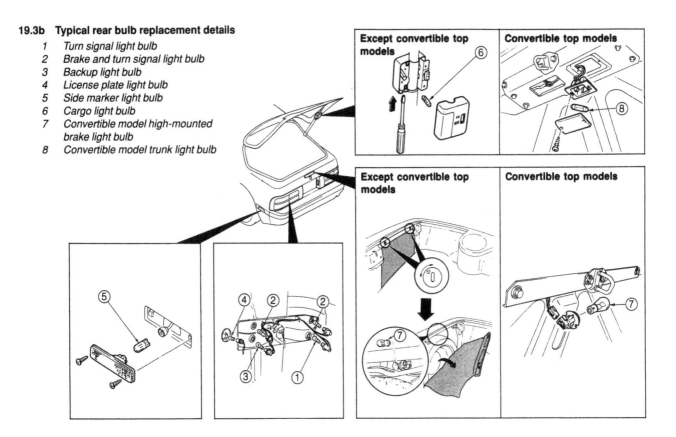

19.3c   Most bulbs are removed by pushing in and turning them counterclockwise

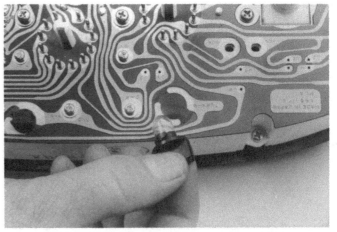

19.4   After rotating the holder counterclockwise, lift it out of the instrument cluster – the bulb can then be pulled out of the holder

Because of the complexity of the cruise control system and the special tools and techniques required for diagnosis, repair should be left to a dealer service department or a repair shop. However, it is possible for the home mechanic to make simple checks of the wiring and vacuum connections for minor faults which can be easily repaired. These include:

a) Inspect the cruise control actuating switches for broken wires and loose connections.
b) Check the cruise control fuse.
c) The cruise control system is operated by vacuum so it's critical that all vacuum switches, hoses and connections are secure. Check the hoses in the engine compartment for tight connections, cracks and obvious vacuum leaks.

21   Power door lock system – description and check

The power door lock system operates the door lock actuators mounted in each door. The system consists of the switches, actuators and associated wiring. Since special tools and techniques are required to diagnose the system, it should be left to a dealer service department or a repair shop. However, it is possible for the home mechanic to make simple checks of the wiring connections and actuators for minor faults which can be easily repaired. These include:

a) Check the system fuse and/or circuit breaker.
b) Check the switch wires for damage and loose connections. Check the switches for continuity.

PRECAUTIONS
Wiring Color Codes

Two-color wires are indicated by a 2-letter symbol. The first letter indicates the base color of the wire and the second indicates the color of the stripe.

CODE	COLOR
B	BLACK
Br	BROWN
G	GREEN
L	BLUE
Lb	LIGHT BLUE
Lg	LIGHT GREEN
O	ORANGE
R	RED
Y	YELLOW
W	WHITE

23.4a Wiring diagram color codes

c) Remove the door panel(s) and check the actuator wiring connections to see if they're loose or damaged. Inspect the actuator rods (if equipped) to make sure they aren't bent or damaged. Inspect the actuator wiring for damaged or loose connections. The actuator can be checked by applying battery power momentarily. A discernible click indicates that the solenoid is operating properly.

22 Power window system – description and check

The power window system operates the electric motors mounted in the doors which lower and raise the windows. The system consists of the control switches, the motors (regulators), glass mechanisms and associated wiring.

Because of the complexity of the power window system and the special tools and techniques required for diagnosis, repair should be left to a dealer service department or a repair shop. However, it is possible for the home mechanic to make simple checks of the wiring connections and motors for minor faults which can be easily repaired. These include:

a) Inspect the power window actuating switches for broken wires and loose connections.
b) Check the power window fuse and or circuit breaker.
c) Remove the door panel(s) and check the power window motor wires to see if they're loose or damaged. Inspect the glass mechanisms for damage which could cause binding.

23 Wiring diagrams – general information

Refer to illustrations 23.4a and 23.4b

Since it isn't possible to include all wiring diagrams for every year covered by this manual, the following diagrams are those that are typical and most commonly needed.

Prior to troubleshooting any circuits, check the fuse and circuit breakers (if equipped) to make sure they're in good condition. Make sure the battery is properly charged and check the cable connections (see Chapter 1).

When checking a circuit, make sure that all connectors are clean, with no broken or loose terminals. When unplugging a connector, do not pull on the wires. Pull only on the connector housings themselves.

Refer to the accompanying tables for the wire color codes and symbols applicable to your vehicle **(see illustrations)**.

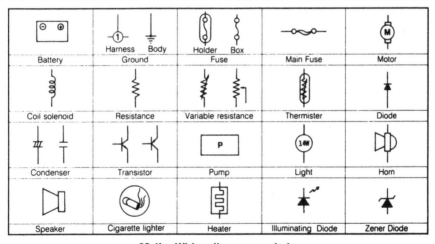

23.4b Wiring diagram symbols

WIRING DIAGRAMS START ON NEXT PAGE

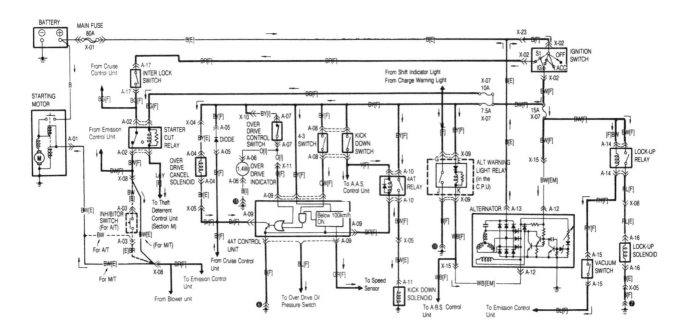

Starting, charging and automatic transmission overdrive and lockup system (non-turbocharged models) wiring diagram (1987 shown, 1986 similar)

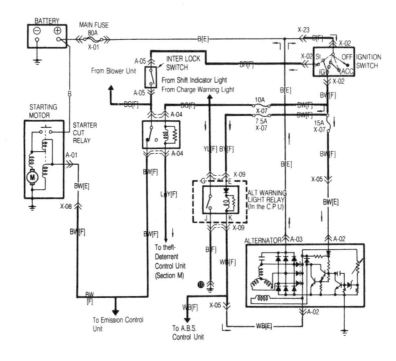

Starting and charging system (turbocharged models) wiring diagram (1987 shown, 1986 similar)

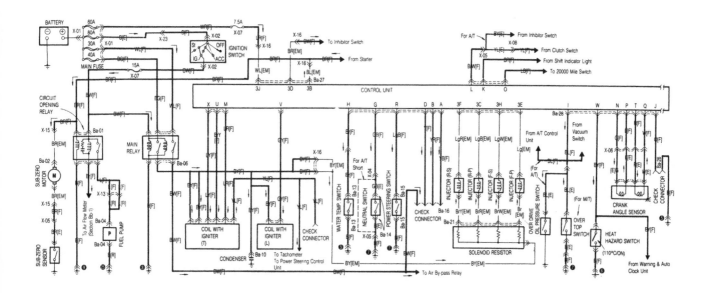

**EGI, emission control, fuel pump, sub-zero starting system (non-turbocharged models) wiring diagram
(1987 shown, 1986 similar)**

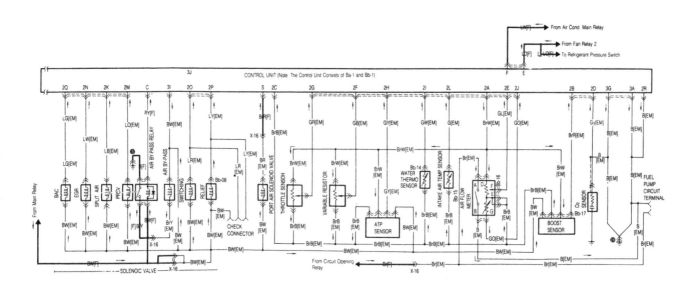

**EGI, emission control, fuel pump, sub-zero starting system (non-turbocharged models) wiring diagram (continued)
(1987 shown, 1986 similar)**

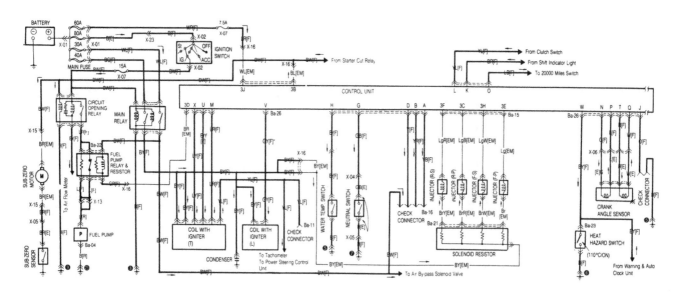

EGI, emission control, fuel pump, sub-zero starting system (turbocharged models) wiring diagram
(1987 shown, 1986 similar)

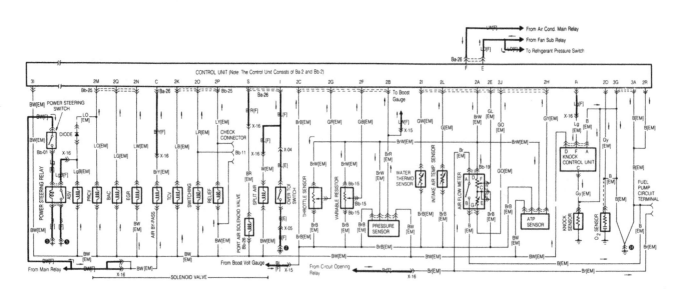

EGI, emission control, fuel pump, sub-zero starting system (turbocharged models) wiring diagram (continued)
(1987 shown, 1986 similar)

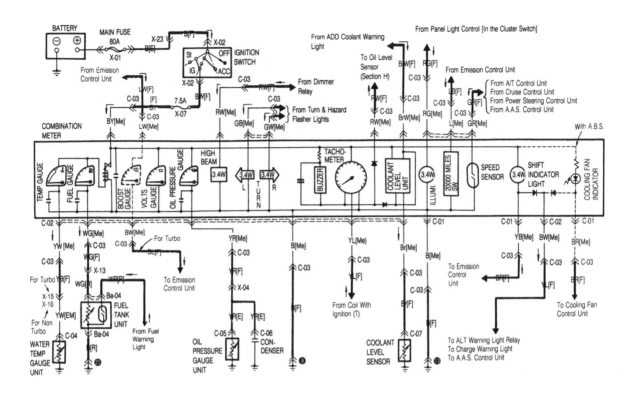

Instrument cluster (combination meter) and warning light system wiring diagram (1987 shown, 1986 similar)

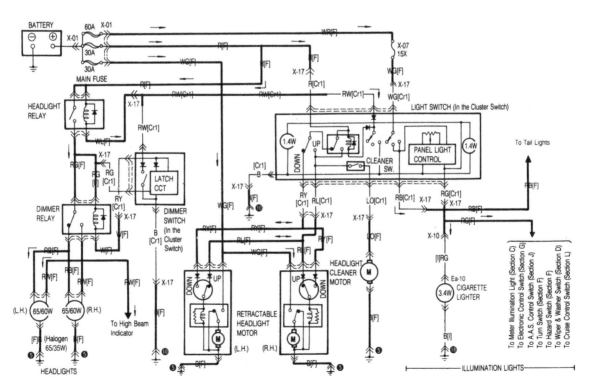

**Headlights, retractor motor system, headlight cleaner and illumination light wiring diagram
(1987 shown, other models similar)**

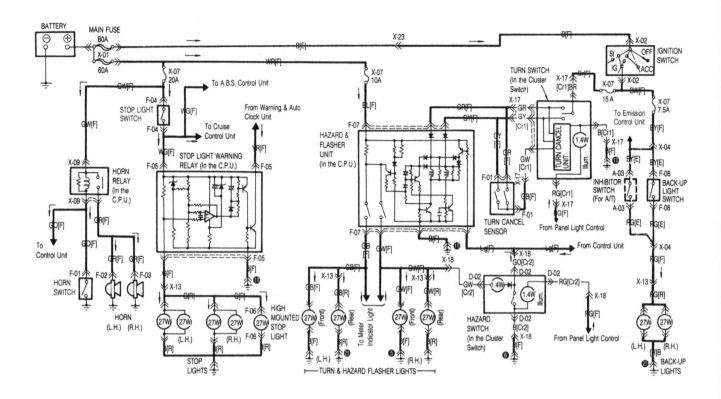

Horn, brake, turn and hazard signal and backup light wiring diagram (1987 shown, 1986 similar)

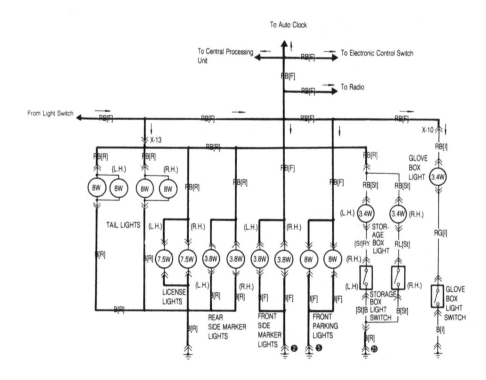

Tail, license plate, front and rear side marker, front parking, storage box and glove box light wiring diagram (1987 shown, 1986 similar)

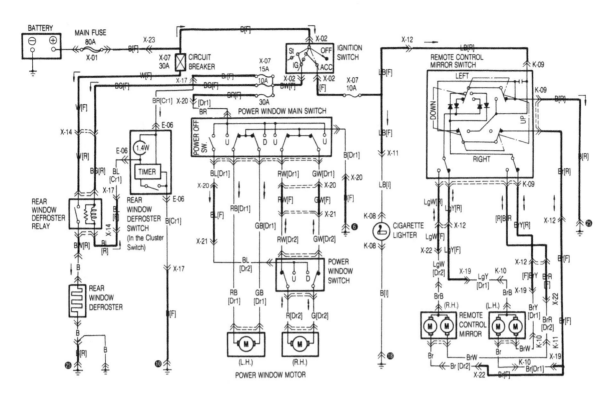

**Rear window defroster, power window, cigarette lighter and remote control mirror wiring diagram
(1987 shown, 1986 similar)**

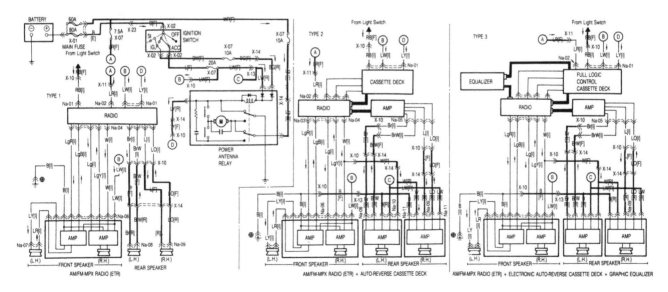

Audio system and power antenna wiring diagram (1987 shown, 1986 similar)

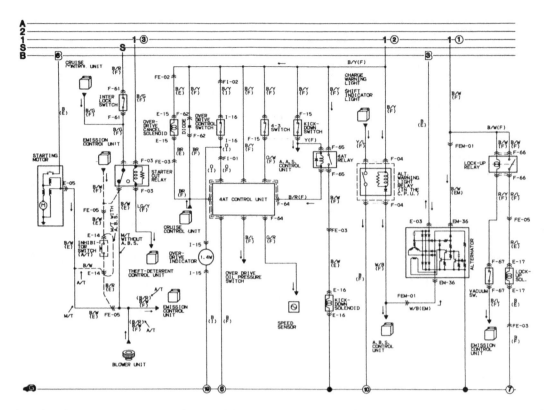

Starting, charging, automatic transmission overdrive and torque converter lockup system (non-turbocharged models) wiring diagram (1988 shown, 1989 and later models similar)

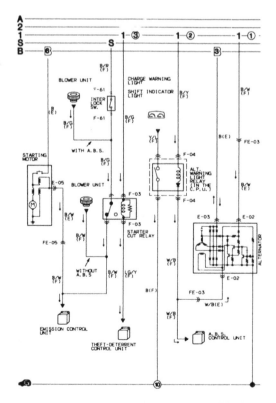

Starting and charging system (turbocharged models) wiring-diagram (1988 shown, 1989 and later models similar)

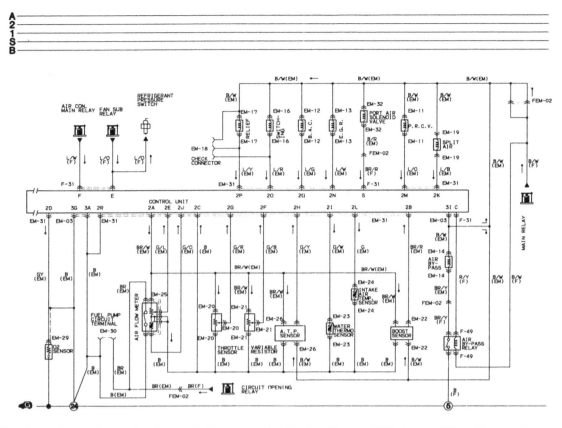

EGI and emission control system (non-turbocharged models) wiring diagram (1988 shown, 1989 and later models similar)

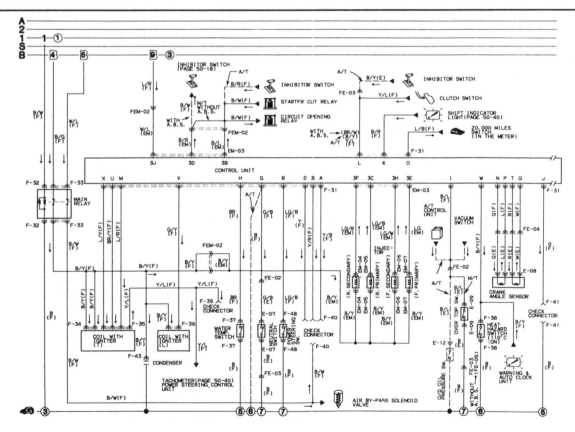

EGI and emission control system (non-turbocharged models) wiring diagram (continued) (1988 shown, 1989 and later models similar)

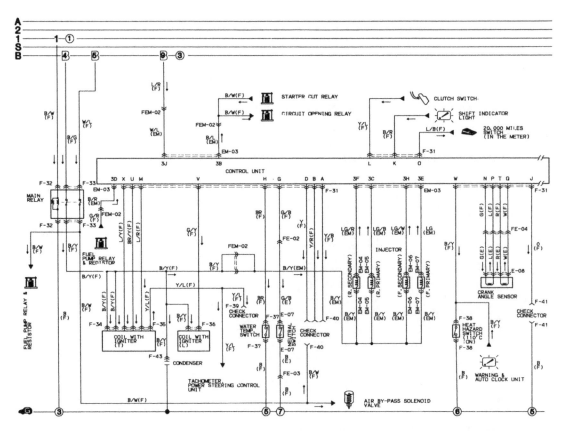

EGI and emission control system (turbocharged models) wiring diagram (1988 shown, 1989 and later models similar)

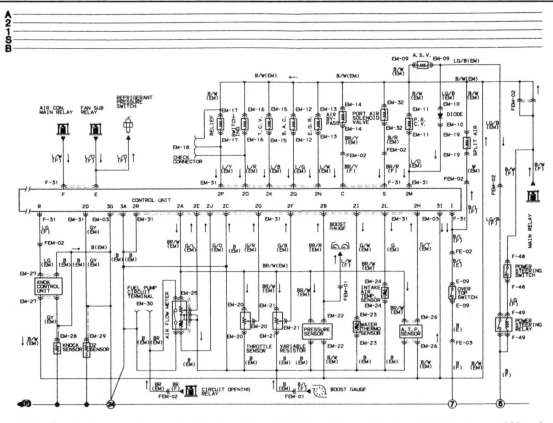

EGI and emission control system (turbocharged models) wiring diagram (continued) (1988 shown, 1989 and later models similar)

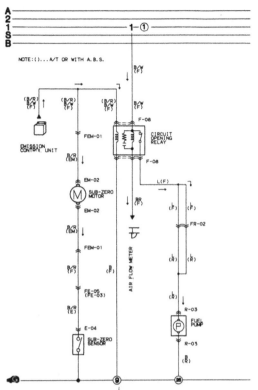

Fuel pump and sub-zero starting system (non-turbocharged models) wiring diagram (1988 shown, 1989 and later models similar)

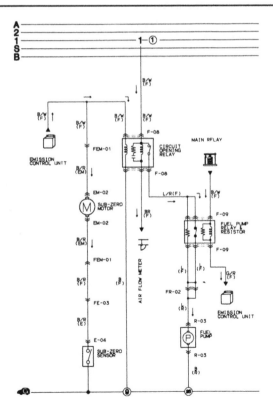

Fuel pump and sub-zero starting system (turbocharged models) wiring diagram (1988 shown, 1989 and later models similar)

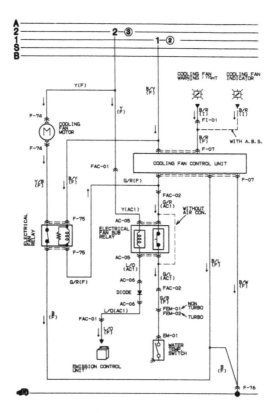

Typical cooling fan system wiring diagram (1988 shown, 1989 and later models similar)

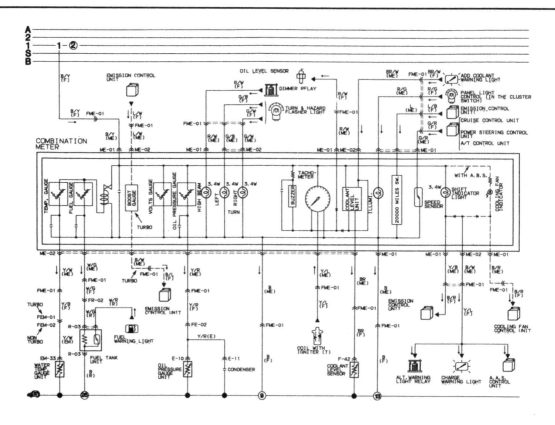

Instrument cluster (combination meter) and warning light system wiring diagram (1988 shown, 1989 and later models similar)

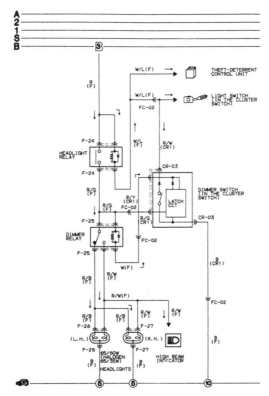

Instrument cluster (combination meter) and warning light system wiring diagram (continued) 1988 shown, 1989 and later models similar)

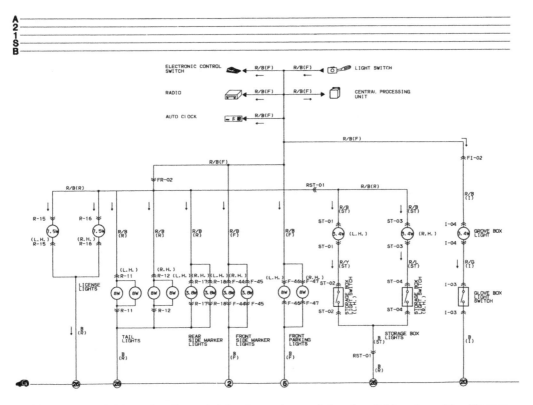

Tail, parking and side marker, license plate, storage box and glove box light system wiring diagram
(1988 shown, 1989 and later models similar)

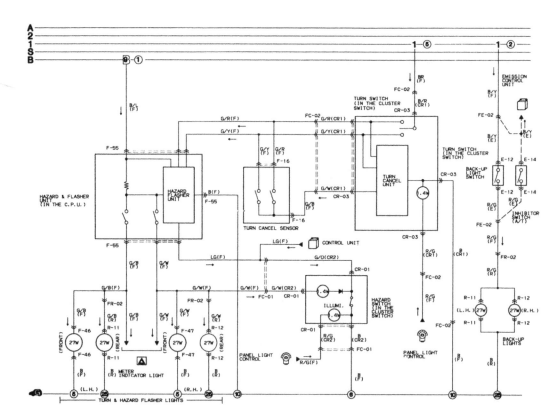

Turn signal, hazard flasher and backup light system wiring diagram (1988 shown, 1989 and later models similar)

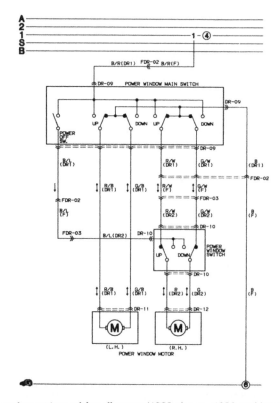

Power window motor system wiring diagram (1988 shown, 1989 and later models similar)

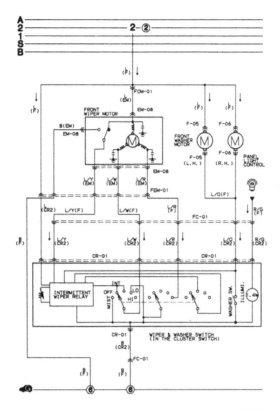

Windshield wiper and washer system wiring diagram (1988 shown, 1989 and later models similar)

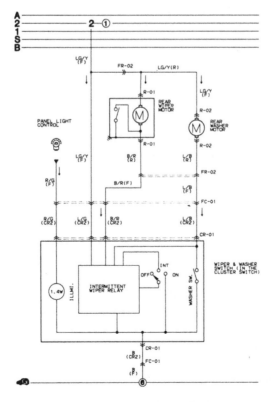

Rear window wiper and washer system wiring diagram (1988 shown, 1989 and later models similar)

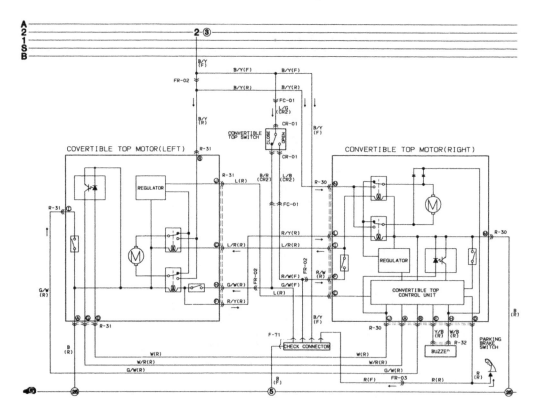

Convertible top system wiring diagram (1988 shown, 1989 and later models similar)

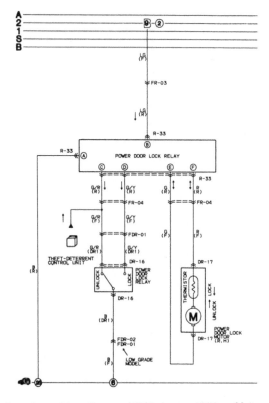

Power door lock system wiring diagram (1988 shown, 1989 and later models similar)

Index

A

About this manual – 5
Air cleaner – 127
Air conditioning system
    blower unit – 107
    check and maintenance – 108
    compressor – 111
    condenser – 111
    control assembly – 108
    receiver/drier – 110
Air filter – 49
Alternator
    brush check and replacement – 158
    check – 156
    drivebelt check, adjustment and replacement – 46
    general information and precautions – 155
    removal and installation – 156
Antenna removal and installation – 277
Antifreeze – 100
Automatic transmission
    fluid and filter change – 50
    fluid level check – 37
    general diagnosis – 185
    general information – 185
    mount check and replacement – 177
    neutral safety switch check, adjustment and replacement – 188
    oil seal replacement – 175
    removal and installation – 189
    shift linkage check and adjustment – 186
    specifications – 27, 185
    speedometer cable replacement – 177
    torque specifications – 185
Automotive chemicals and lubricants – 16

B

Battery
    cable check and replacement –152
    check and maintenance – 38
    jump starting – 14
    removal and installation – 152
Blower unit (heater/air conditioner) – 107
Body
    bumpers – 254
    console – 260
    dashboard trim panels – 257
    door latch, lock cylinder and handles – 263
    doors – 261
    door trim panel – 254
    door window glass and regulator – 265
    exterior mirror – 265
    general information – 251
    hinges and locks – 263
    headlight door
        adjustment – 261
        manual operation – 273
    hood – 253
    maintenance – 252
    rear hatch – 263
    repairs
        major damage – 253
        minor damage – 252
    seat belts – 266
    seats – 266
    trunk lid (convertible models) – 263
    upholstery and carpet maintenance – 252
    windshield – 253
Brakes
    anti-lock brake system (ABS) – 212
    bleeding – 226
    check – 45
    disc – 218
    fluid level check – 33
    fluid replacement – 56
    front brake caliper – 215
    front brake pads
        check – 45
        replacement – 213
    general information and precautions – 211
    hoses and lines – 225
    light switch – 231
    master cylinder – 222
    parking brake
        adjustment – 228
        cable replacement – 228
    pedal – 230
    power brake booster – 227
    proportioning bypass valve – 225
    rear brake pads
        check – 45
        replacement – 220
    rear disc brake caliper – 221
    specifications – 210
    torque specifications – 211
    troubleshooting – 24
Bumpers – 254
Buying parts – 7

C

Capacities – 28
Carpet maintenance – 252
Charging system
  alternator
    brush check and replacement – 158
    removal and installation – 156
  check – 156
  general information – 155
  precautions – 155
Chassis and body fastener check – 48
Clutch
  bleeding – 199
  check – 193
  description – 193
  fluid level check – 33
  general information – 193
  inspection – 194
  installation – 195
  master cylinder – 196
  neutral safety switch check – 47
  pedal
    freeplay and height check and adjustment – 43
    removal and installation – 199
  release bearing – 195
  release cylinder – 199
  removal – 194
  specifications – 28
  torque specifications – 192
  troubleshooting – 23
Compression check – 74
Conversion factors – 18
Cooling system
  antifreeze – 100
  check – 39
  coolant level check – 34
  coolant level warning system – 55
  coolant reservoir – 105
  draining, flushing and refilling – 53
  fan and clutch – 101
  general information – 100
  hoses – 40
  radiator – 102
  specifications – 99
  temperature sending unit – 106
  thermostat – 100
  torque specifications – 99
  troubleshooting – 22
  water pump – 105
Crank angle sensor – 154

D

Differential
  lubricant
    change – 51
    level check – 44
  output shaft seal replacement – 208
  removal and installation – 207
Distributor – see Crank angle sensor
Door
  adjustment – 261
  glass and regulator – 265
  handles – 264
  key lock cylinder – 264
  latch – 264
  removal and installation – 261
  trim panel – 254

Driveaxles
  boot check – 45
  boot replacement – 202
  CV joint overhaul – 202
  general information and check – 201
  removal and installation – 201
Drivebelt check, adjustment and replacement – 46
Driveline inspection – 200
Driveshaft removal and installation – 200

E

Eccentric shaft
  end play adjustment – 95
  inspection – 90
Electrical system
  alternator
    brush check and replacement – 158
    check – 156
    drivebelt check, adjustment and replacement – 46
    general information and precautions – 155
    removal and installation – 156
  battery
    cable check and replacement –152
    check and maintenance – 38
    jump starting – 14
    removal and installation – 152
  circuit breakers – 271
  clock/warning light assembly – 278
  coolant temperature sending unit – 106
  CPU – 268
  general information – 268
  headlight
    adjustment – 274
    replacement – 273
    retractor motor manual operation – 273
  ignition switch – 272
  instrument cluster – 277
  instrument panel – 276
  lights – 279
  neutral safety switch – 188
  power door locks – 280
  power windows – 281
  radio and speakers – 274
  rear wiper motor – 274
  relays – 271
  specifications – 267
  starter motor
    check – 158
    general information and precautions – 158
    removal and installation – 159
    solenoid – 159
  troubleshooting – 22, 268
  turn signal switch – 272
  voltage regulator – 156
  windshield wiper
    blades – 40
    motor – 274
  wiring diagrams – 281 thru 296
Emission control systems
  catalytic converter – 171
  control system and trouble codes – 174
  crankcase and evaporative emission control system – 53, 172
  deceleration control system – 169
  EGR system – 170
  evaporative emissions control system check – 53
  general information – 160
  information label – 160
  secondary air injection system – 165
  vacuum hose diagrams – 161 thru 164

Engine
apex seal and spring inspection – 88
cleaning – 85
compression check – 74
coolant warning system check – 55
corner seal and spring inspection – 90
disassembly – 77
eccentric shaft end play adjustment – 95
eccentric shaft inspection – 90
exhaust manifold removal and installation – 59
final assembly and installation – 97
flywheel/driveplate removal and installation – 61
front and rear oil seal replacement – 60, 63, 90
front bearing and oil pump assembly installation – 96
general information – 58, 74
housing inspection and overhaul – 85
initial start-up and break-in after overhaul – 98
inspection – 251
intake manifold removal and installation – 58
metering oil pump check, removal and installation – 65
mount check and replacement – 71
oil and filter change – 41
oil level warning system check – 47
oil pan removal and installation – 64
oil pump removal and installation – 66
oil seal and spring inspection and replacement – 88
overhaul
    disassembly sequence – 77
    general information – 74
    initial start-up and break-in – 98
    reassembly of internal components – 91
    rebuilding alternatives – 77
removal and installation – 75
removal methods and precautions – 75
repair operations possible with the engine in the vehicle – 58
rotor bearing replacement – 88
rotor inspection and repair – 87
side seal and spring inspection – 89
spark plug replacement – 54
specifications – 57, 72
stationary gear and main bearing replacement – 87
torque specifications – 57, 73
troubleshooting – 20
water pump removal and installation – 105
Exhaust system
check – 44
servicing – 149

F

Fasteners – 7
Filter replacement
air – 49
automatic transmission – 50
fuel – 49
Fluid level checks – 33
Flywheel/driveplate – 61
Front wheel bearing check, repack and adjustment – 51
Fuel filter replacement – 49
Fuel hose – 40
Fuel pump
check – 124
removal and installation – 125
Fuel injection system
air flow meter – 127
atmospheric pressure sensor – 144
auxiliary port valve system – 137
boost/pressure sensor – 143
bypass air control system – 128

dynamic chamber/surge tank – 134
EGI main fuse – 142
EGI main relay – 143
extension manifold/VDI manifold – 137
general information – 114
hot start assist system – 144
idle speed – 47
idle speed control system – 130
injectors – 140
pressure regulator – 140
pressure relief – 114
priming – 114
pulsation damper – 140
solenoid resistor – 142
specifications – 113
sub-zero starting system – 48
tank
    cleaning and repair – 127
    removal and installation – 127
throttle body – 132
throttle cable – 132
torque specifications – 114
Fuel tank
cleaning and repair – 127
removal and installation – 127
Fuses – 268

G

Glass replacement – 253, 265

H

Headlight
adjustment – 274
door
    adjustment – 261
    manual operation – 273
removal and installation – 273
retractor motor – 273
Heater
blower removal and installation – 107
core removal and installation – 107
Hood – 253
Hose
check and replacement – 40
removal tips – 10

I

Ignition system
check – 152
coil/igniter assembly – 152
crank angle sensor – 154
general information – 152
ignition timing – 155
spark plug replacement – 54
spark plug wire check and replacement – 55
specifications – 28, 151
switch – 272
Instrument cluster
housing switch replacement – 271
removal and installation – 277
Instrument panel – 278
Introduction to routine maintenance – 33
Introduction to the Mazda RX-7 – 5

J

Jacking and towing – 15
Jump starting – 14

L

Lights
    bulb application – 267
    bulb replacement – 279
    headlights – 273, 274
Lock cylinder replacement – 264
Lock maintenance – 253
Lubricants (recommended) – 16, 27
Lubrication system
    metering oil pump – 65
    oil and filter change – 41
    oil cooler – 104
    oil level warning system – 47
    oil pan – 64
    oil pressure – 72
    oil pressure control valve – 69
    oil pump – 66
    oil type – 27
    specifications – 57, 72
    torque specifications – 57

M

Maintenance (routine) – 27, 33
Maintenance schedule – 29
Maintenance techniques, tools and working facilities – 7
Manual transmission
    general information – 175
    lubricant
        change – 51
        level check – 44
    mount check and replacement – 177
    oil seal replacement – 175
    overhaul general information – 180
    removal and installation – 178
    shift lever removal and installation – 176
    specifications – 27, 175
    speedometer cable replacement – 176
    starter safety switch check – 47
    torque specifications – 175
    troubleshooting – 23
Master cylinder – 222
Metering oil pump
    check – 65
    removal and installation – 66
    specifications – 57
Metric conversion tables – 18

O

Oil
    change – 41
    filter change – 41
    level warning system check – 47
    level check – 33
    viscosity recommendations – 27
Oil cooler – 104
Oil pan – 64
Oil pressure check – 74
Oil pressure control valve – 69

Oil pump – 66
Oil seal replacement (eccentric shaft)
    during overhaul – 90
    in-vehicle
        front – 60
        rear – 63
Overhaul general information – 74

P

Parking brake
    adjustment – 228
    cable replacement – 228
Parts (buying) – 7
Pilot bearing and seal inspection and replacement – 196
Pinion oil seal replacement – 207
Power brake booster – 227
Power Steering
    fluid level check – 37
    gear removal and installation – 246
    pump removal and installation – 248
    system bleeding – 249

R

Radiator – 102
Radio and speakers – 274
Rebuilding alternatives – 77
Recommended lubricants and fluids – 27
Rear wiper motor – 274
Rotor (brake disc) – 218
Routine maintenance – 29, 33

S

Safety – 17
Sealants – 16
Seatbelt check – 47
Shock absorber removal and installation
    front – 237
    rear – 241
Solenoid removal and installation – 159
Spark plug replacement – 54
Spark plug wire check and replacement – 55
Speedometer cable replacement – 176
Stabilizer bar removal and installation
    front – 233
    rear – 240
Starter motor
    check – 158
    general information and precautions – 158
    removal and installation – 159
    solenoid removal and installation – 159
Steering system
    check – 43
    fluid level check – 37
    front wheel alignment – 248
    gear boot replacement – 247
    gear removal and installation – 246
    general information – 233
    intermediate shaft removal and installation – 246
    knuckle and hub removal and installation – 240
    steering wheel removal and installation – 245
    tie-rod end removal and installation – 247
    torque specifications – 233
    troubleshooting – 25

Sub-zero starting system check – 48
Suspension and steering checks – 43
Suspension system
   balljoint check and replacement – 237
   check – 43
   control arm removal and installation – 236
   control link removal and installation – 243
   front strut/shock absorber and coil spring
      assembly removal, overhaul and installation – 237
   lateral link removal and installation – 243
   rear shock absorber and coil spring
      assembly removal, overhaul and installation – 241
   rear trailing arm removal and installation – 242
   stabilizer bar and bushing removal and installation
      front – 233
      rear – 240
   subframe removal and installation – 243
   sublink removal and installation – 243
   toe control hub and bearing assembly
      removal and installation – 244
   torque specifications – 232
Switches
   headlight – 271
   ignition – 272
   turn signal – 272

T

Thermostat check and replacement – 100
Throttle cable
   adjustment – 132
   check – 132
   replacement – 132
Timing check and adjustment – 155
Tires
   check – 35
   general information – 289
   pressure check – 35
   rotation – 41
Tools – 7
Towing – 15

Transmission, automatic – see *Automatic transmission*
Transmission, manual – see *Manual transmission*
Troubleshooting
   automatic transmission – 24
   brakes – 24
   clutch – 23
   cooling system – 22
   electrical system – 22
   engine – 20
   fuel system – 22
   manual transmission – 23
   suspension and steering – 25
Tune-up general information – 33
Turbocharger and control system – 144

U

Upholstery maintenance – 252
Underhood hose check and replacement – 40

V

Vacuum brake booster – 227
Vacuum hoses – 40
Vehicle Emission Control Information (VECI) label – 6, 160
Vehicle identification numbers – 6

W

Water pump
   check – 105
   replacement – 105
Wheel alignment general information – 248
Window glass removal and installation – 253, 265
Window washer fluid level check – 34
Wiper blade inspection and replacement – 40
Wiper motor removal and installation – 274
Wiring diagrams – 281 thru 296
Working facilities – 13

Haynes Automotive Manuals

NOTE: If you do not see a listing for your vehicle, please visit **haynes.com** *for the latest product information and check out our* ***Online Manuals!***

ACURA
12020 **Integra** '86 thru '89 **& Legend** '86 thru '90
12021 **Integra** '90 thru '93 **& Legend** '91 thru '95
Integra '94 thru '00 - *see HONDA Civic (42025)*
MDX '01 thru '07 - *see HONDA Pilot (42037)*
12050 **Acura TL** all models '99 thru '08

AMC
14020 **Mid-size models** '70 thru '83
14025 **(Renault) Alliance & Encore** '83 thru '87

AUDI
15020 **4000** all models '80 thru '87
15025 **5000** all models '77 thru '83
15026 **5000** all models '84 thru '88
Audi A4 '96 thru '01 - *see VW Passat (96023)*
15030 **Audi A4** '02 thru '08

AUSTIN-HEALEY
Sprite - *see MG Midget (66015)*

BMW
18020 **3/5 Series** '82 thru '92
18021 **3-Series** incl. Z3 models '92 thru '98
18022 **3-Series** incl. Z4 models '99 thru '05
18023 **3-Series** '06 thru '14
18025 **320i all 4-cylinder models** '75 thru '83
18050 **1500 thru 2002** except Turbo '59 thru '77

BUICK
19010 **Buick Century** '97 thru '05
Century (front-wheel drive) - *see GM (38005)*
19020 **Buick, Oldsmobile & Pontiac Full-size (Front-wheel drive)** '85 thru '05
Buick Electra, LeSabre and Park Avenue; **Oldsmobile** Delta 88 Royale, Ninety Eight and Regency; **Pontiac** Bonneville
19025 **Buick, Oldsmobile & Pontiac Full-size (Rear wheel drive)** '70 thru '90
Buick Estate, Electra, LeSabre, Limited, **Oldsmobile** Custom Cruiser, Delta 88, Ninety-eight, **Pontiac** Bonneville, Catalina, Grandville, Parisienne
19027 **Buick LaCrosse** '05 thru '13
Enclave - *see GENERAL MOTORS (38001)*
Rainier - *see CHEVROLET (24072)*
Regal - *see GENERAL MOTORS (38010)*
Riviera - *see GENERAL MOTORS (38030, 38031)*
Roadmaster - *see CHEVROLET (24046)*
Skyhawk - *see GENERAL MOTORS (38015)*
Skylark - *see GENERAL MOTORS (38020, 38025)*
Somerset - *see GENERAL MOTORS (38025)*

CADILLAC
21015 **CTS & CTS-V** '03 thru '14
21030 **Cadillac Rear Wheel Drive** '70 thru '93
Cimarron - *see GENERAL MOTORS (38015)*
DeVille - *see GENERAL MOTORS (38031 & 38032)*
Eldorado - *see GENERAL MOTORS (38030)*
Fleetwood - *see GENERAL MOTORS (38031)*
Seville - *see GM (38030, 38031 & 38032)*

CHEVROLET
10305 **Chevrolet Engine Overhaul Manual**
24010 **Astro & GMC Safari Mini-vans** '85 thru '05
24013 **Aveo** '04 thru '11
24015 **Camaro V8** all models '70 thru '81
24016 **Camaro** all models '82 thru '92
24017 **Camaro & Firebird** '93 thru '02
Cavalier - *see GENERAL MOTORS (38016)*
Celebrity - *see GENERAL MOTORS (38005)*
24018 **Camaro** '10 thru '15
24020 **Chevelle, Malibu & El Camino** '69 thru '87
Cobalt - *see GENERAL MOTORS (38017)*
24024 **Chevette & Pontiac T1000** '76 thru '87
Citation - *see GENERAL MOTORS (38020)*
24027 **Colorado & GMC Canyon** '04 thru '12
24032 **Corsica & Beretta** all models '87 thru '96
24040 **Corvette** all V8 models '68 thru '82
24041 **Corvette** all models '84 thru '96
24042 **Corvette** all models '97 thru '13
24044 **Cruze** '11 thru '19
24045 **Full-size Sedans** Caprice, Impala, Biscayne, Bel Air & Wagons '69 thru '90
24046 **Impala SS & Caprice and Buick Roadmaster** '91 thru '96
Impala '00 thru '05 - *see LUMINA (24048)*
24047 **Impala & Monte Carlo** all models '06 thru '11
Lumina '90 thru '94 - *see GM (38010)*
24048 **Lumina & Monte Carlo** '95 thru '05
Lumina APV - *see GM (38035)*
24050 **Luv Pick-up** all 2WD & 4WD '72 thru '82
24051 **Malibu** '13 thru '19
24055 **Monte Carlo** all models '70 thru '88
Monte Carlo '95 thru '01 - *see LUMINA (24048)*
24059 **Nova** all V8 models '69 thru '79
24060 **Nova and Geo Prizm** '85 thru '92
24064 **Pick-ups** '67 thru '87 - Chevrolet & GMC
24065 **Pick-ups** '88 thru '98 - Chevrolet & GMC
24066 **Pick-ups** '99 thru '06 - Chevrolet & GMC
24067 **Chevrolet Silverado & GMC Sierra** '07 thru '14
24068 **Chevrolet Silverado & GMC Sierra** '14 thru '19
24070 **S-10 & S-15 Pick-ups** '82 thru '93, **Blazer & Jimmy** '83 thru '94,
24071 **S-10 & Sonoma Pick-ups** '94 thru '04, including **Blazer, Jimmy & Hombre**
24072 **Chevrolet TrailBlazer, GMC Envoy & Oldsmobile Bravada** '02 thru '09
24075 **Sprint** '85 thru '88 **& Geo Metro** '89 thru '01
24080 **Vans - Chevrolet & GMC** '68 thru '96
24081 **Chevrolet Express & GMC Savana** Full-size Vans '96 thru '19

CHRYSLER
10310 **Chrysler Engine Overhaul Manual**
25015 **Chrysler Cirrus, Dodge Stratus, Plymouth Breeze** '95 thru '00
25020 **Full-size Front-Wheel Drive** '88 thru '93
K-Cars - *see DODGE Aries (30008)*
Laser - *see DODGE Daytona (30030)*
25025 **Chrysler LHS, Concorde, New Yorker, Dodge** Intrepid, **Eagle** Vision, '93 thru '97
25026 **Chrysler LHS, Concorde, 300M, Dodge** Intrepid, '98 thru '04
25027 **Chrysler 300** '05 thru '18, **Dodge Charger** '06 thru '18, **Magnum** '05 thru '08 **& Challenger** '08 thru '18
25030 **Chrysler & Plymouth Mid-size** front wheel drive '82 thru '95
Rear-wheel Drive - *see Dodge (30050)*
25035 **PT Cruiser** all models '01 thru '10
25040 **Chrysler Sebring** '95 thru '06, **Dodge Stratus** '01 thru '06 **& Dodge Avenger** '95 thru '00
25041 **Chrysler Sebring** '07 thru '10, **200** '11 thru '17 **Dodge Avenger** '08 thru '14

DATSUN
28005 **200SX** all models '80 thru '83
28012 **240Z, 260Z & 280Z** Coupe '70 thru '78
28014 **280ZX** Coupe & 2+2 '79 thru '83
300ZX - *see NISSAN (72010)*
28018 **510 & PL521 Pick-up** '68 thru '73
28020 **510** all models '78 thru '81
28022 **620 Series Pick-up** all models '73 thru '79
720 Series Pick-up - *see NISSAN (72030)*

DODGE
400 & 600 - *see CHRYSLER (25030)*
30008 **Aries & Plymouth Reliant** '81 thru '89
30010 **Caravan & Plymouth Voyager** '84 thru '95
30011 **Caravan & Plymouth Voyager** '96 thru '02
30012 **Challenger & Plymouth Sapporro** '78 thru '83
30013 **Caravan, Chrysler Voyager & Town & Country** '03 thru '07
30014 **Grand Caravan & Chrysler Town & Country** '08 thru '18
30016 **Colt & Plymouth Champ** '78 thru '87
30020 **Dakota Pick-ups** all models '87 thru '96
30021 **Durango** '98 & '99 **& Dakota** '97 thru '99
30022 **Durango** '00 thru '03 **& Dakota** '00 thru '04
30023 **Durango** '04 thru '09 **& Dakota** '05 thru '11
30025 **Dart, Demon, Plymouth Barracuda, Duster & Valiant** 6-cylinder models '67 thru '76
30030 **Daytona & Chrysler Laser** '84 thru '89
Intrepid - *see CHRYSLER (25025, 25026)*
30034 **Neon** all models '95 thru '99
30035 **Omni & Plymouth Horizon** '78 thru '90
30036 **Dodge & Plymouth Neon** '00 thru '05
30040 **Pick-ups** full-size models '74 thru '93
30042 **Pick-ups** full-size models '94 thru '08
30043 **Pick-ups** full-size models '09 thru '18
30045 **Ram 50/D50 Pick-ups & Raider and Plymouth Arrow Pick-ups** '79 thru '93
30050 **Dodge/Plymouth/Chrysler** RWD '71 thru '89
30055 **Shadow & Plymouth Sundance** '87 thru '94
30060 **Spirit & Plymouth Acclaim** '89 thru '95
30065 **Vans - Dodge & Plymouth** '71 thru '03

EAGLE
Talon - *see MITSUBISHI (68030, 68031)*
Vision - *see CHRYSLER (25025)*

FIAT
34010 **124 Sport Coupe & Spider** '68 thru '78
34025 **X1/9** all models '74 thru '80

FORD
10320 **Ford Engine Overhaul Manual**
10355 **Ford Automatic Transmission Overhaul**
11500 **Mustang '64-1/2 thru '70 Restoration Guide**
36004 **Aerostar Mini-vans** all models '86 thru '97
36006 **Contour & Mercury Mystique** '95 thru '00
36008 **Courier Pick-up** all models '72 thru '82
36012 **Crown Victoria & Mercury Grand Marquis** '88 thru '11
36014 **Edge** '07 thru '19 **& Lincoln MKX** '07 thru '18
36016 **Escort & Mercury Lynx** all models '81 thru '90
36020 **Escort & Mercury Tracer** '91 thru '02
36022 **Escape** '01 thru '17, **Mazda Tribute** '01 thru '11, **& Mercury Mariner** '05 thru '11
36024 **Explorer & Mazda Navajo** '91 thru '01
36025 **Explorer & Mercury Mountaineer** '02 thru '10
36026 **Explorer** '11 thru '17
36028 **Fairmont & Mercury Zephyr** '78 thru '83
36030 **Festiva & Aspire** '88 thru '97
36032 **Fiesta** all models '77 thru '80
36034 **Focus** all models '00 thru '11
36035 **Focus** '12 thru '14
36045 **Fusion** '06 thru '14 **& Mercury Milan** '06 thru '11
36048 **Mustang V8** all models '64-1/2 thru '73
36049 **Mustang II** 4-cylinder, V6 & V8 models '74 thru '78
36050 **Mustang & Mercury Capri** '79 thru '93
36051 **Mustang** all models '94 thru '04
36052 **Mustang** '05 thru '14
36054 **Pick-ups & Bronco** '73 thru '79
36058 **Pick-ups & Bronco** '80 thru '96
36059 **F-150** '97 thru '03, **Expedition** '97 thru '17, **F-250** '97 thru '99, **F-150 Heritage** '04 **& Lincoln Navigator** '98 thru '17
36060 **Super Duty Pick-ups & Excursion** '99 thru '10
36061 **F-150** full-size '04 thru '14
36062 **Pinto & Mercury Bobcat** '75 thru '80
36063 **F-150** full-size '15 thru '17
36064 **Super Duty Pick-ups** '11 thru '16
36066 **Probe** all models '89 thru '92
Probe '93 thru '97 - *see MAZDA 626 (61042)*
36070 **Ranger & Bronco II** gas models '83 thru '92
36071 **Ranger** '93 thru '11 **& Mazda Pick-ups** '94 thru '09
36074 **Taurus & Mercury Sable** '86 thru '95
36075 **Taurus & Mercury Sable** '96 thru '07
36076 **Taurus** '08 thru '14, **Five Hundred** '05 thru '07, **Mercury Montego** '05 thru '07 **& Sable** '08 thru '09
36078 **Tempo & Mercury Topaz** '84 thru '94
36082 **Thunderbird & Mercury Cougar** '83 thru '88
36086 **Thunderbird & Mercury Cougar** '89 thru '97
36090 **Vans** all V8 Econoline models '69 thru '91
36094 **Vans** full size '92 thru '14
36097 **Windstar** '95 thru '03, **Freestar & Mercury Monterey Mini-van** '04 thru '07

GENERAL MOTORS
10360 **GM Automatic Transmission Overhaul**
38001 **GMC Acadia** '07 thru '16, **Buick Enclave** '08 thru '17, **Saturn Outlook** '07 thru '10 **& Chevrolet Traverse** '09 thru '17
38005 **Buick Century, Chevrolet Celebrity, Oldsmobile Cutlass Ciera & Pontiac 6000** all models '82 thru '96
38010 **Buick Regal** '88 thru '04, **Chevrolet Lumina** '88 thru '04, **Oldsmobile Cutlass Supreme** '88 thru '97 **& Pontiac Grand Prix** '88 thru '07
38015 **Buick Skyhawk, Cadillac Cimarron, Chevrolet Cavalier, Oldsmobile Firenza, Pontiac J-2000 & Sunbird** '82 thru '94
38016 **Chevrolet Cavalier & Pontiac Sunfire** '95 thru '05
38017 **Chevrolet Cobalt** '05 thru '10, **HHR** '06 thru '11, **Pontiac G5** '07 thru '09, **Pursuit** '05 thru '06 **& Saturn ION** '03 thru '07
38020 **Buick Skylark, Chevrolet Citation, Oldsmobile Omega, Pontiac Phoenix** '80 thru '85
38025 **Buick Skylark** '86 thru '98, **Somerset** '85 thru '87, **Oldsmobile Achieva** '92 thru '98, **Calais** '85 thru '91, **& Pontiac Grand Am** all models '85 thru '98
38026 **Chevrolet Malibu** '97 thru '03, **Classic** '04 thru '05, **Oldsmobile Alero** '99 thru '03, **Cutlass** '97 thru '00, **& Pontiac Grand Am** '99 thru '03
38027 **Chevrolet Malibu** '04 thru '12, **Pontiac G6** '05 thru '10 **& Saturn Aura** '07 thru '10
38030 **Cadillac Eldorado, Seville, Oldsmobile Toronado & Buick Riviera** '71 thru '85
38031 **Cadillac Eldorado, Seville, DeVille, Fleetwood, Oldsmobile Toronado & Buick Riviera** '86 thru '93
38032 **Cadillac DeVille** '94 thru '05, **Seville** '92 thru '04 **& Cadillac DTS** '06 thru '10
38035 **Chevrolet Lumina APV, Oldsmobile Silhouette & Pontiac Trans Sport** all models '90 thru '96
38036 **Chevrolet Venture** '97 thru '05, **Oldsmobile Silhouette** '97 thru '04, **Pontiac Trans Sport** '97 thru '98 **& Montana** '99 thru '05
38040 **Chevrolet Equinox** '05 thru '17, **GMC Terrain** '10 thru '17 **& Pontiac Torrent** '06 thru '09

GEO
Metro - *see CHEVROLET Sprint (24075)*
Prizm - *'85 thru '92 see CHEVY (24060), '93 thru '02 see TOYOTA Corolla (92036)*
40030 **Storm** all models '90 thru '93
Tracker - *see SUZUKI Samurai (90010)*

(Continued on other side)

Haynes Automotive Manuals (continued)

*NOTE: If you do not see a listing for your vehicle, please visit **haynes.com** for the latest product information and check out our **Online Manuals!***

GMC
Acadia - *see GENERAL MOTORS (38001)*
Pick-ups - *see CHEVROLET (24027, 24068)*
Vans - *see CHEVROLET (24081)*

HONDA
42010 Accord CVCC all models '76 thru '83
42011 Accord all models '84 thru '89
42012 Accord all models '90 thru '93
42013 Accord all models '94 thru '97
42014 Accord all models '98 thru '02
42015 Accord '03 thru '12 & Crosstour '10 thru '14
42016 Accord '13 thru '17
42020 Civic 1200 all models '73 thru '79
42021 Civic 1300 & 1500 CVCC '80 thru '83
42022 Civic 1500 CVCC all models '75 thru '79
42023 Civic all models '84 thru '91
42024 Civic & del Sol '92 thru '95
42025 Civic '96 thru '00, CR-V '97 thru '01 & Acura Integra '94 thru '00
42026 Civic '01 thru '11 & CR-V '02 thru '11
42027 Civic '12 thru '15 & CR-V '12 thru '16
42030 Fit '07 thru '13
42035 Odyssey all models '99 thru '10
Passport - *see ISUZU Rodeo (47017)*
42037 Honda Pilot '03 thru '08, Ridgeline '06 thru '14 & Acura MDX '01 thru '07
42040 Prelude CVCC all models '79 thru '89

HYUNDAI
43010 Elantra all models '96 thru '19
43015 Excel & Accent all models '86 thru '13
43050 Santa Fe all models '01 thru '12
43055 Sonata all models '99 thru '14

INFINITI
G35 '03 thru '08 - *see NISSAN 350Z (72011)*

ISUZU
Hombre - *see CHEVROLET S-10 (24071)*
47017 Rodeo '91 thru '02, Amigo '89 thru '94 & '98 thru '02 & Honda Passport '95 thru '02
47020 Trooper '84 thru '91 & Pick-up '81 thru '93

JAGUAR
49010 XJ6 all 6-cylinder models '68 thru '86
49011 XJ6 all models '88 thru '94
49015 XJ12 & XJS all 12-cylinder models '72 thru '85

JEEP
50010 Cherokee, Comanche & Wagoneer Limited all models '84 thru '01
50011 Cherokee '14 thru '19
50020 CJ all models '49 thru '86
50025 Grand Cherokee all models '93 thru '04
50026 Grand Cherokee '05 thru '19 & Dodge Durango '11 thru '19
50029 Grand Wagoneer & Pick-up '72 thru '91 Grand Wagoneer '84 thru '91, Cherokee & Wagoneer '72 thru '83, Pick-up '72 thru '88
50030 Wrangler all models '87 thru '17
50035 Liberty '02 thru '12 & Dodge Nitro '07 thru '11
50050 Patriot & Compass '07 thru '17

KIA
54050 Optima '01 thru '10
54060 Sedona '02 thru '14
54070 Sephia '94 thru '01, Spectra '00 thru '09, Sportage '05 thru '20
54077 Sorento '03 thru '13

LEXUS
ES 300/330 - *see TOYOTA Camry (92007, 92008)*
ES 350 - *see TOYOTA Camry (92009)*
RX 300/330/350 - *see TOYOTA Highlander (92095)*

LINCOLN
MKX - *see FORD (36014)*
Navigator - *see FORD Pick-up (36059)*
59010 Rear-Wheel Drive Continental '70 thru '87, Mark Series '70 thru '92 & Town Car '81 thru '10

MAZDA
61010 GLC (rear-wheel drive) '77 thru '83
61011 GLC (front-wheel drive) '81 thru '85
61012 Mazda3 '04 thru '11
61015 323 & Protegé '90 thru '03
61016 MX-5 Miata '90 thru '14
61020 MPV all models '89 thru '98
Navajo - *see Ford Explorer (36024)*
61030 Pick-ups '72 thru '93
Pick-ups '94 thru '09 - *see Ford Ranger (36071)*
61035 RX-7 all models '79 thru '85
61036 RX-7 all models '86 thru '91
61040 626 (rear-wheel drive) all models '79 thru '82
61041 626 & MX-6 (front-wheel drive) '83 thru '92
61042 626 '93 thru '01 & MX-6/Ford Probe '93 thru '02
61043 Mazda6 '03 thru '13

MERCEDES-BENZ
63012 123 Series Diesel '76 thru '85
63015 190 Series 4-cylinder gas models '84 thru '88
63020 230/250/280 6-cylinder SOHC models '68 thru '72
63025 280 123 Series gas models '77 thru '81
63030 350 & 450 all models '71 thru '80
63040 C-Class: C230/C240/C280/C320/C350 '01 thru '07

MERCURY
64200 Villager & Nissan Quest '93 thru '01
All other titles, see FORD Listing.

MG
66010 MGB Roadster & GT Coupe '62 thru '80
66015 MG Midget, Austin Healey Sprite '58 thru '80

MINI
67010 Mini '02 thru '13

MITSUBISHI
68020 Cordia, Tredia, Galant, Precis & Mirage '83 thru '93
68030 Eclipse, Eagle Talon & Plymouth Laser '90 thru '94
68031 Eclipse '95 thru '05 & Eagle Talon '95 thru '98
68035 Galant '94 thru '12
68040 Pick-up '83 thru '96 & Montero '83 thru '93

NISSAN
72010 300ZX all models including Turbo '84 thru '89
72011 350Z & Infiniti G35 all models '03 thru '08
72015 Altima all models '93 thru '06
72016 Altima '07 thru '12
72020 Maxima all models '85 thru '92
72021 Maxima all models '93 thru '08
72025 Murano '03 thru '14
72030 Pick-ups '80 thru '97 & Pathfinder '87 thru '95
72031 Frontier '98 thru '04, Xterra '00 thru '04, & Pathfinder '96 thru '04
72032 Frontier & Xterra '05 thru '14
72037 Pathfinder '05 thru '14
72040 Pulsar all models '83 thru '86
72042 Roque all models '08 thru '20
72050 Sentra all models '82 thru '94
72051 Sentra & 200SX all models '95 thru '06
72060 Stanza all models '82 thru '90
72070 Titan pick-ups '04 thru '10, Armada '05 thru '10 & Pathfinder Armada '04
72080 Versa all models '07 thru '19

OLDSMOBILE
73015 Cutlass V6 & V8 gas models '74 thru '88
For other OLDSMOBILE titles, see BUICK, CHEVROLET or GENERAL MOTORS listings.

PLYMOUTH
For PLYMOUTH titles, see DODGE listing.

PONTIAC
79008 Fiero all models '84 thru '88
79018 Firebird V8 models except Turbo '70 thru '81
79019 Firebird all models '82 thru '92
79025 G6 all models '05 thru '09
79040 Mid-size Rear-wheel Drive '70 thru '87
Vibe '03 thru '10 - *see TOYOTA Corolla (92037)*
For other PONTIAC titles, see BUICK, CHEVROLET or GENERAL MOTORS listings.

PORSCHE
80020 911 Coupe & Targa models '65 thru '89
80025 914 all 4-cylinder models '69 thru '76
80030 924 all models including Turbo '76 thru '82
80035 944 all models including Turbo '83 thru '89

RENAULT
Alliance & Encore - *see AMC (14025)*

SAAB
84010 900 all models including Turbo '79 thru '88

SATURN
87010 Saturn all S-series models '91 thru '02
Saturn Ion '03 thru '07 - *see GM (38017)*
Saturn Outlook - *see GM (38001)*
87020 Saturn L-series all models '00 thru '04
87040 Saturn VUE '02 thru '09

SUBARU
89002 1100, 1300, 1400 & 1600 '71 thru '79
89003 1600 & 1800 2WD & 4WD '80 thru '94
89080 Impreza '02 thru '11, WRX '02 thru '14, & WRX STI '04 thru '14
89100 Legacy all models '90 thru '99
89101 Legacy & Forester '00 thru '09
89102 Legacy '10 thru '16 & Forester '12 thru '16

SUZUKI
90010 Samurai/Sidekick & Geo Tracker '86 thru '01

TOYOTA
92005 Camry all models '83 thru '91
92006 Camry '92 thru '96 & Avalon '95 thru '96
92007 Camry, Avalon, Solara, Lexus ES 300 '97 thru '01

92008 Camry, Avalon, Lexus ES 300/330 '02 thru '06 & Solara '02 thru '08
92009 Camry, Avalon & Lexus ES 350 '07 thru '17
92015 Celica Rear-wheel Drive '71 thru '85
92020 Celica Front-wheel Drive '86 thru '99
92025 Celica Supra all models '79 thru '92
92030 Corolla all models '75 thru '79
92032 Corolla all rear-wheel drive models '80 thru '87
92035 Corolla all front-wheel drive models '84 thru '92
92036 Corolla & Geo/Chevrolet Prizm '93 thru '02
92037 Corolla '03 thru '19, Matrix '03 thru '14, & Pontiac Vibe '03 thru '10
92040 Corolla Tercel all models '80 thru '82
92045 Corona all models '74 thru '82
92050 Cressida all models '78 thru '82
92055 Land Cruiser FJ40, 43, 45, 55 '68 thru '82
92056 Land Cruiser FJ60, 62, 80, FZJ80 '80 thru '96
92060 Matrix '03 thru '11 & Pontiac Vibe '03 thru '10
92065 MR2 all models '85 thru '87
92070 Pick-up all models '69 thru '78
92075 Pick-up all models '79 thru '95
92076 Tacoma '95 thru '04, 4Runner '96 thru '02 & T100 '93 thru '08
92077 Tacoma all models '05 thru '18
92078 Tundra '00 thru '06 & Sequoia '01 thru '07
92079 4Runner all models '03 thru '09
92080 Previa all models '91 thru '95
92081 Prius all models '01 thru '12
92082 RAV4 all models '96 thru '12
92085 Tercel all models '87 thru '94
92090 Sienna all models '98 thru '10
92095 Highlander '01 thru '19 & Lexus RX330/330/350 '99 thru '19
92179 Tundra '07 thru '19 & Sequoia '08 thru '19

TRIUMPH
94007 Spitfire all models '62 thru '81
94010 TR7 all models '75 thru '81

VW
96008 Beetle & Karmann Ghia '54 thru '79
96009 New Beetle '98 thru '10
96016 Rabbit, Jetta, Scirocco & Pick-up gas models '75 thru '92 & Convertible '80 thru '92
96017 Golf, GTI & Jetta '93 thru '98, Cabrio '95 thru '02
96018 Golf, GTI, Jetta '99 thru '05
96019 Jetta, Rabbit, GLI, GTI & Golf '05 thru '11
96020 Rabbit, Jetta & Pick-up diesel '77 thru '84
96021 Jetta '11 thru '18 & Golf '15 thru '19
96023 Passat '98 thru '05 & Audi A4 '96 thru '01
96030 Transporter 1600 models '68 thru '79
96035 Transporter 1700, 1800 & 2000 '72 thru '79
96040 Type 3 1500 & 1600 all models '63 thru '73
96045 Vanagon Air-Cooled all models '80 thru '83

VOLVO
97010 120, 130 Series & 1800 Sports '61 thru '73
97015 140 Series all models '66 thru '74
97020 240 Series all models '76 thru '93
97040 740 & 760 Series all models '82 thru '88
97050 850 Series all models '93 thru '97

TECHBOOK MANUALS
10205 Automotive Computer Codes
10206 OBD-II & Electronic Engine Management
10210 Automotive Emissions Control Manual
10215 Fuel Injection Manual '78 thru '85
10225 Holley Carburetor Manual
10230 Rochester Carburetor Manual
10305 Chevrolet Engine Overhaul Manual
10320 Ford Engine Overhaul Manual
10330 GM and Ford Diesel Engine Repair Manual
10331 Duramax Diesel Engines '01 thru '19
10332 Cummins Diesel Engine Performance Manual
10333 GM, Ford & Chrysler Engine Performance Manual
10334 GM Engine Performance Manual
10340 Small Engine Repair Manual, 5 HP & Less
10341 Small Engine Repair Manual, 5.5 HP to 20 HP
10345 Suspension, Steering & Driveline Manual
10355 Ford Automatic Transmission Overhaul
10360 GM Automatic Transmission Overhaul
10405 Automotive Body Repair & Painting
10410 Automotive Brake Manual
10411 Automotive Anti-lock Brake (ABS) Systems
10420 Automotive Electrical Manual
10425 Automotive Heating & Air Conditioning
10435 Automotive Tools Manual
10445 Welding Manual
10450 ATV Basics

Over a 100 Haynes
motorcycle manuals
also available

10/22

Haynes North America, Inc. • (805) 498-6703 • www.haynes.com